THE SPEARS OF TWILIGHT

THE SPEARS
OF TWILIGHT

LIFE AND DEATH IN
THE AMAZON JUNGLE

Philippe Descola

Translated from the French by
Janet Lloyd

THE NEW PRESS / NEW YORK

© 1993 by Librairie Plon
English translation © 1996 by The New Press/HarperCollins *Publishers*
Etched full-page drawings by Philippe Munch
Small drawings by Philippe Descola
Photographs by Philippe Descola and Antonino Colajanni
Maps by Ken Lewis

LIBRARY OF CONGRESS CATALOGING-IN-PUBLICATION DATA

Descola, Philippe.
    [Lances du crépuscule. English]
    The spears of twilight: life in the Amazon / Philippe Descola;
      translated from the French by Janet Lloyd.
      p.   cm.
    Includes bibliographical references and index.
    ISBN 1-56584-438-6
    1. Jivaran Indians—Social life and customs. 2. Amazon River
      Region—Social life and customs. I. Title.
    F2230.2.J58D4713   1996
    981'.1004983—DC20
                                     96-12955
                                        CIP

First published in French as *Les Lances du crépuscule* by Librairie Plon in 1993
Published in the United States by The New Press, New York
Distributed by W.W. Norton & Company, Inc., New York

*Established in 1990 as a major alternative to the large commercial publishing houses,
The New Press is a full-scale, nonprofit American book publisher outside of the
university presses. The Press is operated editorially in the public interest, rather
than for private gain; it is committed to publishing, in innovative ways, works of
educational, cultural, and community value that, despite their intellectual merits,
might not normally be commercially viable. The New Press's editorial offices are
located at the City University of New York.*

The New Press is deeply grateful to the French Ministry of Culture and Communication
for its generous translation support.

Printed in the United States of America

9 8 7 6 5 4 3 2 1

For Anne Christine

Contents

MAPS   ix

LIST OF ILLUSTRATIONS   xiii

PROLOGUE   1

I: TAMING THE FOREST

1   Apprenticeship   33

2   Early Morning   44

3   Village Rumours   52

4   Pause   65

5   Bartering   69

6   Garden Magic   84

7   Dreams   103

8   A Hunting Expedition   120

9   Reflections in the Water   134

II: MATTERS OF AFFINITY

10   Selective Friendships   149

11   A Visit to the River People   165

12   Love in the Plural   182

13   Images from Without, Images from Within   201

14   Travelling Downstream   210

15   To Each His Due   231

16   Drinking Party   252

17   The Art of Accommodating Enemies   265

18   Scenes in a House of War   279

III: VISIONS

19 Paths of Revelation   299
20 The Shaman's Song   315
21 Craftsmen of the Imaginary   335
22 Holy Writ   350
23 The Dead and the Living   363
24 Dénouement   384

   EPILOGUE   401

   Spelling   413
   Glossaries   415
   Bibliographical Outline   426
   Postscript: Ethnological Writing   443
   Index   447

MAPS

1. Jivaro country in South America

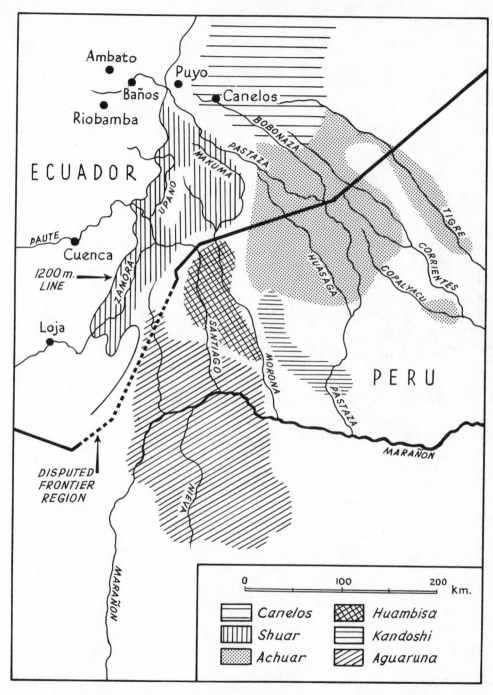

2. The Jivaro Tribes

Ambato

Baños

Riobamba

Puyo

Canelos

ECUADOR

PAUTE

Cuenca

1200 m.
LINE

Loja

DISPUTED
FRONTIER
REGION

MAKUMA

UPANO

ZAMORA

PASTAZA

BOBONAZA

SANTIAGO

MORONA

HUASAGA

PASTAZA

COPALYACU

CORRIENTES

TIGRE

NIEVA

MARAÑON

MARAÑON

PERU

0   100   200 Km.

Canelos

Shuar

Achuar

Huambisa

Kandoshi

Aguaruna

Illustrations

BY THE AUTHOR   *page*

Chimpui stool of the master of the house   43
Pininkia bowl for drinking manioc beer   64
Muits, jar in which manioc beer is fermented   102
Oar   119
Tunta, quiver for blowpipe darts*   164
Tsukanka akitiai, masculine ornaments†   200
Cotton bracelet worn by men after they have met with *arutam*   314
(the zigzag pattern is known as *utunmiamu*)
Tuntui drum made from a hollowed-out tree-trunk   362

* The round gourd contains a supply of kapok fibre for making the wads placed at the end of darts; the piranha jaw is used for notching the tips of the darts; and the jagged handle is used for carrying small birds hooked on to it by their feet.

† These are passed through the ear lobes or attached beneath the *tawasap* crown. They are made from *karis* tubes tipped by a bunch of toucan feathers and a lock of human hair.

Anku nanki winiawai, uchi, uchirua
Pee awemarata
Etsa uchirua, anku nanki winiawai
Pee awemarata
Emesaka tamawa
Ayawaitramkaimpia, uchi, uchirua
Natemkamia waitmakaimpia
Aak aak weakume
Uwi uwi upujkitia.

The spear of twilight is coming, son, my son
Quick, dodge it!
The hollow spear is coming, son, my son
My son, Sun, the spear of twilight is coming for you
Quick, dodge it!
The *emesak*, as it is called
Let it not lie in wait for you, son, my son
Let it not behold you with the clear vision of *natem* trances
As they gradually bear you away
Let each of your steps be disguised as a chonta palm.

Prologue

'However much individuals may come and go, it
would seem that philosophy never travels.'

JEAN-JACQUES ROUSSEAU,
Discourse on the Origin of Inequality

THE FRONTIERS OF CIVILIZATION seldom present an attractive
face, even to the unprejudiced eye. All over the planet a very real
frontier conflict is being played out in these barely civilized places. It
began just over a century ago, setting a handful of tribal minorities
in opposition to a rush of people seeking to dislodge them from their
last refuges, a motley legion of mixed and opposed elements: wretched
peasants seeking land, large-scale cattle- or plantation-owners, prospectors for gold or precious stones, and multinational companies
exploiting petroleum, tropical timber or mining reserves. In this
inglorious conquest, the frontlines are invariably a desolate sight.
Settled amid the anarchy of everything provisional and, in many cases,
beyond the reach of national law, their distinctive mark is a persistent
absence of any kind of urbanity. Their mongrel nature is perhaps more
distinct in Amazonia than anywhere else. From the Orinoco to the
Andes and from the Llanos of Colombia to the plains of the Bolivian
Oriente, at the foot of over-populated highlands and along navigable
rivers, clustered around temporary landing-strips and edging newly
cut roads, thousands of identical little towns mushroom endlessly, each day putting out new tentacles, each day increasingly
ramshackle and still without the power to swallow up the great
forest. Too chaotic to hold the visitor's curiosity for long and too
hybrid to elicit sympathy, these towns of corrugated iron convey a
degenerate image of all the worlds that they bring into confrontation,
an image that is a mixture of tenuous nostalgia for a long-forgotten
European culture and lazy prejudice against the unknown that lies
so close.

1

It is in one of these gloomy observation posts that ethnographic research usually begins. I embarked upon mine in Puyo, a town of colonists immersed in the graceless present, situated at the foot of the eastern slopes of the Ecuadorian Andes. For anybody from Europe or even from one of the old colonial cities perched in the upper valleys of the Cordillera, Puyo comes as a surprise, for it is a world without any real past. Admittedly, this little provincial capital is less than three-quarters of a century old; but the older western outposts in the upper Amazon are hardly better endowed, and some of them were founded under Charles V. History has not been generous to these fringe villages, each day forced to repeat the derisory or tragic efforts of the days of their foundation. It has left them no collective store of memories, no commemorative monuments; nothing now remains to testify to their antiquity except perhaps a few bundles of papers mouldering away in some forgotten archive. Yet in the sixteenth century some Amazonian ghost towns were known to all literate Europeans who, with the aid of maps as splendid as they were inaccurate, attentively followed the progress of the unprecedented conquest then taking place. Jaén, Borja, Sevilla del Oro, Santander, and Valladolid are all geographical markers, fragrant with a nostalgia for native Spain, that have survived in men's memories purely thanks to the laziness of several generations of map-makers: the towns that the *conquistadores* established during the earliest surge of the Spanish invasion were already lying in ashes a hundred years later. As it occurred to nobody to check that they still existed, atlases continued to record their existence in a misleading way, for the size indicated for these towns was proportionate to that of the immense surrounding void they were believed to control. To give life to the great virgin expanse of unexplored land, copyists would set out the names of lifeless villages in enormous letters, adorning their immediate surroundings with miniatures of imaginary animals and carefully tidied little forests. Unbeknown to their inhabitants, decimated by sickness and Indian attacks, their cluster of squalid huts would be credited with the same dimensions as Bordeaux or Philadelphia. These fortresses of the conquest have by now forgotten the lost glory of the days of their foundation; their past lives on only in the imagination of collectors of old maps or the notes of a handful of historians. Whether old or new, all these little town transplants are now afflicted with amnesia: the oldest of them have forgotten their origins and the more recent do not have any memories to share.

Puyo was indifferent not only to time but also to its immediate environment. I thought that I would be making no more than a short stop here at the end of the negotiable road that takes one in a few hours from the large towns of the central Sierra right down to the Amazonian forest, but I soon realized that I would have to find ways of diverting my impatience. The first thing I had to do was find out where the Achuar Jivaros, whom I hoped to visit, were to be found and by what means I could reach them. All that I knew when I arrived was that they were reported to be present along the lower reaches of the Pastaza river, several hundred kilometres away, in a forest enclave innocent of roads or navigable rivers. To my great surprise, most of the people whom I questioned in Puyo told me that they knew nothing at all about the Achuar. The owner of the family lodging house where I was staying with my companion, Anne Christine, the clients of the eating houses where we took our meals, the municipal and provincial officials and the agents of governmental organizations – all the people with whom it is not hard for a passing traveller to enter into conversation in a small provincial town – appeared never to have even heard of the mysterious tribe that we hoped to find. Discouraged as I was to think that I might be on a wild goose chase, it took me several days to realize that the people with whom we had spoken knew absolutely nothing about the forest and its inhabitants. A few hours' march away from the town was the beginning of a world in which they had never set foot. My earlier reading of a number of ethnological monographs on Ecuadorian Amazonia – which, incidentally, were impossible to find in the country to which their research related – had enabled me to know more about the Indians than the very people who lived within striking distance of them.

The inhabitants of Puyo made up for their ignorance with a bent for storytelling as fertile as it was categorical. In the cantinas and eating houses the most unbelievable legends circulated about the jungle and its strange inhabitants. We were told that cannibalistic Indians there would shrink the bodies of their enemies to the size of a doll, an anatomical exploit that was also taken to indicate that they had discovered a miraculous cure for cancer. Others, in contrast, claimed that colonies of white lepers had from time immemorial lived a self-sufficient life alongside an inaccessible river where even the natives did not dare to attack them. Yet others declared that, hidden in the jungle, there were ruined, formerly grandiose palaces, clear evidence that this forest into which they had never ventured had once been visited by intergalactic travellers or even (given that extraterrestrial beings have to some extent replaced God in popular explanations for the mystery of origins) that it was the crucible for the cosmic genesis of the human species. Amid this jumble of improbable stories it was not hard to recognize, with a certain satisfaction, a number of identifiable fantasies that Amazonia has always conjured up in the West, fantasies that local colour had modified hardly at all: white Indians, an Eldorado of fabulous riches lost deep in the forest, monstrous creatures elsewhere extinct, savage magicians with super-human powers. All these myths have been perpetuated in popularizing works from the sixteenth century down to the present day. Evidence disproving them has never stripped them of a power to fascinate, the source of which lies well beyond any verifiable reality.

The irreducible chasm existing between my own scholarly and rationalist knowledge about the Indians of Ecuadorian Amazonia and the legendary world of which the inhabitants of Puyo told us for me came to represent a prime illustration of an implicit law of the practice of ethnography. Parodying the concise language of a physicist, it might be put as follows: one's capacity for objectivization is inversely proportional to one's distance from the object observed. In other words, the greater the geographical and cultural distance an ethnologist establishes between his own native world and his chosen 'field', the less affected he will be by the prejudices that the locally dominant people nurture with regard to the marginal peoples he is studying. However much closer they may be to civilization, the former will be no more familiar to him than the latter.

Admittedly, a solid education in a large cosmopolitan country does not necessarily protect the credulous against the facile seductions of fantasy. Thus, shortly before our own arrival in Puyo in the autumn of 1976, the Ecuadorian authorities had organized an ambitious international expedition to explore a cavern situated in the foothills of the Andes, at the heart of the country of the Shuar Jivaros. Along with a collection of experts of many kinds – who did not, however, include an ethnologist – the organizers had seen fit to enlist the co-operation of a unit of special British commandos and a world-famous American astronaut. It is not known whether the task of the soldiers was to protect the expedition against possible attacks from the local Indians – who for the past forty years had been subjected to missionary pacification – or whether theirs was a more heroic mission, the nature of which might be deduced from the presence of the astronaut. The rumour spread by the widely circulated publications of one clever European charlatan did in fact suggest that the cave contained vestiges of some extra-terrestrial civilization. Strange figures engraved on some unknown substance were said to glow in the dark, retracing every stage in the Promethean founding of human civilization. And, given that the man from NASA's experience of orbiting the world was assumed to qualify him as particularly adept at establishing relations with beings from outer space, his expertise was no doubt to be depended upon in the event of any unforeseen meetings taking place. The results of the expedition were meagre compared to the costly means employed: a few archaeological shards from an already identified culture, the broken remains of pottery discarded by neighbouring Indians, and a better understanding of the private life of the nightjars that lived in their thousands in these caves.

This anecdote provides a fine illustration of the way in which legends woven around the Amazonian world by the West are perpetuated and enriched. Onto the basis of stories inherited from the first chroniclers of the Conquest, each successive century has grafted its own improbabilities by reinterpreting the supposed curiosities of American nature in the light of the myths of its own period. The magical bestiary of the great forest has absorbed, one by one, all the figures that throng our own imaginary representations, from single-breasted Amazons down to flying saucers. Even the most eminent of thinkers have been known to suspend their critical faculties in the face of the fantastical stories brought back by credulous travellers; legends that, thanks to the prestige of their scholarly authority, have thereupon been converted into scientific truths that even scrupulous observers hesitated to question publicly. Hegel provides the best example. At the time when the great explorer Alexander von Humboldt was publishing his remarkable descriptions of the nature and anthropology of the American continent, the famous philosopher, in his lectures, pumped new life into an old belief already popularized by Buffon, according to which the New World native was a being spiritually and physically diminished by reason of the immaturity of the physical environment in which he had evolved. The development of ethnology has now made such blunders impossible, even for philosophers with the utmost indifference for marginal human groups. However, fables in which the scholarly community no longer believes continued to be propagated by the pens of scribblers of mystery and exoticism. Disguised amid a fog of esotericism or sprinkled with spurious anecdotes that immediately carry conviction with the reader, they are widely accepted as the truth. They are even peddled in the popular volumes sold by the stationers of Puyo, in whose shops these are solidly ensconced alongside the school textbooks and women's magazines.

The myths to which Amazonia gives rise seem to have a double life. Noted down by mildly curious explorers who listen to the 'poor whites' who eke out a living on the edge of the jungle, they eventually find their way back to the places where they were first produced, where the printing press gives them the seal of approval. Then, having once more been swallowed by the autochthonous fable-tellers, they may be regurgitated to the next passing adventurous note-taker. However, in contrast to the Amerindian myths that, over the centuries, have been enriched by the comic or tragic interpolations added by their inspired narrators, the poetic content of this particular kind of imaginary ethnology becomes increasingly impoverished as the demands of modern rationality establish a vice-like grip of semi-probability upon it.

Immunized against the fables of the storytellers of Puyo by our own earlier reading, we were desperately seeking to uncover a path that might lead us to the Achuar. I had been taught that ethnologists are seldom the first to reach the theatre of their enquiries, but arrive there in the wake of some colonial power. All that my generation knew of the colonies, however, was what the uneasy consciences of some of our teachers had conveyed to us. But from this I had gleaned that there are always soldiers or missionaries who can open up a path for an ethnological expedition to follow. Even in this little town of an independent republic, there was no lack of either.

However, the soldiers of the special jungle units knew nothing at all of the Achuar. They did, on the other hand, seem interested in any information that they might get out of us once our mission was accomplished. Their overt bellicosity was fuelled by the proximity of the hereditary Peruvian enemy, who in the 1940s had annexed the greater part of Ecuadorian Amazonia; and they viewed with suspicion any foreigner wishing to travel in these disputed territories. Fortunately, though, the officers of these elite troops were fascinated by the myth of the French Foreign Legion and also disturbed by the unconcern of my companion, Anne Christine, also a budding ethnologist, who was intending to accompany me on an expedition that they considered to be extremely risky. The past exploits of the French colonial army and the admirable audacity of Anne Christine thus won us the soldiers' respect and sympathy. Although they could give us no information on the Achuar, they did provide us with the safe-conduct passes indispensable for visiting them.

The missionaries were more up to date on native matters: as is usual in Latin America, the Ecuadorian State was entirely dependent on them when it came to the integration of native peoples. Our interview with the Dominicans was very friendly but not very productive. They had been established in the region for more than three centuries and had certainly heard of the Achuar, but all their attempts to convert them had ended in failure. A little book that I had consulted before leaving France had nevertheless given me some hope. At the end of the last century, a French Dominican *had* made contact with the very Indians amongst whom we were hoping to live. His pastoral activities had been limited to presenting gifts of cheap jewellery to the leader of a small band of warriors who were lured with great difficulty to the house of a convert. Abbé Pierre had been much impressed by these ferocious savages entirely devoted to the pleasures of warfare and the works of Satan. Upon his return to France, he had published an edifying account of his adventures amongst the Jivaros, cleverly interweaving a missionary apologia with the darkest picture of the mores of these Indians, no doubt hoping thereby to encourage the younger readers of parish libraries to develop a vocation for exotic missionary work. But his exhortation fell upon deaf ears and, close on a century later, the notorious Jivaros of the Capahuari river had still not found amongst the Dominicans the pastor that Abbé Pierre had been seeking. Resigning ourselves to not obtaining from the Dominicans the ethnographical information that my reading of that little book had encouraged me to hope for, we turned instead to sects much less familiar to us.

In marked contrast to the relaxed, typically Latin attitude of the Dominicans, the Protestant missionaries were still proceeding at full blast with the fight for souls. These North American evangelists of strictly fundamentalist inclination combined in a curious fashion strict adhesion to the literal meaning of the Old Testament with mastery of the most modern technology. Most of them came from small towns in the Bible Belt, armed with unshakeably clear consciences and a rudimentary smattering of theology, convinced that they alone were the repositories of Christian values now abolished elsewhere. Totally ignorant of the vast world, despite their transplantation, and taking the few articles of morality accepted in the rural America of their childhoods to be a universal credo, they strove bravely to spread these principles of salvation all around them. Their rustic faith was well served by a flotilla of light aircraft, a powerful radio, an ultra-modern hospital and four-wheel-drive vehicles – in short, all the equipment that a battalion of crusaders dropped behind enemy lines needed. When we tried to find out whether their operations stretched as far as the Achuar we were met by a fog of politely evasive replies. Just as with all our requests for information addressed to the official circles of Puyo, we were made to feel that our behaviour was slightly importunate. No doubt both the military and the missionaries felt that, in the efficient use of their equipment, they had better things to do than satisfy the idle curiosity of foreign ethnologists. All the same, we did eventually learn that a small group of Capahuari Achuar had two or three years ago agreed to establish peaceful relations with these missionaries. They had even cleared a small landing strip for them and this had recently come into operation. Now we were at least reassured as to the existence of these elusive Indians; but we ran up against a polite refusal when we asked to be taken to them: the mission's small, single-engined planes only landed there once or twice a year and it was not possible to organize a flight especially for us in the near future.

With the date of our grand departure delayed by all these setbacks, I tried to make the most of the situation and to focus my attention, as a novice ethnologist, upon the inhabitants of Puyo. After all, this little town in the Andean foothills afforded me a chance to make a somewhat disenchanted but most instructive ethnographic survey. In this (it was hoped) brief interim period, my curiosity might well be rewarded with a field in which to dabble that would no doubt prove considerably more exotic than the large French towns in which many of my colleagues put their skills to work.

Puyo, officially founded in 1899 by a Dominican father, was up until the early 1960s no more than a large cul-de-sac clustering close to the wooden mission buildings served, for the past ten years, by a poor dirt road that ran as far as Ambato, in the Andes. Then the colonists arrived, attracted in ever-increasing numbers by the mirage of a bountiful Amazonia. But their arrival did not fundamentally alter the rustic and untidy aspect of this small trading town that depended for its supplies, as for the maintenance of its morale, upon the umbilical cord that linked it with the major towns of the central Sierra. Puyo is simply a terminus for the urban and trading society whose disparate overflow dribbles into it, and it strives to ape the manners of the Andes, the better to exorcize the wildness of the forest on its doorstep. The ground floors of most of the houses are arranged as shops, daubed in pastel shades, their windows offering the various symbolic attributes of the Ecuadorian *petite bourgeoisie*: electric blenders, radio cassettes, china knick-knacks, imported brands of alcohol . . . Wide concrete sidewalks covered by wooden arcades make it possible to view these treasures sheltered from the torrential afternoon downpours. The street itself is also given over to business: shoeshines – whose task in this world of mud and dust is truly Sisyphean – tropical fruit sellers, and the vendors of cigarettes and sweets hope patiently for a tiny profit. Indians from the Otavalo region, distinguishable by their thick plaits and grey felt hats, peddle bundles of clothes singularly unsuited to the climate: heavy blue woollen ponchos and knitwear in brightly clashing colours. An alert ear can seize upon the *leitmotif* of every conversation: 'sucre, sucre, sucre,' for this is the national currency unit. Repeated in this way, greedily, by thousands of lips, it is the anthem of this town of merchants.

Puyo's smell is typical of all small Amazonian towns, a subtle blend of barbecued meat, overripe fruit and damp earth, sometimes overlaid by the pestilential exhaust fumes of a huge truck or jolting bus. Against the background of this composite odour, the houses produce their own typical, intimate smell, a mixture dominated by kerosene and mildewed wood, the two invariably inseparable since petroleum, liberally sprinkled over all walls and floors, is supposed to protect them from creeping rot. This is the acrid stench that greets a purchaser at the threshold of each of these shops, as if to prepare him for a shambles quite different from the showy window displays. Relegated to the semi-darkness and in total contrast to the television sets and typewriters exhibited in positions of honour, other more humble wares are piled on rickety shelving or suspended in garlands from the ceiling – aluminium cooking pots, machetes, axe-blades, adzes, hooks, fishing lines . . . : on display, the sparkling tawdriness of prestige objects; tucked away in the dim shop, the modest utensils destined for the Indians. Better than any wordy explanations, this arrangement of the merchandise indicates that Puyo is a two-faced town that derives a significant proportion of its wealth from the inhabitants of the great forest of whose close presence it pretends to be unaware.

After a closer look at the passers-by, you soon notice that they move about in very different ways. The white and *mestizo* traders, the agents of local government offices and the clerks employed by the banks or co-operatives, who have been Puyo citizens for at most one generation, go about their business with all the bustle of important people. The most august or wealthy of them pass with pomp in their cars between the five blocks of buildings in which their activities are concentrated. In this country where, as a result of the heavy taxes imposed on imports, even the well-to-do can aspire to the possession of no more than a small 'pick-up', the car is the status symbol *par excellence*. The big, four-wheel-drive Toyotas of the government departments confer enviable prestige upon whoever gets to use them. Outside working hours they are chiefly used to parade the families of office chiefs along the main streets of the town, in a self-congratulatory and triumphal procession that is reminiscent of the confident arrogance affected in past days by the cream of Parisian elegance in their carriages in the Bois de Boulogne.

In the midst of this ballet of automobiles, utterly disregarded by the Whites and awkward in their new clothes, Indians move about in small groups. The rubber boots that they have donned in honour of the town sidewalks give them a characteristic gait, at once shuffling and rolling. Superficially, they in every way resemble the *mestizo* colonists and it is not their clothes or their looks that make them stand out, but the awkwardness of their behaviour in this urban space. Here, on the edge of Amazonia, they are as easy to pick out as farmers lost in the Paris Métro at the time of the Agricultural Exhibition. They are more autochthonous than the citizens of Puyo, since they were its very first inhabitants. But the Indians are not at home in this urban blister that has formed over a few decades on their territory. Their language is Quichua, but in Spanish they are known as Canelos or Alamas. They themselves prefer the appellation *sacha runa*, 'people of the forest'. They were converted to Christianity by the Dominicans several centuries ago and now live in small communities in the forest hinterland of Puyo, a few hours' walk away. These Amazonian Quichuas come to the town as if to a country market, to sell what they have learned to produce in excess of their needs and to buy what they no longer desire to do without. In exchange for a few baskets of *ishpingo* or *naranjilla*, peccary pelts and bundles of palm fibres, they can obtain cooking pots, machetes, clothes and rifles.

Most Quichua families are linked to one or other of the traders of Puyo through a 'godfatherly' or *compadrazgo* relationship, an association more political than religious and extremely common in Ecuador as well as more generally in Hispanic America. Those who enter into such an association do so to win the protection of a powerful man who, in exchange for many kinds of services, will become the godfather of one of their children. The merchant thereby wins himself a clientele, in every sense of the term, and also a guarantee that his Quichua *compadres* will unprotestingly accept the systematically unfavourable rate of exchange that he will impose when they come to him to sell their goods and buy manufactured objects in exchange. But there are also a few advantages for the Canelos in the relationship. Through it they acquire the right to put up in their protector's house when they have to stop over in town, and they are promised that he will intercede for them when they have problems with the national bureaucracy. This last advantage is probably the most important in their eyes, since a good number of their visits to Puyo are spent trying to obtain a title deed for their land from the authorities. Since the early 1960s, at the instigation of the government, a flood of small-scale peasants has been streaming to the Oriente, as Ecuadorian Amazonia is customarily called. These mountain Indians and *mestizos* leave poverty-stricken conditions in the over-populated Andes, seeking the easy success that they have been promised in this new Eldorado. Day after day, the ancient buses that ply between the Sierra and Puyo discharge their cargo of poor wretches who have been forced by their disastrous earlier existence to take this leap into the unknown. Some become the responsibility of the State, which assigns them to organized colonization projects; others furtively carve out little estates for themselves in Indian territory. These migrant settlers then try to get their occupation of the land recognized by the Ecuadorian Institute of Agrarian Reform and Colonization, which is not too difficult given that the vast forest regions of the Oriente are legally designated as 'fallow land', part of the State's patrimony that can be ceded to anyone who asks for it.

With very few exceptions, the Indians of this part of Ecuadorian Amazonia thus have no rights over the territories where they have lived for centuries, and their *de facto* sovereignty there remains invalid from the point of view of the juridical apparatus of the State that rules them. This derisory agrarian reform, which dispossesses Indians with no other resources to the doubtful benefit of refugees from the Sierra, exposes the Canelos in the immediate neighbourhood of Puyo to the constant threat of despoliation. The colonists, terrified by their unfamiliar surroundings, never venture very far into the forest. Beyond one day's march from the urban centre the colonizing flood dries up, as if the impetus that it developed flowing down from the mountains was suddenly curtailed. Close to the town, however, there are constant boundary conflicts and the only way for the Indians to protect themselves is to make the same approaches as their invaders to the authorities. Week after week they are subjected to the humiliation of beseeching arrogant bureaucrats to grant them the right to remain on their own ancestral land or of queuing up for hours in the waiting rooms of the offices of specialized lawyers. The consideration of requests made through the normal channels can drag on for years; if a lawsuit is involved a lifetime may not be long enough to gain recognition for one's rights: there is always some document, some signature or some guarantee still needed to end the nightmare.

It is here that a 'godfatherly' relationship can come in useful. By acquiring a *mestizo* or white *compadre* in the centre of things – preferably a trader – an Indian can extend his social network to the edges of administrative power. He is well aware that the influence of his protector is often illusory and that he is paying dearly for it by tacitly accepting being cheated in each and every one of their commercial transactions. The merchants think that the Canelos' apparent docility in the face of this unfair exchange is due to their incomprehension of the principles according to which a civilized society functions. The naive satisfaction that they derive from their business victories over Indians who they assume to be ignorant is implicitly justified in their eyes: small-scale business has a civilizing function, and as the process of learning the laws of the market is a long one, the traders consider it quite legitimate to treat themselves to some reward for the pains they expend upon the Indians whom they are educating. The Indians are more lucid in their pragmatism, having quickly understood that, to get along with this culture based on profit, it is sometimes necessary to give a little in order not to lose a lot. Turning a blind eye to the minor cheating that goes on in their deals is a way to establish a basis for negotiations with the Whites and possibly to defend themselves against the theft of their land.

The Achuar territory begins far beyond the Canelos, several days' march from Puyo, according, at least, to the few works of ethnology in which they are mentioned at all. Their language is not Quichua but a Jivaro dialect said to be very close to that spoken by the Shuar of the south-eastern foothills of the Andes. These scholarly works report that the Jivaro are divided into four tribes, the Shuar, the Aguaruna, the Achuar and the Huambisa, of which only the first two groups have been the subject of any study. Although they are linked linguistically and share common cultural elements, the four groups are clearly distinguished from one another by certain features of their social organization, their material culture and their systems of belief. Their land, which straddles the Amazonian border between Ecuador and Peru, is as large as Portugal but less populated than a single Parisian *arrondissement*. Each tribe occupies a clearly defined territory to which it denies the others access. The Achuar are said to be very isolated and far less numerous than the Shuar and the Aguaruna and to live along the Pastaza river and its tributaries, in thick jungle interspersed with swamps. As a result of the relative inaccessibility of their region and their apparently well deserved bellicose reputation, these seem to have remained isolated from the rest of the world right

13

down to the present day, unlike their fellow Jivaros, the Shuar, who for several decades have been subjected to the acculturation of the missions. This was all that was then known of the Achuar and it was what had made my companion and me keen to undertake extended ethnographical fieldwork.

People will no doubt find it hard to believe that it was not a fascination with their shrunken heads that led me to the Jivaros. Along with the Pygmies, the Eskimos and the Hottentots, the Jivaros are one of those 'primitive societies' that have caught the Western imagination because they have become archetypes of exotic peculiarity and are conveniently identifiable by one particular unusual custom or physical character- istic. The notoriety of the Jivaros is of by no means recent date. By the last third of the nineteenth century Europe was already seized by a fascination with this tribe, although it remained confined, as it is to this day, to its trophies. It was not so much the living society that was intriguing as the methods it employed to produce the end result: an anatomical incongruity that well-intentioned consuls persisted in sending home to museums. With no first-hand observation of the methods of reduction, scholars could do nothing but speculate on the techniques employed – a subject of interminable debate in the Anthropological Society of Paris, in which the great Broca made a particular impact. A few forensic doctors tried to discover the tech- nique by trial and error and ended up producing a number of pre- sentable heads. But of the Jivaros themselves virtually nothing was known and if they had not gone in for shrinking heads, they would probably have remained in the same obscurity as hundreds of other Amazonian tribes that have equally original cultures but lack the particular skill of taxidermy. At the end of the nineteenth century they were one of the rare peoples of the region who for three centuries had victoriously resisted colonial domination; and the world knew nothing of them apart from these macabre trophies that were swapped on the edges of their territory for axe-blades and spear-heads by a few enterprising *mestizos*. Furthermore, when genuine Jivaro production became unable to satisfy the growing demand of collectors in the know, unscrupulous taxidermists in Ecuador and Colombia them- selves turned their hands to producing shrunken heads in large quanti- ties, using the corpses of Indians fraudulently obtained from morgues.

These sinister remains would be offered to tourists passing through the Panama Canal, along with straw hats and fake pre-Colombian ornaments, and would subsequently be set to stand enigmatic guard over the collections of cultivated pre-war travellers, flanked by a Tanagra or an African mask: false, shrivelled evidence that continues to testify to many of the more despicable pretexts for ethnographic curiosity.

The great majority of authentic shrunken heads came from the Shuar tribe, the most numerous of the four groups speaking Jivaro dialects and also the one closest to the southern Andes of Ecuador. The isolation in which they had managed to continue to live began to crack in the 1930s, under pressure from the Salesian missionaries, who had been making attempts to reach them for twenty years. The Shuar were at that time still very difficult to reach since it took almost a week travelling on mule-back along a dreadful mountain track to get from the Andean town of Riobamba to Macas, the last small *mestizo* town, on the edge of their territory. But that path was now tackled and soon a few Shuar families moved to settle around the missionary outposts, while a handful of colonists began to descend to the lowlands, with the encouragement of the missionaries, who counted on their presence to provide the Jivaros with an exemplary model of civilized life. From that time on the way was open for ethnologists and adventurers who, with very rare exceptions, were for a long time content to skim the fringes of the tiny enclave established by the missionaries within the vast forest area occupied by the Shuar.

These forays into missionary territory were to produce a multitude of works more remarkable for their excessive hyperbole than for the quality and originality of their descriptions. Obliged by professional duty to consult this indigestible body of travel literature, I had at every turn encountered the same hackneyed anecdotes, the same erroneous or approximative information, the same insipid verbiage coating a few rudimentary nuggets of ethnographical information gleaned from the missionaries. Amid this jumble, the work of Rafael Karsten alone stands out, distinguished by the subtlety, precision and quality of his observations. In the 1920s this great Finnish Americanist had spent long periods living amongst the Shuar, the Aguaruna and the Canelos. From these he had produced a descriptive monograph that was for many years to remain the only trustworthy ethnographical study on the Jivaro groups, a work that was, moreover, virtually untraceable, having been published by some obscure scholarly society in Helsinki. A photograph in it shows him squeezed into a kind of Bavarian hunting costume, clad in gaiters and sporting a cravat, posed with professorial solemnity against a background of banana trees and palms. In this uncomfortable costume, the Scandinavian scholar nevertheless explored the forest with application and determination and his book barely even hints at the difficulties and dangers that he must have encountered – in happy contrast to the exasperating mixture of self-pity and self-glorification that usually punctuates the prose of explorers of Jivaro country.

In the late 1950s, an American ethnologist took over. Michael Harner spent over a year living amongst the Shuar, studying in particular their social organization and the shamanistic system. However, the book that he eventually published reads more like a catalogue of points of information than a truly anthropological analysis. Although his work complemented Karten's on some points, it failed to illuminate the basic principles that underlay the functioning of Shuar society. Admittedly, those principles did seem particularly difficult to illuminate. The picture that emerges from a reading of Karsten and Harner is the disturbing one of an Amazonian incarnation of man in a state of nature, a kind logical scandal bordering on an anarchistic utopia. None of the interpretation grids used by ethnologist seemed adequate to explain it. The Shuar, who lived in very dispersed, quasi self-sufficient extended family groups, were clearly without any of the centripetal institutions that generally ensure the cohesion of tribal communities. Knowing nothing of the social constraints associated with village settlements, this multitude of independent households had no need of political leaders or the intermediary social units — clans, lineages or age-groups — that maintain a minimum degree of internal equilibrium in other stateless societies. The Shuars' sovereign scorn for the elementary rules of communal life was compounded by their permanent and enthusiastic involvement in generalized vendettas. Not content to wage intense intertribal warfare, as many other Amazonian ethnic groups did, the Jivaros were constantly engaged in murderous conflicts with close neighbours or relatives. Apart from language and culture, the only link binding together this collection of households scattered through the jungle seemed to be the famous 'war of every man against every man' in which certain philsophers of the social contract, Hobbes first and foremost, believed they had detected the main characteristic of humanity in its natural state. However, the endemic permanence of intertribal warfare did not justify its being regarded as a pathology or accidental disfunctioning of society. Nor could it represent the survival of a hypothetical state of nature of the type imagined by classical philosophers since, on the contrary, all the evidence seems to suggest that warfare was a relatively late invention in the history of the human race.

Michael Harner provided some interesting data on the motivation and organization of the conflicts of the Shuar, but he was certainly a long way off solving the riddle of this internal warfare, set up as the sole institution of a people seemingly without any other social rules. In the early 1970s the Jivaros thus presented the curious paradox of still remaining on the periphery of ethnographical knowledge even though their name had a familiar ring throughout the West, as a result of a sinister reputation cultivated for close on a hundred years by travellers in search of exotic adventure. It was this strange discrepancy between ignorance and notoriety that had aroused our curiosity, not some fascination with human trophies. Furthermore, the few scholarly anthropological studies on the Jivaros were exclusively devoted to the Shuar, leaving the other, more inaccessible tribes in total obscurity. Nothing was known of the Achuar except that they lived to the east of the Shuar, were their hereditary enemies and had no contacts with Whites. If we were to try to resolve the sociological puzzle upon which our predecessors had been able to shed no light, the path seemed to lead to them.

Such information as could be gleaned from specialist libraries of the Old World conferred upon the Achuar the distinction of the unknown, something by now rare in the Amazonian world. We had just learned in Puyo that their lines of defence had recently been dented by American evangelists and also, much further to the south, by one Salesian priest, but that most of the tribe had still not succumbed to these missionary sirens. The most convenient way of taking our first steps into this *terra incognita* seemed to be to start by visiting the Achuar who lived on the Capahuari, a tributary that ran into the northern bank of the Pastaza. These Indians had recently accepted occasional visits by Shuar converts sent out as scouts by the Protestants, and it seemed reasonable to hope that they would be equally tolerant of us. As we could not reach them in the comfort of a mission aircraft, we would be forced to make a much longer journey: first on foot to the Dominican mission of Canelos, on the Bobonaza, then down the river by canoe as far as the Quichua village of Montalvo, and from there strike into the forest, heading south, to reach the Capahuari.

The journey as far as Montalvo seemed unlikely to present major difficulties. It had already been made by a whole cohort of missionaries, adventurers and soldiers. The Bobonaza was the only waterway navigable by canoe in this part of Ecuadorian Amazonia and, ever since the second half of the seventeenth century, it had been used as a link between the Canelos mission and the lower reaches of the Pastaza, where Jesuits had established themselves at Maynas. Beyond the Jesuit mission, the Pastaza provided access to the Marañon and thus to the fluvial network of the Amazon. If one set out by canoe from Canelos, it would be reasonable to hope to reach the Atlantic coast in just under a year.

A number of our predecessors on this interminable aquatic route had won fame in Paris from their travels: Abbé Pierre, of course, but also the explorer Bertrand Flornoy, who had travelled down the Bobonaza in the thirties, and above all the extraordinary Isabelle Godin des Odonnais. This tragic heroine of a great conjugal love affair was the wife of a minor member of the geodesic mission sent to Quito by Louis XV to measure a meridian arc at the latitude of the equator. In October 1769 she decided to join her husband, who was waiting for her in Cayenne, not by the then usual route that circumnavigated the Pacific and the Atlantic, but by cutting straight across the continent. The intrepid Doña Isabelle accordingly embarked in a canoe at Canelos with her two brothers, her young nephew, a doctor, a black slave, three chambermaids and a mountain of luggage. She was soon to live through an appalling adventure in the heart of what is now Achuar territory.

Her troubles began when the native canoeists abandoned the little group of travellers under cover of night, after two days proceeding down the Bobonaza. As nobody was capable of manoeuvring the heavily loaded craft, it was decided that the whole company should disembark while the doctor and the black slave were sent ahead to seek aid from the mission at Andoas, several days' journey downstream. When three weeks had passed with no news of the two emissaries, Isabelle and her family built a ramshackle raft on which to try to reach Andoas. At the first eddies it fell apart and, although everybody managed with difficulty to escape the whirlpools, all the provisions and luggage were lost in the catastrophe. Now all they could do was make their way laboriously along the Bobonaza on steep banks covered with inextricable vegetation, taking it in turns to carry the child. To spare their already dwindling strength, the marooned band tried to take short cuts across the loops: a fatal mistake as they soon lost the guiding thread of the river and became lost in the jungle, where one by one they died of exhaustion and starvation.

Isabelle Godin des Odonnais was the sole survivor. Having lost her clothes and shoes, she was reduced to stripping the corpse of one of her brothers, to cover herself. She even managed to find her way back to the Bobonaza and followed it for nine days before coming across Indian converts from the Andoas mission, who finally led her to safety. Her sufferings were over, but not her travels. It took her over a year to rejoin her husband at the other end of the Amazon. The story of this involuntary heroine, relayed from mouth to ear the length of the whole great river, meanwhile became the stuff of legend, embellished with fabulous episodes and risqué anecdotes that deeply shocked the lady's austere modesty. The memory of this epic has now been obliterated from the minds of the riverside dwellers as thoroughly as the camp that the marooned travellers set up two centuries ago on the banks of the Bobonaza. All that remains, in the mind of one ethnologist, is a fleeting vision of a woman in a farthingale struggling through the despairingly empty forest he himself is preparing to enter.

Just over twenty-five years before these events, Charles de la Condamine, the most illustrious member of the geodesic expedition, had also explored the Amazonian territories of the Audience of Quito. Once the triangulation measurements and the astronomical observations that had occupied him in the Andes were completed, this famous geographer had decided to return to France by way of the Amazon, making an exact map of the river as he did so. His journey, which

THE SPEARS OF TWILIGHT

began in May 1743, unfolded more smoothly than that of the luckless Isabelle. He had opted for the route, quite popular at the time, that led from Loja, in the Sierra, to Jaén, on the banks of the Marañon, thereby making a large detour around the *terra incognita* inhabited by the Jivaros. In fact, he hardly mentions them in his account of the journey, merely noting the terror that they inspired in the riverside dwellers of the Marañon, who were regularly subjected to their blood-thirsty raids. La Condamine remained more or less unconcerned about them, preoccupied as he was with mapping the course of the river accurately and establishing its depth and the force of the current. It is true that the seven years spent in the Andes, minutely checking the shape and size of the planet, had inured him to the wildest of adventures. Along with his scientific companions, Louis Godin, Pierre Bouguer and Joseph de Jussieu, he had encountered every kind of obstacle, triumphed over every kind of setback and undergone every kind of humiliation that could assail a scientific expedition to the edges of the civilized world.

These extremely youthful Academicians, passionately interested in mathematics, botany and astronomy, were prepared scarcely better than I was to confront the practical difficulties of the task that faced them. Far removed from the austere satisfactions of work in the seclusion of their book-lined studies, in order to carry out their mission they had been obliged to become now surveyors, now mountain climbers, now foremen, now diplomats. They had had to cajole colonial authorities who suspected them of spying and exhaust themselves in administrative bickering each time they returned to Quito for a rest after a measuring expedition. Bombarded by lawsuits and threatened by expulsion, they would then set off once again to camp in the mountains, suffering from hunger and cold and surrounded by hostile Indians, in order to complete the unusual project that was to transform men's knowledge of the earth. In one respect they resembled modern ethnologists: for them adventure was not an end in itself but simply the spur that lent zest to their research work or, on occasion, obstructed it. They accepted it as an inevitable component of fieldwork, perhaps vaguely hoped for it before setting out, and occasionally relished it when some unexpected but amusing incident broke into their painstaking routine. In this distant land where they had preceded me so many years ago, those young scientists remained in my thoughts, perhaps because I was in need of the immodest comfort of the glorious precedent that their behaviour afforded me.

The profession of ethnologist presents a curious paradox. The public perceives it as a pastime for erudite explorers, while those who practise it place themselves, rather, amongst the ranks of the orderly community described by Bachelard as workers for proof. The world to which we are accustomed is not so much that of the steppe, jungle and desert, but rather one of lecture halls and nocturnal struggles with the blank page, an ordeal repeated *ad infinitum* and far more daunting than any encounter with some unamenable member of the Amazonian bestiary. In a training devoted essentially to the carefree study of the humanities, there is nothing to prepare an apprentice ethnographer for the discomfort of camping that some imagine to be the hallmark of his vocation. If such a vocation exists at all, it is born more of an insidious sense of inadequacy *vis-à-vis* the world, too powerful to be successfully overcome yet too weak to lead to a major revolt. Distant curiosity cultivated as a refuge ever since childhood is not the prerogative solely of ethnologists. Other observers of humankind make use of it in a far more spectacular fashion, bringing it to fruition with talents that the ethnologist lacks. Ill at ease in the great plains of imaginary representation, we are obliged to knuckle under to the servile obedience to reality from which poets and novelists liberate themselves. The observation of exotic cultures thus becomes a kind of substitute: it enables the ethnologist to enter into the Utopian world without submitting himself to the whims of the imagination. Directing a vacillating desire for power into the net of rational explanation, we are in this way able to appropriate through our thoughts societies whose destinies we should never be able to influence. No yearning for the heroic exploit is involved. Our contemplative world is not the world of men of action.

I myself was trained for textual criticism and reflective studies. I knew how to establish a genealogy and identify a kinship terminology. I had been taught how to measure a field using a compass and a surveyor's chain, but nothing in my earlier life had prepared me for the role of a trapper. As an apathetic *normalien* and an undistinguished philosopher, in my perusal of the classics of sociology I had discovered welcome compensation for the purgatory of amassing qualifications. My escape was a lonely one. My companions, devoted to the uncompromising cult of epistemology, considered the social sciences an insufficiently rigorous kind of distraction, deplorably lacking in the 'scientificity' that they aimed to track down in Aristotelian 'physics' or the mathematical texts of Leibniz. My interest in ethnology thus won me a reputation for amiable futility, and the nickname 'Feathers'.

Yet it was a former member of the *École normale* who had guided me in this direction. During the few months when he was responsible for teaching economic anthropology there, Maurice Godelier had introduced within our walls the beginnings of legitimacy for the social sciences. This young *'cayman'* (the term for a young, temporary lecturer, in the slang of the *École normale supérieur*) bathed in the prestige of his first book, and showed us that it was possible to undertake a rigorous analysis of the interactions between economics and society, even among archaic peoples whose institutions lacked the functional transparency to which sociological dissection of the modern world had accustomed us. Dissatisfied with philosophical exegesis and total dedication to purely theoretical work, I decided to desert my classmates, leaving them to their metaphysical fervour. Instead of holding forth on the pre-conditions for the production of truth, I would plunge into the darkness of empiricism and strive to give a rational account of the facts of society.

At Maurice Godelier's suggestion, I made a pilgrimage to the Collège de France in order to consult Claude Lévi-Strauss in his sanctuary. My underlying *normalien* arrogance was of no help to me in such a formidable situation. The idea of approaching one of the greatest minds of the age plunged me into unprecedented terror. Having installed me in the depths of a vast leather armchair, the seat of which was almost at floor level, the founder of structural anthropology listened to me with impassive courtesy from the heights of an upright wooden chair. The comfort of the seat in which I was stuck did nothing to dissipate my stage-fright. I felt as if I were on a grill made red-hot by the attentive silence of my examiner. Increasingly convinced of the insignificance of my plans as I unfolded them, and conscious that my chatter must be interrupting tasks of the greatest importance, I stammeringly brought this oral examination of a new

22

kind to a close. To my astonishment, my ordeal was crowned with success. Claude Lévi-Strauss not only showered me with affable encouragement but even agreed to direct my research and supervise my thesis.

Loath to reproduce in ethnology the kind of abstractions that had alienated me from philosophy, I was determined to submit myself forthwith to the test of monographic enquiry. This rite of passage, which marks one's entry into the brotherhood of ethnologists, may take extremely varied forms now that social anthropology has annexed 'fields' less and less distant. But a certain romantic idea of this initiatory experience, nurtured by my reading of the great French and Anglo-Saxon classics of exotic ethnography, deterred me from settling for some working-class suburb, multinational company or village in the Beauce. My aspiration was to immerse myself in a society where nothing would be obvious and where the way of life, language and forms of thought would become intelligible only gradually, after a long apprenticeship and much patient, ascetic analysis. What I was after, in short, was a miraculously closed society, calibrated so as to suit the surveying skills of a single individual. Such a project furthermore demanded pioneering work. I had to deny myself the prop of the erudition of others and strive on my own to seize upon the spirit of a free and solitary people as yet untouched by civilization. Of all the great ethnographic regions, Amazonia seemed to me the most propitious in which to take up this intellectual challenge, for the grandiloquence of which I took full responsibility. To be sure, history is not unknown in this region of the world. Yet Amazonia is not West Africa or southern Asia. Its peoples have not been divided up and recomposed by caste systems or conquering states, they have not been fragmented or amalgamated by the slave trade, they have not wandered off along interminable trading routes, nor have they experienced the imposition of strict political hierarchies based upon the separation of functions and skills; nor, last but by no means least, have they been affected by the imperious expansion of the major religions. The absence of all these unificatory currents and the formidable disintegration caused by epidemics over the past five centuries have made contemporary Amazonia an assemblage of miniature societies that exerts a strong attraction upon ethnologists who prize uniqueness. In a career in which you are identified first and foremost by the people that you study, and in which intellectual affinities often grow out of the complicity engendered by comparable ethnographic experiences, it is rarely the case that the initial choice of your continent of enquiry is a matter of pure chance. Each region in the world and each kind of society exercises its own attraction upon particular characters, producing a subtle typology that fieldwork tends to confirm. Thus, the squabbling that is a feature of the discipline often simply expresses a mutual incomprehension between different styles of relating to others; and theoretical disagreements may mask far more fundamental incompatibilities relating to different ways of being in the world. Amazonia disconcerts engineers of social mechanics and those with a messianic temperament. It is preferred by reasonable misanthropes who love the echo of their own solitude that they find in the isolation of the Indians; they are passionate in their defence when their survival, culture or independence is threatened, not because they wish to lead them to a better destiny, but because they find it hard to bear seeing others subjected to the great common laws they themselves have always been tempted to evade.

Besides, a number of scholarly arguments did reinforce my personal inclinations. In the course of my reading of the Americanist literature, I had been struck by the great gaps in our knowledge betrayed by the ethnographic inventories of the Amazon and Orinoco basins. Despite the pillage and genocide to which the inhabitants had been subjected over four centuries, this great forest still sheltered isolated ethnic groups about whom nothing, apart from a name and an approximate location, was known. Claude Lévi-Strauss himself had often drawn his colleagues' attention to the need to develop research in this cultural area, where he had made his first forays and which had since supplied him with many of the myths analysed in his *oeuvre*. Being particularly interested in Jivaro mythology and aware of the urgency of the task yet to be accomplished, he had encouraged me to embark without delay upon my projected research on those Achuar still under temporary reprieve from assimilation. Having, through his intercession, obtained funding for my mission from the *Centre nationale de la recherche scientifique*, I was finally in possession of the magic 'go ahead' that all ethnographic expeditions require.

It was this – it must be said – quite modest support that I was eating away in Puyo with my preparations for departure. Since the

Achuar were clearly beyond any monetary circuits, it was important for us to obtain small tradeable goods with which to repay them for their hospitality. In Paris I had been advised to procure glass beads. These ornaments, made in Czech workshops and aimed exclusively at exotic markets, were hard to come by in Latin America, where the Indians continued to consider them precious, highly desirable objects. Equipped with a chit duly stamped by the accounts department of the Collège de France, I had purchased jars of these multicoloured beads in a little shop situated behind the Bastille, possibly the very same one once visited by my thesis supervisor before his departure for Brazil. The idea of soon having to distribute this junk, as had the bearded explorers in nineteenth-century engravings, as their palan-quins overlooked the Zambesi Falls or they parleyed with Kaffirs at the gates to a *kraal* in southern Africa, seemed totally unreal. These anachronistic preparations set a bygone tone and filled me with a parodic pleasure that owed more to the reminiscences of Jules Verne than to my gloomy memories of scouting. It was, moreover, prompted by a literary loyalty to the spirit of pre-war ethnographic expeditions – and as a kind of *hommage* to Henri Michaud, who had preceded us to this country – that we travelled slowly to Ecuador by cargo-boat, to unload our trunks and supplies at the port of Guayaquil, where nothing appeared to have changed since Paul Morand stopped off there.

As a result of my contacts with the prosaic merchants of Puyo, my romantic preconceptions had been adjusted to reality: our supplies of glassware would certainly be well received, but it was impressed upon us that the Indians would also appreciate articles of ironmongery. Admittedly, nothing definite was known of the tastes of the Achuar in these matters, but the chances were that they would conform with those of the Canelos who came shopping in the town stores. On the advice of the store-keepers we accordingly purchased lengths of cloth to make loincloths – measured in *varas*, the *ancien régime* measure-ment – nylon fishing lines and hooks, machetes and axe-heads, knives and needles, not to mention a good supply of mirrors and hairslides to please the girls.

While I was methodically working out the costs of our river transport and accumulating all this *bric-à-brac* in the overheated concrete cell that served as our bedroom in the Hotel Europa, the chance of an immediate departure for Montalvo came up. A small Ecuadorian Air Force plane was due to fly there the next day, with supplies for the military outpost, and could offer us places on this flight, thereby sparing us the long journey by canoe down the Bobonaza.

At the first glimmer of dawn we presented ourselves at the Shell-Mera aerodrome, situated a few kilometres from Puyo at the foot of a steep circle of cliffs surmounted by the peaks of the eastern Cordillera. On that morning the sky was, for once, clear and to the south we could see the snowcapped cone of the Sangay volcano, flushed by the rays of the rising sun and hanging there like a huge floating island enfolded in mists above the still dark barrier constituted by the first spurs of the Andes.

As our plane gained altitude, detaching itself from the bluish foothills and striking towards the blinding morning sun, the orderly arrangement of tea plantations gave way to a scattering of cleared areas. Here and there the tin roof of a colonist made a splash of brightness. Soon the clearings became increasingly rare and the last traces of the pioneer frontier were eventually swallowed up in a sea of little green hills gently undulating away to an indistinct horizon. Beneath our wings, the forest looked like a huge, lumpy carpet of broccoli, interspersed with the paler plumes of thick clusters of palm trees. After just a few minutes airborne we had left behind us a landscape that though only skimpily indicated by a number of familiar signs spoke of human activity to plunge into an anonymous, infinitely repetitive world with no reference points at all. There were no holes, no rent in this mantle of greenery occasionally embroidered with a silvery thread by the reflection of the sun in a tiny twisting rivulet. No signs of life on the beaches, no solitary wisp of smoke; nothing betrayed any human presence beneath that monotonous canopy.

I was torn between anxiety at having soon to find my way through the undergrowth of that immense deserted place and exaltation at finally setting eyes on the real Amazonia, the deep forest in whose existence I had in the end begun to doubt. Living for a while in Puyo had fostered the illusion that the entire jungle resembled the town's distant cleared suburbs, a sort of semi-savannah dotted with residual copses and thickets of bamboo, its denuded hillsides scarred with muddy patches of erosion. Yet we had left that degraded border

26

behind us in less time than it takes for a ship to cast off from the harbour and reach the open seas.

We had been flying over this ocean for nearly an hour when Montalvo came into sight, a straw-coloured gash within a curve of the Bobonaza. A row of rectangular barracks with sheet-metal roofs bordering the landing-strip signalled the military base, while the small huts roofed with palms in which the Canelos lived wound around the outer rim of the clearing and along the banks of the river. A captain and his two lieutenants welcomed us in friendly fashion, pleased at the unexpected irruption into the crushing boredom of this garrison outpost. As expected, they knew nothing of the Achuar of Capahuari. After much consultation, we were presented with two Canelos guides who claimed to be able to lead us to them the very next morning. If we made good time, we would reach our goal in two days, taking a path that the Indians of Montalvo sometimes used in order to barter goods with the Achuar.

The afternoon and evening were spent in the mess, discussing the attractions of Paris, the merits of General de Gaulle and, inevitably, the exploits of the Foreign Legion. Alone in one corner, a very young second lieutenant was reading *Mein Kampf* in a well-thumbed Spanish translation. Like all the officers of the Ecuadorian land forces, our hosts were expected to serve part of their time in Oriente outposts close to Peru. These young men from the middle classes of the larger towns of the Sierra and the Pacific coast underwent this episode of Amazonian purgatory in resigned isolation, knowing as little about the forest and the Indians so close to them as if they had been stationed on a lightship in the mid-Atlantic. The few hours exchanging polite military conversation that we spent with them were like something from the pages of a colonial novel in the manner of Somerset Maugham: we really had nothing to say to one another, but as we were the only socially acceptable Whites for hundreds of kilometres, it was necessary to keep up a façade of the kind of awkward urbanity that testifies to complicity between civilized people in the midst of savages.

At dawn we plunged without transition into the opposite camp, on the trail of the parallel continent that we had chosen to make ours for the next few years. Our two Quichua guides took us in a rickety little canoe across the Bobonaza, then immediately halted at a native

27

hut on the river bank. Once their cargo had been distributed a Canelos woman served them several gourdfuls of manioc beer while they cracked jokes in the Quichua language, no doubt at our expense. As we took our leave she emptied the contents of her gourd over one of them, making a number of ironical remarks that provoked general hilarity. We had understood nothing of what they said, nothing of what they did: it was a typical ethnographic situation.

Having crossed the garden surrounding the house, we began to move into the jungle, taking a narrow, muddy track, already drenched by the dew from the manioc leaves that had spattered us as we passed. I have now only a vague memory of that first forest march that was to be followed by so many others. Our guides adopted a short but very rapid stride, their feet barely leaving the ground, the better to ensure the stability of each step. This steady, rapid pace soon got the better of any inclination of mine to contemplate nature. Barely an hour after our leaving Montalvo the path had become almost indistinguishable and I was plodding ahead as if in blinkers, my eyes fixed on the ground, hardly aware of the riot of plants just beyond my field of vision, trying to place my feet exactly in the tracks of the guide in front of me and every so often tripping over roots or slipping on the damp clay underfoot. The path was very uneven, for we were constantly climbing up or down steep little mounds separated from one another by streams of water. We forded the streams, paddling through the clear water, but the deeper rivers had to be crossed on bridges formed by flexible, slippery tree-trunks, the sole evidence of human activity along this indistinct track.

Towards late afternoon one of the guides killed a toucan with my rifle and soon after we halted to prepare it. A small shelter with a lean-to roof was soon erected, using a few sticks and bracken fronds, and the fowl was plucked and arranged on a spit. One of the Canelos kept its long multicoloured beak to make a powder container while the other took possession of its tongue, which he planned to use as an ingredient in a love potion. Our companions ate this small specimen of game with great relish, but I was not impressed by its gastronomic virtues. I felt I could have appreciated it better in an aviary in the Jardin des Plantes than in a billycan of lukewarm rice.

By six o'clock next morning we were already on the march, moving like automata in torrential rain that the canopy of trees did little to fend off. At midday we at last reached the Capahuari. The river was wider than any we had crossed so far, flowing between high terraces with slopes covered by impenetrable vegetation. The path twisted upstream, following the sheer raised edge of the plateau and keeping close to the constantly looping course of the river. Here and there the steep bank was pierced by little lateral combes that we had to scramble down in order to cross a stream joining the river. The clouds had dispersed and in the heavy midday heat the forest was slumped in a profound silence hardly disturbed by the bubbling eddies from time to time caused by a dead tree-trunk obstructing the river.

We had been following the edge of the Capahuari for about two hours when we heard a dog barking in the distance. Almost immediately the path led into a large clearing planted with manioc and dazzlingly bright after the semi-darkness of the forest. In the middle stood an oval-shaped house with a roof of palms but no outer walls. At our approach a pack of scrawny dogs surrounded us in a threatening circle and some little naked children, who had been playing in a stream, dashed for the safety of the house, leaving one sitting on the ground in tears, too paralysed by fright to run away. From beneath the projecting roof two women clad in blue cotton loincloths stared at us in silence. One of them sported a little wooden tube fixed beneath her lower lip and her face was covered with red and black patterns. Their men were absent and they indicated unequivocally that we should continue on our way. Despite our weariness, of which the thwarted hope of a halt had made us more aware, we were obliged to plunge back into the forest.

The sun was beginning to set by the time we arrived at a small esplanade with its entire length cleared, which must have served as a landing-strip for the planes of the evangelist mission. A few hundred metres below this strip stood a much bigger house than the one we had seen earlier, in which could be glimpsed a group of men engaged in conversation. They wore their hair long, gathered into pony-tails, and their faces too were striped with red lines; some of them rested rifles on their knees. They had long since noticed us but haughtily ignored our presence, pretending to be absorbed in their discussion.

At twenty paces from the house our two guides put down their burdens and exchanged a few words in Quichua with a young man who had been peering out at us from inside the house, slightly apart

29

from the others. Then, turning to us, the Canelos announced that we had arrived at the home of Wajari, an Achuar famous the whole length of the Capahuari, and that they had to return immediately to Montalvo now that their mission was completed. Taken aback by this unexpected departure, I asked them at least to explain to the Achuar why we were there. But they merely shook their heads in an embarrassed fashion. When pressed, they eventually admitted to me that they preferred to spend the night in the forest rather than sleep among the Achuar. Having vouchsafed this rather alarming explanation, they departed rapidly in the direction from which we had come, without any gesture of salutation to the Indians, who went on talking among themselves, totally indifferent to our presence. It was the penultimate day of October 1976, the feast-day of Saint Welcome.

I

TAMING THE FOREST

Everything on this earth multiplies: fecundity is the soul of Nature and the agent of its preservation. Each species has a constant and unvarying lesson to teach us: men who do not follow her are useless on the earth, undeserving of the food that she provides for all in common yet that they are so ungrateful as to use solely for their own maintenance.

BARON DE LAHONTAN,
Dialogues with a Savage

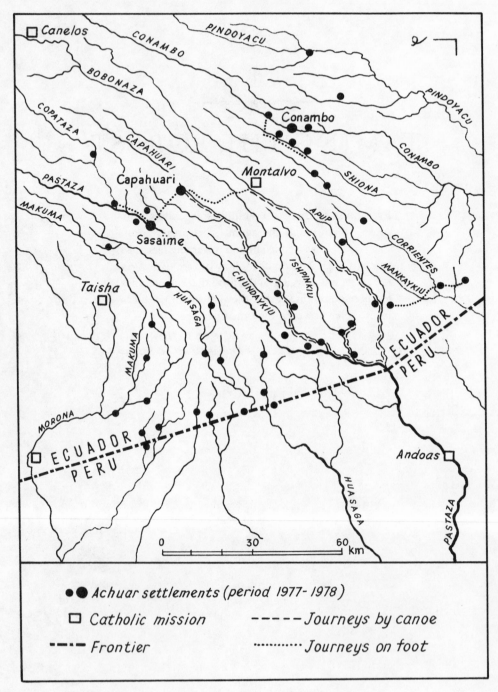

3. Achuar country in Ecuador

CHAPTER 1

Apprenticeship

WAJARI RETURNS FROM his bathe adjusting his old *itip*, a loincloth with vertical stripes of red, yellow, white and blue that reaches to mid-calf. Like most of the men here, he usually wears a pair of shorts or trousers, keeping his traditional costume for home use. The brown swirling water of the Capahuari flows past below the house, but a little inlet in the bank makes safe bathing possible. Here, the current is slowed down by a huge tree-trunk, barely submerged athwart the river bed and used by the children for diving. A few steps made out of logs are set in the steep incline of the bank, making it possible to reach the river without slipping down the clay slope. Secured by a thick creeper to the roots of a kapok tree-stump, a hollowed-out wooden canoe is pulled halfway up the bank. Its horizontal prow sticking out over the river provides a convenient place for washing clothes or dishes or for filling large pear-shaped bottle gourds with water. Dozens of yellow butterflies flutter about inside this floating sink-hole and above the river mud, competing with columns of tiny ants for the remains of the last meal. The people here use the name Kapawi for this stretch of water that the Ecuadorian maps and the Quichuas of Montalvo call Capahuari, a deformation of the Achuar word, itself an abbreviation of Kapawientza, 'the river of the *kapawi*', a species of flat fish.

It is late afternoon but still hot, the heat hardly tempered by the little breeze that circulates freely through the wall-less house. Inside, the dimness is obliquely crossed by long shafts of light that stripe the beaten-earth floor, occasionally catching a thin thread of smoke or the erratic flight of a fat bronze-tinged fly. Seen from inside the house, the vegetation of the garden and the forest is dazzling beneath the dark line of the roof's overhang, an uninterrupted panel of shades of

33

nothing but brilliant green. This *pointilliste* background makes the dwelling darker by contrast and melds into a dominant sepia the pinkish sand of the floor, the blackened brown of the thatch, the dark hue of the bedsteads and the bright ochre of the large jars in which manioc is fermenting.

Wajari has silently sat down on the small, carved, wooden seat that is reserved for him: a concave tree-trunk section set on top of a pyramid-shaped base and ornamented by a jutting lozenge shaped like the head of a reptile. He is a man of thirty or so with dark, almost curly hair, a hooked nose and eyes full of irony beneath his sooty brows. His movements are deft despite his slight stoutness. He has been away hunting with his blowpipe since dawn and has only recently returned, shouldering a plump, white-lipped peccary. On his return the women and children fell silent, each feigning indifference at the sight of this choice booty. Without a word, he dropped his burden at the feet of Senur, the eldest of his wives, then went off to bathe in the Kapawi, after carefully tidying away his blowpipe in a vertical position on a little rack fixed to one of the posts holding up the house. Soon afterwards, Senur brought him the peccary, which he proceeded to skin and bone in a trice, using an old machete-blade as sharp as a razor.

Now Wajari is staring at the ground, avoiding looking in my direction, his elbows resting on his knees, apparently absorbed in profound meditation. His face looks darker than usual as his bathe did not altogether wash off the rocou dye painted on before setting off on his hunting expedition. I am seated opposite him on the little wooden bench reserved for visitors, leaning against one of the posts supporting the roof's overhang at the outer edge of the house. I model my attitude on his and pretend to take no notice of him, absorbed in a Jivaro lexicon put together for pastoral purposes by one of the Salesian missionaries.

Suddenly the master of the house loudly exclaims, '*Nijiamanch! Wari, jiamanch, jiamanch, jiamanch!*' It is time for the women to serve the manioc beer, *nijiamanch*, the smooth, slightly alcoholic drink that constitutes the ordinary, everyday beverage. My companions never drink pure water and the manioc beer serves as much to slake their thirst as to fill their stomachs and lubricate conversation. A few extra days of fermentation turns it into a strong drink that is

consumed in repeated libations on festive occasions. As Senur is busy disembowelling the peccary at the river's edge, it is her sister Entza, the second wife, who hurries to her husband's side with a *pininkia*, a large earthenware bowl coated in white and delicately decorated with red and black geometric patterns. With one hand plunged into the white liquid, she kneads the manioc paste to help it to dissolve in the water, now and again discarding fibres that float to the surface. Good beer must be smooth, without lumps, creamy to the palate and not too watery. But Wajari ignores the bowl proffered by his wife and, without looking at her, mutters what seems to be a reprimand: '*Apach!*', 'The White!' Having handed me the *pininkia*, Entza fetches a second one for Wajari, then positions herself a few paces behind him with a large gourd full of beer that she mechanically continues to mix, ready to refill our bowls. With her forearm folded across her opulent bosom to protect it against the mosquitoes that plague us at this hour of the day, and her rounded belly protruding like that of a pregnant woman, she watches complacently over her husband.

Nijiamanch is drunk according to a precise code of seemly behaviour, which I assimilated within a few days, since learning about an unknown culture always begins with table manners. It would be unthinkable to refuse a bowl offered by a woman. To do so would be interpreted as a grave indication of distrust of one's host, implying a suspicion that he had poisoned the brew. Apparently only the dying or overt enemies would reject *nijiamanch* offered to them, thereby through this very behaviour giving a clear sign of their true condition. However, it is important not to receive the *pininkia* with too much eagerness: a great show of reserve is expected, and under no circumstances should a stranger to the household look at the woman who serves him, under pain of being taken for a seducer. This evasive behaviour makes the matter of drinking all the more complicated since it is unseemly for a male to touch manioc beer: it is the women who exercise full control over it right up to the moment when it is swallowed. So when, as frequently happens, an insect attracted by the milky liquid is struggling to avoid drowning in it, all a man can do is blow gently on the surface to help it to alight safely on the rim. Touched by the drinker's efforts, his hostess will then come over to rid him of the importunate fly and once again knead the fermented paste in his *pininkia*. The guest turns his head ostentatiously away from her as he holds out his bowl at arm's length for her to do so.

It is with a similar gesture, using the appropriate kinship term to call her, that a man requests a refill. Having been served three times, courtesy and an exhibitionist sense of frugality dictate that each subsequent round of drinks be weakly declined, while at the same time the laws of hospitality rule that the women take no notice of this show of politeness. Protestations become more forceful as one refill succeeds another, but they are usually ineffectual. It is more or less taken for granted that a man can never drink less than half a dozen bowlfuls without deeply offending the hostess who is serving him. But when several women are ministering to him simultaneously, it is acceptable for him to return at least one of his *pininkia* before reaching that fateful mark. Only great inventiveness in one's excuses and great vehemence in their formulation will finally assuage the self-respect of the woman serving the beer and enable one to be relieved of one's inexhaustible *pininkia*.

The wives are total mistresses of this little game which, despite the Achuar's fondness for their drink, sometimes ends up by resembling the barrel torture. The initial sound of appreciative smacking lips is soon replaced by discreet burps, one's stomach swells up like a balloon, the slight acidity of the beverage produces an unpleasant taste in the mouth, and one's irrepressible desire to empty one's overfull bladder has to be controlled for the sake of good manners. When the women are feeling malicious, the pleasures of conviviality thus eventually evaporate, as their false solicitude becomes an unrelenting weapon in the unequally balanced contest of strength between the sexes.

Today, fortunately, that is not the case. In fact, as Wajari is busy all day long, away from the house, the evening *nijiamanch* session is one of the rare moments when I can pursue my task, to get the person known in French anthropology by the rather unpleasant name of 'informateur' to talk to me. In truth, I find it very hard to consider Wajari as *informateur*, as the term, conflating as it does the meanings of informer and informant, cannot but evoke to my mind one of those shifty figures in crime or spy stories who peddle their information for money secretively. No doubt we owe that inelegant terminological legacy to the tradition of the pre-war Africanist ethnologists who, surrounded by their boys, porters and interpreters, would, during working hours, dispense payment from their verandas to the native wise men, just as if they were tipping a gardener. Admittedly, the ethnographers of Amazonia are themselves no angels in this respect and also make handouts for all kinds of reasons, both bad and good: you cannot invade the privacy of total strangers without offering some repayment for their goodwill and ensuring, by presenting some offerings immediately upon arrival, that they will not turn you out.

That was what we had counted on when we made our way to the Kapawi with no edible provisions but plenty of small trade goods, as indeed Wajari seemed to understand when he invited us to stay in his house, in the evening of our first meeting. After our two Quichua guides' precipitous departure for Montalvo, the young Achuar who had spoken with them in their language had invited us into Wajari's house in very basic Spanish. Tseremp had acquired his multilingual skills whilst working for a few months as an unskilled worker for a company prospecting for petroleum on the Rio Curaray, to the north of the Achuar territory. I had explained to him that we would like to spend a few days there, learning the Jivaro language, and he had assumed that we were American Protestant missionaries – a belief that, in altogether bad faith, I had neither corrected nor confirmed. Tseremp had then acted as our interpreter *vis-à-vis* the master of the house and, after a long discussion to which we had listened with anxious incomprehension, he had transmitted Wajari's invitation to us to stay in his home.

That very evening I had given Wajari a large machete and a length of material for each of his wives, which he had accepted in silence, seeming to attach no importance to the gifts. During the week that we had been sharing the life of the household he seemed to have accepted our presence almost as though it were natural, keeping a friendly distance but attentive to our needs in a manner both discreet and unservile. Once or twice we had given his wives and children small presents and dispensed medicine to alleviate a crisis of malaria or a small baby's diarrhoea. But I did not feel that these gifts were corrupting nor that they turned Wajari into an *informateur* duly remunerated for disclosing the secrets of his culture in response to my inquisition.

My host continues, in silence, to knock back the manioc beer that his wife is liberally serving him. He takes a last swig, then suddenly turns to me, looking me straight in the eye. According to etiquette, conversation is now permissible and the initiative falls to him, as always with visitors.

'Is everything all right?'

'Yes, fine.'

'And your wife, is she all right?'

'Yes, she is fine.'

So far, nothing too difficult. The little Roneoed Shuar–Spanish dictionary of Father Luigi Bolla makes it possible, despite the differences of vocabulary between the two dialects, for me to sustain this scintillating dialogue. Emboldened by success, I try a slightly less banal line.

'And what is that?' I ask, pointing to his seat.

'It is a *chimpui*.'

I already knew this; the missionary's invaluable lexicon explains that a *chimpui* is a small, wooden, sculpted stool. But I am intrigued by its zoomorphic appearance, and what I am after is its symbolic significance.

'Yes, it is a *chimpui*, but what is it?'

'It's a complete *chimpui*, a true *chimpui*.'

I do not know many ways of asking a question but, as well as 'what is it?' I do know how to say 'why?'

'Why the *chimpui*?'

Wajari answers with a long sentence in which I think I can make out that 'our ancestors' and 'my father' have from time immemorial considered it inconceivable to sit on anything but a *chimpui*. It is the typical vicious circle of explanations in terms of tradition, from which the ethnographer can escape only by taking startling action or else by inventing some complicated yet plausible interpretation. I settle for audacity rather than imagination and, in defiance of all convention, I approach Wajari's *chimpui* and touch the little lozenge shaped like the head of a reptile, repeating my question. 'And this, what is it?'

Another gloss follows. I can catch only the opening words, *yantana nuke*, which, upon frantic consultation of the lexicon, turn out to mean 'cayman's head'. Wajari enthusiastically proceeds with a commentary that remains totally unintelligible to me. Anxious at least to respect appearances, I punctuate his speech with vigorously appreciative interjections such as 'that's the truth, that's the truth,' and 'well said!' as I have heard the Achuar do in their conversations. But inside, I feel desperate. What Wajari is so obligingly telling me is probably his people's myth of origins and, to crown it all, I have forgotten to switch on my tape-recorder. The arrogant protocol of ethnographic investigation is taking a lamentable knock, my probing conversation is turning into a rout, my enquiry into the oral tradition is sinking into the sands of incomprehension.

My conceited scorn for interpreters and those who resort to them is beginning to crumble. Perhaps it would be better to put up with the unverifiable interpretations of native specialists in cultural popularization than to suffer from the persistent ignorance engendered by the language barrier. However, we have no choice. Tseremp's Spanish is much too rudimentary for us to turn him into a translator and nobody else here is bilingual. In fact, the main reason why I find it hard to regard Wajari as the *informateur* patented by the textbooks of ethnography is that I cannot understand a word of what he is telling me. I feel that he is playing his role perfectly, without ever having learnt it, whilst I am failing in mine, despite having prepared for it for years.

Silence once more falls between us and I console myself for my scientific doubts with the memory of a piece of advice that Claude Lévi-Strauss gave me as I was leaving. When I had finished swamping him with a detailed account of the enquiry techniques that I planned to use and the subtle problems that they would enable me to resolve, he had brought our conversation to a close with the simple words, 'Just let yourself go along with the lie of the land.' At this point, there is nothing else I can do.

Senur has returned from the Kapawi having cut the peccary into quarters and washed the innards. Before setting about preparing the animal for cooking, she has first grilled the liver and kidneys on a little spit, then offered them to her husband. When invited to share this snack, we are all the more appreciative given that, in a cuisine dominated by the blandness of boiled dishes, the giblets of hunted animals are the only morsels that are eaten roasted. Entza and Mirunik have meanwhile constructed a smoking grid of green wood over a hearth, where the game will be set to smoke. The smoking grid is used by the entire household, but the meat has already been shared out between Senur and the other wives. As the senior wife, she has kept two haunches and a nice section of chine. The rest is divided between the other two wives.

For supper, each wife chooses a choice piece from her share and sets it to simmer in a pot of manioc or taro. Each in turn comes to deposit at our feet a helping of the stew served on *tachau*, large earthenware plates with a black glaze. Wajari has been similarly served and summons his two adolescent sons, Chiwian and Paantam, to share his meal, while Senur, Entza and Mirunik gather their respective children around them for a little family feast. Although the wives sometimes eat together, each usually prepares the food for herself and her own children. Even within the family group such occasional commensality does not lead to shared dishes. The Achuar have clearly never heard of primitive communism.

A gourd of water is passed round as a ewer, for the pre-meal ablutions: a gulp to rinse one's mouth, then a gulp ejected in a thin stream, to wash one's hands. The master of the house then invites me to begin with the stereotyped injunction, 'Eat the manioc!' to which one has to respond with embarrassed acquiescence and a show of surprise at suddenly discovering the steaming dishes at one's feet. Sweet manioc is the staple food of the Achuar, as synonymous with nourishment as bread is in France and, even when taken as an accompaniment to a dish of choice game, it is always this modest root that one is deprecatingly invited to eat. It is good form for the guest to continue for a while to ignore this invitation, as if already well-satisfied and incapable of swallowing a single mouthful. Only under the duress of the laws of politeness does one finally force oneself to peck at the dishes until then painstakingly ignored.

When the meal is over, the gourd of water is again passed around and then it is Mirunik's turn to serve the inevitable manioc beer. Wajari is talking quietly to his eldest son as he sips his *nijiamanch*, which relieves me of making another unhappy attempt at an oral enquiry. The sun has sunk behind the surrounding forest wall with the suddenness that is inevitable in this latitude, leaving behind it a mixture of cobalt blue and vermilion against which the tall, delicate stems of the chonta palms are silhouetted. Lost amid this extravaganza of colours, a tiny cloud lingers in the west, like a glowing Venetian lantern set in the treetops. The absolute stillness of the air makes the clumps of vegetation merging into a single foreground seem even more static as they stand out against the backdrop of the heavens, like a flat piece of stage scenery.

Submerged in its green monotones, nature here is not of the kind to inspire a painter. Only at twilight does it deploy its bad taste, in line with Baudelairean aesthetics, exceeding the artifice of the gaudiest of coloured images. The inhabitants of the forest become exceptionally agitated during this brief debauchery of colour. The animals of the daytime noisily prepare for sleep while the nocturnal species awaken for the hunt, their carnivorous appetites whetted. Smells are also more definable now, for the heat of the long late afternoon has given them a consistency that the sun can no longer dissipate. Dulled during the daytime by the uniformity of nature's stimulants, the sensual organs are suddenly assailed at dusk by a multiplicity of simultaneous perceptions that make it very difficult to discriminate between sight, sound and smell. Thanks to this brutal onslaught on the senses, the transition between day and night in the forest acquires a dimension of its own as if, for a brief moment just before the great void of sleep takes over, the human body is no longer separate from its environment.

This is the long-awaited time when we can at last drop our guard. Our attentive inspection of our hosts is clearly unrelentingly reciprocated, but at nightfall a truce to this little game of mutual observation is called. The children, in particular, stop spying on us and commenting on our every action in whispers smothered by laughter. For the moment they are too busy hunting frogs, using little bamboo tubes fitted with pistons that, under compression, project small pellets of dried clay. We can hear their shrieks of joy in the bushes bordering the river whenever they score a hit on one of their targets. 'Watch out for snakes!' Senur calls out to them, then grumbles in the semi-darkness by the fire she is fanning, no doubt lamenting their carelessness in the face of the dangers of the forest. I talk quietly with Anne Christine about the events of the day, the slowness of our progress, and all that we have left behind us. Without this interlude of intimacy offered us each evening, it would no doubt be much harder for us to bear the constraints of our new life, and I must confess that already I sometimes wonder how some of our colleagues found the strength of soul to remain alone for several years in similar conditions.

This evening Wajari, no doubt tired after his day of hunting, does not seem of a mind to stay up late. The signal for bedtime comes when he points to the visitors' bed and simply tells me, 'Sleep!' Unlike many other Amazonian tribes, the Jivaros use not hammocks but rectangular bedsteads covered by flexible slats of palm wood or bamboo. You sleep in a strange position there, with your feet projecting into the void as they rest on a little bar set over a smouldering hearth. This arrangement is inspired by an old piece of popular lore according to which you never get cold so long as your feet are warm. Provided someone gets up at regular intervals to keep the dying embers glowing, this is the way to ward off the damp cold of the early hours just before dawn.

The beds in the house are enclosed on three sides by wooden slats. In this dwelling without walls these offer a small island of privacy, rather like the enclosed bed of a Breton household, set up in the common living room. But our bed lacks this feature of refinement. Positioned alongside the outer roof supports, barely sheltered from the rain by the roof's overhang, it is so open to the garden and the forest that you might think you were on a raft still tenuously moored to the house but ready to drift out into the shadows of the jungle as soon as your vigilance is overcome by slumber. Here on this 'apron stage', the sporadic sounds of the sleeping household are supplanted by the nocturnal echoes of the wildlife: a strident chorus produced by frogs and crickets and the throbbing bass of the toads are punctuated by the melancholy cries of predators and the three descending notes of the nightjar's whistle. It seems almost incongruous when the sobs of a child or the whimpers of a dog remind you that a human world is close at hand, so totally does the night here wipe out the patient works of man.

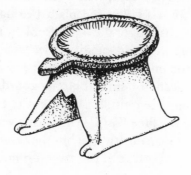

CHAPTER 2

Early Morning

A TREMBLING GLIMMER suddenly licks the underside of the palm-roofing, catching the chequerboard arrangement of battens and rafters. A soft orangish light, occasionally invaded by a huge shadow, gradually picks out the details of the roof structure with the regular rhythm of expertly controlled breathing. In the darkness of what is still the night a woman has just rekindled the fire. Dawn is still a good two hours away, but already the household is awakening to the routines of the new day. Movement is neither immediate nor general, for the penetrating dampness is hardly conducive to it: apart from Senur and Wajari, no one has yet risen. A few tousled children's heads emerge from the enclosed beds, then burrow in again to linger in the inviting softness. The master of the house is seated on his *chimpui*, presenting his broad back to the invigorating warmth from the hearth. His wife returns from the river, looming out of the darkness with a large gourd of fresh water. Chiwian, a lad of about fifteen, joins his father in silence, sitting, like him, with his back to the fire, astride one of the logs.

Senur places the *yukunt* on the *tankamash* hearth. In this wide, shallow, black bowl with its hollow stem the *wayus* is prepared. *Wayus* is an infusion made from a cultivated plant belonging to the same family as the famous herb used for the *maté* drunk by the Argentinians. The bulbous funnel of the stem contains the leaves and prevents them from spreading into the infusion, from which people are expected to help themselves by means of small oblong gourds. As Wajari has invited me to join him, I regretfully abandon the tranquillity of my bed to do my duty by the fire. *Wayus* is not just a version of morning tea: like manioc beer, it is an institution; but the protocol surrounding it is less strict. Only men partake of this sweetish infusion with mildly

44

emetic qualities which, for a short while in the intimacy of the ending night, puts off the strict formality of daytime etiquette.

By inviting a male visitor to join him by the fire like this, the master of the house for a moment does away with the invisible barrier that consigns strangers to the very edge of the domestic space. The Achuar house, which is roughly oval in shape, is divided across its width by an invisible line that separates it into two unequal parts: the *ekent* and the *tankamash*. The *tankamash*, reserved for masculine sociability and the reception of strangers, occupies roughly one third of the house, from one semi-circular end up to the first row of the main roof-bearing pillars. It is here that Wajari sits enthroned on his *chimpui* and that guests and unmarried male adolescents of the household sleep. It is here too that the *tuntui* is kept. This is a huge drum made from a hollowed-out tree-trunk, which is kept in a semi-vertical position by a liana tied round its upper rim and attached to one of the tie-beams. For reasons that are still a mystery to me, this long, hollow-sounding cylinder is also extended at each end by lozenges shaped like reptile heads. In the *tankamash* the master of the house and his guests are each provided with their own hearth composed of three large logs arranged in the shape of a star. The woods chosen for this purpose are particularly dense and burn extremely slowly. To get the flames going, all you need to do is place the ends of the logs in contact, add a little kindling and blow for a moment or two on the glowing wood. These fires for the men are not expected to serve the prosaic purposes of cooking but are used only to warm the chilly night hours and to welcome the circle of *wayus* drinkers.

The *ekent*, in contrast, is the domain of the women and of family life. The household's beds are set up all around the edges, while the centre is occupied by the cooking fires and an impressive array of *muits*, the large earthenware jars in which manioc is left to ferment. Baskets of groundnuts and maize cobs are suspended from the joists, beyond the reach of hungry mice and greedy children. Racks made from palm wood are stacked with domestic utensils, parcels of clay and dyes for pottery, blocks of the grey salt produced by the Shuar of Mangosiza, fishing lines, cotton reels – all the humble *bric-à-brac* of daily life.

Petrified at the thought of behaving in some unsuitable way that would compromise our apparently friendly reception, but forewarned by our reading of previous visitors to the Jivaros, Anne Christine and I lost no time in learning the few rules governing movement about the house that would avoid blunders. In this open dwelling where the entire interior can be taken in at a glance, there is a protocol that determines where men and women can go, depending on whether they are members of the household or strangers. The *ekent* is in principle out of bounds for me, as for all male visitors, and I am supposed to restrict my movements to the part of the *tankamash* assigned to me, except when Wajari invites me to his fireside to drink *wayus*. The wives and daughters of the master of the house are under equal constraint, since they may only cross the imaginary line that separates them from the *tankamash* in the course of their duties, that is to say when serving the men their meals or taking round the manioc beer. Wajari, clearly, is allowed anywhere in his own home, in this space that he himself has constructed, and this manly privilege also extends to his two grown sons.

Thanks to her rather peculiar status, Anne Christine enjoys great freedom of movement. As a woman, she has free access to the *ekent*, where she spends part of the day with Wajari's wives, but the obligations imposed on her sex are partly overridden by the extreme distance introduced by her foreign origin. Whereas a visitor's wife is ordinarily admitted to the *tankamash* only in order to share her husband's bed at night, Anne Christine is free to choose for herself whether to join the women in their special quarters or whether to sit quietly beside me, as would an adolescent boy visiting with his father. She good-humouredly accepts the appearance of submission that opens up to her the doors of two worlds, one of which is virtually irremediably closed to me.

Wajari is telling Chiwian a long story that began with the expression 'Yaunchu', the opening phrase of all myths and stories, which might be translated as 'Once upon a time'. There seem to be many changes of fortune in this story, interspersed with expressive, onomatopoeic expressions and melodic changes of rhythm, and I am again cursing the linguistic incompetence that is depriving my curiosity of this probable treasure of Jivaro culture. Captivated by his father's recitation, young Paantam has also joined us. But this curiosity does not appear to affect the other members of the household: Senur has returned to bed and the other two wives have not yet risen. Overlooking the scene

46

from their platform beds, they are playing with their children or chatting quietly with them.

The *peak*, as the enclosed beds are called, each encompass a whole little world. Each contains one wife and her younger children, sometimes as many as four or five of them. They do not leave their mother's bed until they are about twelve years old. At this point the boys go and sleep in the *tankamash* and the girls acquire a bed of their own in the *ekent*. As for Wajari, each night he honours the *peak* of a different wife in accordance with a rotation that, so far as my observation of such trifles can make out, seems to be quite equitable. The married women are thus the mistresses of a quite separate little territory, where their peripatetic husband comes to lie with them. Each woman's territory furthermore extends beyond her *peak*, according to the rules that give them exclusive use of their own domestic utensils. Senur, Entza and Mirunik each have their own cooking fire that Wajari must supply with large logs fetched from the forest. The domestic utensils and tools that they do not make for themselves – machetes, tin-plate cooking pots, stakes for digging – are also scrupulously shared out. The only piece of kitchen equipment that they all share is the manioc mortar, a large, round, slightly hollowed-out section of a tree-trunk.

The bed of each wife is flanked by another, a miniature version of it, the resting place of half a dozen aggressive, skinny dogs. The packs of dogs are the exclusive responsibility of the women, who care for them with pride, raising them with love and training them with skill. They also feed them carefully, with a tasty purée of sweet potatoes which they set out for them in hollow tortoise shells. The distressing thinness of these poor flea-ridden beasts is certainly not caused by any parsimony on their mistresses' part, but rather by the daunting vigour of the parasites by which they are afflicted. But despite their bony spines and their skeletal frames, the Achuar dogs are brave and tenacious hounds. They also provide an effective guard force for the houses, surrounding any intruder in a threatening ring from which it is sometimes difficult to escape unharmed. They are seldom allowed to run free and, to prevent battles, the packs of the various wives are kept tethered to their respective platforms by leashes made from bark.

Tucked up in a little hammock suspended from the frame of the enclosed bed, Entza's baby is crying. His mother rocks him with her foot, meanwhile placidly delousing a little girl's tousled hair and humming a lullaby to soothe the infant. When this ploy fails, Entza abandons her hygienic pastime and lifts the baby down to suckle him. But no sooner has she grasped him than she shrieks and rushes towards us. His little head is all sticky with semi-coagulated blood, his body unhealthily pallid in contrast. Wajari, concerned, halts his storytelling and takes the baby in his arms. He looks carefully at his bloody skull, muttering in a threatening tone, then asks me to take a look. Just under the ear, the mark of a little bite tells its story: during the night a vampire bat has paid a visit. The wound is not serious, but it has bled a great deal. The bite of such a bat is only superficial, but the creature leaves a secretion that anaesthetizes the victim and prevents the blood from coagulating properly. These vampires are not much bigger than a mouse and a nocturnal nip from them is not serious; nevertheless, if they return to molest an already sickly baby, they may eventually cause an anaemia that is believed to be fatal.

This is the second time since our arrival that this infant has been attacked, and his father seems very upset. While Entza washes the baby's head with warm water, Wajari gently bounces him on his knee, trying to stop him crying, then he lifts him up at arm's length and briefly sucks his penis. As he demonstrates his paternal tenderness, our host presents a curious mixture of brute force and delicacy. His muscular torso and powerful neck and his strong, virile features accentuate the contrast with the quasi-feminine grace of the black locks that brush his shoulders. The baby has calmed down and now gurgles with pleasure as he plays with his father's glossy hair. He tries to catch hold of his jaguar-teeth necklace and the multicoloured ribbons wound about his wrists. In this culture, long hair and precious ornaments are part of a man's prerogative, and the baby grasps at Wajari as though at a beautiful bourgeois Mama with perfumed hair and a dazzling pendant necklace.

Faced with this touching but uncontrived scene, what are we to make of the sinister reputation ascribed to these head-hunting warriors? Admittedly, Wajari does not always dote so on his children and only in rather exceptional circumstances is he to be seen playing with a baby like this. As soon as a child begins to walk, especially if it is a girl, his attitude towards it becomes more constrained and he desists from embracing it at all. But this reserved behaviour cannot mask the affectionate pride in his eye as he quietly contemplates his little horde. It is as if we have landed up with the only pacific Indians in this reputedly bloodthirsty society, or else that, for our benefit, they are deliberately miming out a Rousseauesque fiction for which nothing in the ethnographic literature has prepared us.

The milky gleam of dawn is beginning to supplant the firelight. The mist rising from the river swathes the outlines of the garden and drowns the first rays of the as yet invisible sun in a curious uniformity. From time to time a rent in the mist reveals a tree top, but the ground is carpeted by a cotton-wool cloud that swirls and rises around the vegetation like artificial vapour created in a theatre. The *wayus* rite draws to its inevitable conclusion. This morning beverage has more than a social purpose. Its effects are above all of an emetic nature. Taken in small doses, *wayus* produces no particular effects. However, here it is swallowed without respite, in the same way as the manioc beer, until the large black bowl is empty, and it soon induces a per-sistent nausea that lasts until such time as you can relieve your stomach of its liquid bulk. So off I go with Wajari into the undergrowth bordering the Kapawi, where I tickle my tonsils with a feather, as is expected of me, and, surrounded by the morning mists, make the daily sacrifice of vomit. The men would not be able to start the day without this forceful purge that restores to the body the virginity of an empty stomach. By means of the expulsion of their physiological residues in this way, the Achuar have found a convenient means of wiping out the past and being reborn into the world every morning, refreshed by this bodily amnesia.

Wajari does not return to the house with me, but serenely announces that he is going to defecate in the river. The purge is supposed to be carried right through to the end, which involves immersing oneself in the still cold waters of the Kapawi and evacuating the last of one's residues into the current. I really owe it to our burgeoning camaraderie to accompany him in an activity that men linked by affection always perform in tandem, but so far I have drawn the line at such excessive submission to the obligations of a partici-pating observer. Slightly downstream from the little cove reserved for the household's cleansing activities, Wajari is now making an unholy racket. He splashes the water with his hands, uttering a sustained roar that rises above the vapours of the river like a foghorn: 'I am Wajari! I am Wajari! I am strong! I am a jaguar that prowls in the night! I am an anaconda!' This presents a striking contrast to the gentleness of the earlier domestic scene. Gone the tender father, the attentive host; here is a warrior proclaiming his glory to the receptive dawn.

Dripping and shivering, Wajari returns from this rowdy expedition, confident in his reaffirmed virility. And as the spice of any exploit depends upon it being shared, he grabs three or four pups and goes off to toss them into the Kapawi. Dogs, like men, must be trained, and there is nothing like a swim to strengthen their courage. However, Chiwian and Paantam make no move to follow their father in these ascetic ablutions designed to forge the qualities of masculinity. Nor is their softness reprimanded for, from the age of twelve or thirteen on, boys here seem to be their own masters. Wajari never orders his sons about or raises his voice at them.

The hapless puppies are not so lucky. They yap piteously each time their inflexible trainer returns them to the river with forceful encouragement. Shivering with cold, at last they stumble up the bank, only to be faced with a new trial. Set on its mettle by their whimpers, no doubt, the trumpet-bird that guards the house has, goodness knows why, decided to bar their route. These birds are the size of a hen but with very long legs and, if caught young, are easily tamed. With arrogant dignity they then parade their elegant ash-grey, olive-gleaming plumage all round the immediate vicinity of the house. Despite its pompous and elegant bearing, the trumpet-bird loves to play watchdog, announcing the arrival of any stranger with the indignant, shrill cry from which it gets its name. Wajari's bird sometimes gets carried away, interrupting its dandified patrol to throw itself in unseemly fashion upon an animal or visitor that does not find favour with it. It is very difficult to escape from its hysterical attacks, as the poor puppies learn to their cost. Meantime, the rest of the dogs have all begun to bark at the cheeky bird. The pet marmoset is jumping from side to side on its perch, with piercing high-pitched shrieks, and all the terrified babies are convulsively wailing. Finally Senur leaps up, cursing, and sorts out the scrap, laying about her with a stick; and the odious creature returns to its guard duties with sarcastic satisfaction.

The sun has dispersed the mist, apart from a few twisting scarves at the forest's edge. The pellucid sky heralds another day of heat which, however, will not make itself felt until mid-morning. By my

50

watch it is half past six, and at last breakfast appears in the shape of a general round of manioc beer accompanied – for our benefit – by a plate of boiled taros. Wajari settles down to his drink. As is his custom, he will eat nothing until the only proper meal of the day, in the late afternoon, which should include either game or fish to qualify as such. A small snack of grilled manioc, yam or taro sometimes helps to fill a gap and make it possible to hold out until dinner time, but it has to be eaten in one's fingers, more or less furtively. Gluttony is regarded with horror here, and the young children are constantly reminded to check their natural greed. Food is both varied and abundant, so it is not the spectre of famine that gives rise to this restraint, simply the feeling that temperance in all its forms is the mark of a superior human being. Excepting manioc beer, which may be quaffed in considerable quantities, table manners impose upon the men a show of frugality that becomes the more ostentatious the larger the company to witness it.

Straddled on his *chimpui*, Wajari has embarked upon his toilette with all the concentration of a Venetian courtesan. First he combs his hair carefully, then divides it into two braids, one each side of the thick fringe that encroaches upon his eyebrows. Each braid is wound about with a string of red cotton, and his long pony-tail is caught up in a ribbon woven with a geometrical design, while its other end is adorned with red and yellow toucan feathers that nestle like a little posy on the nape of his neck. Next, he seizes his *karis*, two thin bamboo tubes about thirty centimetres long, decorated with a pattern of lozenges etched in by fire. At the end of each tube is a rosette of feathers and a long strand of black hair. Having moistened the tubes with saliva, to make them more slippery, Wajari pulls out the two little sticks that he wears in the lobes of his ears and carefully replaces them with these cumbersome ornaments. He then asks one of his daughters to fetch a pod from the rocou bush that grows alongside the house, as befits a cosmetic in general daily use. With a stem dipped into the pod, he draws a complicated design on his face, examining his reflection with a critical eye in the little mirror I gave him a few days ago. At last satisfied with his appearance, our host grasps his big machete, invites me to stay at home, and sets off with a joyous step to visit his brother-in-law, Pinchu, who has bidden him help to clear a new garden. Yet another long day of enforced idleness opens up before me.

51

CHAPTER 3

Village Rumours

THE FINE DRIZZLE that has been falling all night has given way to one of those gloomy mornings that make getting out of bed a small act of courage. Fortunately, Wajari has skipped his usual stomach purging and his bathe took place quietly. He is now busy rummaging in his *pitiak*, a closely woven basket with a lid in which he keeps his personal belongings and from which he extracts a horrible nylon shirt of many colours, in the Hawaiian fashion. Having given it a sharp shake to dislodge the many cockroaches that had found refuge in it, he emits a melodious 'tou-tou-tou-tou', summoning the chickens to peck at the panic-stricken insects fleeing in all directions. Despite the vulgarity of his shirt, Wajari does not look ridiculous, just a bit incongruous. The reason why he is deferring to the fashions of the Tropics in this way is so as to do honour to his brother Titiar, who has asked us to go and help him build his house today.

Titiar lives not far off, on the opposite river bank. The rains of the last few days have drastically increased the level of the water, submerging the great tree-trunk that normally serves as a bridge over the Kapawi, so we cross the river in a little canoe, buffeted about by the current. The house of Wajari's brother stands on a wide, sandy terrace at the confluence of the Kapawi and a stream of pellucid water coursing through a small, luxuriant ravine. It is flanked by the skeleton of an extensive roof structure already completely fitted out with beams but still lacking its palm-leaf covering. Unlike our host's house, this one is surrounded by walls of palm wood, pierced at each end by a solid door. At the moment all that emerges from its closeted privacy are loud bursts of talking.

We enter by the *tankamash* door, announcing our arrival with the customary tautological 'I come!' A little time is needed to accustom

52

our eyes to the semi-darkness and make out the circle of guests along the *tankamash* wall facing the silhouette of Titiar, enthroned upon his *chimpui*. Having navigated between a profusion of *pininkia* scattered in great disorder over the floor and on the benches, a small space is made for us in the ranks of the visitors. Wajari is not alone in having donned his Sunday best; a number of other men also sport shirts that would not shame a Samba school. These flamboyant clothes contrast sharply with the gravity of their faces, their formal behaviour and their exotic native finery. All the men's faces are delicately painted with rocou designs and some of them wear *karis* tubes in their ears and crowns of toucan plumes or coronets of macaw feathers.

Titiar is a handsome man with velvety eyes and a slow, melodious way of speaking, whose ostensibly confident demeanour from time to time betrays a hidden apprehension. For the moment, he is engaged in conversation with Tsukanka, a formidable 'old man' of about fifty, short, stocky, with the features of a gargoyle, who is the fortunate possessor of six wives and is even more grouchy than a trumpet-bird. I have never seen him either laugh or smile, which is possibly a blessing as his teeth, briefly glimpsed occasionally, are coated with a black film that gives them the look of a mantrap. Whatever the situation, Tsukanka always speaks fast and loudly with a barely concealed violence that makes you forget his small stature. At the moment he is even more formidable than usual as he is well into the customary visitors' dialogue known as the *yaitias chicham* or 'slow talk' which, belying its name, takes place at a speed that, to my inexpert ears, seems exceptionally fast.

The 'slow talk' is a canonical kind of dialogue between two men in which the responses follow a definite melodic pattern, interspersed with stereotyped formulae that serve to mark the various stages reached and to cue the switches from one interlocutor to the other. This form of expression is employed above all as an introduction to the business in hand on the occasions of visits made by close relatives, but the minute normal interchange looks like centring on any subject of gravity or importance – that is to say of a kind likely to engender a clash – the men almost automatically revert to the ponderous pronouncements and repetitive phrases that characterize the 'slow talk'. As rambling conversations seem unknown here and there appears to be no lack of opportunities for conflict, communication between men generally takes the form of a dialogue that is more or less vivacious or constrained depending upon how pronounced the musical prosody of the 'slow talk' is.

The heads of family present are closely related. The master of the house is married to a sister of Tsukanka, who is himself married to two of Titiar's sisters. According to the logic of the Jivaro kinship system, these relations of mutual alliance extend to include Wajari, since he is Titiar's brother. Naanch is what is called a 'branch brother' (*kana*) of Wajari and Titiar, since their respective fathers were brothers. They call one another 'brother' and regard themselves as such. But Wajari has also married a sister of Tseremp; so Tseremp, along with his two brothers Tarir and Pinchu, is also collectively related by marriage to Wajari, Titiar and Naanch. Furthermore, Tseremp is the husband of a daughter of Tsukanka and would like to take her sister as his second wife. As for Mukuimp, he is Wajari's son-in-law. Thanks to the extended network of categories of kinship and affinity, he accordingly finds himself with three 'fathers-in-law'. Finally, Tayujin and Kuunt are brothers and, given that their sister is one of Naanch's wives, they too have Wajari and Titiar as brothers-in-law; and Tsukanka is also their father-in-law, since Tayujin is married to one of his daughters. The men who belong to this little community do not address one another by their names, but by one of the four kinship terms that denote their interconnections: *yatsur*, meaning 'my brother' (same sex siblings or the issue of siblings of the same sex), *sairu* or 'my cousin-brother-in-law' (the husband of one's sister, the brother of one's wife or the issue of siblings of opposite sexes), *jiichur* or 'my uncle-father-in-law' (the father of one's wife, the brother of one's mother or the husband of a sister of one's father), and *aweru* or 'my son-in-law-nephew' (the husband of one's daughter, the son of one's sister or the son of the brother of one's wife).

I am sitting next to Tseremp. He is about twenty years old, not very tall but well built, with the sympathetic and enthusiastic temperament usually associated in our society with young scout-leaders. In his rustic Spanish he explains to me that this kinship group came to settle here three or four years ago at the instigation of Wajari and Titiar. Before this the families were scattered throughout the region of the upper and middle reaches of the Kapawi, one or two days' march apart, and only visited one another at long intervals despite their close links of kinship. The Kapawi men had for many years maintained hostile relations with the Shuar of the Makuma, about a dozen days' march to the north-east, but when the latter were 'pacified' by Protestant missionaries in the 1950s, my companions took to visiting their erst-while enemies from time to time, to swap their blowpipes and curare for salt, metal tools and guns. The North American missionaries immediately spotted the advantage that they might derive from the occasional exchanges made between their Shuar flock and these rebel-lious Indians amongst whom they had not yet gained a foothold. They accordingly entrusted the Shuar whom they had indoctrinated with the responsibility for persuading their trading partners from the Kapawi to abandon their internal warfare, regroup as a village and build the landing-strip that these flying pastors insisted upon as the first step towards a Christian life. For a long time the people of the Kapawi hesitated. But as the main network of exchange through which they acquired tools and rifles from their Achuar neighbours to the south-east had recently been abruptly broken up by renewed hostilities between Ecuador and Peru, they eventually gave in to the arguments of the Shuar emissaries, in the hope of more easily obtaining from the missionaries the arms and tools they could no longer do without.

By the time we arrived the landing-strip cleared by the Achuar had already been in existence for two years without their deriving any particular advantage from it. A village of about a dozen households had been established close to the runway, to which the missionaries had given the name Capahuari, after the Ecuadorian name of the river. Tseremp told me that from time to time a small plane came to check that the Indians had not massacred one another. If there was a little room to spare on board, one of the Achuar would board the plane with blowpipes and feathered headdresses to be bartered with his Shuar trading partner, thereby saving himself the long journey on foot to the Makuma. A few days later he would return to Capahuari with a sparkling supply of cooking pots and machetes but without any of the presents that he had been expecting from the missionaries. Being firmly convinced of the virtues of free enterprise, the fundamen-talist sects left charity of that kind to Catholic idolaters.

Wajari is winding down his 'slow talk' with Titiar. The two brothers are constantly visiting each other so, with no fresh news to exchange, their conversation has been on the brief side. He finishes off with a stereotyped sentence delivered on a rising scale of notes.

'Well, my brother, as I have now visited you well and truly as our ancestors knew how to, and as I hope to visit you again soon, now I must leave you.'

'Very well! Very well!'

This is pure rhetoric, as we are to spend the whole day working together. In fact, Titiar now gives the signal to get going and we all file out towards the house that is under construction.

At the four corners of a rectangle about twenty metres long and ten metres wide, four weight-bearing pillars support horizontal beams that rest on posts situated halfway along each of the longer sides. The two shorter sides of this parallelepiped bear the triangles carrying the principal rafter that supports the long ridge pole of the roofing. The two narrower ends of the house are prolonged by the semi-circle of short posts fixed in the ground that give it its oval shape. Bamboo rafters are lashed at regular intervals along the lateral sections of the roof and in a fan-like pattern at the two rounded ends. The day's work is to attach to these rafters thin battens to which the palm leaves of the roof covering will be fastened.

The various tasks seem to be allocated spontaneously and nobody, not even Titiar, appears to be directing the enterprise. These men all share the same skills and are thus interchangeable in the chain of operations. But I am impressed at the way it functions without it being necessary first to define each man's particular role. The fact is that the hierarchical pattern of the division of industrial labour – where an engineer programmes operations that a foreman is then responsible for getting the workmen to execute – has made us forget the ancient interlocking customs wrought in the process of collective labour. With every appearance of spontaneity, each man would be attentive to the moods and actions of his fellows, thereby precluding the need for anyone to occupy a position of authority.

The youngest, Tseremp, Kuunt and Mukuimp, shin up to the roofing structure by means of trunks of balsa wood with notches cut into them and start lashing down the battens with lianas. The others prepare battens from palm stems which they split lengthwise through the fibres and then trim carefully. The atmosphere is more relaxed than inside the house and each of them seems to take pleasure in this

common labour. Tayujin jokes with his brother, who is clowning about up on the rafters, telling him he is like a howler monkey.

'You have pissed on me, big-mouthed little brother,' he exclaims, feigning outrage, 'and I am going to kill you and steal your wives.'

The threat does not appear to trouble Kuunt, who now bounces about on the rafters, imitating the hoarse cry of the howler monkey. Tayujin grabs a batten and pretends to be shooting at his brother through a blowpipe.

'I've blown a dart into your arse, little howler-monkey-brother. Now let's see if you can still cover your females.'

Tsukanka is not amused. He lets fly with a forceful string of reproofs, telling his sons-in-law to show a little more dignity. In his day men used not to speak to each other like that; they were proud and strong, and did not mock their brothers. Young men these days are all like Quichuas, totally shameless. They play with words, make you ashamed, but are incapable of avenging their parents.

The scolding of Father Modesty is received in embarrassed silence by the younger generation, who return to work without a word. Actually, the clowning of Tayujin and Kuunt was probably aimed at me. The people of Capahuari have given me an altogether classic Achuar name, Yakum, or 'howler-monkey', because my beard is the same colour as the reddish fur that covers the protruding throat of this animal. During the episode on the roof, sly looks were shot at me, looks that I pretended not to notice for, although I am beginning to understand the Achuar language a little, I reckon it wiser to continue to appear ignorant, so that the men take no notice of me and continue to converse together without reserve. The jokes cracked at my expense are not malicious. They ridicule my clumsiness, and I assume the role of a bogeyman amongst naughty children who calm down immediately when threatened that the great bearded Yakum will gobble them up.

At about eleven o'clock Titiar calls out the long-awaited '*Nijiamanch! Jiamanch, jiamanch, jiamanch! Wari nijiamanch!*' and his two wives set to with pots of manioc beer and piles of gourds and *pininkia*. All the battens are now fixed to the rafters and it is time for a pause. But the men continue to make a show of busying themselves, pretending to be absorbed in useless little finicky tasks, while Titiar presses them all in turn to come and refresh themselves. When each has eventually abandoned his task, seemingly with regret, the *nijiamanch* can at last begin to flow.

The first duty of a man benefiting from the co-operation of his relatives by blood and by marriage is to refresh them liberally. Collective work of this kind is known as an 'invitation', *ipiakratatuin*, and whoever is setting it up first does the rounds of the various households, inviting each man to come and help, using the standard formula: 'Tomorrow you will come and drink manioc beer in my house!' No reference is ever made to the nature of the work to be done – everybody knows that Titiar is finishing the roof of his new house – or even to the fact that there will be work to be done. The drinks and the chat, both formal and informal, occupy a large place in an invitation such as this, and the communal labour seems more a pretext for a little party than a strictly economical necessity.

Given that each household is virtually self-sufficient, a man only resorts to issuing an invitation in the event of certain very specific tasks, such as hacking out a new swidden, setting in place certain particularly heavy parts of a roof frame, or pulling a large canoe on rollers from the place where the tree was felled and fashioned into a canoe as far as a navigable river. Strictly speaking, only the last of those operations requires the use of helpers from outside the family. In the other cases a man and his sons can manage on their own, so collective work is just a way of saving time and minimizing one's efforts. This mutual aid is not subject to strict accountability as to how many days' work are owed by the parties concerned. But since relatives have a duty to assist one another, to decline an invitation is not considered good form, particularly in view of the fact that such an occasion, with its well-lubricated gossip, presents a chance for an agreeable break in the monotony of domestic life.

The yearning for conviviality is less acute now that the Achuar of the Kapawi have regrouped around the landing-strip and can easily visit one another daily. No more than four or five years ago these men had to undertake a march of several days in order to deliver an invitation to all their relatives scattered in the jungle. Although communal labour was, on that account, more infrequent, on the other hand it lasted longer and ended in a big drinking party with dancing until dawn. Having fled the isolation of a scattered habitat by coming together in a little village from which the only exit leads to the sky, the Achuar are now discovering that a measure of promiscuity may diminish the joys of social life.

It is Tsukanka, not Titiar, who eventually gives the signal to return to work. At no point has the master of the house issued any instructions to those who have come to help him except to suggest that they take a break. The only orders that I have so far heard are those addressed by husbands to their wives. On a formal level at least, the men certainly appear to form a community of equals. But Titiar now orders his wives to accompany him to fetch loads of *kampanak* palms that he has cut in the forest more than an hour's march away. This carrying work is the only kind that devolves upon the women in the construction of the house.

Two species of small palm trees are used for covering roofs: they are *kampanak* and *turuji,* which both belong to the same botanical group and mercifully tend to grow together in colonies, which makes it easier to gather them. These are very common plants, but enormous quantities of them are needed to make a roof covering and the copses close at hand are soon exhausted. So when a palm-tree roof begins to rot after a dozen or so years, the only thing to do is to move to another site. However, since Titiar's former house is only eight or nine years old, he is counting on salvaging part of its thatch for use on the new house that he is now constructing.

More than anything else, it is the accessibility of palms and the durability of the roof that condition the cycle of removals to new homes. Whatever happens, a man has to rebuild his house every twelve or fifteen years. If sufficient clumps of *kampanak* and *turuji* remain close at hand, if the game and the plants for gathering remain abundant, and if no war makes a tactical move away from enemy territory necessary, he will build his new dwelling alongside the old one, so as to be able to continue to make use of his manioc gardens. But if that is not the case, he will have to select a new site for his home, one or two days' march away, and set about the laborious business of moving, which involves clearing the ground for new gardens, transplanting cuttings, building a new house and furnishing it, etc. In Capahuari this semi-nomadic cycle has of late been interrupted by the formation of a village, but this upheaval in the Achuar way of life is already beginning to pose problems. Titiar was complaining about having to go quite far afield now to find palms for his roofing and the right kind of wood for his rafters. In this forest where natural resources are abundant but widely dispersed, a concentration of dwellings such as this and the switch to a sedentary life soon make for upsets in the traditional modes of making use of nature; and my companions are just beginning to measure the cost of this. However luxuriant nature may seem in these latitudes, it is hard put to withstand even modest demographic pressures.

With several bundles of *kampanak* already deposited beneath the roof structure, work can continue in Titiar's absence. Each palm leaf is separately tied to a batten by its stem, placed in such a way that it overlaps the last one. The work of setting the palm leaves in place begins with the battens of the roof-overhang and progresses upwards towards the ridge, each new band of palm leaves partially overlapping the band below so as to ensure perfect watertightness.

The work pace has slowed down considerably and I make the most of this to ask Tseremp to tell me more about the animated conversations inside the house that morning. As I suspected, a vendetta is being plotted, but it is not yet clear who the protagonists are to be since the *casus belli* remains obscure. The first part of the affair is generally known: a certain Ikiam who lived at the confluence of the Copataza and the Pastaza, three days' march from here towards the north-west, was a few months ago abandoned by his wife, Pinik, whom he had been beating. Probably with the complicity of one of her kin, Pinik made her escape in a canoe, travelling for several days down the Pastaza until she came to a small group of Achuar houses situated at the point where the river joins the Kapawi. A certain Sumpaish, living in the neighbourhood, promptly fell in love with the fugitive and took her for his wife.

What happened next in this drama, which had not so far been known to anyone present, was this morning reported by Tayujin, Tsukanka's son-in-law, who had just paid a visit to his brother Narankas, on the Sasaïme river. Furious at being cuckolded, Ikiam had last month decided to go and kill his unfaithful wife and her new husband. One fine day he had set out alone in a canoe with a muzzle-loading gun and a good supply of powder and lead, and had not been seen since. Nobody here has the slightest doubt that he has been killed, but there are two theories as to the identity of his murderer. Some think that he was shot by Sumpaish, as indeed seems the most likely. Well aware of the probable consequences of his marriage, Pinik's new husband was on his guard and is believed to have caught Ikiam prowling round his house. According to another rumour, spread by the people of Sasaïme, the jealous husband was killed by one of his brothers-in-law, a certain Kawarunch, who lived a day's canoe journey downstream from him. Kawarunch is said to have fired at the unsuspecting Ikiam as he passed by, bent on vengeance on the lower Pastaza. Kawarunch's presumed guilt is based upon no evidence other than his reputation as a bad-tempered man. Tseremp says he is a dangerous fellow with quite a few killings to his name. Given that the Achuar of the Copataza seem determined to mount a raid of vengeance and that everybody at Capahuari is distantly related not only to the victim but also to one or other of his presumed murderers, the question is which side each man involved will take.

The return of Titiar and his two wives under their burden of palms signals the imminent end to the day's work. Having expressed his thanks to them all, the master of the house soon bids everyone return to the old house where a copious meal prepared by his daughters, in their mothers' absence, awaits us. Apart from laying on floods of *nijiamanch*, whoever issues an invitation such as this is also obliged to offer his helpers a good dinner and that means plenty of meat. For the past two days Titiar has been scouring the woods for supplies for his little party, but with no more than meagre success: two capuchin monkeys, one agouti and a toucan. I get the hands of one of the monkeys, blackish little clenched fists swimming in a greasy stew like the leftovers of some cannibal feast. This is the choice morsel reserved for guests whom one wishes to honour, so I am obliged to suck at these sad fingers with a show of conviction befitting a well-mannered guest.

A new round of manioc beer follows the meal. It is much more alcoholic than the previous rounds and soon helps to hot up the conversation. Two 'slow talks' are taking place simultaneously, one between Titiar and Naanch, the other between Tsukanka and Wajari. Pretending to be unaware of the parallel conversation, each of the interlocutors shouts at his opposite number, spitting repeatedly. The controlled expulsion of saliva is one of the social talents always displayed when paying a visit, a stylish outlet for the acidity of the fermented manioc beer. But in the context of a 'slow talk', spitting acquires a truly semantic value. With one elbow resting on his knee and his hand cupped round his mouth, the forceful speaker conceals his bared teeth and the rhythmic phrases echo round the house, their all-too-human origin masked, as if escaping from a muzzle. At regular intervals two raised fingers pinch the speaker's lips into a whistling position and expel an elegant arching jet of saliva that lands several metres away. The graver the subject discussed, the more frequent these emissions become, mounting a continuous bombardment within the still space in which the two unmoving speakers are interlocked, like statues. The spitting punctuates, underlines, lends emphasis. Its hissing sound makes the dialogue sound rhymed. The humble physical action of spitting, midway between a word and a gesture, here acquires the dignity of a technique of rhetoric.

The Ikiam business is at the centre of all this codified clamour. Despite the absence of any plausible motive, the majority present believe Kawarunch to be guilty. The vindictiveness directed against him clearly antedates this latest drama. Two of Kawarunch's neighbours are at the source of the accusations levelled at him: Tukupi and Washikta live at the mouth of the Sasaïme and have both acquired considerable fame thanks to their warrior exploits. Both are 'brothers-in-law' to Kawarunch but at present are not on good terms with him. In the past, before rivalry undermined the team that they had formed, this redoubtable trio together used to launch numerous raids against the Achuar of the south. The Capahuari people who are related to them by marriage honour Tukupi and Washikta with the title *juunt*, 'great man', reserved for the bravest and most experienced of military leaders. Kawarunch, on the other hand, is merely a *mamkartin*, a 'killer', for he kills without panache, preferring cautious ambushes to glorious face-to-face encounters.

All the assumptions of the guilt of one person or another stem from what the Achuar call *pase chicham*, 'bad words', a fog of rumours, accusations and half-lies that are a particularly effective means of encouraging the outbreak of wars. As a result of the wide dispersion of the homes of the Achuar, news, even of the most anodyne nature, tends to be systematically distorted as it is carried from one house to another by a series of different visitors. These messengers, sometimes quite well intentioned, sometimes less so, interpret the facts to suit their own personal interests and relay the most unlikely slanders to people only too happy to believe them. And when some old grudge is refuelled by a new crop of slanderous stories or some long-deferred vendetta is given new life by a recent pretext, then a man's life depends upon his unfailingly vigilant prudence.

The crude statistics of the genealogies that we have begun to trace testify to the proportions of these vendetta wars. In the generation that has just passed away, one man out of two died fighting. Behind the serene façade proffered by our hosts and the endearing routine of their daily life, a more tumultuous world is gradually taking shape. No one feels any need to conceal its echoes from me, possibly because of my presumed incomprehension but more probably because here violent death lurks at the crossroads in every man's destiny.

CHAPTER 4

Pause

TWO MONTHS ALREADY since we arrived in Capahuari! Time seems to be standing still, with neither depth nor rhythm, waiting for something to happen. Biological routines are all that lend a small measure of animation to our uneventful existence. The changes that they bring sometimes introduce a note of originality. An asphyxiating spice, a pretty caterpillar that inflicts an acid burn, mosquitoes that prevent you from sleeping, jiggers that eat away at your legs and abdomen, infected insect bites that suppurate, lice that infest your head, athelete's foot that makes your feet stink, colic that wrenches your entrails – in short, all the minor infirmities customary in the tropics combine to draw attention to, as it were, the alien nature of our own bodies in which these successive aches and pains find a home. Perhaps we should be grateful for the way that, through this cycle of new experiences, our animal nature supplements the imperceptible cycles of the nature of vegetation that, here, never changes! *Semper virens*, evergreen, is the botanists' description for this forest that never loses its leaves, and whose modest, unappealing flowers evoke nothing but the unexceptional process of reproduction. Accustomed as we Westerners are to gauge the passing of time by the colour changes of the successive seasons, it is hard for us to apprehend the flow of a monochrome duration.

The Indians of Amazonia react to this absence of seasonal variations in voluntarist fashion. In this part of the world the juxtaposition of bright colours is an attribute of culture; by using it to introduce definite stages, its pre-eminence over an unchanging nature is confirmed. Headdresses of red, yellow and blue feathers, patterns painted in rocou, necklaces of bright glass beads, and multicoloured bracelets and loincloths adorn the person, thereby extending the chromatism of the small fraction of the animal order that discreetly enlivens nature with its many-coloured liveries. In this monochrome world the macaws, toucans, motmots and cocks-of-the-rock stand out, thanks to their dazzling appearances, and when the Indians imitate their ostentation, donning their recomposed plumage, they do so to show that they consider them somehow as their equals. Birds possess a number of other special qualities that draw them close to human beings. The stages of their growth and the radical changes that these produce – all the features that differentiate the chick, the fledgling and the adult bird, the progression from down to feathers, the distinctive appearances of the two sexes, etc. – are particularly well suited to symbolize the changes of status that rites of passage are designed to express. So it is not surprising that in Amazonia the initiation of adolescents, admission to a warrior society or to a particular age group, acceptance as a leader, or the culmination of a shaman's apprenticeship should frequently be marked by the wearing of a distinctive set of feathers. The fidelity of mated birds, the devotion of parents to their brood, their altruism, and the highly organized lives of sociable species all suggest analogies with the ways in which human affectivity is expressed. Finally, birdsong presents a melodic complexity virtually unparalleled in the animal kingdom and the trills, which the Indians can reproduce with astounding precision, suggest to them a capacity to formulate messages that is closer to the language of human beings than any other animal's vocal expression. In most Amazonian cultures certain birds with exceptional plumage, such as macaws and toucans, thus become exemplary metaphors for the human condition at the very heart of nature. However, whether it is upon a bird or upon an item of human apparel that they confer their brilliance, these contrasting colours that are the stamp of sociability are only displayed on certain short-lived occasions. They do not mark out the temporal periodicity that, for want of any distinguishing signs, has become imperceptible.

To be sure, there are days of sun and days of rain. The former go on for ever under the harsh light from the zenith that eats away at all the happy expectations of the morning and the social pleasures of the afternoon. The latter, as anywhere else in the world, are just gloomy, housebound, rainy days. Some sunny days darken in the afternoon beneath a pall of stormy clouds. The heavy shower that follows lasts only a moment and soon evaporates into steam rising from the overheated earth. Rainy days too are sometimes interrupted; a sudden break in the clouds around midday arrests the small deluge that looked as though it would never stop. In either eventuality, a rainbow sets its seal upon the unexpected. It is a celestial metamorphosis of the anaconda, the great water snake whose gleaming skin evokes and intermingles the entire spectrum of the prism. Like that snake, it spells danger and its presence is greeted with the word *pasun*, 'bad omen', murmured fearfully by the women. The rainbow is also the sign of a transition, an interval, a fleeting separated moment. The colours that it displays indicate an unusual discontinuity in the homogeneous flow of time. But this many-coloured mirage is itself so fleeting that the gap that it is its function to indicate is soon forgotten: either the rain returns or the sun reasserts its rights.

Our fieldwork diary is our 'Robinson Crusoe' calendar. As on a ship, January and July lose their seasonal savours and become nothing more than markers along the course of passing days. The minute chronicle of daily life is thus stripped of any cosmic reference, to be totally dominated by the rhythm of social life. Family quarrels, accusations of witchcraft, and hunting tales provide its principal themes, punctuated from time to time by a panicky rumour of impending war.

The peoples of solitude, as Chateaubriand called them, lead a social existence that is limited by the very small number of events that occur within a restricted circle of relations. Their past seldom goes back beyond childhood memories and is soon lost in the adjacent world of mythology. Few of the Achuar know the names of their great-grandparents, and the tribal memory that covers four generations at the most is periodically swallowed up in confusion and oblivion. The friendships and alliances that men inherit from their fathers obliterate the older configurations set up by their fathers' fathers, for there are no memorialists interested in celebrating high deeds accomplished decades earlier by people whose names no longer mean anything to anyone. Apart from the rivers, fleeting spaces that are constantly changing, no place is named here. The sites of human habitation are temporary, seldom occupied for more than about fifteen years, after which they vanish again beneath the all-conquering forest. Even the memory of a clearing fades away with the death of those who cleared it. How could these nomads in space and time not seem puzzling to us, who set so much store by the perpetuation of lineages and lands and who live in part on the patrimony and fame amassed by our ancestors?

In this tiny, shallow social world, even the most insignificant happening eventually takes on a cosmic dimension. An injury suffered by a dog out hunting becomes as significant as the death of a child or a projected marriage. All are events that are equally commented upon and interpreted in the light of the surrounding circumstances. With the routine of daily tasks unchanging all the year round, only the changing topics of conversation give one a sense of the passing of time, as if the pages of a chronicle of news items were slowly turning. Wars, the abandonment of a spouse, and removals to set up home on new sites are the major events that punctuate this monotonous sociability. The life stories that we have begun to piece together boil down to a succession of chaotic accidents: birth somewhere that has now vanished; father murdered; flight to take refuge with an uncle; a murderous vendetta; mother carried off; marriage somewhere that has now vanished; murder of spouse; flight once again; another marriage; another war; and so on. In between these recurrent crises, life takes over as before, weaving a new web of more ordinary joys and sorrows. So far, I have only encountered distant echoes of these great explosions of violence that dissipate the prevailing boredom. I have before me the closed system of which I have been dreaming and, after spending no more than a few weeks observing it, I am already wishing it were more open. Despite our ever-alert curiosity and the routines of our research work, each day that passes is trapped in the filaments of eternity. Our existence is quietly consigned to a parenthesis.

CHAPTER 5

Bartering

AT DAWN, YESTERDAY, Wajari set out for Montalvo to swap a bundle of peccary skins for powder, fishing hooks and lead shot. He would also like to bring back some Peruvian curare, reputed to be much stronger than what he makes himself. The rate of exchange is derisory: one peccary skin for an ounce of black powder and a small packet of fishing hooks, or three skins for one pound of lead shot. In this region, where money is totally unknown, the peddling *regatones* of Montalvo exercise an almost exclusive monopoly over trading and have no difficulty in imposing their exorbitant rates upon the Achuar. It is not hard to imagine the number of middlemen with fat profits in a trading chain that conveys the skin of a peccary killed by Wajari all the way to a shop window displaying fine leather goods! Through a curious paradox of international commerce, an industry based on ostentatious superfluity finds itself depending for its raw materials upon the modest by-products of an economy of strict necessity that itself has no use for them.

As is customary, Wajari's *chimpui* is laid on its side to show that the house is empty, being temporarily without its master. This unequivocal sign is designed to be a warning: no male visitor must cross the threshold, under pain of being suspected of wanting to seduce the women. For me Wajari has made an exception to this rule, even urging me, before he left, to take good care of the household – and this despite the fact that Wajari's wives are all very attractive. Senur and Entza have the same sturdy build, strong shoulders, a well-shaped bottom and a generous bosom, the elder more serious but given to irony, the younger always with a wide grin that a slight squint makes curiously alluring. As for Mirunik, she is still a girl, with a slim and supple figure whose remarkable grace is in no way concealed

69

by a reserved expression. Perhaps Wajari's faith in me rests upon the reassuring presence of Anne Christine, or perhaps it simply reflects his opinion of the Whites' mode of enjoying themselves.

It is true that a brief trip to Puyo from which we returned a few days ago noticeably altered our standing in the community. Making the most of a landing of the North American missionaries' little plane on the Capahuari strip – the sole purpose of which appeared to be to check out the rumour that we were living here – we had managed to get a lift on the next flight to the Shell-Mera aerodrome. Unfore-warned of the plane's arrival, we had dashed out to the landing-strip as soon as we heard it approaching. I had been working in a tree-felling team and, like all the other men, had my face painted with rocou. It was with disgusted consternation that the pilot, an immaculately dressed, blond, rosy colossus, took in the sight of this hirsute, daubed tramp who was, however, expressing himself in English. He had eventually resigned himself to negotiating a lift for us, at cost price, to transport us to the civilized hygiene that we clearly badly needed. Having initially refused to take us to the Achuar, the evangelists seemed to have decided to tolerate our presence in their zone of influence, since they had no right to oppose it. It would have been churlish now to deny us the succour of their little plane.

The small red and white Cessna had indeed returned to Capahuari on the appointed day. As such a spectacle was a rare one, most of the village inhabitants had invaded the landing-strip to watch us set off. The men and adolescent boys swanked around the stationary aircraft while the women chatted amongst themselves, squatting at a safe distance. In all this happy turmoil, nobody had manifested any particu-lar feelings towards us. When the time came to clamber aboard, a sudden hush fell. Then, like a distant murmur, we heard the quavering voices of the older women droning a melancholy distant dirge.

This ten-day visit to Puyo had enabled us to replenish our stocks of gifts and medicaments and to buy a small, second-hand outboard motor and a number of cans of fuel. Air transport for all this equipment now made a long stay amongst the Achuar possible. Capahuari would serve as a base for expeditions by canoe to more inaccessible regions not yet visited by the missionaries.

The men had been unable to disguise their astonishment at our return to the community: despite our promises to come back as soon as possible, they were not expecting to see us again. With the exception of one legendary Salesian, far away in the south, they knew of no Whites who had ever lived for so long amongst the Achuar. The length of our first stay had already seemed sufficiently remarkable to rule out any idea of a longer one. By returning amongst them and bringing, as agreed, some of the manufactured objects they had told us they needed, we had given a new twist to our relations: clearly Yakum and Anchumir – Anne Christine's native name – were not just passing through and would now have to be reckoned with on a more lasting basis.

The people of Capahuari still did not understand the motive for our long visit, but in the long run this had become a secondary preoccupation, as the reality of our sharing in daily activities was of more immediate concern. They had soon realized that we were not Protestant missionaries, since we made no secret of our taste for tobacco. On the basis of mysterious theological reasons, the evangelists forbade recourse to this comfort for which we are so much in the Amerindians' debt. Nor could we be Catholic missionaries, for they had heard it said that these were solitary men whose lack of a penis ruled out their living with a woman. We apparently had no colonizing ambitions: I had even declined the proposal put to me towards the end of our first stay to start a garden and build a house, and this had no doubt strengthened their belief that we should soon be leaving them. Finally, the language that we spoke together did not sound like Spanish, so we must belong to some distant tribe, probably one related to the North American missionaries but distinguished from them by different customs. As it was impossible to define our identity by reference to existing types, the people of Capahuari had decided to regard us as a new variety of Whites, made to seem quite distinct by the dearth of accessible comparisons. By returning amongst them, we added to this first picture of us the dimension of duration. All the indications were that we should be around for a long time, and what had seemed during the early weeks a bizarre and temporary curiosity about their language, myths and the names of their grandparents now had to be considered as a lasting desire to share in their life.

The trip to Puyo had also produced another, more unexpected effect upon our relations with the Indians. Far from undermining the rudiments of Jivaro that we had managed to acquire by applying

71

ourselves to a systematic study of it, this gap of a few days had, on the contrary, helped to break through a barrier to our comprehension of the language. Being obliged to speak Achuar upon disembarking from the little plane, we had found to our surprise that both of us had achieved this exploit quite naturally. The sense of a sudden rent in the fog of words had been strengthening ever since. Admittedly, professionalism demanded that we record on our tapes the words whose meaning was difficult to summarize or translate directly, so as to be able to transcribe and interpret them later, in peace and quiet. However, the daily chatter had to a large extent become comprehensible to us, revealing to our suddenly cleared ears a flow of talk, most of which was banal in the extreme.

Wajari had been more surprised than anyone by our return. He had asked me, with no real conviction, to make a few purchases for him in Puyo – an axe-blade, some lengths of cotton material, some machetes and blankets – and I had asked him, in return, to set aside for me a blowpipe that he had been planning to barter. I had scrupulously fulfilled my side of the bargain but Wajari, who had clearly counted on never seeing me again, had meantime given the blowpipe to a Quichua from the Bobonaza in exchange for two or three battered cooking pots. Without asking for anything in return and with perverse ostentation, I had handed over to my former host the little bundle of supplies that everyone had had time to eye as it was unloaded from the plane.

His breach of the punctilious etiquette of exchanges had plunged Wajari into a consternation that was compounded by the fact that all the men in the community knew about it. For the Achuar are extremely strict where reciprocity is concerned and are loath to allow their internal transactions to be tarnished by too obvious imbalances. Everyone knows whose debtor he is and the absence of money does not prevent anyone knowing the going rate for the objects that are usually bartered. To mask his embarrassment, Wajari had immediately invited us to live in his house, and he had diligently set about making a quiver that was to make up for the vanished blowpipe. In the eternal cycle of gifts and counter-gifts, I had established a lead that would, at least for a time, guarantee us a bed and a roof over our heads.

Whenever an Achuar asks us for a machete, a knife, a length of material or some glass beads, we ask for something in return: an earthenware *pininkia* bowl, a little curare, a gourd, occasionally a basket or a traditional ornament of little value. We have little use for these ordinary objects in common use which the Indians, for their part, soon replace. So they pile up in an abandoned hen-run alongside the landing-strip, awaiting a hypothetical transfer to civilization, where we are believed to be going to distribute them amongst our kin. The Achuar reckon that they do well out of these more or less symbolic swaps against goods that are much coveted, and we thereby avoid being subjected to excessive or unjustified demands. The only exceptions to this bartering rule are the currently available medicaments, of which we have amassed quite a large and diverse stock and which, of course, we dispense for nothing to all who come to consult us.

It may seem paradoxical or petty for us to have deliberately made use of the canons of native reciprocity to claim from the Achuar objects that contribute nothing to our material comfort in exchange for these indispensable manufactured goods that cost us so little. Parsimonious though they are, the funds provided by the French Republic would suffice for us to distribute the shoddy goods from Puyo with liberality and without asking for any return apart from our modest daily nourishment and a roof to shelter us. However, when we chose to live among the Indians we decided to make a show of adopting their habitual modes of behaviour, in the first place to get ourselves accepted but also so that our presence would not upset more than necessary the fragile balance of their independence. The Achuar recognize that certain objects possess a value and should not be given away for nothing. They draw a clear distinction between things that cannot be the object of any transaction because they are, as it were, extensions of an individual person – manioc gardens, a house and its furnishings, food or work – and things that have an objective value since they are independent of the individuals who possess them and can, accordingly, be converted into any equivalent, whatever it may be, with those same properties. This applies both to goods exchanged between Indians – weapons, curare, salt, ornaments, dogs, canoes, etc. – and to those bartered, in both directions, with the *regatones* of Montalvo – tools, cloth, utensils, peccary skins, jaguar or ocelot skins, etc. Certain things in the first category may be exchanged in return for their like, although this does not imply any strict reciprocity since their inseparability from those who offer them prevents them from being quantified: offering a meal and taking part in a tree-clearance operation are part of the mutual obligations that exist between kin and are thus not subject to any strict accounts. Despite the absence of money, objects in the second category are, in contrast, subject to the rules that govern a system of circulation that is altogether orthodox in that it does not tolerate flow in a single direction. Several months or even years may elapse between the two moments of exchange, but the time elapsed does not wipe out the obligation to reciprocate with something of more or less equivalent value as the object obtained.

By conforming to the models of exchange culturally sanctioned by the Achuar, we avoid causing the kind of conflicts that a general and indiscriminate distribution of manufactured objects might provoke: jealousy over supposedly unfair treatment, exaggerated demands, the disruption of traditional circuits, etc. As the people of Capahuari have no experience of charity, our little deals thus make it possible for us to exhibit *vis-à-vis* the world of objects a mode of behaviour that is easily recognizable. This makes our presence less exotic and our characters more predictable; and quite apart from the parity of attitudes that it establishes, this ostensible adhesion to the rules of barter is the only way for us to procure ourselves food and shelter. In common with all societies not governed by market prices, the Achuar rule out lucrative transactions where food is concerned. This ban on haggling for profit over goods that are indispensable for survival is sometimes interpreted as a happy way of preserving the solidarity of a community of equals. However, it does not make the survival of an ethnologist any the easier. What good are his dollars to him if he cannot get himself anything to eat? Food and hospitality are offered without counting the cost to kin who come to visit, but the Achuar make no provision for strangers offering payment for such things. However fascinating this ignorance of mercantilism may be for a mind charmed by ancient morality, it can lead to plenty of stomach twinges: when nobody else is concerned about your empty plate, you find yourself thinking wistfully of the conveniences of a world in which money can buy anything.

Thanks to the barter system, however, we have become substitute kin. In the same way that the Achuar welcome in distantly related visitors who then make the most of their hospitality to engage in barter, we are offered the hospitality indispensable for the correct functioning of the circulation of things. In return for the hospitality and sustenance that Wajari offers us, we simply reciprocate more generously than we do to other Achuar. The surcharge that we systematically add to our reciprocity has thus become a way, understood by everyone, to negotiate for our welcome while at the same time saving the appearance of gratuity of goods needed for one's subsistence.

The temporary absence of Wajari has somewhat relaxed discipline in the household. Admittedly, it is raining cats and dogs even though the season of heavy rains has not yet begun. The climate of the Upper Amazon is notoriously erratic thanks to the formidable barrier formed by the Andes, which hook to their peaks the great downpours carried in from the east. So the women have decided not to get soaked by venturing into the garden. There is still a large supply of manioc beer left, not enough to cater for long for the unslakeable thirst of the master of the house, no doubt, but certainly sufficient for our more modest capacity until tomorrow.

Senur is bent over a cooking pot in which she is softening the bark chippings of a variety of stramonium used especially to strengthen the character of dogs. Imbibing this preparation provokes delirium accompanied by extremely powerful hallucinations that are caused by the strong doses of atropine and scopolamine that stramonium contains in its natural state. The people of Capahuari cultivate several varieties close to their houses, each of them reputed to serve a particular purpose: 'stramonium for blowing at little birds', *chinki tukutai maikiua*, reinforces the strength of a hunter puffing into his blowpipe; 'celestial water stramonium', *yumi maikiua*, is used as a poultice to heal gangrenous wounds suffered in warfare, for example, or for snake-bites; 'great stramonium', *juunt maikiua*, provokes several days of violent delirium punctuated by alternate phases of narcosis and excitation, during which the Achuar enter into contact with the *arutam*, ancestral spirits; finally, 'stramonium for dogs', *yawa maikiua*, is used to improve the animals' scent, courage and pugnacity, plunging them momentarily into a state of hypersensitivity that heightens all their faculties.

This treatment is destined for an emaciated bitch of an indefinable colour that answers to the martial name Makanch, the fer-de-lance snake whose bite can cause death within a few hours. Contrary to optimistic expectations, the poor beast does not identify with her daunting homonym: she is a whimpering weakling and her mistress is ashamed of her. The languor of this bitch is supposed to be due to the liquefaction of her bone marrow caused by a fart from a great anteater. According to a quite common Amazonian belief, the flatulence of this creature is supposed to be more dangerous for the dogs pursuing it than its long, sharp claws that cause even jaguars to give it a prudent wide berth. It is true that, with its long tubular muzzle from which a quivering snake-like tongue darts out, this large anteater seems condemned to suffer from such unusually narrow upper orifices that it is perhaps naturally forced to express itself solely through its anus. The lethal force of its farts assures the great anteater of total immunity, as is the case in all animals that 'stink badly' and whose flesh is in consequence declared to be nauseating. The most notorious in this category are the tamandua, the tapir, the coati, the opossum, the red brocket deer, and the anaconda, as well as the predators and carnivore species in general. This collection of fetid animals stands in polar contrast to animals that 'smell good' and, as such, are honoured by being eaten as game by the Achuar. The Indians' sense of smell is certainly remarkable, for they claim to detect the presence of an animal by its particular odour before they have even caught a glimpse of it. Yet this distinction between animals that smell good and animals that smell bad does not have much to do with the alchemy of the nose: while it is true that certain animals, such as the opossum, do emit pestilential exhalations, it does not seem to me that the whiff of the peccary – choice game if ever there was – is any sweeter than that of the graceful kinkajou (honey bear): both secrete a particularly redolent type of musk.

This classification of game according to smell does not exclude other classification systems that draw on an extremely varied set of criteria. Like all ethnologists embarked upon their first stint of fieldwork in an exotic culture, I have for the past few weeks devoted much of my time to drawing up exhaustive lists of plant and animal names, striving to identify the recognizable species and amassing as much information as possible about each one. The Achuar have names for just over 600 animal species, of which barely a third are regarded as edible. The category of edible species includes the animals that smell good, together with all species hunted or caught in daylight. In contrast, nocturnal animals are in general rivals of men as hunters – feline, rapacious, flesh-eating predators – and their own taste for flesh makes them unsuitable for eating because, by virtue of their diet, they are insufficiently distinct from the Indians. Quite apart from their flatulence and their glandular exhalations, inedible animals are inedible because, being carnivorous, they 'have bad breath'.

Their gastronomic qualities aside, animals may also be classified according to whether they are 'of the forest' or 'of the river'. The latter group obviously includes fish, but equally all creatures that enjoy being in the water even if they do not live in it all the time: foremost amongst these are anacondas, otters, grisons, crabs, racoons, hog-nosed skunks and certain members of the cat family. Similarly, the animals of the forest are not exclusively terrestrial. But whether they be quadruped or winged, their existence unfolds in the space of vegetation closed in by the canopy formed by the tallest trees. These constitute the largest category of fauna and game, for only a handful of predators are classified as being 'of the sky', where they wheel endlessly to spot their prey below, amid the uninterrupted carpet of foliage. The river creatures are also defined by the fact that they bite or grip, while the animals of the forest are either delvers that scratch at the earth – armadillos, anteaters, peccaries or Penelope-birds – or peckers with prominent or sharp beaks – toucans, caciques, wood-peckers, puffbirds, trumpet-birds, etc. Edible animals fall into four classes according to the ways in which they are caught and how they are cooked. Feathered or furry 'game', *kuntin*, is hunted with a blow-pipe or rifle and is served boiled; 'fish', *namak*, is caught with a fishing line or a harpoon and is boiled in slices or fillets, whilst 'small fry', *tsarur*, is caught by fishing with poison and cooked and eaten wrapped in banana leaves; finally, 'small birds', *chinki*, shot by means of a blowpipe in the garden, correspond to our buntings and are roasted on spits. Lifestyles, habitats, smells, practical uses and modes of defence thus combine to create a network of signs that impose order upon the animal world according to a logic of the concrete in which imaginary attributes are not totally absent.

After the misfortune of the great anteater's fart, poor Makanch clearly has no idea where she fits in amid all these subtly distinguished sensible qualities. Unsuspecting of the rotten trick about to be played on her, she is scratching at her fleas on the big platform reserved for Senur's pack of hounds. Tethered as she is by a leash of bark, she unprotestingly allows herself to be seized by her mistress, who in a trice binds her paws in a rudimentary hobble. Lying on her back, unable to move and with her mouth now forced open with a stick, the unhappy beast squeals wildly and gargles whilst Namoch, one of Naanch's wives, forces into her muzzle and down her throat copious draughts of stramonium which then dribbles into her eyes. Finally, on the point of asphyxia, Makanch is released and wanders out into the rain, staggering about with her tail between her legs. She stumbles and slips on the sodden earth, bangs into tree-trunks and from time to time falls flat, then painfully struggles up. Now motionless and shivering, now careering at full speed after goodness knows what monstrous vision, the bitch exhibits all the symptoms of a delirious trance. The little naked boys who were playing at sliding on their tummies through the viscous clay have prudently desisted from their game. Caked from top to toe in mud, they have gone off to bathe, leaving the pitch free for the capers of the hallucinating Makanch.

Squatting beneath the roof projection, Senur is watching her bitch, humming between her teeth a little song that I shortly afterwards prevail upon her to record. Each phrase ends in a kind of guttural staccato strangely reminiscent of the 'quilisma', the ancient vocal technique of Gregorian plainsong that Monteverdi restored to honour in his sacred music.

My bitch of Patukam, daughter of the tapir, running in the woods
Always my little bitch, daughter of the tapir, running in the woods
Seeing you, the woman Sunka, the woman Sunka rejoices
Domesticated creature of the woman Nunkui
You who make friends, you who have friends amongst those that roam
    in a pack
Going along like that, my tayra bitch, my little tayra bitch.

We have recently begun to appreciate the importance that the Achuar ascribe to these brief chanted invocations that they call *anent*, since a Shuar preacher visiting Capahuari for a few days helped us to translate into Spanish the recordings that we have made of them. The *anent* serve to transmit messages to the spirits and creatures of nature in tones that are now threatening, now humble. The spirits are entreated to help or to intercede; the natural creatures, whether plants or animals, are warned to conform to the ideal norms of their species. These supplications may also be addressed to human beings: through them, it is possible to transmit one's most secret thoughts to people far beyond earshot and thereby to affect their feelings, actions or even destinies. By these means one can arouse love, overcome rifts between relatives, strengthen conjugal harmony, ward off the dangers that hover over a dear one, or avert the risk of being abandoned. Widows, who are inured to misfortune, are experts in this last-mentioned register, to which they resort almost automatically each time a departure reawakens their own memories of being left behind, as their quavering voices movingly demonstrated when we ourselves left by plane.

As in many manifestations of Achuar affectivity, these *anent* are characterized by great restraint: seldom are the desired outcome or the being invoked explicitly named. Although it is addressed to Makanch, Senur's *anent* does not refer to the object of her anxiety except through metaphorical figures that weave around the bitch an increasingly dense network of desirable qualities embodied by emblematic creatures. Ferocity and skill when hunting in a pack are evoked by the reference to 'the hounds of Patukam', the fierce, untameable little bush dogs which, as a pack, will even take on large specimens of game such as tapirs. Although the Achuar recognize no genetic kinship between their domesticated dogs and these bush dogs, the latter are regarded as the archetype to which all hunting dogs should approximate, and an invocation to this wild canine cousin that is of no use to human beings always serves as an introduction to any *anent* addressed to the human hunter's helpers. As for the tayra, a great devourer of chickens, it manifests all the cunning and clever qualities of the weasel, which it resembles in a much larger format. Finally, the reason why Makanch is called 'daughter of the tapir' is to make her breasts fill with as much milk as that corpulent symbol of ideal maternity that suckles its young for many months, after carrying it in its womb for over a year.

Just as they may be addressed to a wide range of creatures, *anent* are appropriate in a wide range of circumstances. But it is still difficult to get a clear idea of them since, in contrast to myths, which belong to the common Achuar patrimony, these magic songs, each one different from all the rest, are individual treasures that are jealously guarded and not supposed to be heard by any beings but those they invoke. So they are not sung in public, or if they are it is only in the singer's head, and meanwhile his or her countenance betrays nothing. Considerable diplomatic efforts on our part are needed in order to record *anent* discreetly on our tapes. We are allowed to do so only if we satisfy the singers' curiosity about those who have preceded them to our magnetic confessional, whose *anent* they get us to play back to them.

However, this does not mean that we have become traffickers in *anent*, since they are only divulged with the consent of those who allow us to record them. Besides, it is not possible to appropriate these magic songs simply by listening to them. It would also be necessary to know their purpose and the circumstances in which they may be used – conditions that their extremely allegorical nature does not, in most cases, make it possible to guess. When I am favoured with an explanation of how an *anent* can be used, it is only with the assurance that my machine is switched off and, I suspect, only in the cases of *anent* to which their owners attach little value. And yet the tape-recorder also plays a positive revelatory role, since it restores the *anent*'s true dimensions by rescuing it from the erratic secrecy of an individual memory. The words used in these incantations are considered truly to embody the entities to which they refer. They are invisible yet almost material substitutes which the singer appropriates and uses in the manner of a talisman, to act upon the world. Thus *anent* can be passed on as though they were material things, and their concrete and impersonal realization, in the form of a magnetic tape confined within a box, in no way diminishes their power but, in the eyes of the Indians, rather confirms their quality as magic objects.

Apart from a few stylistic variations, the words of the *anent* differ from the ordinary vocabulary only thanks to the virtues that are ascribed to them. These produce a metamorphosis that changes them into elements in some kind of natural language in which things, beings and properties are called by different names from those they bear in reality – names which are, however, their true ones, those that have for ever defined them. To avoid confusion, each *anent* is adapted to a most precisely defined situation: the sowing of maize in seed holes,

(above) The Pastaza

(right) An Achuar garden on the banks of the Pastaza

(far right) A forest path!

Previous page:
Morning ablutions in
the lower Makuma

A house under construction

A house at Sasaïme

Outside a house in Capahuari: an ocelot skin is drying on a frame

A fortified house, Mashumarentza

(above) Women serving manioc beer in a house on the Surikentza: the master of the house is seated in the middle, his rifle on his knees even in this domestic intimacy. His son-in-law is on his right

(left) A martial welcome at the door of a house at Sasaïme

Previous page:
Interior of a house at Numpaïme: view of the female part, the *ekent*

the planting of a manioc cutting, the encouragement of milk in a bitch. Furthermore, the song is said to be truly effective only if it is accompanied by the affectionate thoughts of the person who taught it to the singer, for the intention ascribed to its magic character is then amplified by an emotive purposefulness. Women usually learn *anent* from their mothers or from their aunts. They learn them in adolescence, memorizing the words after drinking some green tobacco juice to sharpen their mental faculties. Once equipped with her little repertory of *anent*, as it were her spiritual trousseau, a young girl is ready to become a married woman.

In this arsenal of chanted invocations, those supposed to act upon dogs occupy an important place that correlates with the high value the women set upon these domesticated animals. An appropriate *anent* can bring about all kinds of desirable results: it can stimulate a bitch's milk, restore its scent and pugnacity, encourage numerous litters, protect it from sickness, incite it to follow a scent or flush out a quarry, or encourage it to attack predators that invade the garden. This conversion of the dog into a mystical interlocutor is not prompted by the normal affection ordinarily felt for a pet that provides company. Rather, it stems from its mistress's constant desire to see it surpass its fellows. An Achuar dog is not a confidant; rather, it is a kind of symbolic projection of the skills of its mistress. A woman is judged by the way in which the essential qualities of the feminine condition are more or less manifest in the products of her labours. Handsome, brave dogs, a rich garden, a creamy manioc beer, fine, delicately ornamented pottery, and cloths with clever designs win respect from the men and envious admiration from other women. These things testify to a woman's exceptional zeal in her work, her know-how and her skill and, above all, her great mastery of the symbolic efficacy without which all the rest would be useless. A dog is thus a stake in a woman's covert battle to win prestige, and the care that she lavishes on it is an expression not so much of her solicitude, but rather her own desire for success.

But a dog's value is not measured solely in the light of personal considerations. It also depends upon market values that turn the best hounds into extremely precious possessions. Whereas pups that have not yet revealed any intrinsic qualities are generally given away for nothing, adult dogs are bartered at rates that vary according to their status and their origins. The rarest dogs with the best reputations are those courageous and agile enough to get the better of ocelots or even jaguars. These may only be acquired, without haggling, in exchange for a canoe or a breach-loading rifle. Such an exorbitant price – it takes several weeks of continuous work to make a canoe – is partly justified by the profits the new owner reckons on making in the illegal fur trade; but it also reflects the disproportionate importance that men attach to doing battle with a jaguar, an animal with a legendary reputation whose skin will guarantee him fame as a great hunter. This big cat is the embodiment of all combative qualities and the symbol of all dangers, for it is a universal predator which competes with men and sometimes kills them; it is an assistant to shamans, as is the anaconda, and it shares with the latter the privilege of inspiring a respectful fear based, in part, on its supposed powers of metamorphosis.

Dogs from far away are also highly prized, whatever their visible qualities. The Achuar are very keen to get hold of them from neighbouring peoples, and vice versa. Yet the dogs of the Shuar and the Canelos, indefinable mongrels with a vague look of a degenerate greyhound about them, are remarkably similar to those of the Achuar. Moreover, they are not even such good hunters, as a result of not having much practice in an area where the big game has vanished under pressure from the advancing front of colonization and demographic expansion. So this circulation of dogs cannot be justified objectively by the qualities of the hounds from distant places. Its cause lies in something common to all the Jivaro groups: the fantastical value set on certain material or immaterial things – shamanistic powers, for example – upon which a foreign origin is supposed to confer strength and qualities far superior to those of identical things that are obtainable locally. This willing dependence upon the external world is bound to encourage bartering, since the things one possesses oneself are necessarily less estimable than others that are invested with all kinds of merits purely because they have moved from one place to another.

Except for the pups, the women's dogs are bartered by the men, who alone have the right to trade objects of value. So a woman does not really own the pack that her husband allows her to use, since he may at any time carry off one of its members and trade it for something else. In practice, it is quite rare for a man to take away a dog to which his wife is attached without promising to replace it with something of equal value, either another dog or else some precious object for her own exclusive use, such as a coil of glass beads. This overlapping of rights where dogs are concerned certainly reflects the animal's ambiguous status: placed entirely in the dependence of the women and raised, cared for, fed and trained by them, it is mainly used by the men in one of the most distinctively masculine occupations.

The ambiguity of the dog is also expressed in other areas. The life that it lives associates it closely with human beings since it is the only animal that sleeps on a bed and eats cooked food; yet the dog's bestial nature is revealed by its lack of discrimination in matters of feeding and sexuality: it will eat scraps of every kind, including excrement, and couple with its own parents, in defiance of the prohibition against incest that regulates society. Furthermore, it is known by the same generic term, *yawa*, that designates the jaguar and a number of other cats, whose essential nature and behaviour it is thus supposed to share. Yet this shared wildness is at the same time deflected to man's advantage, for the dog simultaneously represents the archetype of domestication, *tanku*, an epithet also applied to it to distinguish it from its false, untameable cousins. It is furthermore given a name of its own, a privilege granted to no other tamed animal. Standing at the intersection of what is natural and what is cultural, what is masculine and what is feminine, what is social and what is bestial, the dog is a composite and unclassifiable being. Its strange position in the Jivaro bestiary probably indicates the lateness of its arrival in the forest of the foothills: it is as if its place in the animal hierarchies is not yet firmly established.

CHAPTER 6

Garden Magic

OUR CONVERSATIONS IN the early hours of the mornings have become more fluent. Alone at the fireside, Wajari and I seek each other out by means of words, as if suspended between sleep and the dawn by the circle of fire that isolates us from the shadows. In low but intense tones, Wajari is describing to me the dream that he has just recounted to Entza in the intimacy of their closed bed. During the night, Nunkui, the spirit of gardens, has appeared to him in the form of a stocky little female dwarf with her face painted with rocou. Seated on a log, as serenely still as a toad, she was surrounded by a shimmering red halo. Wajari was surprised, for Nunkui is more inclined to visit the dreams of women, whom she helps with advice relating to their gardening work. Bidding him follow her, she led him to a steep bank of the Kapawi. There, with a forceful jerk of her chin, she drew his attention to a pebbly promontory projecting from a little landslide. Amid the stones a speck began to glow red, like the end of one of the thick cigarettes that Wajari rolls himself in dried maize leaves. In a thin thread of a voice Nunkui then hummed a song and Entza appeared at her side. Then the two of them suddenly vanished, as did the glow of fire in the drift of pebbles. According to Wajari, this unusual dream is an omen, or rather a prefiguration of the discovery of a Nunkui stone. These extremely powerful charms, also known as *nantar*, favour the growth of cultivated plants by passing on to them the energy that they contain. Women lucky enough to possess one guard it jealously, for it imparts to their garden a showy opulence that is a source of both prestige and envy.

At sunrise, barely pausing to down a dish of sweet potatoes, we set off in search of the magic stone. Wajari finds it in the spot indicated, no more than three curves of the river downstream from the house.

84

It is a little sliver of silicate, its reddish surface sparkling here and there with shiny little specks. Entza, for whom it is destined, wraps it carefully in a cotton rag and places it in a *pininkia* bowl which she stows away in her basket-hod. Then she returns to the house, ties her baby to her in a sling, seizes her machete and a fire-brand, unleashes her dogs, signals to her little daughter to follow her, and the whole little troop makes for the garden. Anne Christine goes with them and I follow, with studied nonchalance, a few paces behind. Men are not welcome in gardens.

It is, of course, the men who clear the ground but, once they have felled the bigger trees with an axe and slashed back the residual bushes with their machetes, they call upon the women to burn what is left. Then, once a thick carpet of ash covers the future garden, their last contribution is to plant the rows of banana trees that are to mark out the plots of the various co-wives. After this symbolic gesture that expresses the social appropriation of the garden, they retire from the scene, leaving it to their female companions. With the aid of digging sticks of chonta wood, the women first plant manioc cuttings all over their plots, then distribute in apparent disorder yams, sweet potatoes, taroes, beans, squashes, groundnuts and pineapples. All that then remains to be done is to plant the trees whose seasonal fruits help to vary the somewhat monotonous everyday diet: chonta palms, avocado trees, sweetsop trees, caïmitos, ingas, cocoa trees and guava trees. These tend to be planted along the edge of the area, totally cleared of grass, that surrounds the house, a collective space that is not subject to the exclusive jurisdiction that each wife exercises over her own parcel of land. Here also are the plants that are used communally by one and all: pimento, tobacco, cotton, bushes of clibadium and lonchocarpus – the juices of which asphyxiate fish caught with the poison – gourd plants, rocou and genipa for face-painting and, last but not least, herbal remedies and narcotic plants such as stramonium. When mature, the garden resembles an orchard set in amongst a vegetable garden standing high with produce. The tall papaya stems rise above a most impressive tangle of plants; the taroes spread like monstrous sheaves of arum lily leaves, the peeling banana trees intertwine and stoop beneath the weight of enormous bunches of fruit, the squashes swell like balloons at the foot of charred stumps, carpets of groundnuts border thickets of sugar cane, arrowroot flourishes along the great fallen tree-trunks left over from the felling operation, and everywhere the bushes of manioc unfurl the tentacles of their finger-like leaves.

Entza has halted in the shade of a wild sapote tree, spared at the time of the felling for the sake of its succulent fruits. She lodges her baby in a little hammock, one end of which is attached to the tree, the other to a post driven into the ground. Then, in a trice, she lights a fire using a few blackened twigs left over from the burning. Here she is in her realm, at the heart of the plot she has created, which is marked out in the household's great garden by a little path that separates it from Senur's territory and by the trunk of a huge felled bombax tree, which erects a barrier taller than a man between her domain and Mirunik's. On the side bordering on the forest, an edging row of banana trees indicates where the domesticated space ends.

Now it is time to deal with the Nunkui stone. Entza takes the *pininkia* bowl containing it, covers it with another *pininkia* exactly the same size and buries this little receptacle in a deep hole at the foot of a tree-stump. Imprisoned there, the *nantar* will exercise its beneficent power without endangering the baby. For these magic stones are endowed with a life of their own that enables them to move by themselves. If allowed to wander freely, they would surreptitiously move close to the children to suck their blood. Fortunately, Entza knows an *anent*, learnt long ago from her mother, that will enable her to placate these mineral bloodsuckers so that they will not attack human beings. In response to this invocation, *nantar* glow like fanned embers and the life-giving energy they derive from Nunkui is diffused into the plants. To complete these propitiatory rites, the cannibal *nantar* should be regularly irrigated with infusions of rocou, a metaphorical substitute for the blood to which they are so partial.

However, the Nunkui stones cannot, on their own, take care of all the gardening. Hard work is also necessary. Progressing in concentric circles as she squats there, Entza is busy weeding, using her machete. Every day she attacks the weeds that are competing with her cultivated plants. It is a patient chore that takes up most of the time spent in the garden. Mythical tradition has it that these clumps of parasitical grasses developed from the down covering Hummingbird, who strewed them over the earth's surface to punish human beings for their excessive horticultural zeal. After being disobeyed by two sisters,

Wayus and Mukunt, who, not trusting his promise that cultivation would be effortless, laboured, bent double, planting manioc cuttings, in defiance of his advice, Hummingbird had pronounced a curse that put paid to easy work. Henceforth men would have to labour hard to clear the land for gardens and women would be condemned to the task of weeding in perpetuity.

Decreed by an irascible hummingbird it may be, but this horticultural imperative in truth appears to stem not so much from practical reasons as from aesthetic preoccupations. To an Achuar woman, it is a matter of personal pride to present to the critical gaze of her sisters a garden under perfect control, in which no weed may be found to remind one of the chaotic disorder of the jungle so close at hand. The apparent confusion of plants that strikes an unversed observer at first glance is in reality the product of the careful equilibrium struck between groups of plants that vary greatly in their appearance and needs. They are set out, according to their affinities, in beds separated one from another by little sandy paths as carefully raked as those in a Japanese garden. To be sure, the weeding does slightly prolong the life of the garden beyond the three or four years after which the exhaustion of the not very fertile soil inevitably dictates that it be abandoned. However, the obsessive care with which the Achuar women tend their plants seems to stem above all from the pleasure they derive from the design and harmony of their kitchen gardens, an observation apparently confirmed, *a contrario*, by the fact that many other Amazonian Indians do not bother to weed their clearings, yet do not go hungry on that account.

Apart from their fastidious and, in part, unnecessary maintenance work, it is true that tropical horticulture does not demand great efforts. Here, there is no need to turn the earth, hoe the clods, water or mulch young seedlings, enrich the soil, prune off unnecessary shoots and battle against parasites. Most plants are propagated vegetatively, either by cuttings, as in the case of manioc, or by planting a shoot – from a banana tree, for example – or, as in the case of a yam, by burying a portion of the tuber. Manioc, the numerous varieties of which constitute the major part of daily nourishment, is a lazy gardener's dream. Each cutting produces from two to five kilos of roots easily unearthed by a shove with a machete. Once these are collected, a couple of slashes suffice to reshape the stem into a little rod which, stuck carelessly into the earth, is soon covered with leaves and produces a new set of roots within the space of a few months. Like the yam, this accommodating plant can be left in the earth well beyond the point when it reaches maturation without danger of the roots spoiling. Stockpiling of food supplies is consequently unnecessary since, without the dead seasons to be faced by cultivators of cereals, here the garden remains a reserve of flourishing starch-producing crops that will provide for one's needs throughout the year.

It is true that there are a few furtive tuber fanciers around, but all in all their depredations are relatively modest. Pacas, acouchis and above all agoutis are the most assiduous of the nocturnal delvers that come to the gardens to claim a few roots for themselves. The men are well able to cope with their rapidly detected misdeeds: efficient traps are laid on the paths worn by these stout rodents whose rather greasy flesh is highly prized. The most common of the traps takes the form of a little tunnel of twigs from which a heavier log is suspended. When the animal enters this trap laid in the path of its usual route, it trips on a little rod which causes the log to fall.

Sometimes more direct methods of reprisal are preferred. For instance, the other night Wajari borrowed my electric flash-light and stationed himself with his old blunderbuss in wait for an agouti that had recently been stealing manioc from Senur's garden. It was not long before he potted it, awakening the entire household with a dreadful report. The pleasure of the ambush, always keen for a hunter, was complemented by the satisfaction of wreaking gastronomic revenge on this portly, elongated version of a guinea pig set on weasel-like legs. Rather than enclose their gardens, the Achuar prefer to allow free access to the predators on which they themselves feed, philosophically accepting that it is sometimes necessary to lose something in order to gain something else.

The sun has already passed the zenith and Entza is finishing off her weeding. With the help of her little daughter Inchi, aged six or seven at the most, she scoops up the weeds and piles them on to the fire, which is soon belching thick spirals of white smoke. Like all little Achuar girls, at a very early age Inchi was initiated into the distinctive tasks of her feminine condition: gardening, cooking, housework, water-fetching, looking after the smaller children, and so on. It is in that last capacity that she is the most useful, rocking the baby while her mother is busy, and keeping the bothersome flies away. Though the help she gives Entza may be modest still, she is learning her future role as a wife and a good gardener. The simplicity of the horticultural methods may obscure the fact that the garden is a very complex world in which thousands of plants, belonging to at least a hundred species, must all co-exist. Some species, such as manioc and sweet potatoes, have several dozen varieties. To master this vegetable society, about which their husbands know virtually nothing, women depend upon a botanical knowledge that they have been acquiring patiently since childhood.

Inchi's little brother, in contrast, is totally free from constraints. Unkush spends his days as he pleases, without it ever occurring to anyone to request the smallest service from him, and this leisure will continue up until his adolescence. Precariously balanced on a log, he is at the moment busy reaching for papayas with a long stick. But the papayas are not yet ripe and remain obstinately impervious to the blows that the little chap is dealing them. Stretching too far, he eventually tumbles into a bed of beans from which he picks himself up with a '*chuwa!*' of disgust.

With Inchi still in attendance, Entza has approached a manioc plant and is eyeing it critically. It is a new variety that she planted a few weeks ago, having obtained the cutting from her sister Chawir, who lives on the banks of the Pastaza. Its roots are much thicker than those of the varieties cultivated at Capahuari and its rather bland taste predestines it exclusively for the production of manioc beer. But the soil here is different from the soil of the Pastaza. It is dense and clayey and said to be less fertile than the black, sandy soil alongside that great river. For this reason, Entza worries that the plant will not be able to acclimatize. Squatting before the manioc plant, she softly sings it a little song of supplication.

Being a Nunkui woman, I am always calling nourishment into existence
The sekemur roots, there where they push, there where they are, I
    made them be like that, nicely separate
Being of the same species, when I have passed by, they continue to be
    born
The sekemur roots have become divided into 'species'
They are now coming to me

Being a Nunkui woman, I am always calling nourishment into existence
Behind me, in response to my call, it continues to be born.

The power of words is once again affirmed: for the irrepressible
vampirism of the Nunkui stones to be contained, or for a manioc
cutting to flourish despite being transplanted, it is necessary to sing
an appropriate *anent*, to touch the souls of these dumb but attentive
entities. For speech to be effective, however, precautions are needed.
Although addressed to a manioc cutting, Entza's *anent* does not refer
to the object of her anxiety except through a metaphor, that of the
sekemur, a vegetable soap, whose voluminous roots evoke those of
the manioc. The souls of plants, like the souls of dogs, cannot tolerate
being addressed too directly. The sensitivity of these touchy interlocutors would be affronted by an explicit account of what human beings
were expecting from them, so it must be allayed by indirect injunctions
that mask the crudity of the demands being made of it and even the
very name of the being that is expected to respond to them.
  Whatever their addressee, all gardening *anent* refer in one way or
another to Nunkui. She is the creator and mistress of cultivated plants,
as is attested by a myth that even the youngest children are able to
tell me. I obtained the following version – our first shot at a translation
of a myth – from old Chinkias, the mother of Wajari and Titiar.

A long time ago, a long, long time ago, people had no gardens. They
were constantly hungry, for they lived on roots and leaves that they
gathered in the forest. One day a woman went off to collect shrimps in
a little river. Standing at the water's edge, she noticed manioc peelings
and plantain skins floating down the river. Making her way upstream to
see where these peelings were coming from, she saw a woman peeling
manioc. This woman was Nunkui. She said to Nunkui, 'Little grandmother, for pity's sake, give me some manioc,' but Nunkui refused and
said, 'Rather, take my daughter Uyush (sloth) with you; but I beg you
to treat her well. When you reach home, you must tell her to call the
cultivated plants by their names.'
  The woman did so and the child Uyush named all the garden plants:
manioc, plantain, sweet potato, taro, yam, all the garden plants, and
then they truly did exist. People were happy, for there was no longer a
lack of food. One day when Uyush found herself alone with the other
children of the household, they asked her, for fun, to call into existence

a spider, which she did. Then a scorpion, which she also did. Then they insisted that she call the harmful Iwianch spirits. At first she refused, but at length gave in to their demand and some horrible Iwianch invaded the house. Totally terrorized, the children wanted to revenge themselves on Uyush and threw handfuls of hot ash into her eyes. Uyush took refuge on the roof of the house.

There, she began to sing softly to the giant bamboos, the *kenku*, that grew close to the house: '*Kenku, kenku*, come and fetch me, let us go and eat groundnuts; *kenku, kenku*, come and fetch me, let us go and eat groundnuts.' Blown by a sudden gust of wind, a bamboo crashed on to the roof and Uyush caught hold of it. The children tried to reach her, but she crawled into the bamboo and from there pronounced a curse upon the cultivated plants, naming them one by one. Thereupon these began to shrink, until they were tiny. Then Uyush slipped inside the bamboo, defecating regularly as she went. Each of her excrements formed a knot in the bamboo. Now Uyush lives underground with Nunkui.

That is what my mother Yapan told me long ago.

Although every variant of this myth begins with the formula *yaunchu*, 'long ago', it does not on that account establish an irremediable break between the present time and the time of origins. Myths certainly are 'discourse about the past' (*yaunchu aujmatsamu*), but here '*yaunchu*' simply means an earlier point that it is impossible to specify precisely in the unfolding of time, by reason of the happy amnesia that the Achuar cultivate. The world of myths came to an end no more than a few generations ago, at the blurred edge of the memories of the more immediate ancestors whom the chain of memory still links with the living. The time of the foundation of culture was thus not so long ago that its actors no longer have any say in the present course of daily events, where their presence continues to be felt as a fading echo of the heroic role that they once played. Daily intercourse with spirits who exist alongside human beings strips them of mystery and extends into their immanent but knowable world the principles of equality that regulate human society. No original separation, no ascent into heaven, no distinction of essences intervenes here, to found the human order upon the basis of a withdrawal on the part of the gods. My companions give no thanks to Nunkui for her creative action, perform no acts of gratitude for her benefits, and make no sacrifices to ingratiate themselves with her. In short, they have contracted towards her none of the irredeemable moral debts that render religions of transcendence so constraining.

This good-natured spirit lives just beneath the surface of the gardens, where she watches over the well-being of her plant-children, apparently holding no grudge against human beings for their former unkindness to Uyush. Women make sure of her presence by singing *anent* to her and enter into an implicit agreement to join her in watching over their cultivated plants. Thanks to their assiduous efforts, the Achuar have succeeded in circumventing Uyush's curse and getting the miniature vegetables she left them to grow again. To some extent, Nunkui is a metaphor for the good gardener. In most of the invocations addressed to her the singer explicitly identifies herself with her as if desiring to appropriate the virtues of her model. The maternal authority that Nunkui exercises over her vegetable progeny is thus ideally conceded to women who know how to maintain good relations with her. In short, gardening can be seen as a daily repetition of the act of creation in which Nunkui gave birth to the cultivated plants through the intermediary of her daughter Uyush. Logically enough, plants are treated as their own children by the women who take care of them and are also represented in *anent* as the adoptive children of Nunkui.

This horticultural mothering no doubt reflects a very real technical necessity: most of the plants cultivated by the Achuar are propagated by means of cuttings and so depend for their existence and perpetuation upon the care that the women lavish upon them. Manioc does not revert to its wild state when left untended, but soon dies without reproducing, strangled by the secondary vegetation that encroaches from the surrounding jungle. Horticulture thus proceeds on the basis of a dialectic deal, according to which the manioc allows itself to be eaten by human beings provided that they assume responsibility for ensuring its continued propagation. This vegetable cannibalism is by no means purely metaphorical to my companions, who regard manioc as a living being, possessed of a soul, *wakan*, and leading an altogether regular family life in the forest clearings. Although always placed under the auspices of Nunkui, most of the gardening *anent* are addressed to this little manioc community, to encourage it to grow and multiply harmoniously.

These leafy children, who are devoured by those who raise them, know where they can find compensation for their fate. Like the Nunkui stones, manioc is believed to suck the blood of human beings, in particular that of their offspring. The anaemia of young infants is often ascribed to this, when vampire bats cannot be held responsible. In contrast to the bats, no traces remain of the manioc, for it slakes its thirst simply through the touch of its omnipresent leaves. That is why the Achuar like to move from one spot to another in their gardens along the great tree-trunks that are left there after being felled. They constitute places of sanctuary raised above the cunning sea of manioc and provide safe paths for those visiting the garden. The women and the children, who are forced into daily contact with the vampire plant, are obviously the most at risk. The children are kept under careful supervision and warned not to stray too far from their mother, for she can weave an invisible protective barrier around them by singing the appropriate *anent*. Her incantations encourage the manioc to turn away from the children and instead attack any strangers who slip secretly into the garden.

> Pierce-him-on-the-spot
> Saying this, I could hear them regenerating themselves
> I could imagine the rocky chaos
> As we, we ourselves, came to gather, I could hear them regenerating
>   themselves
> I roll, I roll
> I could hear them regenerating themselves, making the rocky chaos
>   roll away
> My little garden regenerating itself, I could imagine
> That rocky landslide, I could imagine it.

The manioc is here given an unequivocal order. A monstrous fate depends upon it being obeyed properly: by sucking the blood of intruders, the plant acquires an unstoppable power, its roots swell up and become unbreakable, like a rocky chaos in which the singer is supposed to have provoked a gigantic landslide. However, such injunctions are not always heeded. A few days ago Entza dug up some roots streaked with red, which she immediately interpreted as traces of the blood that the plant had sucked. This threat makes her take particular care, the more so given that the danger is now increased by the new presence of the *nantar*, whose cannibalistic inclinations she is not yet sure she can control.

Gardening presents a curious paradox. The Achuar have turned a carefree, unthreatening occupation into a kind of internecine guerrilla war ruled by the risky balance of a series of blood-lettings. The mother feeds on her plant-children, who in their turn take from her human offspring the blood that they need for their own growth. The fecundity of the *nantar* is proportionate to their harmful vampire powers and Nunkui herself grades her attributes according to a scale of shades of red. First, the vermilion red of rocou, with which the women paint their faces to please her; the brownish red of the manioc cuckoo and the orange-red of the little *wapau* boa, two creatures considered to be Nunkui's helpers or avatars, which the women try to attract to their gardens by means of their alluring *anent*; and the pinkish red of the wild flower *keaku cesa*, the bulb of which is shredded into an infusion of rocou, then poured on to the manioc cuttings when they are first pricked out.

This secret ritual, which Anne Christine has recently been able to observe in the new garden of Suwitiar, Mukuimp's young wife, is usually organized by an old woman of experience. Surutik had been asked to officiate. Bent over her walking stick, with her pendulous breasts and her nose ravaged by leishmaniosis, she presented a sad image of decrepitude and sterility. Yet it was she who poured over the clumps of manioc the gourdful of reddened water and she who exhorted the plants to drink this substitute for human blood and so, in the future, spare any careless children who went too close to them. Surutik had been excluded from the fertility cycle by the menopause, which was no doubt why she could, without risk, dispense to the manioc a semblance of the blood that had ceased to flow in her. A younger woman would have been exposed to a surreptitious nip from the manioc: its slips would prefer the fresh blood of their mistress to the paler substitute being offered to them.

Blood exists in the world as a limited source of energy and it is the progressive dwindling of its flow that brings about ageing. But what is lost for some can only benefit others, in a subtle system of communicating vessels. The relationship between the women gardeners and the manioc is thus of the same order as the strange association that binds certain insects to their 'mothers'. My companions claim that anopheles and sand-flies live in great numbers on animal-mothers that resemble huge dogs, with which they cohabit in a state of symbiosis, forever pumping out their host's blood and reinjecting the blood that they have taken from other creatures. The vampirism of manioc and Nunkui stones would thus appear to be simply a means of restoring a natural equilibrium to a great circuit of physiological exchange, linking together women and both their human offspring and their 'plant-children', for the necessary preservation of blood, since there is only a finite supply of this.

Fortunately, not all the plants in the garden manifest the dangerous disposition of manioc. But many of them are endowed with a soul, *wakan*, the last remaining trace of their earlier humanity from the days before the mythical heroes divided life into the various orders that now embody it. This is the case, for example, with the unfortunate girl, Wayus, condemned by Hummingbird, for her excessive zeal, to be changed into the little bush of the same name; the leaves are used for the infusion consumed before dawn. It is likewise the case with two sisters, Ipiak (rocou) and Sua (genipa), whose voracious, insatiable sexual appetites led to their metamorphosis into the natural cosmetics used by human beings to decorate their faces. Not long ago, Naanch told me their edifying story.

The ancients used to say that long ago there was a young woman called Sua, whom we now know as a plant used for painting our faces; and she had a sister called Ipiak. Both were unmarried and the same thing happened to them as happens to us men when we have no wife and we have a great desire for a woman. For husbandless women, it is just the same. They very much desired to possess a man and together they set out to look for one. They had heard tell of Nayap [a black martin with a forked tail] as of a real male and they decided to look for him and marry him. They met him on a forest path, on his way to hunt birds with his blowpipe. 'Where are you going?' he asked them, and they replied, 'We are going to your house.'

Then Nayap told them, 'That's fine, my mother stayed at home to mill maize, so go and join her.' Then he added, 'A little further along, the path forks; on the path that leads to my house there is the tail feather of a *yusa* parrot and on the path that leads to my brother Tsuna [pus], there is the tail feather of a cuckoo, *ikianchim.* Be very careful not to take the wrong path!'

'Right!' they said, and off they went.

But Tsuna was behind them and had heard everything. Roused by these lovely young women, he made up his mind to marry them himself and rushed homewards to switch the tail feathers around. The young women took the wrong path.

Nayap, suspecting nothing, returned home in the evening with plenty of game for the two sisters. He asked his mother, 'Have the women not yet arrived?'; and she replied, 'No, I have not seen any women.'

Nayap then exclaimed, 'What has happened to them? They told me they were coming here and I gave them the necessary directions.' Then he added, 'Perhaps they went to my brother Tsuna's house instead.' He was very cross about it and decided to forget the whole business.

Meanwhile, the two women had arrived at the home of Tsuna's mother. She was busy kneading clay to make some pots. Surprised at this, they asked, 'You are Nayap's mother, are you not?'

'Yes, yes, that's me,' she hastened to reply.

The two sisters installed themselves and waited for Nayap to return. When night fell and he still had not come, they asked the old woman, 'What about your son? Where is he?' and she told them that he had gone off to hunt birds. They stayed up until quite late but eventually the old woman told them to go to sleep on the *peak*.

At last, in the middle of the night, Tsuna arrived. He looked so repugnant that he was ashamed to show himself in daylight. He returned from his hunting expedition embarrassed, for he had caught nothing but a few river crabs, and his mother grumbled, 'These birds that you have killed are very old and tough!' Then Tsuna went off to sleep between the two sisters and the whole night was passed in caresses and erotic games.

Exhausted, Sua and Ipiak eventually fell asleep just before dawn. When they awoke it was broad daylight and their partner had disappeared. They noticed then that they were covered in a kind of sticky and fetid pus. The two sisters wondered what on earth could have happened and decided not to sleep at all the next night. Once in bed with Tsuna again, they managed to exhaust him so much with their caresses that he soon fell asleep. At dawn they discovered his revolting body covered in pus. They quickly moved away and hid, so that they could watch him.

When Tsuna awoke his mother said, 'My son, you are beginning to lose your shame!' Alarmed, Tsuna leaped up, grabbed his blowpipe and dashed off into the forest. He had forgotten his quiver but did not dare return and called out to his mother to bring it to him; then he disappeared.

The two sisters decided to go to Nayap's house, but he was angry, for he realized from their nauseating smell that the young women had slept with Tsuna. Nayap told them to go and bathe to wash away the pus with which they were coated. After their bathe they rubbed themselves with fragrant leaves and returned to the house. But they still gave off disgusting whiffs and Nayap repulsed their advances. Sua and Ipiak then set out in search of another man. They came to the house of an old woman who had a monster-son. He was of minute stature but had a gigantic penis that he carried wound about his body like a rope. His mother kept him shut up in a large jar set on a grid above the bed. Not knowing this, the two sisters enquired where he was, to which the old woman replied, 'My son is away, killing animals. He is not home yet.'

'Very well,' they said, 'we shall wait here to take him for our husband.'

Every day they asked for news of the son and the mother replied, 'I do not know when he will return.'

Now, every night, the tiny man poked his huge penis out of the jar and unwound it, letting it down to the bed below, where he copulated with the two sleeping sisters. In the morning they realized that they had been penetrated, but could not make out how it had happened. While the old woman was out in her garden, the two young women set about searching the house and discovered the jar and the monster-son. Having found him, they decided to kill him. They boiled some water and poured it into the pot and the son died, boiled alive.

Sua and Ipiak resumed their quest, weeping. They did not know where to go now, for no man wanted anything to do with them. As they went along, they said, 'What could we change ourselves into? A hill, perhaps? No, because men run all over hills, they would mock us and we should be ashamed. Or could we become frogs in a great marsh? No, that would be shaming too. Why not change ourselves into a great alluvial plain? That would not do, for men would jeer at us, saying that a person had turned herself into a plain.'

In the end, Sua came to a decision. 'The best thing would be for me to become Sua, for even young men might say to their wives, "Give me Sua so that I can paint my face!" Then my name would be famous.' Then Sua said to her sister, 'And you, little sister, what do you want to turn yourself into?'

Ipiak replied, 'Well then, I shall become Ipiak, for even young men will say to their wives, "Give me Ipiak so that I can paint my face!" and my name will be famous.'

Sua drew herself up to her full height and set her legs apart. She gave a loud cry and became the *sua* plant (genipa). Ipiak squatted on the ground and became the *ipiak* plant (rocou). That is why rocou is a low bush, whereas genipa stands high. They merged so well into the undergrowth that even the birds flew over them without fear. Then all kinds of people came to visit them, to be painted. Yakum ('howler monkey') was smeared with rocou by Ipiak, as was Kunamp ('squirrel'). Chuu ('woolly monkey') was nicely decorated by Sua, who put genipa on his head, hands and feet. And when they were all thus embellished, they underwent a metamorphosis. That is all.

Humiliated by hideous suitors whom they had immodestly solicited, rejected by a handsome man with a forked tail whom their shamelessness disgusted, and despised by all those whose virility they coveted, Sua and Ipiak learned the lesson of modesty the hard way. By taking it upon themselves to make the first move towards marriage, they exposed themselves to the shame of their all-too-visible lust and condemned themselves to seeing it constantly abused or derided. There could only be one outcome to this excessive love of men: to come as close as possible to the faces and bodies of those who had rejected them and to embellish all those disdainful lovers with their transfigured defilement. While this myth confers a certain tragic grandeur upon the two modest cosmetic bushes growing alongside the house, it also spells out a puritanical morality that is aimed at the Achuar women. The canons of seemliness and the rules of respectable behaviour impose upon them a reserved pattern of conduct to which they must always adhere, on pain of being wiped out from humanity. Like the Cheshire Cat, which slowly fades away among the leaves, leaving only its enigmatic grin to linger, the two lustful women disappeared into the vegetable kingdom, bequeathing to men their pigments, symbols *par excellence* of the domestication of nature for social ends.

Not all the garden plants came by such dramatic fates. The sweet potato and the squash have a feminine soul, the banana tree a masculine one, but no mythical past is known in their cases. The genders attributed to them likewise evoke sexuality, but they are more prosaically derived from metonymic homologies with various organs of reproduction, sometimes recalled in puns laden with double meanings. The humanization of the majority of cultivated plants indicates that these are receptive to the *anent* invocations addressed to them. The soul, *wakan*, with which such a plant is endowed is a faculty of understanding. This makes it able to communicate with other plants of the same species and also to understand both the messages of the women who mother them and the injunctions of Nunkui or the animals linked with her. But it is only in dreams and hallucinatory trances that these leafy beings can readopt their long-lost human shape and speak to the Achuar in their own language.

The Achuars' animation of plants is not confined to their gardens. As with the graceful dryads of antiquity or the curly-headed alders of German legends, the frail or majestic appearance of many of the forest trees masks a consciousness just beneath their bark. These are the creatures of Shakaim, Nunkui's brother (or husband, according to a different interpretation), who cultivates the jungle as a huge plantation and shows men the most appropriate spots in which to open up clearings. The outer boundaries of nature are pushed back by this socialization of plants, and the forest that looks so wild becomes simply the supernatural garden where Shakaim uses his talents as a horticulturist. When human beings create clearings in which to cultivate their crops, they are simply replacing the plantations of Shakaim by those of Nunkui, but both kinds of plantation are domesticated, to their advantage, by these accommodating spirits.

Senur has come out to join Entza by the slowly dying fire. Pointing her machete threateningly at a clump of sickly banana trees, Entza grumbles in a throaty voice, as might a woman angered by the indifference or waywardness of her husband.

'My banana trees are ailing, little sister. For a whole moon they have been drying up, consumed by the heat. Might they perhaps be dying as a result of jealousy?'

'We must wait and see, my little sister. You may be right.'

'My little sweet potatoes are like big papayas from the Pastaza, my manioc roots are as round as a tapir's belly, all my little store of food is multiplying. Given that I am a Nunkui woman, little sister, how could the children of my garden die? Could it not be the jealousy of a bad woman that is making my little banana trees waste away? Could they not be dying from a curse?'

There. The word has been pronounced: *yuminkramu*; the curse of an envious woman has perhaps fallen upon Entza's garden, borne there by *anent* so secret that no woman will admit to knowing them.

Senur, the elder wife and Entza's confidante, proffers advice and consolation.

'You may be right, little sister. Bad women do that when the food that they grow is sickly. In her jealousy, what such a woman thinks is: "My sister's cuttings are fine and many, but let's just see if her cuttings will wilt." To be sure, you must think, little sister. Might it not be a woman who has come to your garden? Might it not be one who said, "Little sister, your banana trees are as splendid as those of the Kukam, downstream. Mine are as thin as the wild *winchus* of the water's edge; for pity's sake, tell me how you make them grow!" A bad woman does not speak straight, my sister, and jealousy lies in her heart. Think back, little sister; remember who has visited you with crooked words. It is she, certainly she who has set a curse upon you.'

Now Entza will have to cast her mind back over all the women who have come to see her garden. Amongst them lurks the one who, with her excessive praises, betrayed her jealousy. By means of an *anent* specially designed for the purpose, the very curse that is affecting the banana trees will have to be returned to the garden of the woman who first pronounced it. This way of distributing justice can sometimes miss the proper target but, with domestic witchcraft, that is an inevitable hazard.

It is by now late afternoon and the gardening chores are almost completed. While Senur returns to the house, Entza digs up half a dozen manioc roots and swiftly replants the stems, after piling the roots into her wicker hod. She adds a few sweet potatoes and two large yams, then makes her way to the river to wash and peel the tubers, which are encrusted with mud. With this task completed, she deposits her basket in the house and takes her children to bathe in the river. On the way she passes Wajari, who is in high spirits, his blowpipe on his shoulder and two empty-eyed howler monkeys slung down his back. Quite a way downstream thick smoke is lazily rising from Tseremp's new clearing, its smell of burning, damp wood spreading as far as us. A pair of squawking macaws wing their way into the sunset, too high to shoot down. This is said to be a sign that some Achuar woman has been carried off by Shuar warriors. A small catfish has been caught on Chiwian's line: it twists this way and that, its moustache quivering, and is finally pulled up on to the bank and dispatched by a sharp blow with a stick. With peals of laughter, the

100

children are splashing each other in the river, their skin gleaming like polished leather. Their disorderly movements churn up the sand, which rises in whirling columns like aquatic clouds, refracting the light in a thousand tiny flashes. All this peaceful agitation, this tissue of insignificant happenings, brings Entza back down into the bosom of the household, suspending the internal dialogue begun in the garden.

CHAPTER 7

Dreams

FOR THE PAST FEW DAYS we have been installed in the home of
Pinchu, Mirunik's brother. His large house is situated slightly
upstream, on the opposite bank of the Kapawi, very close to our
former lodgings. From it we can hear Wajari's shouts as he takes his
morning bathe, just as from his house we could hear the melancholy
notes of Pinchu's flute floating down the dawn mists. However, it is
not Pinchu's musician's soul that has drawn us to his home, nor the
attractions of his more spacious house, but rather the need to diversify
our mentors and avoid offending the other few men who have insistently repeated offers of hospitality to us. Wajari greeted our decision
good-naturedly, particularly as he gets on well with his brother-in-law.
He is certainly sorry to see us go, partly because of my little presents,
but also partly because he thinks we had become mascots for him and
our continued presence in his house afforded him an unusual source
of distraction and conferred a mark of distinction discreetly capitalized
upon with the other men. It is also possible, finally, that the burgeoning friendship that I feel for him is reciprocated and that his
affectionate words at our parting were not dictated solely by the
protocol of hospitality.

In contrast to Wajari, Pinchu is frail-looking and his movements
are exuberant. His delicate limbs with their fine joints and his relaxed
gait give him a slightly dandified air that is enhanced by a smile full
of charm and two permanently shadowed wide brown eyes. His two
wives also present a contrast on every count. Yatris moves with languid
grace and has an arresting Gioconda-like face illuminated by a mysterious half-smile. Santamik, on the other hand, is a robust girl brimming
with tomboyish energy. The bands that she winds tightly round her
ankles show off the swell of her calves to graceful advantage, attracting

103

the furtive glances of all male visitors. The house reflects the personalities of these likeable hosts. Its architecture and furnishings are no different from other houses, yet everything about it seems more elegant and better finished, probably as a result of its subtly balanced proportions. In a society where respect for tradition rules out the very idea of constructing a house that does not conform with the canonical model, originality and a love of beauty can still find expression in the harmonious relations between the various elements of the roof structure, even though the general arrangement is nothing out of the ordinary.

Pinchu rises slightly later than Wajari, that is to say seldom before 4 a.m., but his attitude towards the *wayus* libations is equally ceremonious. This morning it is Santamik who has prepared the infusion, and she is openly amused at the sight of her bearded 'brother' complying with the custom. I have acquired this fictitious kinship thanks to the classificatory properties of the Jivaro kinship system, which make it possible to deduce my relationship to any of my interlocutors by working it out logically from some other relationship that is already known. Since Wajari called me 'brother', I have inherited his own infinitely extended family and have thus, *ipso facto*, become Pinchu's 'brother-in-law' and, conversely, the 'brother' of his wives. This little exercise in permutation will suffice to show that we have finally acquired an identifiable position within our hosts' network of relations, and have thereby entered upon an existence that is socially acceptable.

Right now our host is thoughtful and silent, slowly sipping his sweetish infusion of *wayus*. He is listening with concern to mysterious whistling sounds that are piercing the night above the house. They are not predators' cries, nor are they the hooting of owls. The sound is more like that of the high-pitched whirr of a rhombus projected into space at high speed.

'Wait, brother-in-law, listen. Can you not hear a *juij, juij, juij* sound up there?'

'Yes, I hear it, brother-in-law.'

'It must be *tsentsak* passing overhead. They come from far away, these darts, all the way from the Kupatentza or the Kunampentza. There are many bad shamans there, who want to eat us. Here, we do not have shamans. So they want to wipe us out with their *tsentsak*:

tsak! they fly into your arms, *tsak!* they fly into your legs, *tsak!* they fly into your stomach, and soon you die.'

'Is it true, brother-in-law, that there is no shaman here?'

'Well, brother-in-law, there is Mukuimp, the son-in-law of your brother Wajari: he knows a bit; but he is not much good, he has not learned much. He cannot fight on equal terms with Chalua or Yuu. He has no Quichua *tsentsak*; he only knows how to suck out the darts that are easy to unhook from the body.'

'Truly, brother-in-law; and these darts of the shamans, are they like those used in blowpipes?'

'Yes, they are of the same kind; but only the shamans can see them, when they have drunk **natem**. Then they can see them wherever they are stuck in the body, like the reflection of a fish beneath the surface of the water. We ordinary folk cannot see them, but we can hear them flying.'

I too have become accustomed to prefacing my remarks with the appropriate kinship term and to ornamenting my responses in this litany with the indispensable interjections without which a conversation would lose its *raison-d'être*. I must confess that I derive a somewhat satirical pleasure from this, for the rhetorical additions that give the conversation its personal tone and its stamp of truth are so very similar to the stereotyped speech of comic-book Red Indians that I sometimes feel I am deferring to the conventions of fiction rather than to the rules of real sociability.

The shamanistic darts passing overhead have clearly greatly disturbed Pinchu, who sinks once again into gloomy silence. Yatris and Santamik are whispering together in a corner, no doubt commenting on the event, but I cannot make out what they are saying. I make an effort to restart the conversation.

'What are you going to do today?'

'I am going to the forest. I shall exercise the hounds. I have had a **kuntuknar** dream. I was on a forest path and I heard men coming towards me. I hid and saw a band of Shuar carrying rifles. They were painted as for war, but were marching along carelessly in single file, showing off. They kept bragging, "I am going to kill! I am going to kill! I am going to kill!" They were on their way to attack us. That, brother-in-law, is a good enough **kuntuknar** dream to send one into the forest! Today I shall show what I too am capable of!'

Contrary to what might be assumed to be its message, this dream does not presage a skirmish with other warriors, but rather an encounter with a herd of white-lipped peccaries. *Kuntuknar* constitute favourable hunting omens and their latent meaning is interpreted by a term-for-term reversal of their superficial meaning. A dream is usually classed as a *kuntuknar* if it is about human beings who are either aggressive or particularly inoffensive, enigmatic or very numerous, in despair or very attractive. Thus, to dream of a buxom woman inviting you to make love by displaying her sexual organs or to dream of a crowd of people bathing noisily in a river prefigures a meeting with white-lipped peccaries, while a dream in which you see an angry man making threats should be considered as a favourable omen for hunting collared peccaries. The interpretation rests upon unobtrusive homologies of behaviour or appearance. A gaping vulva symbolizes the slaughtered carcass of a peccary, a bellicose attitude evokes the aggressive temperament of animals, the aquatic frolics of a crowd of people is reminiscent of the tumult caused by a herd fording a stream.

Depicting the human world as something wild thus operates as an omen for many types of game. A vision of tearful women's faces floating in the trees like ripe fruit, for example, foretells a successful hunt for woolly monkeys, since that pathetic image suggests the despair exhibited by the females of a group of monkeys when one of their males is killed. To dream of a fat, dimpled little baby becomes, through an almost cannibalistic metaphor, the sign of a plump agouti. A wan face glimpsed in a dream becomes the pale little visage of a sapajou monkey. The gaze of an impassive warrior painted with rocou evokes a jaguar poised to spring, and a man with a reddish beard prefigures a howler monkey. The latter dream has become less improbable since my arrival has given it a material basis and I am happy to think that by haunting the sleep of my companions I am at least giving them hope of successful hunting at their awakening.

The interpretation of a *kuntuknar* by dint of the metaphorical naturalization of mankind is but one of the possible forms of inversion used to explain its prophetic meaning. Thus, to dream that one is shooting at birds up in the branches of a tree augurs well for a fishing expedition, just as a dream about catching fish foretells of success in a bird hunt. The cross-referencing of terms is systematic: an airborne creature, still and visible, killed at a distance by a blowpipe dart becomes an aquatic animal, mobile and invisible, caught at close hand with a fishing net or a harpoon. Another form of reversal plays upon the ability of women to have *kuntuknar* dreams for their husbands: a dream representing a typically feminine activity will be a favourable omen for the eminently masculine action of killing an animal. Interpretation may also be based upon extremely tenuous gestural or visual resemblances. When a woman dreams that she is threading beads, this means that she will soon have to gut the intestines of some hunted animal; to dream of spinning cotton means that she will soon be plucking the white breast of a hocco bird; and to dream of carrying a wicker hod brimful of manioc tells her that she will soon have a peccary, killed by her husband, to carry home on her back. The images of confrontation, seduction or distress that dominate the dreams of men are replaced, in the dreams of women, by more peaceful domestic visions, in conformity with the day-to-day organization of tasks according to which the women reign over the household world, only venturing into the forest as helpers to the hunters.

As they convert the contents of oneiric visions into favourable hunting omens, the Achuar make extremely imaginative use of the properties of the subconscious as manifested in dreams. Like other Amazonian societies, they play upon a rule of conversion that assumes there is a correspondence between domains of practical behaviour and sets of concepts that appear to be irreconcilable: human beings and animals, above and below, the aquatic and the airborne, fishes and birds, the activities of men and those of women. By these means the Indians exploit for their pragmatic ends the characteristic way in which dreams fasten upon the various relations that exist between the dreamer and his environment, rather than upon the particular objects that are involved in those relations, so that every dream becomes an expression of a relationship that the dreamer may experience when in a state of consciousness. And the Achuar are quite right to attach less importance to the terms involved in dream relationships than to the relationship that the dream expresses, a relationship of a purely logical character which, on that very account, lends itself easily to these permutations by homology, inversion or symmetry, from which the dream's prophetic message flows. Thus, when a woman dreams that she is threading glass beads, it is not those highly desirable ornaments that she charges with a symbolic significance but, instead, the altogether ordinary operation of placing small, hard, hollow objects upon an elongated, flexible support – an operation identical to, albeit a symmetrical reversal of, the operation that she performs when she removes an animal's intestines, making soft, solid objects slip out of a hollow support or container that is likewise flexible and long. The gestures of her hands are similar although opposed, just as there is an opposition between the natural and the artificial nature of the objects involved and the relation between the container and what is contained.

Such a method of interpretation turns out to be at once very normative and totally open-ended. It selects from the infinitely diverse material of dreams relational systems that can be endowed with a prophetic function by following a few simple rules of conversion. So the *kuntuknar* examples that I conscientiously collect each morning should not be regarded as elements in a vast table of correspondences between stereotyped oneiric symbols and categories of omens. Rather, they testify to my hosts' inventiveness in the exercise of analytic faculties which their desire to establish a hold over the future makes them press into constant use. There is no need to resort to any set of equivalences exhaustively classified by tradition into a key for dreams, since all interpretations of hunting dreams become valid so long as they conform with these laws of derivation which the Achuar do not formulate explicitly but know how to exploit to their advantage.

Although it has been daylight for some time already, Pinchu makes no move to set off hunting. It is true that a fine, persistent rain is falling, the kind that sets in for the whole day and soaks you to the bone. The rhythm with which the rounds of manioc beer are succeeding one another shows no sign of slackening and Pinchu is drinking heavily, in shameless contravention of the abstinence that all hunters impose upon themselves before setting out for the forest. He has set his gourd of curare poison to warm by the fire and has taken from his quiver a dozen darts, which he is sharpening with the penknife that I have given him. Proceeding with the tranquil care of a man who is in no hurry, he then dips the darts into the curare – softened by the heat – coating the tips with a thin layer of the shiny black paste. He then sticks the darts into the loose earth surrounding the fire to allow them to dry.

The amorphous appearance of curare masks the fact that it is a living substance that feeds on the blood of animals. It must accordingly be treated with consideration if it is to fulfil its function. The strength of the curare can be gauged by its bitterness (*yapau*), tested by the sensation that it produces when rubbed lightly on one's tongue. It must be kept out of contact with animals that smell bad, so as not to make it sick, and one should sing *anent* to it if it is feeling weak. The bitterness of the curare does wear off – and with it the effectiveness of the poison – when it is accidentally combined with other savours of natural origin such as anything nauseous, *mejeaku*, or of cultural origin, such as anything salty, *yapaku*, sweet, *yumin*, or spicy, *tara*. The volatile essence of the hunting poison causes the Achuar men to take complex precautions when preparing and handling it. In the first place, they must be chaste, retaining their vital energy for its benefit; and they must not eat foods or spices characterized by a savour that is antithetical to it. The presumed touchiness of curare thus condemns hunters to a bland, tasteless diet, for only thus can they avoid affronting it with substances whose strong taste could weaken its power.

Having served me, Yatris places a few pieces of grilled manioc at Pinchu's feet and he accepts them without demur. She has clearly interpreted her husband's procrastination as signifying that he has given up his hunting plans for the day.

'Are you going to the forest today?'

'No! Can't you see that it's raining? Do you imagine that I am like Amasank, the mother of hunted animals, who lives out there in their midst? How could I find the animals when the noise of the rain prevents me from hearing what they are saying? Let us stay here and talk.'

A *kuntuknar* dream is a necessary condition for hunting, then, but not a sufficient one. It is certainly necessary, for no man would go hunting in the jungle unless either he or a spouse had during the night received a discreet omen presaging game, the interpretation of which, upon awakening, settles the pattern of the coming day. Hounds and other predatory animals would likewise be incapable of catching their prey had they not been forewarned by a dream, a product of the imagination that bends even the forest dwellers to its whims. This necessary precondition does not so much specify a result as render an action possible. The *kuntuknar* does not ensure automatic success, but is indispensable for success to be possible. To that extent, a hunting expedition begins long before the hunter plunges into the misty half-darkness of the undergrowth, for it is triggered by his meanderings through the labyrinth of sleep. However, one can, equally, decide not to heed the portents of one's dream if the circumstances are not favourable: a passing indisposition, previous engagements, pouring rain . . . So a hunt cannot be reduced to a preordained fulfilment of the omen that makes it possible. Like all the activities in which the Achuar engage, it requires complex knowledge and certain physical qualities abetted by magical means, quite apart from a measure of good luck for which all the above ingredients could never completely compensate.

Jorge Luis Borges used to lament the fact that the Spanish language makes no distinction between dream and sleep. For both, the word is *sueño*. As a meticulous chronicler of dream worlds, he was exasperated by such a confusion between the fantastical reality of dreams and the daily small death that those dreams enliven. But terminological imprecision does not necessarily mean that a particularly high value is set on that period of oblivion. The Achuar, who are equally guilty in this respect, on the contrary imply that sleep is nothing but a long dream (*kara* is the term indiscriminately used for both). As soon as waking consciousness is abolished, the soul leaves the inert body to wander in a parallel world and, upon waking, still retains vibrating echoes of it.

The extremely acute oneiric memory displayed by the Indians probably results to some extent from a broken sleep that is divided into a series of short snatches interrupted by a wailing child, a suspicious noise, the barking of a dog or an insistent sensation of discomfort when the dying fire no longer palliates the night chill. Upon surfacing from each of these little excursions of the soul, its dreams are briefly recalled, perhaps even communicated in a whisper within the closed bed, so the final morning awakening provides a rich collection of images to be interpreted. Their interpretation occupies the small hours just before dawn and is regarded as being of considerable importance since, to my companions, almost all dreams are taken to be omens of future happenings. The Jivaros' practice of subjecting the future to dream interpretations, which is common to many pre-modern civilizations, was noticed very early on. In the sixteenth century a conquistador was already remarking that their religion amounted to no more than 'the deceptions of dreams and a few birdsongs'. It must be said that the soldier's laconic words do contain a grain of truth, for this invisible world to which sleep provides access is a world where, with the constraints of space and time abolished, guardian spirits, the creatures of nature and figures of mythology can present themselves immanently to human beings.

Pinchu's temporary idleness and his communicative mood encourage me to enquire further into the twists and turns of oneiric omens. The interpretations of dreams that I have been collecting each morning indicate the existence of two other categories of dreams that are just as common as the *kuntuknar* and are known respectively as *karamprar* and *mesekramprar*.

'*Mesekramprar* is when we dream things that foretell misfortune, sickness perhaps, or death. War too, when our enemies come to kill us, or when we meet them unexpectedly on a path – that too we dream. Those whom we fight are like mad beasts; are they not perhaps killers like the jaguar or the anaconda? When I dream of the jaguar prowling around the house, growling *juum, juum, juum*, to kill our dogs, I know that those from downstream, in the same way, will surround us to shoot at us. And now I dream that the anaconda is coiling itself around me, to stifle me; perhaps I shall die, and for nothing. Is it not Pujupat who is going to kill me with his rifle, hiding at the water's edge? In the same way, white-lipped peccaries, before charging in a herd, go *taash, taash, taash*, clashing their tusks; and the old black male, the fiercest of all, which roars before attacking; that too I dream and it tells me of war. I shoot at the peccaries, but they are many, as are our enemies.'

'So *mesekramprar* is always to foretell war?'

'No! Listen to me carefully! I am strong, I am, and not afraid to die; just let those enemies come and see! I've killed plenty of them: do you imagine that I'm a woman, afraid of death? *Mesekramprar* is a bad omen [*pasun*], death through evil spells or diseases. We are sad because we think with compassion of our wives and our children when they suffer. What can we do against bad shamans? Your medicines and your injections, what good are they against *tsentsak* darts? Some dreams make us suffer because we are powerless before what they presage. I dream that my children are losing their hair and that their teeth are falling out and perhaps they will die; and it's the same when

I dream I am drinking a soup made of palm-tree grubs. When my father was killed, on the Kashpaentza, I dreamed just before that a human-headed Penelope-bird was flapping off heavily. For a long time I could hear its cry, *wiaa, wiaa, wiaa*. And when I was young, before I had married Santamik, I dreamed I was copulating with a very beautiful pale-skinned woman, who was hugging me with her thighs. After that dream I was bitten by a fer-de-lance snake during a tree-clearing operation and for a long time I was close to death, my leg full of worms. A shaman from the Bobonaza, it was, who cured me. That is the way it is, brother-in-law!'

A dream of bad augury seems to be a kind of inverted *kuntuknar*. It foretells death and calamities and expresses the wickedness of men through images borrowed from nature, whereas a hunting dream announces its catch of game through familiar images of human beings. And this transposition is reversible in the rare cases in which animals present themselves in the guise of aggressors, for the misfortune that they may provoke is always revealed by a dream that excludes them. Thus the snake-bite is suggested by the transparent analogy of coitus, or in a dream of an anodyne prick caused by the clumsy handling of a needle, hook or dart. Similarly, the unlikely attack of an anaconda is shown in a dream about being smothered by a mosquito net. Yet, by foretelling a natural danger from a dream about peculiarly human activities, the Achuar exegesis does re-establish an order of responsibilities. Jaguars, anacondas and venomous snakes are zealous helpers of shamans and the threat that they represent to the Indians is in the last analysis simply an expression of the more real peril of which they are the willing instruments. Dreams of ill omen proclaim that nature is less to be feared than the animosity of other human beings. In this oneiric theatre of misfortune, animals play only walk-on parts, serving as metaphors for human enemies who can be named; and when, as occasionally happens, the labour of interpretation reveals that they stand for anonymous dangers, it is still a daunting human figure that they symbolize: the shaman.

With the exception of violent death, all misfortunes are reputed to come from a shaman if their gravity, or simply their persistence, appears to rule out a more ordinary causality. Sickness, accidents, melancholy, bad luck and death are not flukes of destiny but manifestations of some malevolent plot that dreams can warn of without necessarily indicating their source. Shamans are thus implicitly designated by most dreams that foretell adversity, even when their interpretation goes no further than simply to reveal the hostility of animals well known to serve them. This automatic attribution of responsibility explains why some *mesekramprar* are simply descriptive metaphors of symptoms or states that everyone knows to be caused by shamans. Thus, the innocent palm grubs to which the Achuar are so partial are a monstrously magnified image of the maggots that thrive in carrion. The disintegration of the body that follows death is similarly expressed in visions of mutilation – teeth or hair falling out – or by the sleeper being lost in a fog so thick that he can no longer make out where his own body ends, so hopelessly has it become diluted in the uniformity that surrounds it.

Sometimes the correspondences are more rigorous. For example, a dreamer of countless asphyxiated fish carried downstream by the current after a fishing operation using poison betokens an epidemic. When Wajari produced this exegesis, a little while ago, I was very gratified. The poisoning of fish and epidemic diseases are analogous in a number of respects: they occur suddenly and the ravages that they cause amongst the fish or the people involved are spectacularly greater than with other, more usual causes of death. The fact is that the logical connection established by Wajari in his interpretation of a dream had already been suggested by Lévi-Strauss in his conclusion to a complex thesis advanced to resolve the problems posed by the analysis of a group of Amazonian myths about the origin of diseases and fish-poisonings. When made explicit in an Achuar prediction, the structural relationship detected through an analysis of mythical material foreign to the Jivaro culture acquired the unquestionable density of lived reality. I had therefore found myself in the situation, well known to physicists, in which an experimentalist 'discovers' the actual existence of a phenomenon already predicted in theory. Far from blunting the freshness of direct observation, a measure of scholarly erudition may eventually favour an ethnologist with one of those little demonstrations through reality that enliven fieldwork with the thrill of discovery.

'A true dream, *penke karamprar*, is a soul's visit to someone we know. We see those whom we know and we talk to them as I am talking to you now. In contrast, the people who appear to us in *kuntuknar* or in *mesekramprar* are unknown to us, their faces have no names. When my brother pays a visit far away, I think of him with affection, but I worry because I fear that he might be killed. He comes to visit me in a dream and I am happy, for then I know that he is well. When I awaken I am full of nostalgia, as the dream reminds me of his absence. Sometimes we dream of the dead, soon after their passing. The dead come to us to complain. They bewail their solitude and beg insistently for something to eat, as they are always hungry. Then we have to fill bowls with food and manioc beer and place them on their tombs, otherwise they will not leave us in peace. The dead are unhappy and they take it out on us.'

'Can the dead harm you?'

'Yes. They try to draw us to them. They want to make us the way they are. It is very dangerous to dream of the dead; it weakens us and we may die too. Later, when time has passed, they no longer have the power to harm us. Listen! I'll tell you. A long time ago, my brother Tseremp shot at an *iwianch japa* (a red brocket, similar to a little roe deer). Four times he shot and the deer kept on coming towards him. My brother was very young at the time and, out of bravado, he disregarded the injunction of the ancients. The rest of us never kill red deer, as the souls of the dead sometimes lodge in them. And how could we eat the dead? Furthermore, only clumsy people wound animals without finishing them off. Why cause suffering to creatures with a soul like our own? They go off to see their own shamans, to be cured, but they bear us a grudge and take care never to expose themselves again to us. That is how it is that hunters often return empty-handed.

'When he had used up all his supply of powder, my brother returned to the house of father-in-law Tsukanka, for he had just got married. All of them were then living far away from here, on the Chundaykiu. Tseremp took the dogs and finally forced the deer to take flight, and killed it. When he brought the beast home, it was noticed that the flesh did not cook. It was an *Iwianch*, the spirit of a dead person.

'That night Tsukanka was visited in a dream by a dead man called Tiriats. His head was all bloody and he complained bitterly about the aggression of which he had been victim. Tiriats had already been dead for a while. He used to live on the Ishpinkiu and Tsukanka used to know him, as they had once waged war together against those of the

114

opposite bank of the Pastaza. Tseremp, on the other hand, had never seen this Tiriats. The dead man told Tsukanka that he should teach his son-in-law better, and that it was not done to shoot at Iwianch deer in which the souls of the dead were embodied. Tsukanka, as you know, is a man who is prone to raise his voice. The next day he lectured Tseremp. He was furious and his reprimand lasted a long time. My brother was upset and he nearly abandoned his wife.'

'And the enemies that you have killed, do they too come to visit you in dreams?'

'Yes, and we fear them. When they are killed, their souls thirst for vengeance, they become *emesak*, "the harmful one". *Emesak* comes to torment the killer in his sleep and frightens him. He dreams of horrible things. Sometimes *emesak* takes the form of the dead man in order to threaten and terrify and sometimes *emesak* causes accidents. But gradually "the harmful one" grows weaker, then disappears from our dreams. What can become of him then? I don't know.'

Unlike *kuntuknar* and *mesekramprar* dream omens, which set up silent tableaux, a *karamprar* dream is a real dialogue of souls. The former two types of dream are interpretable on the basis of visual indices presented anonymously, whereas the immediate meaning of the third type is to be found in the verbal messages that are its *raison d'être*. With these dream conversations the first thing to do is identify the interlocutor; then, in his sleep, the dreamer can pursue an interchange that has been interrupted by his interlocutor's temporary or definitive absence. The dead themselves never pay visits to any but those whom they know: that is why Tiriats went to bother his former comrade-in-arms, not the young whippersnapper who attacked him in his animal shape. The oneiric incursions of the dead into the world of the living give rise to sadness, nostalgia and, above all, anxiety, and are regarded by the Achuar as a regrettable but necessary evil. This modest outlet for the dead in their unenviable condition is at least an assurance that they have truly crossed the frontiers of human existence, beyond which only distant echoes of their dissatisfaction are perceptible. The principle of *emesak* vengeance is itself to a large extent disarmed when confronted with the victorious killer who has provoked its apparition. The victim's ghost certainly assuages his vindictiveness by filling the murderer's nights with terrifying nightmares, but these very temporary inconveniences amount to very little compared with the glorious feat of arms of which they are the consequence.

It is thus up to the dead from time to time to end a separation that is no doubt more painful to them than to the living, who soon put the sorrows of death out of their minds. However, dream visits from the dead are not always a cause of anxiety or ill omen. Sometimes they provide a chance briefly to renew links between divergent destinies, yet without risking tribulations of the kind suffered by Orpheus. A little while ago Entza recounted a moving dream in which a still-born son of hers appeared to her as a loving little boy. Emerging from the edge of the garden in which she was working, he had rushed into her arms for an all-too-brief embrace. Periodically, such dreams recurred and each time the child's appearance was slightly different, as he reached a new stage in his growth, which death had not had the effect of interrupting. This harmless foetus, snatched from human social life as a result of his premature birth, continued to grow pointlessly, punctuating his progress with nostalgic reunions with the mother he never knew. For him, as for Entza, the dream was a last chance of impossible consolation.

As well as making it possible to speak with the wandering souls of both the living and the dead, *karamprar* dreams are a valued means of communication with various beings on the fringes of humanity: guardian spirits, representatives of animal species, personal genies, magical helpers, etc. These elusive entities are generally only perceptible in the singular state of clairvoyance produced by sleep or hallucinogenic drugs. Freed from the limitations of the physical senses, the soul is able to wander as it will and to pass to other planes of reality that are ordinarily inaccessible. That passage takes the form not so much of an ecstasy as of a refinement of lucidity, a sudden purging of the physical conditions of seeing and speaking. Dreaming fleetingly makes it possible to pass beyond the constraints of language. It creates a means to communicate with all those beings which are naturally bereft of the powers of linguistic expression; in dreams, at least, they can clothe their essence with an appearance that is accessible to human understanding. One example of such metamorphosis is provided by the *nantar*, those dangerously vampiric gardening charms, which sometimes appear in dreams in the form of young girls, to complain to their mistress of not being refreshed with enough rocou.

Dreams provide a practical demonstration of the arbitrariness of ontological frontiers: natural entities, which are receptive to the *anent* sung to them but incapable of replying to them in the language of men, choose dreams as their means of declaring that they are not dumb. Beneath the illusion of distinctions of form can be glimpsed a continuum in which beings are ordered according to, not so much the modalities of their existence, but rather their various ways of communicating. This effect of immanence is best expressed in human beings' relations with guardian spirits, since it is through dreams that human presentiments of their benevolent actions are repeatedly confirmed. Nunkui and Shakaim are probably the most regular of these nocturnal counsellors who dispense their advice to the Achuar. Their visits are expected, even hoped for: before undertaking an important or delicate task – clearing a swidden for a new garden in the case of a man, or sowing a difficult plant in that of a woman – spouses refrain from all sexual dealings, since carnal pleasures are reputed to deter dreams and thus prevent the spirits from delivering their advice. Gardening is an activity that is to some extent oneiric, just like hunting: both call for a preparatory and paradoxical sublimation shared by both sexes.

But if all dreams are auguries, they do not all prophesy in the same fashion. Some are a prerequisite to some future action with a positive outcome (*kuntuknar*); others presage unfortunate or confrontational events to come (*mesekramprar*). But what dreams of hunting and dreams of war do have in common is that their true meanings need to be worked out in an early-morning exercise of exegesis that reduces their imagistic content to a logical formula of symmetrical inversion: the attributes of natural beings can be translated into human ways of behaving, whilst cultural human activities provide a register for relations with animals. In these two kinds of dreams the interpretation is strictly metaphorical. On the other hand, a true dream, *karamprar*, is intelligible without such mediation since, in contrast to the two other kinds, its essential feature is that it is a meeting that involves a dialogue. Its message is thus directly revealed by someone who is known to the dreamer, although distant from him either spatially or in terms of the scale of beings. Here, the interpretation is not metaphorical but literal.

But in all cases, dreams seem to place constraints upon fate by introducing into daily life particular instances of determinism that could be called into question simply by the contrary evidence of reality. Like all magical techniques, oneiromancy must thus achieve at least a minimum of efficacy simply to ensure its perpetuation. The Achuar are aware of this risky element that makes their future actions depend upon the caprices of their oneiric memory. So it is that, through the work of interpretation, meticulously carried out each day upon emerging from the night, they bend the contents of their dreams to the needs of the moment. That is certainly true in the cases of *kuntuknar* and *mesekramprar* dreams, which are defined as such at the moment of exegesis on the basis of the extensive possibilities of inversion that they offer. These reservoirs of metaphors proffer oneiric images that can be manipulated according to basic rules of permutation that make it possible to ascribe to them a meaning that is of instant practical use. By rejecting the idea of a key to dreams in which each symbol noted would require a single, invariable translation, the Achuar have in effect engineered for themselves a wide field of manoeuvre. Each and every element in a dream becomes significant provided it can undergo a transformation provided for in the rules, such as an inversion between container and what is contained, a switch between the natural and the cultural codes, homologies of form or behaviour, etc.

The Achuar interpretation of dreams thus presents curious analogies with the method of structural analysis that Lévi-Strauss uses for myths. Lévi-Strauss brings to light the intellectual problems that a myth attempts to resolve by studying the relations between the latent properties of its characters, situations and narrative sequences; the Achuar, for their part, dissect the oneiric material in order to extract basic relations that are themselves homologically suggestive of other relations that could be realized by some desirable or dreaded happening. The anthropologist deconstructs the mythical data in order to discover within it the formula of relations between ideas; the Indians deconstruct nocturnal images, reducing them to minimal logical units in order to derive practical information from them. The paradoxical affinity of their respective methods suggests an affinity between their objects. The long-suspected connection between myths and dreams probably rests upon their similar ways of proceeding from the sensible domain to the intelligible, from the concrete to the abstract. The individual subconscious and the collective subconscious seem to be connected not so much by contiguity or derivation as by the use of identical methods of codifying the diversity of reality in terms of basic systems of relations.

But if Achuar oneiromancy presents features shared by the structural analysis of myths, it certainly differs from the psychoanalytical interpretation of dreams. The difference lies firstly in the fact that Freud – and, even more, Jung – never doubt the realistic concept of oneiric symbols. On the strength of the common basis of mythography and folklore, the founder of psychoanalysis believes it possible to establish a universal lexicon of the equivalences between, on the one hand, certain types of images and situations and, on the other, certain phenomena mostly of a sexual nature. Impulses that are everywhere identical are supposed to correspond, term for term, to a finite register of products of the imagination that are common to the whole of humanity – in short a register that constitutes a transcendental dictionary of symbols scientifically guaranteed by the psychoanalyst's couch. The Achuar have explored a different path. Far from attributing to the symbols that throng their dreams a meaning that is unchanging, they on the contrary seek to efface them behind the logical operations that they reveal. It is not the metaphorical quality of the objects dreamed about that takes on a divinatory power, but the metaphorical attributes of the relations between them. In valuing form above content and the properties of signs above their figurative message, my companions have turned their backs on an interpretation of symbols whose creation Freud, with a cast of mind typical of his age, preferred to attribute in its entirety to primitive peoples, rather than contemplate the possibility of its being of a relative nature.

CHAPTER 8

A Hunting Expedition

THE PATH SNAKES ALONG the crest of the cliff, separated from the void by a thin curtain of vegetation through which the pale light of dawn is filtering with difficulty. Once in a while a gap opened up by a landslide affords a glimpse of the valley below through which the Kapawi flows. Down there in the hollow bordered by the steep plateau edges, it is hard, amid the trails of mist, to make out the paler patches that are gardens and the odd palm-leaf roof from which a lazy coil of smoke rises. Far away upstream the regular sound of hacking rings out with surprising clarity. Ahead of me, Pinchu is moving with short, rapid steps through the twilight, his long blowpipe balanced on his shoulder and his quiver swinging on his back. Santamik follows me, armed with a small machete and grasping the leash of her pack of five dogs, which are snuffling at my heels. We left the house before daybreak to hunt for a herd of peccaries.

Pinchu awoke very early, telling me that he had had a *kuntuknar* dream that augured well for collared peccaries: during a drinking party, when the whole company was rather drunk on fermented manioc beer, a violent quarrel had broken out between Wajari and himself. The two brothers-in-law had threatened each other with their weapons, then exchanged a few blows. So improbable was it that he was much amused at the picture: quite apart from the fact that each brother-in-law usually appears well satisfied with the other, they would never settle a dispute with their bare hands. The Achuar despise their Quichua neighbours to the north, who dare not fire at their enemies but fight with their fists, shameless and without dignity, like children or scrapping dogs that have to be separated by the blows of a stick. Such violent familiarity is viewed with horror here, where even the most extreme hostility is always settled from a distance, with a rifle

120

shot. Dreams clearly provide a useful outlet for all the repressed aggression that the punctilious dignity of the Achuar prevents from bursting out. Presented undisguised in the innocence of dreams, the thousand and one baffled animosities of social life are converted into pretexts for hunting expeditions.

Although Pinchu expounded his interpretation of his *kuntuknar* quite openly, he did not actually say that he would be going hunting. The dream indicated an encounter with a herd of peccaries, but said nothing about the fate reserved for them. After hastily gulping down his manioc beer, as the night was drawing to an end the master of the house had simply stood up, exclaiming to nobody in particular, 'Let's take the dogs for a walk!' It was Santamik's turn to accompany him, since he had spent the night with her, and Yatris had been to the forest with him three days earlier. The Achuar take such care not to make their hunting plans known that the very word 'hunting' does not exist and is replaced by all kinds of circumlocutions from which any suggestion of death is systematically banished. Such semantic hypocrisy is considered a wise precaution: no point in risking annoying the spirits that watch over game. Automatically, out of habit, Pinchu has both expounded his divinatory dream and concealed his intentions but, in truth, today he could have dispensed with these propitiatory measures since his circumspection is fed by certainty: a herd of peccaries was definitely foraging for food yesterday not far from the Kusutka, on the edge of the little marsh where the swamp palms grow. As he was returning from gathering plants in the late afternoon, his wicker hod filled with sections of *machap* liana to make curare, Pinchu noticed that the earth had been churned up by rooting snouts and that there were crusts of mud, freshly scraped, at the foot of the trees. For a while he had followed the tracks, which left a clear trail leading up towards the Achuentza. It was a fine group of about twenty animals, including a number of young. Running out of time, he had hurried home, where he had made all his preparations for today. The first of these, at sunset, had been to play on his long flute an *anent* specially designed to summon a *kuntuknar*: an admirable precaution supposed to reduce risks doubly since, by ensuring the dream, he at the same time forearmed himself against the hazards of the hunt. An Achuar man acts in this way in order to assure himself of a favourable dream, the effect of which will be to justify the resolution to go hunting that he has already reached, either because the women are complaining of a lack of meat or because fresh animal tracks have recently been sighted. This technique of autosuggestion, adopted shortly before retiring to sleep, encourages the mental imagery and emotive predisposition most propitious for provoking the desired nocturnal visions. Dreams that tell of hunting – and equally those that presage fighting – are thus not totally spontaneous or fortuitous, but rather constitute predictable confirmations of pre-existing intentions. They have the quality of deliberate actions and this to some extent cancels the determinism that oneiromancy introduces into the conduct of the affairs of daily life.

Suddenly leaving the crest of the hill, the path veers off to the west and soon becomes an indistinct winding track, a mere scuffle through the dead leaves. The plateau is regularly cleft by steep dales containing pellucid rivulets with an almost bucolic crystalline babble. But the mounting heat and the sweat-flies clinging in bunches to one's skin soon banish any romantic illusions, the more so since the forest now seems as thorny as a bramble patch: on every side there are sharp points, spikes galore, twigs that whip at you, roots that trip, hostile ants and twisted lianas. These obstacles, more or less negotiable on flat terrain, become impassable on the steep sudden descents where a thin covering of fallen leaves treacherously masks toboggan runs of clay. On no account catch hold of anything to arrest your fall. The handy branch will pierce your hand with needles or disclose a colony of ants; the creeper that you seize as a last resort will buckle under your weight, precipitating a deluge of tiny stinging insects down your neck; the fine, smooth trunk that you grab as you pass will crumble at your touch, eaten away by decay. While I slide about in the slush, at each step lifting huge clods of clay sticking to the soles of my encrusted boots, Pinchu runs lightly ahead of me on the tips of his prehensile toes.

The chaotic landscape through which we are progressing with countless detours seems as familiar to my guide as that of an everyday walk. Just as a country man will regale you with anecdotes relating to a fountain, a calvary or a crossroads, Pinchu punctuates our journey with little stories of an amusing or tragic nature. Here is the ravine into which Tsukanka once fell during an ambush. Having by some miracle escaped the salvo of shots, he crawled away at full speed, bottom uppermost, leaving his *itip* impaled on thorns. There, at the foot of this bombax tree, Tayujin lay for several days awaiting *arutam* visions, drunk on green tobacco and stramonium. Just overlooking the Chirta, at its confluence with this little stream, Tarir hollowed out a fine, big canoe; he had to get lots of people to help him drag it on rollers to the Chirta.

Although it looks deserted, this territory is in fact crisscrossed with the memory of thousands of events which, even better than famous landmarks, furnish the anonymous forest with all the historical substance that those points of reference provide. It is true that, barely two hours' walk away from Pinchu's house, we are still more or less in his back yard. The Chirta, which we crossed a little way back, represents the frontier of the domesticated space in which the women and children lead their lives. Within that zone they collect wild honey, gather seasonal fruits and catch fish in the rivers, using poison to stun them. Beyond the frontier the real hunting country begins, the domain that is uninhabited. Travelling westwards, two days' march is needed to reach the nearest house, which belongs to Kawarunch, on the banks of the Pastaza. To the north, it takes three days to reach Yaur's house, where the Kupatenza debouches. To the south-east, it is even worse: the path that used to lead one in a week to Nayapi's place, at the confluence of the Kapawi and the Chundaykiu, has disappeared. In these immense fastnesses it is never by chance that you come across a human being.

Around mid-morning we cross the Kusutka and strike southwards, along a barely perceptible track. This is one of Pinchu's hunting trails, discreetly marked out from time to time by a broken branch whose leaves present a contrast with the surrounding foliage, a track without any apparent logic or destination. My mentor, who has for a while been treading extremely carefully, comes to a halt at the foot of a tree and sniffs at its bark.

'They have pissed here,' he whispers.

'Who? The peccaries?'

'No, no, the parrots.'

Motioning to me to follow him with care, Pinchu climbs a little hill, pausing at regular intervals to point out the remains of wild cocoa at the foot of certain trees.

'They've certainly had a feast, those parrots!' he chuckles quietly.

Santamik has remained at the bottom of the hill with her dogs. Once at the top, we notice random movements in the branches of a gigantic tree. Dozens of half-glimpsed reddish shapes are moving fearlessly about. Pinchu slots a dart into his blowpipe, slips two into his thick hair, to have them immediately to hand, and cautiously moves to the foot of the tree in which the woolly monkeys are perched. Calling them 'parrots' was a classic ruse to trick them for, it seems, their ears are well attuned to the sound of their own name. Throwing his head back and holding the heavy blowpipe completely vertical, Pinchu has now silently blown his first dart and immediately reloads. The projectile has caught in the throat of a large male who, taken by surprise, sharply pulls it out. It makes no difference, for the tip, coated with curare, has remained stuck in the wound. The extremity of the dart has been carefully notched by means of the piranha jaw that Pinchu always carries attached to his quiver.

Just as he is positioning himself to shoot at a second animal, the distant bark of a dog provokes a commotion among the band of monkeys. The larger animals fling themselves in every direction and the one selected by Pinchu moves out of reach. In an attempt to engage its curiosity and lure it closer, Pinchu quietly emits a guttural sound: '*Chaar, chaar, chaar,*' the rallying cry of this species of monkey. But a second dog's bark ruins the effect and the entire band suddenly scatters. Only the first victim remains, crammed into a fork in the boughs and convulsively clinging to a thick secondary branch, its tail desperately wound around another. Death is not long in coming but still does not resolve the hunter's problem. With staring eyes, the creature obstinately remains clinging to its perch, stiffened into *rigor mortis*. Above its tabular buttresses, the tree towers upwards with not a single handhold. Without an axe to cut some steps in it, it is clearly impossible to climb. Gazing at his unattainable prey, Pinchu murmurs a resigned *anent* between his teeth. However, the magic call produces no result. The woolly monkey is not going to fall.

'Tcha! I have wasted my breath for nothing! My little curare has sucked the monkey's blood for the benefit of the vultures. It's the vultures that will gorge themselves on all that good fat. But, after all, my *kuntuknar* was not about woolly monkeys . . . Well, that's that. Come along, brother-in-law! We must not linger here or the *amana* might see us.'

125

The *amana* of the woolly monkeys is, in a way, their protector: an ancient, hoary male, but of gigantic proportions, always crafty enough to elude the eyes of hunters. The *amana* is the ultimate incarnation of all the species' aptitudes and is their emblematic representative, rather in the manner of the essential forms of Platonic philosophy that exist for ever in the empyreum of ideas, like so many models for the elements of the world. The *amana* watches over his fellow-creatures with goodwill; thanks to his ability to be everywhere at once, he can listen to the boasts of bragging hunters and warn the other monkeys of whatever threatens them. It is not that he is against hunting, but he does require that it take place in accordance with the proper rules. To leave a monkey's corpse stuck up in a tree, for the vultures, is lacking in dignity and Pinchu's hasty departure seems an acknowledgement of his unease, an implicit recognition that he has failed to live up to the ethics of hunting.

The very existence of the *amana* to some extent rests upon this need to hold up a personal mirror to the hunter's regret. Although it is for their own pleasure as much as to provide a modicum of food for their families that my companions hunt on a daily basis, they are not insensitive to the fact that they are putting to death feathered or furry creatures to which they attribute truly human feelings. Now, an animal species is nothing but an abstract category; it allows the mind to subject minor differences in the appearances of particular individuals to the more essential generic differences that distinguish them collectively from other living kinds. By embodying this purely nominal category in a single being that can represent it as a whole, it is possible to give dynamic expression to the ambivalent feelings that the suppression of a life cannot fail to arouse. In the face of the manifest innocence of every slaughtered animal, the idea of all those victims within each species inevitably engenders the vindicating image of a judge.

Rejoining Santamik, we find her busy chastising one of her dogs with a cane, amid an uproar of whines and curses. Wampuash, still young and inexperienced, had not been able to resist yapping at a fieldmouse scampering away into the dead leaves, thereby causing the monkeys to flee in alarm. Despite his annoyance, Pinchu makes no comment, leaving his wife with full responsibility for controlling her pack.

On the banks of a marshy tributary of the Kusutka we see the first signs of the collared peccaries. After rolling in the blackish mud, the beasts have rubbed themselves hard against the palm trunks, releasing from their musk glands the acrid discharge that is so distinctive. It is not long since they were here: bubbles are still rising to the surface of the iridescent muddy puddles and a strong smell of pigs floats in the air, given off by the putrid mud. The trail is not easy to follow as the peccaries have made their way through the shallow swamp, no doubt huddled closely around the old boar leading the herd. In this greenish slime that swallows up every visible sign of whatever has passed through it, the dogs are now very useful for sniffing out the quarry. Tightly gripping her machete, her eyes glittering with excitement beneath the overhang of her fringe, Santamik is the very picture of a tropical Diana. She urges on her pack quietly but urgently with repeated exclamations of 'sik, sik!', the encouraging injunction that leads up to the final charge. From time to time she affectionately murmurs the name of the leader of the pack, a black bitch called Shuwinia.

Approaching an islet covered with tall bracken, Pinchu freezes our little band with a wide backward sweep of his arm and jerks his chin towards a long hump rising above the dark waters.

'Can't you hear them? They're going tush, tush, tush.'

Sure enough, we can clearly make out the sound of tusks clicking together. It resembles a muted background din of rattles. The animals must have discovered a windfall of fruits with hard rinds.

Pinchu gives his last instructions to Santamik before the final approach:

'You stay back here with the dogs. When you hear the beasts running, with juu, juu, juu noises, release Shuwinia first and then, a bit later, the others. They are not very brave; they mustn't get themselves gored.'

We cross this arm of the marsh in total silence, to the delight of the sandflies, clouds of which make the most of the chance to bombard us with impunity. The peccaries are widely scattered, as always when they stop to forage. At such a moment there is less danger of being charged by the whole herd.

The first pig that we encounter is alone in a little clearing, about thirty metres away. Its heavy head outlined by the greyish collar and its bristles stiff on its hackles, it is grunting softly as it burrows under the roots of a fallen tree-trunk. Hiding behind a tree, Pinchu takes careful aim and blows a dart into its flank, just at the shoulder joint, as close as possible to the heart so that the curare will act swiftly. The animal immediately takes to its heels with loud guttural grunts, provoking an indescribable commotion. Pinchu dashes after it into the undergrowth, yelling to the dogs to follow, while the other pigs flee blindly in all directions, panic-stricken by the frantically barking pack of dogs. Struggling in Pinchu's wake through the tangled undergrowth, I catch up with him a little further on, just at the moment when the peccary, paralysed by the poison, falls heavily forward, its hind legs shaking violently.

Meanwhile, the tumult has abated. All that can now be heard in the distance is the furious din of the dogs, clearly at a standstill before their quarry, which has gone to ground. Leaving the creature to its last death-throes, we return to the pack. With stiff hackles and snarling teeth, the dogs are standing in a menacing semi-circle around the entrance to a barely visible cavity between the roots of an enormous tree, from which a clacking of mandibles can be heard. Each time Shuwinia tries to approach a head lunges out of the burrow, slashing at the air with its sharp tusks, then hastily withdraws. The young Wampuash, the dog guilty of frightening the monkeys away, is whimpering on his own, his shoulder already torn by a deep gash that he is cleaning with painful little licks. Making the most of a lunge from the peccary, nimbly dodged by Shuwinia, Pinchu lodges a dart in its neck. This is the *coup de grâce* that brings the hunt to an end, as the rest of the herd is by now too far away for us to catch up before nightfall.

After all this hue and cry, cutting up the game seems quite a prosaic anticlimax. The two peccaries are disembowelled on the spot by Santamik, who plunges her hands into the steaming cavity and pulls out lengths of bluish entrails. Normally, the intestines are not considered food to be sniffed at, but each of these animals weighs over thirty kilos and the load has to be lightened for the long trek home. The liver is carefully preserved, however: grilled on spits, it makes a welcome reward for a hunter's efforts.

Pinchu extracts the musk gland situated at the base of the tail and energetically rubs the dogs' muzzles with it so as to impregnate them thoroughly with the powerful odour that is, as it were, the hallmark of the peccary. He then throws them these smelly, kidney-shaped organs, not in order to train them to scent the wild boar, but so that, by eating the organ that produces the creature's distinctive smell, they will acquire some of its ferocity. Ever since at least the time of Gaston Phoebus, who mentions the practice in an ancient hunting treatise, hunters in the Pays d'Oc have faithfully been following this same custom when out hunting wild boar. In Jivaro country, as in the Comminges or the Pays de Foix, the occasional incorporation of the humours of wild animals helps to impart extra savagery to dogs that have become over-domesticated; their reacquired bestiality thereby becomes a more deadly weapon and, distanced from mankind, they become better servants of the masters to whom they had grown too close.

One of the peccaries is cut into pieces without more ado: the head, loins, breast and haunches are wrapped, all bloody, in large leaves and packed into Santamik's wicker hod. Using a liana, Pinchu binds together the four legs of the other animal and fixes the whole burden on to his back with the aid of a band of bark secured around his chest. Thus laden, my hosts set off rapidly for home, no doubt thinking wistfully of the joys of love that are denied them by my inquisitive presence. Such information as I have gleaned from the younger men all tallies on this point. A hunting expedition provides an opportunity for spouses to indulge in the pleasures of the flesh with a freedom that they have to repress in their embarrassingly over-populated house. When a man invites one of his wives to accompany him to the forest (always taking care to respect the rota, so as not to attract the anger of them all), it is partly in order to fulfil his conjugal obligations. This woodland sexuality is no doubt not purely a matter of convenience: as they lie there in each other's arms in that immense solitude but with the eye of nature upon them and possibly right alongside their kill, they may well be seeking to recapture in their pleasure the excitement of the chase and the paroxysm of death in which it climaxed.

With legs aching after our ten-hour march, we finally reach home. Refreshed by a bathe and cheered by the sight of the peccaries piled up on a smoking rack, Pinchu is in the mood for a chat.

'Tell me about the *amana* of the collared peccaries, brother-in-law; what is he like?'

'Their real *amana* is Jurijri, the mother of peccaries. You know, Jurijri is as pale as you are. He has a beard and long hair; and also, he speaks every language, ours, Quichua, Spanish and yours too, the one that you speak with Anchumir. Jurijri wears boots and a metal helmet and he carries a sword. At the nape of his neck he has a mouth with big teeth. And with that mouth he eats people, the ones who mock the animals and kill them for no reason, just for pleasure. He lives underground, Jurijri does. There are many of them there and they come out through burrows and hollow trees. The collared peccaries live with them, like dogs; there are lots of them around their houses.'

Now it is easier for me to understand the furtive insistence with which, in the early days, the adolescents would examine the back of my head. They were looking for sharp teeth! There was I, bent on placating these head-hunters and they, meantime, took me for a cannibalistic swineherd who lived in the bowels of the earth, a sinister metaphor for the white man, clad in the tawdry finery of a conquistador! Throughout most of Amazonia, the Indians regard the peccaries as domesticated pigs controlled by fierce, supernatural masters who tend to keep them shut up in vast enclosures from which they are from time to time released to confront the projectiles of hunters. So they never kill an animal purely for the sake of doing so. It is important to have the consent of its invisible guardian, for he will not hesitate to hold his beasts back if he suspects that respect has not been shown them.

Strangely enough, the example set by the spirit protectors of wild animals has not been imitated by the Indians, who have never made any serious attempts to domesticate any of the wild species that might have proved suitable. To be sure, they take in the young of animals that they have hunted and they usually treat them with the rather rough kindness reserved for orphans of any kind. But only the young of their victims are adopted in this way, possibly to compensate for the fate that the hunters have meted out to their parents – as if to get rid of a feeling of guilt that they dare not express. What is more, the Amerindians seldom eat these tamed companions, not even if they die naturally. There are not many species that obdurately resist such a life in the midst of human beings and some Capahuari houses resemble positive Noah's Arks, in which many species of Amazonian fauna have resigned themselves to living together: macaws, marmosets, toucans, sapajou monkeys, parrots, pacas, trumpet-birds, woolly monkeys, etc. Pinchu himself dotes on a very young peccary which, to the great disgust of the dogs, frolics around the house as freely as the companion of Saint Anthony.

However, their random contact with tamed animals has not led the Indians of the forest to undertake any true domestication, that is to say any attempt to impose human control over the reproduction of certain species. Apart from those introduced by the conquistadors, Amazonia has no domesticated animals. The reasons for this are probably cultural more than technical. Certain autochthonous species that are occasionally tamed, such as the peccary, the tapir and the agouti, would no doubt eventually have proved possible to raise in semi-captivity, thereby providing the tropical equivalent of pigs, cows and rabbits. But the idea of any such enterprise à la Robinson Crusoe would be unrealistic for, while taming may seem a natural correlative of hunting, domestication would represent its very negation. Herd-raising implies a relationship of reciprocal subjection for both man and the animals concerned, for each sees in the other an obvious source of food and well-being. This mutual dependence, founded in part upon recognition of the stomach's demands, presents itself as a mask of conviviality that holds no surprises: the very opposite of the sportsman's fervour that inspires the Indian hunter as he pursues his daily pleasure – hunting.

The absence of domesticated animals in this part of the world does not seem attributable to any lack of skill on the part of the Amerindians, for they are great experimenters where anything to do with living matter is concerned, well aware of all its properties and past masters in the techniques of plant propagation. More than 5000 years have passed since manioc began to be cultivated in Amazonia, and this was followed by the cultivation of hundreds of species of plants with countless different varieties, each adapted to the tiniest variations of soil and climate. Yet, in contrast to what happened in the Middle East, this extremely ancient domestication of a large range of plants was never accompanied by the domestication of animals. It is true that this would have been more or less redundant anyway since, along with the Achuar, many Amazonian tribes regard the beasts of the forest as subject to the spirits that protect them; accordingly they are already as domesticated as they possibly can be. The idea of raising them in herds must have seemed pointless, or even perilous, on account of the conflicts over ownership and prior rights that would inevitably have arisen with the animals' supernatural masters, who would have jealously guarded their prerogatives. Domesticated animals could clearly not have belonged simultaneously to more than one master. And although the spirits allow men, on certain conditions, to draw upon their woodland herds in order to feed themselves, they surely would not tolerate being totally dispossessed. Hunting thus proceeds as a right to temporary benefits which the animals' keepers like to see constantly renegotiated. It presupposes a contractual ethic and a philosophy of exchange that have nothing in common with the undemanding morality of the stable and the chicken-run.

'What was the *anent* that you were singing, brother-in-law, when we were going to shoot at the woolly monkeys?'

'Listen, it goes like this:

'Little *amana*, little *amana*, if we are both *amana*, what are we to do?
I efface myself, like the Shaam, like the Shaam
Little *amana*, little *amana*, send me your children!
On this very mound, let them cry *churururui, churururui, churururui*
Let them go *waanta, waanta, waanta*, as they shake the branches.'

A clever supplication, if ever there was one, playing throughout on the equivocacy of identifications! First there is the identification with the *amana* of the woolly monkeys, the exemplary animal that represents the interests of that species and whose connivance the hunter requires, as is expected among people of quality. Then, also, an identification with the Shaam, one of the spirits that watches carefully over the fates of wild animals. This invisible inhabitant of the marshes and dark undergrowth is reputed to carry its heart slung on its chest like some palpitating jellyfish, but nothing is really known of it except the plaintive moans that it emits at dusk.

'And when the woolly monkey stayed up there, caught in the branches, what *anent* did you sing then?'

'Little brother-in-law, little brother-in-law, little brother-in-law, bend the branch down to me!
My little hook, my little dart, how, how can it not have pierced you?
My own brother-in-law, I have killed you in distant lands.'

132

The woolly monkey, like the toucan, is an emblematic representative of wild, hunted animals and it is regarded by the hunter as a brother-in-law, that is to say as a taker or giver of wives. This alliance through marriage that binds the two partners in a mutually inextinguishable debt is not without problems for the Achuar. The behaviour of brothers-in-law, based on mutual dependence and indispensable amenities, thus constitutes a model of ambiguous camaraderie that is an appropriate metaphor for the equivocal relationship that binds the hunter to his prey. This contorted affinity stands in contrast to the open spirit of the egalitarian appeal to the *amana*, for it is as a peer that the *amana* is asked to deliver up his dependants.

'But the woolly monkey was dead. How could he hear your *anent*?'

'He was dead; you're right. But his *wakan* was still close to him. Those to whom we sing our *anent*, they do not hear them as you hear me at the moment; they do not hear the words that we speak. But the thoughts that we put into our *anent*, they enter the *wakan* of those whom we invoke and there they establish themselves, as in a house. Then, without fully realizing it, those for whom we sing desire what we desire. They bend themselves to our thoughts because it is our desires that fill them.'

While we were chatting, the pet peccary had trotted up and had settled at my feet in a hollow of the beaten earth floor into which it fitted snugly. Sprawling in its sandy bed, the animal was nudging my ankles with its snout. As usual, it wanted me to scratch it. While talking, I have been running the toe of my boot over its hairy head. Whenever I pause in this stroking, the creature half-rises and fixes me with an indignant stare, its grunts of pleasure giving way to discontented grumbles. Tiring of this, eventually I desist altogether. Now the peccary gets up and comes to rub itself hard against my legs, its little button-eyes fixed on me, intent upon exerting the tyranny of a favoured pet. Just behind us a large wooden frame is propped against the posts that support the roof's overhang, exposing to the evening sun the skin of the animal carried home by Pinchu. It is grotesquely stretched by the lianas by which it is attached and is still spotted here and there with blood-stains over which green flies are swarming, but my tormentor remains totally oblivious to the remains of its dead fellow.

CHAPTER 9

Reflections in the Water

WAJARI AND MUKUIMP are working on the overspill-shoot of the little dam, raising their voices to make themselves heard above the constant splash of falling water.

'In my basket-trap I may catch a beautiful, white-skinned Tsunki with a magnificent bosom and long, black hair,' Mukuimp exclaims happily.

'Yes, but Tsunki women can only live in the rivers. You will have to follow her to her father, to the great house with banging doors under the water; and I don't want that, as you are my son-in-law and must stay with my daughter, close to me.'

'Who knows? The Tsunki father-in-law may have several daughters to give me! From what one hears, he's not niggardly.'

'And what will you do with these river wives when you have to live in the water and the piranhas have crunched up your rod?'

It is not long after sunrise and the slanting rays are piercing the foliage bordering the Kusutka, here and there leaving wide sweeps of light upon the green pool upstream that lies, flat and secret, beneath the vault of trees, like some romantic spring. The river-bed, normally narrow, is here pinched even more, so that only some five metres separate the two steep banks which rise almost to the height of a man. It is a well-chosen spot for the temporary dam that Wajari and Mukuimp have constructed with a view to some poison fishing. Four trestles set upright in the middle of the Kusutka support a thick, horizontal cross-bar, secured at each end to trees on either bank. Along this cross-bar is fixed a row of posts, set solidly in the river-bed, forming an oblique wall that slants upstream, rather like a huge comb. The lower part of this palisade remains watertight thanks to layer upon layer of leaves kept in place by the pressure of the current.

134

Between the central trestles, a large platform serving as an overspill-shoot rests on a flat framework. Standing about a metre above the tail-bay, it channels the overspill of water, which cascades down. It is a construction at once elegant and ingenious; it merges with the forest background, appearing to be a natural extension of it, not so much an obstacle to the lazy, even flow of water as a means to enhance it with a silvery splashing sound.

By the time we reached the Kusutka yesterday morning the dam had already been erected. Wajari and Mukuimp had been working on it the whole of the preceding day and all that remained to be done was to seal the base of the palisade with large canna leaves. We had set off at dawn from Wajari's house, where we have once again taken up residence, and it took only three hours of easy walking to reach here. On the way the dogs killed a sapajou monkey that was probably too sick or too old to get away, and we ate it, sitting at the water's edge. In the afternoon Mukuimp wove a big basket out of thin *kaapi* lianas, while Mirunik and Senur went off to gather fruits from the *kunkuk* palms that have just come into season. Until dusk began to fall, we chatted, sucking at the oily flesh that forms a thin, sweetish envelope around the huge stone. To amuse his little sister, Paantam had some-how stuck a big green buzzing fly on to the tip of a little stick that he waggled in front of the delighted baby. As soon as night fell we stretched out on the ground on a mat of palm leaves, squeezed together like a string of onions in the little lean-to shelter next to the river.

The rudimentary hut in which we slept is a kind of hunting lodge, which Wajari repairs or rebuilds each time he comes to spend some time on the banks of the Kusutka. It is surrounded by a tiny garden planted with manioc, banana trees and clumps of sweet potatoes smothered by weeds. Lonchocarpus bushes surround these sickly vegetables, no doubt serving to protect them from being totally annihilated by chomping agoutis, pacas or peccaries. The loncho-carpus root contains a toxic juice that the Achuar use to asphyxiate fish, and it is for this purpose that they cultivate it in all their gardens. Yesterday we dug up vast quantities of it, ready for today's fishing, carefully replanting part of each root.

Most of the Capahuari men own a hunting lodge like this, situated a few hours' march away from their main residence. These shelters, miniature versions of a normal house or simply temporary huts, are designed for short stays and play a similar role to the dove-shooting lodges of southern France, providing a chance to interrupt the routine of rural life with an amusing interlude for which some countryside task provides a pretext. But these Jivaro hunting lodges definitely have a practical function too, for they extend the range of the hunters' field of action, affording them immediate access to areas better stocked with game than the overused neighbourhood of their main residences. And as now, they also afford an opportunity to mount an operation of fishing with poison in faraway rivers without having to carry the necessary loads of lonchocarpus roots over long distances. These tucked-away retreats also serve as temporary refuges in times of war, for in most cases there is no discernible path leading to them. However, the Achuar regard their hunting lodges principally as places of recreation, as the holiday atmosphere that has reigned here since yesterday testifies. They all go about their tasks here with a marked nonchalance, amid bursts of laughter and good-natured jokes that contrast sharply with the at times quite stiff formality of the usual domestic etiquette.

Yesterday afternoon Wajari and Mukuimp made their harpoons, spending less than an hour on the job. Using a well-honed machete, which they whetted on a stone, they notched two heavy nails that Wajari had brought back from a trip to Montalvo, separating out a thin splinter on each side to form little hooks. The hafts were made in a trice from good straight *taun* stems hollowed out at one end to hold the mobile tip, as was the cord of plaited chambira palm fibre used to secure the latter to the haft. My companions' skill at instant improvisation for many of the things they need never fails to amaze me: a harpoon for fishing, a balsa raft to cross a wide river, a rope to moor a canoe, a long pole to punt it along, a basket to carry an unforeseen load, a loom for weaving or a bedstead for visitors – all these things are produced on the spot when the circumstances demand it, often to be abandoned once the need for them has passed. Admittedly, the equipment of the Indians may seem rudimentary to an unaccustomed eye, but the fact is that the Achuar scorn to encumber themselves with utensils that, with ingenuity and a few moments of easy work, can be recreated whenever necessary. This wise way of going about things has been wrongly interpreted by our own technical civilization. Ever since early colonial times it has fuelled the accusa-

136

tions of improvidence that we never fail to level at peoples who have rejected the accumulation of objects so as not to hamper their freedom of movement.

Wajari and Mukuimp complete the sealing of the overspill-shoot with a flexible wattle that prevents the fish from passing yet allows the running water to filter through. Then the two of them move upstream, where they immerse some of the fishing poison while I, along with the women, station myself at an intermediary post, about 300 metres above the dam. Here, lonchocarpus roots are piled up on a platform made of tree-trunk sections at the river's edge, and my task – for this is an operation that can only be carried out by a man – is to hammer them with a small log in order to express the whitish juice. The women have meantime felled two adjacent palm stems with their axes. Once my task is completed, we install ourselves comfortably on the bank to nibble at their hearts as we await the arrival of the film of poison. Right opposite us, a large hoazin perched above the river berates us in its croaking voice, shaking its shabby crest. Its stinking flesh saves it from the cooking pot, but not from the insulting mimicry that the women hurl at it in response. Attracted, no doubt, by the tumult, a featherless baby bird emerges from the platform-like nest, looking quite obscene in its clumsy, pinkish nudity. A pebble tossed at it by Mirunik makes it lose its balance and it plummets like a stone into the river, where it immediately swims under water with consummate ease before landing amongst the arum lilies on the bank, helping itself along with the little claws positioned on its wings, rather like those of a bat. The playful animosity born of idleness that the women display towards the little hoazin is not so much cruel as experimental. The Achuar never tire of getting nature to confirm its peculiarities.

It is not long before Wajari and Mukuimp join us in great excitement. The poison that they have put in the water upstream will soon be reaching us. A milky film is indeed just rounding the last curve, clouding the hitherto pellucid water. Now the men stuff the roots that I have crushed into baskets, then dip these into the Kusutka, shaking them in every direction so as to spread the juice everywhere. Once this is done, we all jump into the shallow water, the men and adolescent boys armed with harpoons or machetes, the women with baskets, and slowly we make our way towards the barrage.

Lonchocarpus, known as *barbasco* in the Spanish spoken in the Andean foothills, and its cousin clibadium both have the effect of asphyxiating the fish in waters that they have contaminated but produce no durable effects upon those that manage to get away. Hence the need for a barrage and also to catch the prey quickly, before they recover. Soon, as expected, the river begins to churn with quivering flashes of silver, dozens of fish leaping in every direction, desperately straining to escape being suffocated. Many land up in the bushy vegetation along the river banks, where the women and children can simply scoop them up. Beneath the barrage, a huge catfish is twisting about, flapping its tail right alongside Mukuimp, who is triumphantly brandishing a sting-ray at the end of his harpoon, no doubt relieved at having avoided its redoubtable hooked dart. Carrying over his shoulder a dozen small fish threaded through their gills on a liana, Chiwian is trying to club a piranha that is refusing to die. He must take care as he seizes it: even in the throes of death, it could sever his thumb! Everyone is wildly exuberant, laughing, shouting and joking. Only little Nawir is weeping bitterly. She upset her basket of fish into the river as she tripped over a large submerged bough and all her booty is being swept away for the benefit of her brothers and sisters stationed further downstream. Whether fishing with poison is conducted as a communal operation involving several households or, as on this occasion, takes the form of a family affair, the custom is for each individual to catch as many fish as possible. Disparities between the catches are not evened out by any subsequent redistribution. The collective nature of the enterprise does nothing to diminish the punctilious individualism that governs all the actions of our hosts.

Standing on the overspill platform, ankle deep in a wriggling magma of fish, Wajari is methodically collecting those trapped by the barrage: mostly hatchet-fish, *titim*, a few *pushin*, similar in appearance and taste to red mullet, and the kind of perch that the Achuar call *yutui*. The miraculous catch is over: in a few hours of carefree splashing about, it has procured us over 200 fish.

This is mid-January; in other words – according to the Achuar – these are the last few days of low water levels, before the start of the heavy rains that will continue until August, making fishing expeditions of this kind impossible in the swollen rivers. The period now coming to an end is called 'the time of low waters' or 'the time of the fish';

this dry season – from which, however, the rain is never truly absent – is thus placed under the sign of the river. The peaceful currents of this season make it possible to undertake long canoe trips that become extremely difficult in the time of floods, in particular when one has to struggle back upstream for days, pushing on long punting poles. In the period of low water the fish are easy to catch everywhere: in the dead arms of the rivers and the branch channels where they become trapped when the floods recede, in the little plateau rivers such as the Kusutka, where the transparent flow becomes easy to dam, and in the deepest meanders and *pongos* where the whirlpools become less danger-ous. Between August and October big water turtles are also easier to catch, as they come to lay their tasty eggs in the sandbanks exposed by the receding waters. Furthermore the caymans, attracted by this deli-cacy, to which they are as partial as the Indians, flock in large numbers to these beaches, where hunting them likewise is no problem.

Aquatic provender disappears or dwindles with the arrival of the season of heavy rains which, however, brings along its own sequence of resources. First comes 'the time of wild fruits', the benefits of which we are already enjoying, as it begins in mid November and lasts until the end of April. Dozens of species produce their fruits simultaneously and in the case of some – such as the sapote, the wild mango and cocoa trees, the granadilla, the bread-fruit tree and the inga, and the swamp, ivory and chambira palms – it seems a shame that the Achuar have not applied their zeal for domestication to them. Meanwhile, in accordance with the logic of generalized predation that links jungle dwellers in a great food chain of dependence, the animals, now better nourished, become more desirable prey for the hunters. After a period of relative deprivation, the game needs three or four months to fill out again, so not until March is it the start of the season that the Achuar, with anatomical accuracy, call 'the time of the fat of the woolly monkey' – a reference to the fine layer of fat that this creature's body has by then accumulated.

Here, as in much of the Amerindian world, fat is a rarity, given the absence of domesticated animals, and is fancied all the more because opportunities for eating it are few and far between. This taste for fat goes far beyond the simple needs of metabolism. It reflects the high value that these societies set on stoutness and dimpled flesh, which are considered signs of health and beauty. The Indians believe that the attraction of fatness must be universal. An old Andean belief shared by many tribes in the foothills attributes to some perverted Whites an insatiable appetite for the fat of natives, which they are believed to satisfy by boiling the unfortunate ones that they catch in huge cooking pots or by scraping them as empty as water-skins. Some claim that these macabre practices in truth serve to lubricate and fuel the gigantic machines thanks to which the Whites have imposed their dominion over the world, monstrous steel molochs that must be fed by constant sacrifices. These demons so avid for fat, who are called *pishtaco*, are feared and hated all the more because there is nothing to distinguish them from other Whites. It is consequently extremely dangerous for pale-skinned men to venture into certain regions, where their supposed cannibalism might bring them to a very sticky end, as some naive explorers have recently discovered to their sad cost. Unprepared to accept the notion of such collective responsibility, they were no doubt unaware that all Whites are considered potentially *pishtaco*: the merciless exploitation to which the Andean Indians have for centuries been subjected by their colonizers has found its most accurate expression in this metaphor of rapacity that has become progressively more literal over the years.

The women have constructed smoking shelves, large trays of green wood mounted on posts, where they are now piling up the fish, after gutting them. Suddenly Senur interrupts her task to peer at a small coloured concretion which she has picked out of the entrails of a large cat-fish. Wajari, called in for consultation, bends briefly over the find and, approvingly and with satisfaction, exclaims, *'Pai! pai! namurkaiti!'* Sure enough, it is a *namur*, a hunting charm. Through one of those systematic reversals favoured by Achuar thinking, the stones discovered inside fish serve as magic aids for attracting game, while those from birds and mammals are used for fishing. With a peremptory and, it must be said, quite convincing air, Wajari adds, for my benefit, that Amasank, one of the spirits known as the 'mothers of game', recently foretold this discovery to him in a dream, even specifying that this particular charm was to be used for hunting toucans. Each of the *namur* is supposed to possess a power of attraction for one particular species of game, determined either by its shape and colour or by the animal in which it is discovered; and it is pointless to try to extend its use or to substitute another.

The inversion between the origin of the magic charm and the use for which it is destined determines the efficacy of these *namur* according to a mental procedure reminiscent of the interpretation of the omens of *kuntuknar* dreams. As in certain dreams, the connection established between bird and fish is based upon a term-for-term table of contraries: the airborne and the aquatic, the visible and the invisible, the upper and the lower, the static and the mobile, the noisy and the dumb. The apparently arbitrary spontaneity of the magic thought at work in these associations is in reality dictated by a strict determinism, for the causal relation that it establishes between specific objects or phenomena is entirely based upon the characteristics peculiar to them; it cannot be extended to cover other domains in which the terms present might display properties of a different nature. Far from reflecting a vague participative philosophy that indiscriminately connects every level of the cosmos in one great indistinct original mass, magic objects and divinatory practices testify to the minute attention that the Indians pay to a classification of phenomena in which each effect requires its own particular cause. In common with the positivism that triumphed in the last century, and in contrast to modern science, this physics of particularity rejects the notion of chance.

Making the most of the last rays of sunshine, the men go off to bathe together slightly downstream from the now dismantled barrage. Mukuimp is in a smutty mood this evening, pretending to copulate with the water, puffing noisily the while, to the delight of his young brothers-in-law.

'Well, father-in-law,' he says to me with an ironic smile, 'did you see, this morning? I made love with the river. It became white with my sperm; and it was the Tsunki woman who rubbed my tail with *piripiri* herbs; she made me a huge rod to fuck her with because, you know, she has a vulva that could swallow up your head.'

'And who is this Tsunki woman you keep talking about? Is Suwitiar not enough for you, so that you want another wife?'

'I have never seen a Tsunki woman myself, but Nayapi, who lives at the mouth of the Chundaykiu, in the lowlands, he told me about her. One night, in a dream, he saw a kindly old man with very long hair, who said to him: "Give me your daughter, and I will give you mine in exchange, to marry." The old man returned in dreams several times, with the same request. It was Tsunki. One morning, after one of these dreams, Nayapi went off to hunt upstream along the Chundaykiu. There he saw an extraordinarily beautiful woman bathing in a waterfall. Her skin was very white and her long hair was jet-black. She offered herself to him, saying that she would be his in exchange for his daughter. She was quite shameless, parting her legs to show her sweet potato and flicking her tongue as women do when they want your rod, but as she was a Tsunki, a water creature, Nayapi was afraid and went away. He has seen her again several times, in dreams, and she continues to pursue him eagerly. Once, she appeared to him on a beach of the lower Kapawi, not far from where Taish lives. She was just emerging from a bathe and was playing with a litter of pretty black puppies. She went up close to him, and they rubbed noses; and then Nayapi made love with her. Ever since, she has been following him everywhere. She tells him in dreams to come to her more often, as she is missing him. She has a son by Nayapi and by now the puppies have grown up. Now they are huge black jaguars. She lives in the Chundaykiu at the foot of the hill, just below the house. When one of Nayapi's wives is unwilling to go hunting with him, he says, "Never mind, I have a Tsunki wife, who accompanies me with her dogs."'

Night has almost fallen by the time we return to dry ourselves by the fire for the smoking shelves. A delicious smell of smoked fish wafts from our camp. The dogs are whining miserably at the prospect of this feast to which they will not be invited, whilst the children, in contrast, plunged in ecstatic silence, are watching the grease drip slowly into the crackling flames.

'Tell me, brother, are there Tsunki here too, or at Capahuari?'

'Very few,' Wajari replies, 'as the rivers are swift and not very deep. Once I lived much further downstream, in the lowlands, close to Nayapi's present home. When I went to bathe before dawn I could hear people talking under the water, just as we do at *wayus* time. I could also hear the beat of a *tuntui* drum. When I built my house there, a huge anaconda lived in a little lake just below. It was very fierce and spent the time making the earth shake. One night, a huge otter appeared to me in a dream, then it turned into a man with very long hair that fell to his waist. The otter asked to become my *amik*, my ceremonial friend, and promised to help me to fight the anaconda. "If you won't become my *amik*," it said, "the anaconda will eat your wives and children." So I agreed. How could I have put all my family in danger? Tsunki kept his word and the anaconda was never seen again. Tsunki often came to visit me in dreams and I swore I would never again hunt otters, for fear of killing my *amik*. He told me, "If I die, you will soon die too." Then Tii paid me a visit and told me that he had killed two giant otters just before he reached my house, but he had not been able to catch hold of them as they were swept away downstream. Since then my otter friend has never come back to see me. I suppose Tii killed it.'

'So Tsunki can also turn himself into an anaconda?'

'No, I don't think so. Anaconda is one of Tsunki's domesticated animals and obeys him in everything, just like a dog. A few years ago, Yuu – you don't know him, he lives on the Kunampentza – visited Tsunki in his house, and there were lots of anacondas there; he was very scared. This Yuu met Tsunki because he is a powerful shaman, an *uwishin*: he sees things that we cannot. He had built himself a little "dreaming hut" on the river bank and withdrew there regularly to have his visions. He would get drunk on tobacco juice and also *natem*. One night, he told me, a young Tsunki woman sought him out in his visions, but she was not a "haunter" like Nayapi's woman. She told him that her father wished to get to know him, to converse with him, and she took him down to the depths of the river, at the spot where there is a big whirlpool, enveloping him in her long hair. Yuu says that, in the water, the Tsunki have houses just like ours and that they are just like human beings in every way. The old Tsunki man was seated on a coiled anaconda and he had Yuu sit on a big tortoise that poked out its head to take a look at him with its round eyes. Other Tsunki were seated on a cayman lying alongside the wall and enormous jaguars prowled round him, barking like dogs. Yuu saw all these things.'

Eureka! The riddle of the cayman head carved on Wajari's *chimpui* is now partly resolved, the riddle that a few months ago made me realize the full frustrating measure of the ignorance that prevented me from understanding the meaning even of a detail as trivial as the shape of a knob. But it is only partly resolved, for while it is now clear that the stools and benches used by my companions are symbolic representations of the animals used as seats by the Tsunki in their homes beneath the water, the reason for this parallelism between the two worlds is still not immediately apparent. The fact is that we may here have reached the limits of what a willing informant is capable of presenting in a synthetic and explicit fashion, on the basis of the norms of coherence ordinarily used in his culture to give meaning to various ways of behaving.

What ethnologists call a system of representation is generally systematic only in the eyes of the observer who reconstructs it and can understand how it is structured. The underlying logic detected by scholarly analysis seldom rises into the conscious minds of the members of the culture that he is studying. They are no more capable of formulating it than a young child is capable of setting out the grammatical rules of a language that he has, notwithstanding, mastered. The exercise of formalization that I have undertaken in an attempt to understand Achuar oneiromancy is an extension of the attempt to explain what is implicit that is the essential purpose of ethnology. In contrast to ethnography, which reports and interprets, ethnology strives to bring to light the principles that govern the functioning of the various systems that are supposedly identifiable within each society – a political system, an economic system, a symbolic system or a kinship system – thereby paving the way for comparison with other cultures. To be sure, no society can be reduced to any other; it constitutes a whole the meaning of which is impoverished when, for the purposes of analysis, it is deconstructed into relatively autonomous sub-systems, a juxtaposition of formal assemblages that assuredly stands in sharp contrast to the global, subjective gaze which the observer fastens upon the genius of its people. That loss of meaning is the price that has to be paid for a higher understanding of the social situation. The fact is that, although social and cultural phenomena may seem to possess a stubborn uniqueness that, at first sight, renders them incommensurable to one another, the logics that organize their diversity may stem from an order that is less chaotic, for they do possess comparable properties and it is to be hoped that one day we shall be able to formulate the principles according to which they are combined. That, at least, is the fond, founding hope upon which our vocation rests.

The ethnologists' obsession with 'giving an account of things', to use an old Platonic formula, has earned them plenty of criticism. People so often scoff at their pretentious claims to be in a better position than the men and women they have been studying to reveal the fundamental mainsprings of a culture with which they themselves have been no more than briefly acquainted. That ambition has been regarded as evidence of the scorn in which these experts on otherness hold the reflexive knowledge of the societies they claim to be able to explain. Yet the desire to reach beyond mere common sense is not limited to ethnologists. Nobody is shocked when a sociologist explains the reproduction mechanisms of our elites or when a linguist shows us the implicit distinctions that govern the organization of the tenses of French verbs. We accept that, each in his/her own field, these experts have mastered a specialized knowledge able to cast upon our daily reality an entirely new light which our intuitive powers of under-standing would, on their own, be incapable of shedding. So what is so shocking about the fact that some of us have chosen to elucidate the unknown not in our own backyards and using our own languages, but overseas and making use of strange-sounding tongues? It is some-times claimed that it is the peculiarity of societies without writing to be entirely transparent to themselves although, because they are so foreign to our own ways of looking at things, they are bound to remain for ever opaque to us. Far from striking an effective blow against ethnocentricity, this romantic idea leads to re-establishing the old splits between Ourselves and Others. Masquerading as respect for a cultural difference reckoned to be too vast ever to be truly under-stood, the series of incompatibilities that we thought discredited once and for all surfaces once again: sensible knowledge or scientific know-ledge, prelogical mentalities or rational thought, savage or civilized. They are the kind of handy distinctions that racism would all too readily like to see fashionable once more.

Wajari's and Mukuimp's description of the world of the Tsunki is representative of the basic material from which we ethnologists gener-ally derive our interpretations: confidences gleaned in chance circum-stances, a web of anecdotes and reported information that is a compound of picturesque bragging and confessions of ignorance, interrupted by mythical reminiscences and philosophical reflections. All this 'ethnographic data' is anything but a body of established knowledge. It constitutes not a faithful copy of an elusive reality, but a representation of it recomposed by one particular observer using a rather muddled palette from which successive strokes of colour build up an impressionistic cosmology. In this sketched theory of the world, the aquatic spirits play an important role, for in the eyes of my companions they clearly embody all the precepts of ideal sociability. The love-match marriage, the wife who is accomplished both as a lover and as a work partner, and the affectionate deference manifested towards the father-in-law are all enviable features of the happy family life and harmonious relations with in-laws for which the Tsunki provide an unblemished model. In the Achuar pantheon of spirits, these home-makers are the only beings who live in proper houses. In contrast to the Shaam, Amasank, Jurijri, Titipiur and other Iwianch – those deformed and malevolent products of some 'beggars' court of miracles', condemned to live beneath the earth or to wander in the woods and marshes – the water spirits respect the etiquette of social life. They present to human beings, who are always susceptible to charm, a beguiling appearance that is, as it were, their distinctive sign. By sitting on representations of tortoises and caymans, the Indians are no doubt simply evoking within their own domestic life the patronage of these likeable spirits who, in the depths of their rivers, perpetuate the invention of civilized life. In the Achuar cosmology, the surface of the waters, smooth or rough, clear or clouded with silt, fulfils the same function as Alice's mirror, a familiar plane passed through more or less by chance that opens on to a world of such fantastical transpositions that the precedence of the original over its reflection eventually becomes blurred.

II

MATTERS OF AFFINITY

'In the forest as in society, the happiness of an individual may be greater or less great than that of another individual; but I suspect that nature has established limits to the happiness of the greater part of humanity, beyond which there is about as much to lose as to gain.'

ABBÉ RAYNAL,
A Philosophical History of the Indies

CHAPTER 10

Selective Friendships

THE DAY BEFORE YESTERDAY Taish arrived in Capahuari to visit Tarir, his ceremonial friend. He took five days to travel up the Kapawi in a ramshackle, leaking canoe, with his wife Mamati and two dogs. He is a slightly built man with remarkably thin legs and a weasel face beneath his velvety fringe of hair, who always walks with a wary step as if afraid of soiling his dainty feet. Everyone knows that Taish has brought Tarir a magnificent *mayn akaru*, one of the breech-loading rifles that every man in Capahuari covets. These Peruvian weapons of North American origin take 16 mm cartridges and are incomparably superior to the muzzle-loading guns from Ecuador. Both types are called *akaru*, a term probably derived from *arcabuz*, the Spanish arquebus, and they are distinguished more by their immediate provenance than by their ways of functioning. The cartridge rifles are supplied to the Achuar by the Mayn Shuar, Jivaro Indians from Peru – hence their name, *mayn akaru* – while the muzzle-loaders, brought from the Andes by a Jivaro group from the foothills, are known as *shiwiar akaru*, after the Achuar name for this other tribe.

As soon as Taish arrived, Tarir swept him into a whirl of social visits, for everyone here is naturally eager for the news from downstream and happy to gossip on about the ups and downs of all and sundry. It is over a year since anyone has made the trip to or from the lower Kapawi, so Taish resigns himself with a morose kind of satisfaction to the role of gossip-columnist, for which his meagre talents as a *raconteur* in truth hardly predispose him but which allows him to pass his days in continuous bouts of drinking.

Accompanied by Tarir who, with touching pride, is unfailingly eager to show off the gleaming barrel of his fine *akaru*, the traveller is at present in Titiar's house, to which Wajari and myself are also paying a visit. As a choice titbit, he serves up the latest episode in the saga of Ikiam, the man from the Copataza whose mysterious disappearance has for some time been giving rise to the most contradictory rumours. Yaur, Ikiam's brother, seemed convinced of the guilt of Sumpaish, the man living on the lower Kapawi with whom Pinik, the victim's fugitive wife, had found a new home. In the absence of proof of any kind, since the body has still not been found, Yaur assumed that his brother had committed some imprudence as he sought vengeance on his wife and the man who had taken her from him and that the latter had killed Ikiam as a measure of self-protection. It seems that Yaur at first had the idea of going himself to kill Sumpaish for, as Ikiam's closest relative, this was his imperative duty. But, recognizing that Sumpaish had probably got rid of his brother in legitimate self-defence, he had subsequently decided instead to ask for material compensation.

To kill Sumpaish now would be a risky business, for the man would be doubly on his guard. Besides, it would expose his killer to reprisals from the victim's relatives, who would not have accepted that revenge was justified. In cases such as this, the injured party can require satisfaction from the murderer in the form of the gift of a rifle, a transaction that the Achuar call, literally, a blood debt, *numpa tumash*. An exchange of goods and a vendetta, that is to say an exchange of deaths, are both ruled by the same principles; and the same word, *tumash*, is used both in the deal, to designate the obligation to return an object of equivalent value to the object received, and in conflicts such as this one, to denote the situation in which the murderer finds himself, namely under the obligation to pay for the life that he has taken from another either with his own life or else with a rifle, also referred to as '*tumash*'. Yaur had accordingly asked his brother-in-law Kawarunch to go, in his name, to the people of the lower Kapawi to insist on a rifle being handed over in compensation.

In choosing Kawarunch to serve as intermediary, Yaur had perhaps sought to put an ostensible stop to the rumours that were accusing this controversial figure of himself being Ikiam's assassin – rumours that were being bandied about by Kawarunch's own neighbours, his brothers-in-law Tukupi and Washikta, men of some renown whom many people in Capahuari were only too ready to believe. Accompanied by Narankas, a brother of the Tayujin who lives in Capahuari,

Kawarunch had thus travelled down the Pastaza to where the Kapawi debouched, in order first to visit Tii, his ceremonial friend. Tii had then escorted him to the home of Nayapi, who was acting as Sumpaish's representative. Sumpaish was apparently meanwhile prudently lying low in his own house, not far away. Now, according to Taish, who lives only a few hours' journey by canoe away from Sumpaish and Nayapi and who claims to have been present at the great confrontation, it was quite impossible for Ikiam to have been killed by Sumpaish since, at the time that that murder was taking place, the latter had in point of fact gone off with the lovely Pinik to the house of a relative who lived a long way away, on the lower Kurientza, seeking refuge from a possible attack by Pinik's vindictive husband. This alibi was confirmed by several witnesses, to the apparent satisfaction of Kawarunch, who then embarked on the long return journey to inform Yaur of the outcome of his transactions. For the time being, then, the Ikiam mystery remains totally unresolved.

Taish's visit to Capahuari affords us a good chance to glean information on the region from which he hails, which we are hoping soon to explore with the aid of the outboard motor that we brought back from our brief trip to Puyo. We still need to lay hands on a boat, but I have high hopes of securing the use of a large canoe made by the men of Capahuari last year, at the instigation of the North American evangelists, for the purpose of carrying the word to their brothers living further downstream, where they are still lost in the darkness of paganism. This project, later abandoned, would in effect have made it possible for the members of the Capahuari community to go, without too much effort, to barter in the lowlands, since the *gringos* were obliging enough to provide an outboard motor. The reason why the whole project foundered seems to be that the Achuar of the lower reaches of the Kapawi had themselves already set up trading networks with the Achuar and Mayn of Peru, so they did not need to make themselves beholden to the missionaries in order to obtain manufactured goods. Left over from this abortive crusade is the canoe with its (now mainly commercial) purpose of establishing a link with the lower reaches of the river, a purpose that our own outboard motor has opportunely once more made practicable.

Our interest in the Indians downstream is quickened by the fact that their region appears to constitute a kind of cultural island so far protected from missionary incursions by its relative inaccessibility. The habitat there is extremely dispersed: as you descend the Kapawi you first come to Taish's house, about three days' journey away; there then follows an irregular succession of homes set alongside the river all the way down to its mouth and also bordering the Pastaza and its tributaries. The region is thus home to a population that is quite large albeit scattered throughout a partially swampy forest, some way away from the major navigable waterways and inaccessible by plane by reason of the absence of landing-strips. According to Taish, the lower Kapawi is at peace at the moment, but further to the east a war is said to be raging between the people of the Apupentza and those of the Kurientza, in which several lives have already been lost.

Our own curiosity is exceeded by that of the men of Capahuari, who listen attentively to all that Taish can tell them about the situation downstream. The possibility, thanks to our outboard motor, of re-establishing trading links with the lower Kapawi after a long period of interruption is encouraging them to learn as much as possible about the present situation of individuals whom they know either personally or by hearsay, many of whom are distantly related to them but about whose present circumstances, such as the state of their marriage alliances and even where exactly they live, they know nothing. Plenty of the present residents of Capahuari used to live much further downstream and the slackening of their links with the people of the lower river has resulted not so much from any open or latent hostility but from their relative laziness. Without an engine, the return upstream by canoe is extremely taxing, and virtually impossible during the floods. The creation of a settlement at Capahuari has tended to re-orientate its trading networks towards neighbours who are less inaccessible. The men of Capahuari thus have ceremonial friends amongst the Achuar of Sasaïme, two days' march away, one or two on the more distant lower Copataza, and also a few amongst the Achuar of the Bobonaza, and at Tawaynambi and Montalvo. Not many have trading partners further downstream, as Tarir does.

Making the most of Taish's presence, I question him as to the identity of his ceremonial friends in order to piece together the sociological network of which he constitutes the centre and which connects him on the one hand to the people of Capahuari and, on the other, to Indians who live a long way off, such as the Mayn of the upper

Makusar and the Achuar of the Wampuik. Wajari, greatly excited by this conversation, has been making discreet signs to his brother Titiar to get him to say his piece. Seizing the chance afforded by a silence, Titiar now turns to me and, after clearing his throat several times and spitting, he at last declares himself.

'My brother Wajari, in whose home you have been living for a long time with your wife, asks me to tell you that he would like to be your *amik*. When we Achuar think of someone with affection and want to be like a brother to him, we become *amik* with him. Now that you are going to remain amongst us, you ought to have an *amik* to protect and feed you. For you do not really know how to hunt as we the Achuar do and if you have no *amik* to give you meat, what will your poor Anchumir eat? She will be very unhappy and might leave you.'

This manoeuvre has no doubt been carefully plotted by the two brothers. Through this initiative, Wajari makes clear to the whole community the priority rights that he has gradually acquired where we two are concerned. Over the past few days he has been assessing the advantages of those rights – and now I understand why – questioning me discreetly as to the extent of my wealth and making sure, by dint of flowery speeches and circumstantial anecdotes, that I, for my part, am fully aware of the obligations of generosity and assistance that characterize the relationship between *amik*. Quite apart from the fact that it would be hard to refuse such a proposal openly without humiliating Wajari, I think that strengthening the links between us by a formal connection would be rather a good idea. Ceremonial friendship would establish a socially recognized relationship that would make it possible to ratify dealings that have up until now been based upon mutual sympathy as much as upon our coinciding personal convenience – an unstable situation that a system of clearly codified mutual obligations would render less precarious.

No sooner have I agreed than Titiar goes off to fetch a grimy blanket that he spreads upon the floor of the *tankamash*, then he bids Wajari and me kneel down facing each other. In this uncomfortable position we then slap each other warmly on first the right shoulder, then the left, repeating with conviction, 'My *amik*! My *amik*!' Then it is the turn of Anne Christine and Entza, Wajari's third wife, to embrace in ritual fashion, exclaiming, 'My *yanas*! My *yanas*!' Henceforward Wajari and Entza will have to call me 'my *amik*', the formula that I shall also use when addressing Wajari, and I shall call Entza 'my *yanas*', which is also the expression that she and Anne Christine will use when addressing each other. The classic terms of kinship that we used to employ will now be replaced by this network of new appellations, indicating that the old relations of consanguinity or affinity must give way before a link that is stronger because it has been deliberately sought and publicly instituted. Ceremonial friendship introduces an order of its own that sometimes contradicts the sociological principles that govern ordinary relations. By emphasizing the parity established between our two couples, for example, it cuts across the equality of status that obtains between all the various wives of a man, for now only one of them can enjoy the advantages of the new attachment contracted by their husband. Summary though it was, the ceremony to establish our new status delighted me: I still feel a stab of emotion at the thought that customs about which I had up until then had no more than a bookish knowledge are vital enough for me to become an actor in them. It is perhaps this kind of confirmation, repeated by every ethnographic experience, that guarantees the truth of the social abstractions described in anthropological literature and that, ultimately, makes comparison between them possible.

The term *amik* seems to be derived from the Spanish *amigo*, and the brief ritual we have just completed itself resembles the feudally inspired ceremony in the course of which the sixteenth-century conquistadors would confer an *encomienda* upon their deserving soldiers, that is to say commission them to 'civilize' and convert an Indian village or group of villages, a mission which those soldiers would then shamelessly turn to their own advantage by proceeding to extort tribute from the villagers. But despite its Hispanic tone, the institution is almost certainly of autochthonous origin. In the first place, it is significant that the bond of ceremonial friendship excludes strangers in that it is normally established only between partners who speak a Jivaro dialect. Admittedly, the word *amik* is also sometimes used as a mark of respect when addressing certain Whites, missionaries or *regatones*, but without implying on either side any commitment to the system of obligations that characterizes the *amik* relationship. Some of the northern Achuar who maintain regular contacts with the Christianized Quichuas or the few *mestizos* to be found in Montalvo choose instead to formalize their commercial relations through the

154

compadrazgo. As conceived by the Achuar, the reciprocal commitments of the *kumpas* (those engaged by this contract) in practice amount to no more than observation of a minimal code of good behaviour in their trading deals.

In contrast to the *compadrazgo* relationship, ceremonial friendship is truly meaningful only within the Jivaro culture, that is to say for people who speak the same language and share the same values, for whom the principles of behaviour and the subtleties of etiquette refer to the same social code, and who adhere to the same ethic of personal honour. For *amik* are not merely commercial partners, even if that is the function that tends to predominate in the definition spontaneously provided by the Indians themselves. They are also bound by other obligations: to offer assistance and refuge in times of war, to act as intermediaries with their respective enemies, to guarantee each other's safety on visits to hostile territory – all obligations that clearly presuppose a certain geographic, social and cultural proximity. However surprising it may seem, my co-option into such a closed system is not entirely unexpected. It was prompted by a desire to share to a certain extent in the benefits of my supposed wealth and also by Anne Christine's and my custom of respecting the Achuar etiquette of correct behaviour. It is a custom that contrasts so sharply with the behaviour of the other rare Whites our hosts have come across that it must have encouraged them to believe that I would not fail in commitments of a more constraining nature.

Ceremonial friendship is very common in the Amazonian world, which is another reason for believing that the Jivaro variant of the phenomenon owes nothing to the Spaniards. The content of the institution varies greatly from one culture to another. Most commonly, it functions as a means of long-distance trading and as a mechanism of economic redistribution, for the formalization of a bond of friendship ensures the security of exchanges between partners who frequently belong to tribes hostile to each other. Far more rare are the cases in which, as amongst the Jivaros, the ceremonial friends promise each other protection and assistance in times of war. For highly conflictual societies, this is a judicious system since it affords each friend zones of active neutrality or potential alliance. Amongst the peoples of central Brazil, in contrast, where each member of the village finds himself/herself fixed from birth within an intricate

155

network of opposed yet complementary social groupings – clans, ceremonial moieties, age groups, warrior brotherhoods – formal friendship loses its aspect of an elective affinity and becomes a collective relationship like the rest, inherited – as they are – from one's parents. It then simply amounts to a series of strictly codified duties towards particular individuals: to make their headdresses, to adorn them for ceremonies or to organize their burials. Finally, there are certain Tupi tribes that have carried this institution in quite the opposite direction: far from turning it into the basis of obligations of a quasi-liturgical nature, they conceive it as a joyous sharing of body and spirit that extends quite naturally to wives. These friendships are sealed between married couples and involve free nocturnal access to one's partner of the opposite sex.

The sexual reciprocity of certain Tupi societies emphasizes in spectacular fashion a feature that is common to most other Amazonian forms of ceremonial friendship. These friendships are developed alongside ordinary social relationships, as an alternative or even an antidote to them. In this region of the world, both public and private life tend to be organized on the basis of a fundamental division between two classes of people: relatives by blood and relatives by marriage, on the one hand people who are like brothers and sisters to you, on the other those amongst whom you may seek a spouse. The properties of classificatory kinship peculiar to this type of society are such that, through the interplay of logical derivations spreading from a small kernel of genealogically attested relationships, every member of the tribe is bound to be either a blood-relative to you or an affine. Thanks to their relative abstraction, these mutually exclusive categories find a potential field of application that goes far beyond the purely social sphere and, ideally at least, covers the whole of the universe. My companions thus conceive of gardening as a kind of blood relationship between the women and the plants they tend, whilst hunting involves the establishment of a relation of affinity between the men and the animals they hunt. Ceremonial friendship cuts across this somewhat inflexible symmetry, introducing a third type of relationship which combines certain properties of each of the others. The bond between *amik* is comparable to affinity by marriage in that it presupposes a certain distance between the partners who have concluded the pact, yet at the same time it remains marvellously unencumbered by the obligations that you acquire for all time towards the people who supply you with women. Meanwhile, it draws its affective inspiration from the deep mutual confidence that characterizes the relations between brothers by blood. It is always in terms of the behaviour prescribed for brothers that the Achuar describe the duties of ceremonial friendship, revenge obviously being prominent among them. So Wajari's desire to tie the *amik* knot with me is quite understandable: midway between a relationship of blood-kinship, which would seem too unlikely, and affinity, with obligations that would be too heavy, this formal friendship that guarantees us mutual tranquillity and furthermore provides him with access to my little fortune no doubt seemed the ideal sociological slot for the odd bearded stranger and his white companion.

When choosing their *amik*, the people of Capahuari are guided by two apparently contradictory considerations: the one is to strengthen their bonds with very close relatives, such as brothers or brothers-in-law, the other to forge relationships with individuals who are very distant both sociologically and geographically. Yet, to varying degrees, both strategies are a response to the same need: to make sure of loyal and diversified support at every level where it might prove necessary.

Admittedly, ritual friendship between brothers, even uterine brothers, is something of a perversion of the system, probably designed not so much to strengthen flagging brotherly relations, but to warn off potential enemies with the show of flawless coalition. This is the case with Tarir and Pinchu: an inseparable brotherly duo much given to bandying about the ceremonial 'my *amik*' at every opportunity. They are so closely linked that when Santamik, Pinchu's wife, accompanies him on a trip lasting several days, she always entrusts her children to her *yanas*, Nampirach, who is Tarir's wife, rather than to Yatris, the second wife of her own husband. The economic aspect of a relationship such as this is clearly of minor consideration, since the brothers are more interested in the political advantages they may derive from it and each already possesses his own network of distant *amik* with whom he can carry on long-distance trading. All the same, commercial interests and social advantages are often hard to dissociate. A few days ago Pinchu was complaining bitterly that Tarir would not give him any of his curare. The fact was that Taish had brought his *amik* Tarir this curare in return for a muzzle-loading gun that he had earlier received from him, and Tarir wanted to keep the poison in order to present it to his *amik* Washikta, in Sasaïme, from whom he was hoping to receive a breech-loading rifle. 'Brotherly friendship' did not weigh very heavily in the balance against *amik* who, though more distant, might be givers of rare and precious gifts.

Distant friends are not always of the same type, however. Firstly, there are business partners chosen really far afield, from some neighbouring tribe, because they live in a place that is strategic for the procurement of certain items that have become indispensable to the Achuar. For a long time the people of the Kapawi have had Shuar *amik* in the region of the upper Makuma, through whom they obtain manufactured goods that these already accultured Indians themselves procure from the east, from other Shuar who live in direct contact with the front of colonization. This is the route by which not only muzzle-loaders find their way but also many of the knives, machetes, blankets, lengths of cloth and other bartered goods in use here. *Amik* living on the Makuma also serve as middlemen in the supply of salt, traditionally produced from saline sources by the Shuar of Mangosiza and then transported over very long distances in the form of large, compact cakes. Apart from this salt, the exchanges made with Achuar *amik* and Quichua *kumpa* living on the Bobonaza involve the same kind of items since, like the Shuar, these Indians also make the most of their proximity to the *regatones* of Montalvo in order to control the diffusion of Western goods to the Kapawi. The Quichuas furthermore exercise a monopoly over the mineral dyes that are indispensable for the decoration of pots – small concretions enclosed in clay, black for the *kitiun*, red for the *pura*, and white for the *pushan*. As for the Indians to the south, the Mayn, or the Achuar of Peru, they are the suppliers of the three kinds of goods most highly prized by the people of Capahuari: breech-loading guns, *shauk*, and curare.

Shauk are simply glass beads, preferably coral-pink, white, yellow or ultramarine, threaded on to a single string or worn as a coil or else made into a bracelet or a belt. These beads, traditionally manufactured in Bohemia, have gradually replaced the *mullu*, little pink pearls made since time immemorial out of a type of shell very common in the Guayas gulf. Under the Inca empire, these were already being widely diffused throughout much of the Andes and the Amazonian foothills. Even nowadays the Achuar claim that their *shauk* come from 'the people of the sun', and this mysterious provenance may well be a reference to the Inca origin of the pre-Colombian jewellery for which the glass beads of today are a substitute. Despite the fact that glass beads were among the first barter articles brought to Amazonia by the Europeans, they still remain unobtainable in Ecuador and have to be transported from faraway Peruvian warehouses over huge distances before reaching the Achuar. The same applies to high-quality curare, mass-produced in almost industrial quantities by extremely distant indigenous peoples such as the Lamistas and the Cocamas, then collected in centres such as Tarapoto or Iquitos by *regatones* who then ensure their distribution to the Indians of the frontier region.

In exchange for this variety of goods, the Achuar generally give their distant friends two kinds of article for which they are rightly famed in much of upper Amazonia: blowpipes and feathered head-dresses or *tawasap*. Both are produced on a truly commercial scale specifically for inter-tribal trading. Every Capahuari man makes at least half a dozen blowpipes each year and all their houses normally contain a number of these weapons in various stages of completion, ranging from the roughly trimmed basic material – long wooden palm stems that must be left to dry out for at least a year before work can be begun on them to shape them into a demi-cylinder – to the completed tube lacking only the addition of a tip fashioned from the femur of a jaguar. *Tawasap* could never be produced at such a rate, for their silky yellow and red feathers come exclusively from a small tuft situated at the base of the toucan's tail, so that several dozen of these unfortunate birds are needed in order to make this item of masculine finery. It is true that the value of a *tawasap* is much greater than that of a blowpipe. The former can be traded for a brand-new cartridge rifle or a fine canoe, whereas the latter is worth only a nasty nylon blanket or a couple of shirts. My companions also provide their Shuar *amik* and their Quichua *kumpa* with a number of natural resources that are now scarce in the territories of those tribes: sections of certain kinds of trees suitable for making flutes or blowpipes, pieces of the *iniayua* palm for making darts and kapok fibre for their flight fins, and teeth from the fresh-water dolphin, which are used as hunting or fishing amulets, etc. Finally, since the Capahuari people enjoy a monopoly in the distribution networks for goods from Peru, it is inevitably they who supply the Shuar and the Quichuas with the famous triad of riches: curare, *shauk* and *mayn akaru*.

Although it may appear to obey the sensible rationality of economics textbooks, this regional division of trade according to which each trader is supposed to export his own specialized products and resources so as to make up for the deficiencies of nature or industry in his own region, in reality it is more like those artificial devices designed to allow belligerent states to perpetuate diplomatic relations. Apart from the salt – for which there is certainly no equivalent but for which alternative sources do exist in Peru, where they have been exploited over thousands of years – all the native goods bartered with distant *amik* could, in truth, be produced by those who are seeking to acquire them or could be replaced by perfectly acceptable substitutes. For example, there is nothing to prevent the Shuar and the Quichuas from making their own blowpipes, curare and *tawasap*, since all the indications are that they were still doing so in the recent past: the basic material is no longer as plentiful but has not disappeared, and the technology could soon be revived. If they do not do so, it is because they find it to their advantage to obtain products so difficult and time-consuming to make in exchange for relatively cheap goods that are not hard to come by. But quite apart from this obvious selfish interest, the allocation of particular types of craftsmanship to particular tribes also has the effect of making barter an inevitable instrument of regional interaction. Through it, lasting relations of mutual dependence are woven between groups of men who could perfectly well cultivate lives of self-sufficiency. This long-distance trading founded upon artificially maintained scarcities, codified by the mutual obligations of *amik*, and fostered by the erratic detours of a capitalist market thus constitutes a response not only to an economic need but also to a political desire to maintain some form of liaison between people who are not particularly fond of each other.

However, that is not to suggest that trading between friends does away with inter-tribal clashes: for it precedes them and prolongs them; in some cases fosters them, in others may help to suspend them. From time immemorial, the Shuar of the upper Makuma have been the enemies of the Kapawi Achuar as well as their bartering partners: it was to the Kapawi that the Shuar came, no more than a dozen years ago, seeking heads to shrink, and it was, naturally enough, to the

160

Makuma that the people of Capahuari sent their expeditions to exact reprisals. These hostile relations seem not to have prevented the *amik* of the two tribes from visiting one another with total confidence, the host standing as personal guarantor for the safety of his guest for the duration of the visit and even escorting him on his return journey as far as that point where his own safety might be endangered. Ceremonial friends thus enjoy the kind of immunity normally reserved for diplomats. It is well known that this creates a convenient way of spying on enemies, discussing the suspension of hostilities with them or setting up the overthrow of particular alliances. It was through such intermediaries that, not long ago, the first contacts were established between the protestant missionaries of the Makuma and the Achuar of the Kapawi. It was a move that the Achuar eventually decided to favour precisely in order to safeguard their own supply of manufactured goods, which was at that time being jeopardized by the diminishingly permeable frontier with Peru. While death debts and wealth debts combine to shape the general relations between one tribe and another, they never coexist in a personal friendship between a Shuar and an Achuar, for such a pair's commitment to the trading of objects rules out any recourse to vengeance. The paradoxical association of war and trade, ubiquitous in Amazonia, is perhaps a way of resolving a contradiction that confronts all the peoples of the region – that between the irrepressible desire for autonomy felt by neighbours who resemble one another too closely and the need, felt by every human group, to define its own identity by setting itself against another such group.

Such a contradiction also governs the choice of an 'appropriately distant' Achuar *amik*, that is to say a man outside the family circle but still close enough for one to hope to be able to mobilize his active support in a vendetta. For Tarir, that is the case with Taish and with Washikta. Belonging as they do to networks of relatives and friends that are distinct from his own yet not entirely separate, and living no more than a few days' march away, relatively close according to the scale of Achuar country, they would have made perfect enemies in an internal tribe war had ceremonial friendship not converted them into potential allies. Even more than in inter-tribal relations, this type of *amik* bond exploits the cover of trading to cloak a desire to diversify one's alliances. It also makes it possible to distinguish one's social

161

position by relations of antagonism and exchange that define a particular type of otherness and, by contrast, of identity. To each kind of enemy there thus corresponds a particular kind of friend, in a subtle arrangement that gives social life its full piquancy and daily enlivens it with the intriguing uncertainties of a game of politics worthy of the Florentines.

An *amik* relationship is ceremonious as well as ceremonial. It displays to the highest degree the formalism that regulates all masculine sociability, always a combination of inflated rhetoric and conventional posturing that irresistibly evokes all the worst clichés of exploration literature. In my future dealings with Wajari I shall have to be very careful to use the appropriate formulae demanded by courtesy as well as, more generally, attempt to use the flowery language that becomes man-to-man conversations.

Titiar, probably the most pompous of the Capahuari Achuar, is at present providing a model for me. Now that most of the visitors have departed, he chooses this moment to harangue his son-in-law Chumapi, a young man aged about seventeen or eighteen.

'My son-in-law, now that I have given you my daughter, you live in my house and we get along fine, all together, as we should. Did not our ancients tell us that a son-in-law must live with his father-in-law and lend him assistance, and were they not right? We, the Achuar, do as the ancients said we should.'

'That is very true, my father-in-law.'

'The *amik* of my brother Wajari, he too is learning the way of behaving prescribed by the ancients. He knows how to read and write, he knows everything that the Whites know and he may even have travelled to the moon. Nevertheless, he too wants to know what the ancients said we should do, because that is the right way to behave.'

'So it is, father-in-law. Absolutely!'

'Should a son-in-law not help his father-in-law? Should he say bad things about his mother-in-law? Should he turn his back when his father-in-law's enemies act threateningly? No, a son-in-law who did not put himself at his father-in-law's service would be like a mouse that comes to steal groundnuts, a stealer of women, not a man of his word.'

'That is so, father-in-law! A stealer of women, not a man of his word!'

162

'Young people these days have no respect for what the ancients said. They flit from girl to girl, like humming-birds. All they want is to sleep with them: *tsak!* one here, *tsak!* another there. Is it not shameful to behave like that? They don't want to take a wife because they don't want to work. Should one not clear a garden for one's wife? Should one not go hunting for her? Should one not give her *shauk?*'

'You are quite right, father-in-law.'

'Son-in-law, have you not seen that the chicken shed is in ruins?'

'Absolutely in ruins.'

'What is to be done with the hens now? In the night, ocelots and tayras come and eat the hens. As you may recall, I made a trap a moon ago, but they managed to avoid it. Only Inchi, brother-in-law Tsukanka's dog, fell into it, poor imbecile! Our hens are being wiped out. Now what are we going to give the Quichuas? Do we not need shirts and blankets?'

'Very true, father-in-law.'

'The ancients taught us that it was necessary to build chicken sheds to protect the hens. Were the ancients wrong? My brother Wajari's *amik* also says that the Whites construct chicken sheds, where they keep enormous hens, as big as vultures.'

'Absolutely, father-in-law, like vultures! Some of them like eagles!'

'Come, come, son-in-law . . . Tomorrow I invite you, if you are agreeable, to rebuild the chicken shed with me.'

'I agree! I agree!'

After this homily on domestic morality we take rapid leave of Titiar, whose sententious mood looks ready to start him off again. And to think that not so long ago I was kicking myself for being unable to understand these conversations!

On our return to Wajari's house at dusk, we find Chiwian and Paantam in the garden, hunting birds with the miniature blowpipes that their father has made them. They have taken up position close to a *yakuch*, a small, wild tree spared in the clearing operation because its fruits, to which the toucans are partial, serve as a convenient lure. Not far off, Nawir is sitting on the ground, looking cross. Senur tells us that she has been sulking like this since mid-afternoon over something that nobody can remember, despite the fact that they have all, each in turn, tried without success to console her. Wajari is upset and spends a long time talking to the little girl in a comforting voice. In a society that is particularly exercised about quarrels, the sulks of children are taken very seriously, as if it were important to root out any lasting resentment within the family the better to direct aggression outwards.

From the house we notice Naanch passing by on the other side of the river with a fair-sized ocelot over his shoulder. This is at least the third that he has killed over the last few days. Wajari is rather put out as one of his dogs was killed a little while ago by a female jaguar that escaped, whereas Naanch's dogs have all emerged unscathed from their encounters with the big cats.

'I've got a white *amik*,' he says, laughing, 'but as for Naanch, he has become *amik* with the ocelots. That's how it is that no harm ever comes to his dogs. I should have asked him to intercede with his jaguar *yanas*, to get her to spare my dog. You see how it is, a proper man must have *amik* of all sorts!'

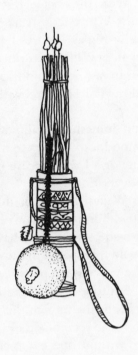

CHAPTER 11

A Visit to the River People

THE HOUSE IS PROTECTED by a high fortification constructed of palm-trunks, but the open door, hewn from a single slab of wood, invites one to enter. The small enclosure inside the palisade is deserted, rain-sodden and strewn with domestic paraphernalia: cracked pots, bundles of palm leaves, worn-out baskets, an untidy heap of wood for fuel. The house itself is also surrounded by a wall of palm slats pierced on the *tankamash* side by a low door, narrowed by the barely parted movable planks that usually serve to close it. Tsukanka, Wajari and Mukuimp precede me into this dark hovel, whilst Auju, Senur and Entza remain outside, as does Anne Christine. Amid the furious barks of the leashed dogs and the shouts of the women correcting them, we seat ourselves on the visitors' *kutank*. Upon entering, each of us pronounced the customary formula, '*Winiajai!*' (I come!) Seated on his *chimpui*, but taking good care not to look at us, Kawarunch each time replied, '*Winitia!*' (Come!)

The craggy face of the master of the house is daubed with bloody splashes of rocou. With his rifle placed carelessly between his legs, and turning aside slightly so as not to see us, he orders his wives to bring us some manioc beer. A long silence descends as we sip the *nijiamanch*, broken only by appreciative claps of the tongue. Following the example of the other visitors from Capahuari, I pass my bowl at arm's length through the door so that Anne Christine, squatting outside with the other women, can also slake her thirst. Behind her impassive look, I sense the beginnings of an ironical smile.

Swivelling round in a single movement to face us, Kawarunch suddenly looks Tsukanka straight in the eye. They then embark upon that extraordinary bravura performance of Achuar rhetoric, the great visit dialogue, the *aujmatin* or 'conversation'.

165

'Brother-in-law, you have come!'

'*Aih!*'

'*Haa!*'

'*Aih!* Brother-in-law, I have come!'

'*Aih!*'

'*Haa!*'

In a confusion made all the more difficult to disentangle by the fact that each of them is bellowing at the top of his voice, the two men then set about simultaneously delivering virtually identical formulaic exclamations, Tsukanka chiming in just after Kawarunch, as in a round.

'*Aih! Aih!* Brother-in-law! We, the Achuar, being here where we are. *Aih!* Brother-in-law! We, the Achuar, being here in our little house, we, the true Achuar, are we not present? And so we remain. *Maah!* So it is that you, sitting there, have come to me, is it not thus that we do it? Remaining thus, just so, at home, waiting for whoever comes, just as our ancients did, that is what we do, and is it not exactly what we should be doing? *Aih!*'

After this introductory medley the real dialogue begins. It takes the form of a litany chanted in rapid rhythm, with each short phrase rising in a continuous crescendo, then suddenly dropping, with much emphasis, to a note slightly below the one on which it started. The interlocutor punctuates the end of each of the decrescendos by interjecting a vigorous agreement. He may add a brief commentary, delivered on the same melodic scale, but much shorter. Having briefly looked each other up and down at the start of this *aujmatin*, both Kawarunch and Tsukanka are now avoiding each other's eye. With one elbow resting on his knee and one hand cupped like a shell before his mouth, each is now connected to the other only by the counterpoint of their powerful voices, the visible origins of which are carefully concealed. One senses that one is witnessing a highly codified skirmish. Following the first sudden eye-to-eye contact, it is seemly to disguise the physical source of both speech and vision, leaving words, now disembodied, to convey the true intentions of those competing in eloquence. There is, however, one exception to the concealment of all physical agents in the dialogue, namely the spurts of saliva that Kawarunch and Tsukanka emit at regular intervals, compressing their lips between two fingers to do so. These projected streams of saliva accompany the trajectory of the words, vouching for their veracity.

'And since you have come to visit as is fitting, so I remain here!'

'That is true!'

'To set about doing what I should, I am here!'

'Brother-in-law, you are here for me!'

'*Haa!* Some of us know how to behave. And him! And him!'

'*Tsa, tsa, tsa, tsaa!*'

'*Haa*, without knowing the news, here I am, at home!'

'*Aih!*'

'To tell me the news that you bring, thus it is that you have come to me!'

'*Haa!* That is true!'

Almost identical in meaning, but with slight variations in their expression, the clichés roll out in rapid succession until Kawarunch suddenly interrupts the harmonious balance of his exclamations to produce one that differs from the rest only in that it is delivered all on one note. This is the signal for Tsukanka to take over. With brio to match his deep conviction he now starts up at the top of his voice in exactly the same vein, whilst Kawarunch in turn stresses each of his visitor's banalities with enthusiastic exclamations of approval. And so the conversation continues, the words flowing from the one to the other according to a set pattern but giving no hint of the reason for our presence other than in the most allusive fashion. Lost in an avalanche of stereotyped declarations of the suitability of visits and the immemorial rules of hospitality, the amount of information passing between the two men is minimal: Tsukanka is on his way to visit his *amik* Washikta, whom he hopes to find at home; yes, Washikta is at home; the Capahuari region is at present free from conflicts; good news, and so is the Sasaïme region. Almost twenty minutes after the beginning of the *aujmatin*, it is Tsukanka who brings it to a conclusion, his words rising steadily up a scale.

'Having thus conversed well, as befits proper men, *haa!* let's see: being obliged now to leave again after visiting you, we shall meet another time. Now I must leave you!'

'Very well, very well!'

'*Aih!*'

Now there is a pause. Kawarunch chats with his wives while the

167

men from Capahuari exchange a few banalities on a note of forced joviality, host and visitors once again deliberately ignoring one another. Then the master of the house turns to Wajari and another *aujmatin* is under way. Its content is as sparse as the last one: Wajari announces that he is on his way to visit his father-in-law Tukupi, accompanied by his son-in-law Mukuimp, his *amik* Yakum – a member of the mysterious Pransis tribe, who has come to learn the language of proper men – and his *yanas* Anchumir. Our presence appears not to surprise Kawarunch in the least and he politely refrains from asking any questions about it.

While this dialogue unfolds its rhythmic sequences, my mind, still sluggish from the fatigue of the march, begins to wander, recalling the impressions left by the journey. We left Capahuari at dawn yesterday and walked, virtually without a halt, until dusk, through a dense, hilly and despairingly deserted forest. Despite my fresh experience as a backwoods man, I was still quite incapable of making out the course of the twisting track that we followed in single file, with the men leading and bringing up the rear so as to prevent the women being carried off in a possible raid by an evil Iwianch spirit. To my gloomy satisfaction, even the Indians several times lost their way and had to pause to discuss which direction to take. Towards evening we came across a noisy group of howler monkeys and, by some miracle, I managed to bring one down for our dinner with my very first shot. The night, spent in a rudimentary palm-leaf lean-to, was chilly, rainy and not very refreshing. Our footwear and clothes, soaking wet after fording several rivers, gave off a mouldy smell. Slipping into them at daybreak, as if into icy winding-sheets, did not help to encourage us in the purpose that had brought us so far.

Around mid-morning we reached the great swamp of the Mente Kusutka, which we crossed, wading through water up to our thighs for over an hour, softly sinking with every step into the squelching, muddy bottom and constantly tripping over roots and dead branches that were impossible to see in the black water. Beneath the raised roots of mangrove trees, at the foot of swamp palms and huge tree-like ferns, the smooth surface of the water was at moments disturbed by some disquieting form of animal life, which caused everybody to freeze in alarm. In its primordial inhumanity, the swamp gradually became confused in my mind with the coloured illustrations in my

childhood encyclopaedias, in which inventive illustrators had represented the most daunting specimens of the Cretaceous mega-fauna cohabiting in an antediluvian setting. Stunned as I was by the exhaustion induced by our march, I should probably not have been at all surprised to see a tyrannosaurus or a pteranodon rising from the waters as we rounded some mossy trunk.

After emerging from the swamp we still had to climb a steep bluff and then for a while continue along its rim before descending its other side by a slippery gully running down the cliff. Then, a sudden vision: through a gap in the vegetation we could see an endless, flat, peaceful landscape. It was the Pastaza plain, cut into by the interlacing dead branches and channels that created a string of low-lying islands bordered by grey shingle beaches. On the larger spits of sandy land isolated by the whimsically winding river, thickets of giant bamboos flourished alongside copses of canna, providing noisy refuges for myriad plovers. Perched on their slender legs, white egrets stalked along the calm water's edge, oblivious to our presence. My breath was taken away by this vision of Eden that presented such a contrast to the Darwinian stuffiness of the swamp. I hardly knew where to look, my gaze suddenly unable to take in the immense sky crossed by a string of fluffy clouds. The distant rumble of the river added to the vastness of the spectacle, its powerful pulsations seeming to extend the horizon.

To explain the extent of my emotion, I should perhaps point out that for months on end our world had been confined to clearings implacably enclosed by a vertical mass of vegetation unbroken by any vista or chink, where the firmament itself was reduced to a tiny window all too soon obscured as the night fell. A few paces across the garden soon trapped us in a submarine gloom that extended in all directions like some eternal and infernal punishment. Even the Indians seemed happy now to emerge from the interminable greenish tunnel through which we had been plodding for two days. They paused to rest for a while on the shingle, silently contemplating the majestic sight of the great river. With his eyes dreamily fixed on the thin green line that marked the point where the forest again took over, Wajari laconically remarked: 'It's beautiful,' the only aesthetic judgement on a view that I ever heard him pronounce. A few minutes later we had come to Kawarunch's house.

He is now engaged in conversation with Mukuimp, who is clearly less at ease than his elders in this rhetorical exercise. His tirades are not so long, sometimes marred by stammering, and are delivered with much less assurance. The *aujmatin* is a daunting trial for young men, despite the fact that they have been preparing for it ever since adolescence, practising with their brothers or cousins in the privacy of the forest, out of the way of the ironical comments that might be made by the adult men. Unlike the *yaitias chicham* or 'slow talk', the more or less natural mode of dialogue for all the men, this kind of conversation is only *de rigueur* on visits to houses that are distant from home either geographically, genealogically or because they are suspected of hostility. Those three grounds for wariness are usually combined, since a distant relative is never to be trusted, particularly if his political alliances operate in a region in which one has few contacts oneself. This is, in fact, the case with Kawarunch, to whom Tsukanka and Wajari are no more than distantly connected by marriage and whom the people of Capahuari suspect of having killed Ikiam, who was the maternal uncle of Auju, Tsukanka's wife. If Kawarunch's guilt were proved, Tsukanka would be in duty bound to help his wife's kin to take revenge on our host – something that they do not appear disposed to do in the immediate future since Yaur, Ikiam's brother, happens to be Kawarunch's *amik* and, as such, recently requested Kawarunch to claim *tumash* on his behalf from Sumpaish, the other possible suspect.

The circumstances of this murky affair are in the minds of all present, but there is no mention of the matter in the series of *aujmatin*. The peculiar feature of this kind of 'conversation' is that it in effect excludes all real conversation. The succession of stereotyped formulae, many of them utterly meaningless, the systematic anaphora, the repetition of a single verb used in several different modes, and the persistent use of synonyms and paraphrases all combine to create a largely redundant discourse in which very few scraps of meaning ever surface. And even these amount to no more than the endless repetition of a handful of the cardinal values of the Achuar culture, namely the importance of visits, the rules of hospitality, the duty of relatives to help one another and the obligation for men to display bravery. Given that the time allowed for each interlocutor is furthermore limited by the alternating pattern of prosody, it becomes impossible to ask any question or develop any theme that falls outside the conventional script. Unlike in normal conversation, it would be equally impossible either to steer the dialogue round to the desired subject or to allow it to develop in an unexpected way. The fact is that the *aujmatin* is a form of verbal exchange in which semantics plays an extremely minor role. The messages transmitted are contained not so much in the words, but rather in the very interaction that they make possible, in the minutely coded stage management that brings into confrontation two characters who have reason to mistrust each other and for whom this preamble affords an opportunity to spy upon each other. Hence the importance of gestures, intonation, forms of address, the ordered succession of phases, the display of finery and weapons, in short the whole setting of the dialogue. The conversation is as much a rhetorical competition as an instrument of mediation, by means of which individuals who start off by drawing attention to the great distance that separates them are progressively led, through their shared reiteration of a common credo, to diminish the social distance between them. By the end of the 'conversation', the hierarchy of the protagonists is re-established and normal sociability can be restored.

Our host has now desisted from torturing Mukuimp and, since I have taken great care not to meet his eye so as to avoid being submitted to a similar harangue, Tsukanka can finally reveal the practical purpose of our visit: we need Kawarunch to convey us across the Pastaza in his canoe so that we can visit Tukupi and Washikta on the opposite bank.

Soon after this we set out, trudging across a labyrinth of beaches and islands until we come to the main branch of the river, where large logs are being noisily swept downstream through the whirlpools of brown water. Two journeys are needed to ferry everyone across this formidable obstacle; the fragile craft is tossed about like a straw in the irresistible current and is several times saved from capsizing only by one of Kawarunch's expert digs with his oar. As we land in a small cove overarched by tall kapok trees, Wajari tells me in detached tones that during the last crossing he made here the canoe being manoeuvred by his *amik* Picham had been forced across the current and had eventually capsized. The river had swept them several hundred metres before they managed to gain a foothold on a pebbly outcrop and little Nawir, who had been carried much further downstream, had remained unconscious for a long time.

Leaving the canoe securely moored, we continue on our way along dead branches of the river-bed carpeted with shingle and, after an hour's march, reach a quiet beach with a path leading from it. At this point the men undertake a meticulous toilette. First they comb their hair, then divide it into three pony-tails wound about by little cords. Then they don their *tawasap* crowns and slip into the gaudy shirts they have been carrying in their string bags. Taking it in turns to dip a stick into a tiny gourd filled with powder made from a base of pounded rocou, we then paint one another's faces. I have finally settled for a design known as 'the anaconda', which consists of double crosses over my nose, a wide band either side of a row of little dots along my cheeks, and an elegant network of lines running from the corners of my mouth to the lobes of my ears. Anne Christine is not so lucky. Like the other women, she has to be content with a more modest pattern; this time it consists of a crescent surrounding a dot on either cheekbone. To look his very best, Wajari borrows my rifle, having recently given his own to one of his *amik*. Arrayed in this splendid finery, we at last reach Tukupi's house.

The garden seems immense and is bordered by a wide, clear stream, the Sasaïme. The house, visible from afar, is larger than any that I have yet seen. Although the dogs heard us coming some time ago, Wajari announces our arrival in the correct fashion, blowing through the rifle's barrel to produce the lowing sound of a hunting horn. The master of the house is seated majestically upon his *chimpui*. He is a thickset, muscular man of forty to fifty years of age with an aura of contained strength that is emphasized by a square face with a determined chin. Strangely enough, his hair has fair, coppery lights in it, giving it an almost Venetian look. A young man is seated a few paces away on a smaller *chimpui*. This is Naychap, his eldest son. He bears a striking resemblance to Tukupi, but his features seem a rougher, hasty copy in which the father's strength is converted into sulky brutality. Two other visitors are present: Asamat, Tukupi's sole surviving brother, whom I soon deduce from his guttural grunts to be deaf and dumb, and Washikta, a lanky sort with the dry, impassive face of a warlord, who is engaged in loud bursts of conversation with the master of the house. Soon after our arrival the latter breaks off his talk and orders manioc beer to be served. He then calls Tsukanka over for a particularly animated *aujmatin*.

The face-painting motifs of these river Achuar, applied profusely in thick smears, are less refined than those fashionable in Capahuari. Their pottery is also less delicate, adorned – if at all – by no more than a few clumsy daubs. Their primitive aesthetics, which spurn any complex ornamentation, are in keeping with the men's fierce, abrupt manner of speech and also with their wary postures. The scene as a whole conveys a distinctive style that is new to me but more in line with the reports of travel literature, in which the Jivaros are represented as seething with violence and inordinate pride. With the exception of Tsukanka, my travelling companions seem somewhat intimidated by Tukupi, particularly Wajari, whose usual bonhomie has virtually dissolved faced with such a formidable father-in-law.

My *amik* came by this marriage alliance in quite martial circumstances. About seven or eight years ago Tukupi and Washikta were involved in a relentless vendetta against two brothers, Jimpikit and Tiriruk, who lived one day's march to the east. The kindred mobilized by each side were of more or less equal strength, so in the clashes between them neither side ever gained a decisive advantage. Tukupi and Washikta had accordingly decided to call up reinforcements from their allies living on the Kapawi; these had included Tsukanka, Wajari and his brother, Titiar. Others were summoned from the Surikentza, much further south. After several deaths on both sides the people of Sasaïme eventually emerged victorious: Tiriruk and Jimpikit were killed, as was Yurank, the latter's son-in-law, laid low by Chumpi, a man from the Surikentza whose brother Yurank had previously killed. Whilst returning from a raid the victors by chance came across the women of the vanquished party, busily engaged in fishing with poison, and seized and carried them all off. Kawarunch took Atinia, Kayuye took Nuis, and Tukupi took Tsitsink, Jimpikit's widow. Tsitsink was accompanied by her daughters, two of whom – Entza and Chawir – were still very young and went with their mother to live in Tukupi's home. The third daughter, Senur, had been Yurank's wife. To reward Wajari for his bravery, as Chumpi did not claim Senur for himself, Tukupi had handed Yurank's widow over to my *amik*, who took her to the Kapawi where he made her his second wife. Accompanying Senur were her daughter Suwitiar – whom Wajari later gave in marriage to Mukuimp – her young son Sumpa and Yurank's mother, Awasant, who now lives in Mukuimp's house. By carrying off Tsitsink,

Tukupi automatically became the 'father' of Senur, Entza and Chawir, her daughters from her first marriage. When Wajari, on a subsequent visit with Senur to his 'father-in-law', had there met the young Entza, he had had no difficulty in winning her for his third wife. However, these tragic events now seem very distant and the harmony that prevails in the households of Wajari and Mukuimp gives no hint of the fact that four of the five women living there were originally war captives, distributed in summary fashion to the very men who had helped to kill their fathers, sons and husbands. The dislocation of family lives caused by vendettas, and the murders, separations and seizures of women that periodically afflict them are thus partially mitigated by the affectionate treatment received by the captives. The abductions and enforced adoptions, initially acts of violence, are in time overcome, and the hostility of the past fades into a domestic intimacy that sometimes proves even more harmonious than it would have been were it the fruit of free consent.

The people of Capahuari regard Tukupi as the 'great man', *juunt*, of the entire Sasaïme region. This is a term of respect given to a courageous man (*kakaram*) whom his peers acknowledge to be the leader of their warrior faction, by virtue of his tactical intelligence and his charisma. In a society where adult men are equal and dependent upon nobody but themselves and in which the supreme masculine quality is bravery in combat and the risks of stopping a bullet are high, to acquire and preserve such pre-eminence is no mean feat. Apart from unfailing courage, attested by many personal exploits, a *juunt* needs a certain theatrical flair and a definite oratorical skill. His mastery of speech in dialogue enables him to convince, win over and dominate, intimidating reticent allies and potential enemies alike as he manifests a strength of character quite outside the common run. The ardent eloquence of an Achuar great man is not designed to promote public well-being, harmony or virtue, as it is in other South American tribes, in which leaders without any effective authority relentlessly churn out edifying homilies to which nobody pays the slightest attention. Unlike those powerless sermonizers, a *juunt* always brings the force of his convictions to bear upon one particular interlocutor whose support or distrust he is anxious to assess. He is a skilful manoeuvrer, adept at resorting to lies when he deems it necessary and passionately committed to his own glorious reputation and the prestige of his own faction. As such, he is more likely to be a warmonger than a peacemaker.

Such a career can only be pursued with the active compliance of a number of wives. To gather together a group of kin and allies willing to commit themselves to armed action with him, a great man must make a show of unfailing hospitality. Here, the help of his wives proves indispensable since it is they who provide the meals and serve the inexhaustible manioc beer. A *juunt* also needs to be a good hunter, with a supply of fresh or smoked meat always to hand, for to fail to serve game to a guest would be dishonouring. The degree of a great man's munificence is gauged in altogether concrete fashion by the size of his gardens and his house, the diligence of his wives and the abundance of his meat, for these are all elements that contribute to his ability to make numerous visitors welcome in all circumstances.

The acquisition of wives is as much a result of a leader's political strategy as it is a means to further his enterprises. Of course, vendettas provide a chance to appropriate the wives of other men without owing anything in return, since the obligations to provide assistance normally contracted towards one's affines are in these circumstances waived by the very state of hostility that made the seizure of the women possible in the first place. The systematic practice of levirate, which provides for a man to marry the widows of his brothers, is also a convenient way of increasing one's family in a society in which many men die before reaching full maturity. Thanks to this institution, familiar to us from the Bible, the bravest or luckiest of a group of brothers may progressively come to profit from the fertility and labour of his sisters-in-law, thus fulfilling some of the social conditions necessary to become a *juunt*. However, as a young Achuar never goes off to war before he is married and normally then does so under the wing of his father-in-law, the cycle of marriages is usually activated in less dramatic circumstances. The choice of a first wife obeys one very simple rule: a man must take her from amongst the daughters of either his maternal uncles or his paternal aunts, and all the young women who fall into this category are addressed by him as *waje*. When marriage to a genuine *waje* proves impossible it becomes necessary to fall back upon more distant 'cousins', the daughters of the brothers or sisters of the spouses of his parents' siblings of the opposite sex. Thus Tukupi married first his *waje* Yapan, the daughter of his father's sister, then Shamich, also a *waje* but a more distant one: the daughter of the brother of Yapan's father. Later, he married Yamanoch, the widow of Yapan's brother – a somewhat irregular marriage – Tsitsink, whom he took from Jimpikit, then Pirisant, the widow of his brother Wampush who had been killed in a vendetta, and finally Ishkui, whom he had seized from Tiriruk but whom the latter subsequently regained.

Marriage between cross-cousins – to use the customary terminology of ethnologists – is common to many peoples in all latitudes. Contrary to what our own customs might lead us to think, this is not considered a marriage between blood-relatives since, in such a system, the brothers of your mother, the sisters of your father and their children are all considered to be relatives by marriage, whereas the brothers of your father, the sisters of your mother and their children are regarded as your blood-relatives. Among the Achuar, marriage with a *waje* periodically helps to tighten already close links between neighbouring kindred, which can in this way reproduce themselves and perpetuate their alliances within a very restricted circle of endogamy. Strengthening the chain of marriages within a very limited social network, whose members are attached to it by one or more genealogical connections, tends to establish a web of family solidarities, constantly sustained by the commitments to mutual assistance expected of close blood-relatives and relatives by marriage. The unassailable complicity that links Washikta and Tukupi in vendetta wars is thus founded upon the extreme intricacy of their relations as affines, for in the first place the mother of Washikta was the sister of Tukupi's father; secondly, each gave the other his own sister in marriage; thirdly, the son of Tukupi's brother, adopted by Tukupi after the father's death, is married to Washikta's daughter; and fourthly, Washikta's son is married to the daughter of Chawir, whom Tukupi carried off years ago along with her mother Tsitsink.

To become the pivot of a faction that is at all durable, a great man needs to create around him a wider kindred than the one bequeathed to him by his parents. His brothers and one or two of his loyal affines – such as Washikta, in Tukupi's case – make up the initial kernel, to which more diversified relatives by marriage are then gradually added. In order to be able to call upon a large group of brothers-in-law who are likely to come to his aid, he must first find himself wives from a number of different families and put their members under an obligation to himself by giving his sisters in marriage to them. The affines of his brothers and the brothers of his own closest relatives by marriage also come to swell the ranks of those from whom he can request aid, although in their case support for his projects is not a foregone conclusion. Eventually, as he grows older, the *juunt* comes to control a group of dependants who owe him personal allegiance: first and foremost, his sons, but also his sons-in-law, who are obliged by custom to live for several years in the house of their father-in-law or at least very close by. The sons of a great man, however, are not subject to such a rule of residence; and it is perhaps this exception to the common norm that most clearly manifests the special status of a leader: to ensure the support of his male children for as long as possible, a great man will arrange for them to marry orphans or the daughters of men who live far away and are marginal figures anyway, incapable of resisting pressure from such a redoubtable relative by marriage. Here again, Tukupi presents an exemplary model of success for, on the strength of his own kindred and that of his brother-in-law Washikta, he can at the present time count upon the active support of half a dozen men of his own generation and a dozen or so younger warriors, all of them sons, sons-in-law or nephews of his.

Constructing networks of alliance and mobilizing them when vendettas arise are easier when the closest of the kin and affines live little more than one day's march or canoe journey apart from one another. The ideal is to marry as close as possible, both genealogically and geographically, that is to say within a zone whose topography and inhabitants have been familiar ever since childhood. The biographies of our Capahuari companions had already suggested to us that this might be so and all that we are learning about the Sasaïme region definitely confirms it. What is new here, though, is the evident political aspect to the role of Tukupi, who is recognized as war-leader by a large proportion of his kindred and who is thus better placed than anyone to represent to outsiders the social identity of the territory in which his presence is so decisive. In Capahuari Naanch and Tsukanka no doubt to a certain extent play the role of great men, but in a very minor way: since the missionaries' influence has begun to make itself felt in their region, no serious conflict has afforded them a chance to confirm their prestige by acting as effective faction leaders.

*　　*　　*

Seizing the opportunity presented by a lull in the series of conversations between Tukupi and the Capahuari men, Washikta turns to Kawarunch and launches into a violent attack on him in the 'slow talk' mode. He asks him if the rumours that he killed Ikiam are true, reproaches him bitterly for disturbing the peace of the region, accuses him of misleading Yaur, the victim's brother, with rancorous talk that incriminates Washikta himself, and calls upon Tsukanka to testify to the gravity of these accusations. This show of virulence is clearly put on solely for our benefit. Given that Washikta lives quite close to Kawarunch, he is most unlikely to have waited until now to tackle him about a matter that already goes back several months. Under the mocking eye of Tukupi, Kawarunch vehemently protests his innocence, invoking the sacred link that binds him to his *amik* Yaur and ascribing to Washikta the responsibility for any troubles that may arise from such unbridled slander. With the fury of the two men mounting, Tsukanka eventually intervenes to calm things down, producing a barrage of mollifying pronouncements on the need to avoid discord between kinsmen and the seemliness that should always be observed in dialogues between them.

Kawarunch is clearly the black sheep of the Sasaïme region. He is brother-in-law to both Tukupi and Washikta and used to be their ally in vendettas, but now he is out in the cold, isolated on the other side of the Pastaza by a fog of malicious gossip. A certain Tuntuam is said to share his disgrace; although a cousin of Tukupi's and a 'branch' brother to Washikta, he too has fallen out with them and pays frequent visits to Kawarunch, whose sister he has married. The faction that a great man such as Tukupi has the power to mobilize when a conflict arises does not necessarily include all the men living in his area of influence. There will always be one or two of his kinsmen who are estranged from him as a result of mutual resentment and will consequently refuse to play his game. The chances for such antipathies to arise and the total freedom of action that each man is recognized to possess stand in the way of the establishment of any real local power, for they make it impossible for anyone ever to exercise lasting authority over kinsmen perpetually liable to fall out with one another. Despite the respectful awe that he inspires, despite the prestige that surrounds him and despite all the warriors upon whose assistance he may call, Tukupi is not a chief, since nobody is forced to accept his authority.

Washikta has invited us to visit him, so we make our long-winded farewells and all depart in his wake, except Kawarunch, who returns home, visibly fuming with rage. Keeping his eyes skinned and his rifle loaded, Washikta for a while leads us through an alluvial forest of tall trees until we reach another big garden. My travelling companions enthuse about the exuberance and wide variety of the cultivated plants, commenting on the vigorous growth of the groundnuts and beans, the size of the cocoa trees, the diversity of the types of pimento and manioc and the thickly spreading banana trees. In contrast to the compact, heavy earth of Capahuari, the soil here is dark and light, its fertility constantly regenerated by the river silt. After all our plodding through the wet clay of the hills and the mud of the marshes, it offers my feet, finally unshod and martyred by blisters, a marvellous, warm and resilient carpet.

A succulent repast awaits us at Washikta's house, our first since the day before yesterday: smoked peccary done to a turn and a peanut soup with boiled manioc leaves masquerading as spinach. But Auju, despite the quiet exhortations of Tsukanka, refuses to eat. Mukuimp later explains to me that, suspecting Washikta of having killed Ikiam, as she does, she fears poisoning if she eats game shot by the rifle that was probably used to kill her uncle. The appetite of the other diners, however, is not inhibited by this instrumental contagion, since it only affects the blood-relatives of the victim. The Achuar belief is that the weapon feeds upon the blood of the creatures it kills and as a result those animals become partially contaminated. Since blood-relatives are reputed literally to share the same blood, serious physiological complaints are caused when their blood comes into contact with itself through the intermediary of some slaughtered animal. In this inside-out kind of immunology, whatever is identical is harmful: hence the taboo known as *kinchimiartin* that obtains against such a rifle.

A large number of women are bustling about in Washikta's household. Of the seven wives married by Washikta, two have been killed in wars and two others died during a measles epidemic. The youngest, a particularly attractive young woman, no doubt helps to console him in his old age. Most of the children remain confined to the *ekent*, but one little girl aged six or seven is serving the manioc beer. She is adorned like an adult, with patterns of rocou on her face, a coil of *shauk* around her neck and many woven ribbons wound about her wrists and ankles. She is married to Samiruk, the son-in-law of the master of the house, a big, strong lad whose cheerfulness seems unaffected by his enforced sexual abstinence until such time as his young wife begins to menstruate. Marriage with prepubescent girls is much favoured by my companions as they believe it engenders in them a lasting attachment to their husband, forged at a time in their lives when learning how to be a wife is still a kind of game. As the child's domestic accomplishments still leave something to be desired, it is Samiruk's mother, Pirisant, who oversees the proceedings. This fat old woman, always wreathed in smiles, is the widow of Wampush, the brother of Tukupi, and was taken over by the latter as his own wife after her husband was killed. She has not been repudiated formally, but she seems to prefer exercising her maternal solicitude in Washikta's household to living with a husband already well provided with other wives.

Night has fallen and only one resin torch now illuminates the *tanka-mash*. The flickering light seems to reanimate the remains of a harpy-eagle pinned to the wall by chonta thorns, its white wings spanning over two metres, like some fantastical effigy. After the tension of our earlier visits, and with the aid of darkness and full stomachs, the atmosphere has become noticeably more relaxed. Washikta picks this moment to present Tsukanka with his rifle.

'Here, my *amik*, take this for me!'

'Right, right,' is the only response of the recipient.

He does not appear particularly bothered by the suspicion that Washikta may have killed Ikiam with this weapon. Despite the gravity of insinuation in Auju's refusal to eat, she has not been deterred from her resolve. Squatting at the edge of the *ekent*, she stares at the long, gleaming object with an inscrutable gaze.

CHAPTER 12

Love in the Plural

WAJARI SEEMS IN excellent heart after his evening bathe with Entza. From Picham's house, where we are staying, I can see them teasing each other like a couple of turtle doves as they return along the sandy path leading from the Pastaza, close by. The reason for Wajari asking Picham for hospitality during our stay at Sasaïme is that Picham is his *amik* as well as sharing the redoubtable honour of being one of Tukupi's sons-in-law. Chawir, our host's wife, is a sister of Senur and Entza, one of the three Graces carried off in the past by Tukupi, along with their mother Tsitsink. Tsitsink now lives with Chawir and the evident happiness that these fate-tossed women clearly feel at being reunited infuses the friendly complicity of Wajari's and Picham's relationship. The master of the house is a jovial fellow anyway, a robust man aged about thirty, who invariably coquettishly sports an *itip*. With his regular-featured but heavy face framed by long, floating locks, he irresistibly puts me in mind of a rugby player in drag.

Gripping the giggling Entza by the ear, Wajari makes a triumphal entrance.

'Look, my *amik*, look at the big fish that I have caught. She couldn't resist my big hook!'

Senur mockingly remarks, 'Yet there's not much flesh on your hook to make it alluring. Perhaps you would do better to go out and hunt a coati!'

Everyone snorts with laughter, in particular Picham whose laughs are punctuated by repeated exclamations of '*hey ya!*' – a sign of the utmost hilarity. Senur's barb was well aimed. The penis of the coati rejoices in a long fine bone that keeps it constantly rigid. This anatomical peculiarity has made a forceful impression upon the imagination of the Indians, and the men make the most of it, grating the bone into a decoction of green tobacco to make a love philtre. Quaffed at the right moment, it is reputed to prevent or remedy any flagging of the male member.

The boldness of Senur's joke took me by surprise. It reflects the general harmony that reigns in Wajari's family and also a certain liberty of tone that I have noticed in my friends since our arrival at Sasaïme. The few days' jaunt away from home has been enough to overcome the modest discretion that normally characterizes relations between the sexes. In public, spouses remain apart, seldom speak to one another and rarely use terms of affection. Even the best-assorted couples refrain from jokes in front of spectators. This restraint is not occasioned by embarrassment but rather results from a deliberate censoring of vigorous sexuality, any excessive manifestation of which seems to be feared. The slightest risqué irony between a man and a woman is normally immediately interpreted as an unmistakable invitation to make love.

Ribaldry amongst men is also frowned upon, as it suggests an offensive derision of virility. 'Am I a woman that you should talk like that to me?' Tarir severely said the other day to his younger brother Tseremp, who was clownishly offering him his penis in exchange for some curare. This fear of blurring the differences between the sexes no doubt explains how it is that overt, or even covert, homosexuality seems unheard of here. To be sure, here as anywhere else adolescent boys are sometimes aroused by sexual desire for the long-familiar bodies of their male companions. When two of Tsukanka's boys were recently discovered trying to sodomize each other everybody made a great fuss, but in a joking way that belied the supposed gravity of their turpitude. Their father, however, was by no means amused and the severity of the drubbing that he meted out to them both perhaps explains how it is that such inclinations tend subsequently to be repressed. The Achuar have on several occasions told me with genuine horror of the existence of 'women-men' amongst the Quichuas of the Bobonaza, homosexuals who make pottery, work in the gardens, prepare the meals and behave in every way as real women. The reprobation prompted by such behaviour expresses not so much a moral judgement as repugnance in the face of any confusion between domains and categories whose absolute separation is deemed necessary for the world to run properly.

183

Senur's quip also testifies to her good relationship with her sister. Wajari and Entza have obviously just been making love on an isolated beach and their happy mood of satisfied lovers prompted Senur to recall with irony her own rights over the virility of the man whom the two women share. It was not really a matter of her being put out, simply an expression of the complicity that has to exist between wives with healthy sexual appetites. Given the jealousy that is always bound to threaten the concord of polygamous households, a husband's successful accomplishment of his conjugal duties calls for various precautions, in particular the avoidance of overt transports of love within the over-populated household precinct. So, when a husband takes one of his wives hunting or to bathe with him in some out-of-the-way place, his other wives are well aware of the pleasures in store for the couple. If the husband scrupulously respects each wife's turn and is vigorous enough to satisfy them all reasonably regularly, this cyclic sexuality is generally tolerated perfectly well. According to Mukuimp's confidences to me, a neglected wife will not hesitate to make her desires explicit by seizing hold of her husband's penis as soon as an opportunity arises. But such familiarities are rare and indicate an exceptional degree of rancour. Modesty dictates that women be more or less passive in the sexual act, and their full and rapid satisfaction does not appear to require any of the erotic subtleties that Mukuimp learned of with increasing astonishment as the systematic questions that I put to him revealed the inventiveness in this domain displayed by other cultures. It must be said that, with its high concentration of unpleasant insects and hostile plants, nature in these latitudes is hardly conducive to prolonged bouts of outdoor amorous dalliance.

To satisfy the carnal desires of a wife is also to contribute to her domestication. Achuar men hold that it is necessary literally to work on their wives' bodies in order to tame their native wildness and train them for conjugal cohabitation. Marrying barely nubile little girls means that the Achuar can make an early start on this labour of familiarization deemed necessary for a successful marriage. By dint of a mixture of sex and physical coercion women captured from enemies are schooled to their new condition. In response to my discreet amazement that Senur had never tried to run away after being carried off, Wajari told me how he had proceeded.

'At first, it is important to get very angry. I told her, "If you do not come along with me, I shall kill you on the spot." She was frightened and followed me. In the early days I never let her out of my sight; I even accompanied her when she went to piss or shit; and I went with her when she fetched manioc from the garden. I never left her side. She cried a lot, never spoke and wanted to run off to her brother. So I threatened to kill her and she kept quiet. I wanted her to forget Yurank, so I made love to her as soon as possible. She didn't want to, she used to cry and hit me with her fists; but women are like us: they can't live without sex, so as I "worked" on her a lot, she soon got used to me.'

The idea that sexuality has a part to play in the taming of women does not simply reflect a male delusion – though the men are prompt, as ever, to disguise the domination they impose upon their companions with fantasies that they like to persuade themselves are shared. For up to a point the women go along with this naturalistic vision of conjugal relations. They like to see themselves as tame little animals, incapable of surviving alone in the big, wide world and dependent upon the patience and tenderness of their master if they are to flourish fully. One gets an idea of the disarming poetic element in this self-image if one listens to the *anent* that wives sing on their own in the garden, unbeknownst to their husbands, in order to influence their feelings. Here is one example, in which Mamati implicitly likens herself to a silky marmoset or a saimiri, one of the little monkeys that Achuar of all ages tend to carry around, clinging to their legs or hair:

My little father, my dear little father, my little father, your little thighs
    delight me
My little father, your little thighs attract me
My dear little father, I talk to your little bronzed testicles
My little father, I withdraw from your little thighs, I talk to them and
    cherish them tenderly
My little father, your little gob of spit, I love it
My dear father, your little thighs attract me
I love your little torso, I miss it when I let go of it.

The use of the term 'father' to refer to a husband is a conventional mark of respect common to all women's *anent*. It implies that subjugation to a husband is simply a prolongation of a father's guardianship over his daughters. Even in the tenderly erotic context of an *anent* which is, in principle, secret, the respect due to the head of the family rules out the use of any affectionate nickname. In contrast, fathers and husbands have no compunction about calling their daughters and wives amusing names: 'mosquito' or 'little thighs' for the former, 'little scrap' or 'little mouse' for the latter.

However, male domination is not as complete as the men like to imagine or as the women are content to let them think. In the first place, the women enjoy the episodic independence afforded them by certain reserved spaces. One is, of course, the garden, their own domain of accomplishment, bathed in the benevolent protection of Nunkui, the theatre of an unrestricted sociability that brings together children, close female friends and the plant people, and a place of refuge where a woman can pour out her sorrow at times of conjugal crisis or bereavement. Equally, there is the *ekent*, the centre *par excellence* of domestic life, where the women are not so much confined as entrenched and from which they exclude all men except their husband. Sole mistresses, as they are, of the cooking and the manioc beer, the women maintain an altogether fearsome hold over their husband through the degree of alacrity they choose to display in serving him; embattled in his arrogant virility, the poor man cannot fend for his own food and drink without losing face. An unwillingness or a refusal to prepare his meals constitutes a classic means for the women to express resentment and as a rule it soon results in bringing a flighty or over-brutal husband to heel. There are, of course, masculine *anent* appropriate to this not uncommon situation. Here is an example, in which Titiar tries to arouse his wife's pity by comparing himself to an abandoned baby bird:

> Your anger, your painful anger has brought me to this
> With nothing to eat, I remain sitting here, abandoned, calling upon
>   the deity
> Drying my ruffled feathers, I huddle here
> Because of your anger, your refusal to nourish me
> Here I sit, alone and full of shame, invoking the deity
> In a leafless tree, drying my ruffled feathers, I huddle here without
>   consolation.

Maltreated wives are not alone in their resentment. The obligation imposed upon young men to live for several years in the house of their parents-in-law, where they are bound to show them an unfailing deference and are constantly under the scrutiny of the entire watchful household, weaves around them such a web of moral constraints that, in these conditions, very few venture to beat their wife. However, Antunish did do so. He is a pretty boy with a languorous eye who has recently arrived in Capahuari from the upper Copataza, fleeing the impossible life to which his father-in-law subjected him on account of his treatment of his wife. Touchy but charming nonetheless, he had made his escape with an extremely pretty girl over whom he can now lord it as he pleases. Even when a young husband at last wins his longed-for independence by setting up his own household, he is not free from the discreet surveillance of his wife's family, particularly her brothers, who make no bones about their displeasure if they discover that their sister is unhappy, as Tseremp's father learned to his fatal cost. Despite the remonstrations of his affines, he continued to beat one of his wives so badly that she eventually fell ill and died. One of her relatives was so angry that, soon after, he killed her husband. The fact is that a wife never belongs completely to her husband; he must always get along with those who gave her to him and who retain lasting rights over her. The only way to avoid being perpetually indebted in this way is to marry an orphan, an inglorious last resort fit only for the 'paltry' (*suri*), dry-hearted men who manage in this way to reign undisputed and without check over waifs of fortune. Unfortunate women with no family depend particularly heavily upon *anent* designed to conciliate a churlish husband or even to frighten him, as in the following desolate song in which Mamati intimates that she is a Jurijri, a subterranean spirit and master of game, who devours over-greedy hunters:

My husband, you anger me so much
That, making the earth shake and disappearing into the ground, I shall
    leave to be reunited with my little children
Making the earth shake, I shall leave
'Yet I knew it would end like this with me losing my temper so badly
    with my wife'
That is what you will say, my little father
Always cross with me
Do not provoke my anger
Reunited with my little children, I shall leave, making the earth shake

My father who will miss me, suddenly switching from resentment to a
longing for my little children.

Some wives have particularly strong characters. It is not that they
are nags; they are simply women with forceful personalities, never at
a loss, and possessed of a sharp tongue. One such is, of course, our
friend Senur who, the other day, seeing Wajari preparing to go hunting alone, grabbed a machete and a basket and, unleashing her dogs,
called out imperiously, 'Wait for me, Wajari, I'm coming too!' an
authoritative action that not many women would dare to take. Her
daughter Suwitiar is not to be outdone, no doubt having learned
from her mother's example. She is a fine woman of twenty-five, with
a powerful build like her mother's and a dimpled, teasing face framed
by thickly flowing, sensual locks. Learning of her husband's plan
to marry another of Wajari's daughters, she told Mukuimp, only
half-jokingly, 'If you marry one of my sisters, I shall take your brother
as my lover!' A discontented wife may take advantage of the presence
of strangers in the household to make a public show of her independence, so as to embarrass her husband. For instance, a wife relaxing
in the *ekent* may pretend not to hear her husband when he asks her
to bring manioc beer for a visitor. If the master of the house gets
angry, usually to no avail, he will be judged to lack the quiet confidence
that is the mark of a proper man; on the other hand, if he takes no
notice he will appear weak, incapable of keeping order even within
his family, and when his wife at last consents to stir and comply, with
a bad grace, to his request, all the mortified husband can do is shoot
a brief, murderous glare at her. No doubt because only very few
women venture to go further, wives are very skilful at inflicting silent
humiliations upon their husbands. The life of an unlucky or inept
hunter is not a happy one. His return from hunting is never commented on, whether or not he brings home game. But when he
returns yet again empty-handed, how very heavy is the silence that
greets him! How tightly lips are pursed when hopes are dashed! And
then, what a clatter of dishwashing, to cover the sighs!

Age and status reinforce the temperaments of certain self-asserting
wives whom the men consider almost as their equals. This is generally
the case with wives who have reached the years of maturity and who
rule as despotic mistresses over a cohort of young girls and terrorize

188

their sons-in-law, women who speak their minds and do not hesitate to intervene in the men's conversations as they serve them manioc beer, or who make loud comments from the depths of the *ekent*. Whether they pretend to ignore them or reply in joking fashion, the husbands and their guests take these interventions from the women's seat of power by no means lightly. A wife with a dominating personality is frequently the first one, the *tarimiat*, since her very chronological precedence bestows on her a certain pre-eminence in the household. Of course, it sometimes happens that a second wife, older than the *tarimiat*, ends up by exercising an authority that the *tarimiat* visibly lacks. This is the case in Wajari's household where, despite the fact that she was married first, Mirunik's position is much less authoritative than Senur's and is undermined by the exclusive complicity that binds Senur to her sister Entza. Generally, however, a *tarimiat* seeks to retain her rank: the other wives address her with respect, especially if they are much younger, and she enjoys certain formal prerogatives, such as the right to distribute the game when her husband has been hunting on his own, and also to make her own particular point of view predominate when a new garden is being divided into allotments.

As new wives come to swell the ranks in the household, the older ones make up for what they lose in demonstrations of affection by what they gain in authority. The men's justification of polygamy is perfectly straightforward: however attractive and tender a young wife may be, eventually a man's erotic ardour tires of her and new attractions must then be found to revive it. Since the sexual novelty of new wives wears off at regular intervals, the only limits to the cycle of remarriage are the husband's vigour and his ability to obtain and support new wives. Tseremp, who has come into marginal contact with the big, outside world in the camps of petroleum workers, cogently sums up the philosophy of repeated marriages: 'Why do the Whites say that you should not have several wives? They have mistresses and they pay to sleep with tarts, whereas we, the Achuar, do not change wives, we simply add to them.' Then he goes on, clearly referring to his own situation, 'It's very hard having only one wife. There are times when you can't make love to her, when she has just had a child and is not yet "dry", when she has the "moon blood" or when she is ill. With several wives, we no longer have to suffer.'

'Adding wives', the expression for polygamous marriage, also makes it possible for a husband to rise above a first, unsuccessful union without repudiating the wife; and this spares him the anger of his father-in-law. Sometimes the initiative comes from the first young wife herself: Chumapi, the son-in-law of Titiar, who was secretly sleeping with the younger sister of his wife Pincian, claims that it was Pincian herself who, probably at the instigation of her mother, pushed the girl into his arms in order to force him to marry her. By making the first move in this way, a *tarimiat* prepares for the future: she ensures that she will not be abandoned if her husband wearies of her and, rather than find herself one day supplanted by a stranger, she herself chooses a close relative with whom she knows she can get along well. In the long run, however, Pincian's manoeuvre failed, as her sister is ardently and platonically in love with the handsome Antunish, despite the favours that she bestows upon Chumapi who, feeling offended, now wants no more to do with her.

Even cumulative unions with sisters cannot guarantee concord in a household. Despite the clout that they wield, the elder wives may find it hard to tolerate the enthusiasm with which their husband regularly slips away with his latest wife and they will miss no chance to get their own back, criticizing the favourite and accusing her of neglecting her domestic duties. Conversely, because the men tend to make up for their lukewarm affections with generous presents of *shauk*, cooking pots and lengths of cloth, the younger wives may complain that the *tarimiat* is getting unfair preferential treatment. Bad relations between wives seldom escalate into guerrilla warfare – the husband sees to that – but they do create a grumpy atmosphere soon sensed by any observer. This is the case, for instance, in Titiar's house, where his two wives Wawar and Wirisam get along notoriously badly. Wawar, a skinny little woman with a bilious face puckered with bitterness, is in every way a contrast to Wirisam, the second wife, a robust matron with a misleadingly cheery look, always spoiling for a fight. In this house where discord reigns, the dogs scrap all day long, no doubt sensing the antipathy between their respective mistresses. The children of the two families quarrel on the slightest pretext, with their respective mothers loudly championing their own brood and criticizing the poor upbringing of the other brats. Meanwhile, Wawar's mother grumbles away in one corner and Titiar's, who tends to favour Wirisam, complains in another, neither of these toothless crones having addressed a single direct word to the other for many a long day. Although a full-blown row never quite erupts, the scene is one of shrill complaints, bitter recriminations, cross faces and constant niggles over nothing.

Such dissension would not be tolerated in Tsukanka's household. Throughout his conjugal career he has imposed domestic order through violence. First he married Masuk, the sister of Wajari and Titiar, next Tsapak, a 'branch' sister of Masuk, and Inkis, a distant cousin. When the Shuar carried off the head of his brother Arias, Tsukanka took over his three wives, paying no attention to the protestations of his other brother, who had naively been hoping to share them. Of those three, Tsukanka killed one, suspecting adultery, the second ran away to escape his ill-treatment and the third, Auju, tried to commit suicide a little while ago by taking a dose of fishing poison. The poor woman was in despair – presumably she loved him – because her insatiable brute of a husband had just obtained Inkis's young sister, for whom he had long been badgering her father Uwejint, a noble old man who had taken refuge with his daughter a day's march away from Capahuari, fearing reprisals provoked by his initial refusal.

Tsukanka is selectively violent, that is to say he spares those wives whose brothers might turn nasty on their sister's behalf. Thus, the unfortunate woman whom he killed with a rifle shot – as she was swimming across the Kapawi to escape from his blows – was never avenged as she had no close relatives. Public opinion, particularly amongst the women, still blames Tsukanka for this crime, judged to be gratuitous since the infidelity of which he accused the dead woman was, it is said, a figment of his own imagination. And while nothing can protect an adulterous woman from being pumped full of buck-shot if she is caught *in flagrante delicto*, in contrast suspicions alone – sometimes well-founded but difficult to prove, given the precautions that lovers tend to take – normally occasion no more than a rain of blows. So Tsukanka's violence is not so much exceptional as deemed to be excessive, for all the men consider they have a right to beat wives who displease them.

Apart from counting on vigilance on the part of her blood-relatives, a woman can do little about such brutality. However moving it may be, an *anent* does not always do the trick. Flight, though common enough, is dangerous; a strike in the kitchen will not work if there is little solidarity between the wives in the household; and suicide, even more rare, does not suit all temperaments. On the other hand, good relations between the various wives, forged in the course of their shared sufferings, may occasionally result in their making common cause against their brutal husband. That is exactly what happened to Tsukanka. Having planned a journey of several days with other Capahuari men to seek out a possible location for a new village, he found himself exposed to public ridicule at the moment of departure because his wives had ignored his instructions to prepare the parcels of manioc paste indispensable as provisions for the journey. Speechless with fury, he was obliged to delay the departure before the amused eyes of the other men.

Marital violence is so much a part of daily life that it is turned into a game by the children. In Washikta's house yesterday, I saw a little boy chasing his sister, yelling imprecations and brandishing a machete, whilst she fled before him, her hands protectively clutching her head, and her pleas for conjugal clemency repeatedly interrupted by peals of laughter. The realism of the game was striking. It is with blows to the head, dealt with the flat side of the machete blade, that men belabour their spouses; more rarely, in bursts of incontrollable rage, they even use the cutting edge, leaving deep gashes in the skin of the wife's skull and causing blood to course down the poor woman's face.

The sight of a woman being beaten is one that severely tests the obligation of neutrality that an ethnologist imposes upon himself on the principle that it is necessary to respect the cultures whose logic he is trying to understand; he is also disinclined to foist upon other people a morality that is of no use to them. Having learned from the missionaries that the Whites frown upon such brutality, the Achuar of Capahuari abstain from maltreating their wives in our presence, the more so since it is not seemly for a man to lose control of himself before a stranger to the household. So it was only in the course of bandaging the wounds and bruises of various women that we learned of their conjugal trials. A little earlier I had already tried to reason with Naanch who, in a fit of anger, had broken the arm of one of his wives. Yet the man certainly does not look like a domestic tyrant: he is a charming forty-year-old with a distinguished and ironical face reminiscent of certain Italian screen actors, and he appears to get along very well with his wives who, moreover, seem from their behaviour to be very much in love with him. In his melodious, serene voice, Naanch had responded to my reproaches by dismissing the affair as one of no importance and observing that he naturally had to impose order when a quarrel broke out between his six wives, that the Achuar had always acted thus without anyone complaining about it, and that he was surprised to hear me talking like the evangelist missionaries, since up until now I had been more inclined to scoff at their absurd ideas.

This lecture in cultural relativism had disconcerted me and, in an attempt to overcome an indignation that repetition ended up by blunting anyway, I had come to interpret the Achuar's conjugal violence not so much as the expression of a natural brutality but rather as a way of inuring their women to social life by blows, similar in its intentions to their symbolic taming of their wives through sexuality. The idea – in truth, a very common one – that women are in the main on the side of nature presupposes not only that men must educate them in the art of day-to-day living (a good wife must be *unuim*, 'receptive to her apprenticeship') but that women are bound also to bear the stigmata of a masculine law that is presented as the incarnation of culture. Just as, in many societies, tattoos and scar marks on a body judged to have been too naked, too natural or too insignificant testify to the social dimensions of an individual's personality and to the collective constraints that fashion it, so too the scars with which Achuar husbands criss-cross the skulls of their wives might be seen as an indelible sign of their successful domestication.

My companions of both sexes furthermore claim that men are temperamentally *kajen*, 'disposed to anger' – not that there is anything particularly natural about this propensity: right from their earliest infancy, little boys' tantrums of rage are received with amused indulgence, even with secret approval, as an indication of their strength of character, whereas little girls are sternly reprimanded if they ever deviate from the reserve deemed appropriate to their condition. Fury thus seems to be considered as inevitably bound up with the masculine condition – not anything to be proud about since it testifies to a lack of self-control, but not really a handicap either, since it promotes a warrior's bravery. In practice, the men do cultivate their anger, just as one cultivates a talent, seeking, as they grow older, to adapt it to the circumstances and to control its theatrical expression, but never attempting to prevent its eruption. The ritualization of warfare and its inevitable strategic considerations generally introduce quite a long delay between a man's flash of anger at an insult and its outlet in combat. In a society in which masculine domination is extremely marked, the women, because they are close at hand, become the victims of this character trait, presumed to be innate in their menfolk, whenever it cannot be used to more glorious ends. Intellectually satisfying though these explanations may be, they are, to tell the truth, of little comfort morally. Yet seeking rational explanations to assuage the feelings of revolt provoked by practices that clash with their own beliefs is the only recourse for ethnologists, who are condemned by the very nature of their task not to set themselves up as censors of those who have given them their trust.

However undeniable and detestable, the all too common violence of husbands does not exclude a delicacy of feeling, even an almost romantic concept of the sensibility of love. Thus, despite the swaggering attitude they are prone to affect, young men are subject to attacks of languor into which they are plunged by an unsatisfied longing for feminine tenderness. Like so many young Chateaubriands wandering in the woods of Combourg in quest of an elusive Sylphide, they roam, lovesick, through the forest, yearning to discover a shared love into which to pour their overflowing, unfocused emotions. Their confused sentimentality can sometimes make do with fleeting and clandestine liaisons with girls of their own age or an older woman, but these affairs do not provide an outlet for a more abstract distress. 'Acting the humming-bird', as juvenile Don Juanism is called, is not devoid of excitement since the risks involved are considerable: a jealous husband will not hesitate to shoot you and you may pay with your life for taking the virtue of a virgin, if her brothers take against you. But adolescent sexuality such as this does not deliver young men from their distress since it belongs to a different register of life: it merely constitutes an initiation to pleasures of love that are seen as play, and it seldom leads to any lasting attachment.

In its most extreme form, lovesickness becomes a pathological melancholy that is recognized as a personality disorder and is inevitably believed to be caused by some malevolent shaman. It mainly affects young people, men or women, regardless of whether or not they are married. Sinking into depression and self-disgust, particularly at dusk, the victim is seized by suicidal impulses and uncontrollable fits of despair. In Capahuari, Shakaim, a still almost adolescent son-in-law of Naanch's, told me of his own distress. His heart heavy with an indefinable dissatisfaction, each day he contemplates the sunrise and the sunset, silently weeping, convinced, despite all the evidence to the contrary, that his tender young wife no longer loves him. Racked with sobs, he told me of his irrepressible desire to leave his family-in-law, for the sight of the sun poised on the horizon was like the promise of a radiant elsewhere that made his present condition all the more unbearable. Naanch, who is worried about the pitiful state of Shakaim, has decided to take his son-in-law to Montalvo, to get a shaman to cure him of his neurasthenia.

The idea that love is a yearning for impossible fulfilment rather than a state of satisfied happiness is well conveyed by the semantics of the term that is the closest Achuar equivalent: *aneamu* closely combines affection, longing, tenderness, memories, and desire for the presence of the loved one. Its organ is the heart, *ininti*, the seat of thought, emotions and meaning, and also the root of a constellation of related words: *aneajai*, 'I cherish', 'I languish for', 'I am nostalgic for'; *anearjai*, 'I am thinking of'; *anent*, the magic incantation; inintaimprajai, 'I remember'; *inintaimsajai*, 'I think of', 'I act in thought upon', etc. Carnal desire, *kunkatmamu*, and copulation, *nijirmamu*, do not belong to this terminological configuration, indicating that, at least so far as the sense is concerned, the domain of affectivity is relatively separate from that of sexuality. Love is, of course, fuelled by a mutual attraction to the body of one's companion and to the physical qualities that make it desirable, but it is also the fruit of an attachment to moral and social virtues that are quite precisely defined. In a man, women appreciate eloquence, courage, energy, a happy temperament, musical talent, excellence in hunting, and technical skill, while the qualities valued in a woman are a smiling modesty, biddableness, gentleness, skill at domestic tasks, and being a good gardener, weaver and potter. Finally, both men and women should possess an extensive repertory of *anent* songs. Prosaic though some of these virtues may be, in combination they form the desirable image that shapes a lover's ideal.

Again, it is the *anent*, truly poetic glosses on day-to-day life, that best convey the idea that love is first and foremost ravished hope, a nostalgic yearning fuelled by separation. Consider, for example, the following *anent*, sung by Chawir to hasten the return of her husband who has gone off to pay a distant visit or to war. It is designed to stimulate the affection of her absent husband by evoking the possibility of a definitive separation.

My little father, my dear little father, my father, my little father.
Waiting steadfastly on the path, my dear little father, waiting for me
    on the path
'I was truly at her side, I was truly in her arms, I could see her perfectly,
    I have lost my wife,' he says, standing there in the path
My little father, all impatient, motionless, you are burning for me
But I have disappeared, my little father, I have left my beloved father,
    I have vanished into smoke
'Oh no! I'm coming!
My own wife, vanished,' he laments, standing there
'Oh no!' suddenly alert
'Oh no! What is happening to me?'
There you stay, losing your wits, my father, my beloved father, standing
    there, wildly longing to be at my side
'My dear wife,' you imagine yourself putting my trinkets away in a
    basket
'If she is dead, what will become of me? Here I am with her mementoes
    in a basket
Oh dear! And despite all this I used to lose my temper with my wife
When I have buried my wife's little treasures in the bottom of the
    basket, I shall be alone
Her garden will revert to the wild and I, being a man, I shall go
    wandering in distant lands
My death will be solitary
Oh dear! Without my wife it is better to die, I shall say
My wife, in truth, is dead because of me
In my wife's garden, this garden that was hers, in the manioc garden
    where she will never be again, I treated her like that!'
With these words, he remained there in the path, standing there waiting
    for me
Oh! my little creature, stuck there for me, my little father, alone with
    his ardent desire.

There is a poignant narcissism in this savouring of the imagined sorrow of a husband suddenly faced with his ruined happiness and a

solitude so unbearable that it leads him to suicide. 'Wandering in
distant lands' means seeking death in foolhardy confrontations with
enemies. Men, for whom absence is more of a stimulant, are no less
narcissistic than their companions, but in a very different mode, as
can be seen from the following *anent* sung by Jempe for his wife who
has stayed at home:

> You, you like a flight of toucans at twilight, and you my wife
> You may be thinking, 'It is just the end of the day'
> But it is me! It's me!
> It is my blazing head that's approaching, I arrive all radiant
> Incandescent yellow, I come to you
> Singing *kirua*, *kirua*, I drown in the setting sun
> So stay there contemplating me, my wife, my wife, all alone
> 'It is just the twilight,' you may be thinking
> But it is I who am coming to you
> My head is rolling towards you
> I'm coming, all radiant, I'm coming
> Fix your impassive eyes on me
> In your intense gaze I'm drowning in the setting sun!

The melancholy and desire felt by the lonely wife are not caused
by the sun, which she is watching as it sets, but by the tender thoughts
of her distant husband that flock together in the sky like a flight
of toucans. The image condenses two themes characteristic of the
language of emotion: twilight is, *par excellence*, the moment of nostalgia, a brief interlude when thoughts fly more easily to those far away,
and it is the time for those whose bodies or hearts are distant to meet
in the echoless dialogue constituted by the *anent*. As for the toucan,
it is a flamboyant symbol of virile beauty, sexual potency and conjugal
harmony. Wajari tells me that once upon a time the bird was an
ordinary man and it was the lovely Sua who, having tenderly adorned
him with genipa, rocou and cotton, gave him his present appearance.
When this showy bird sings, it is to thank Sua for all his finery.

These songs are certainly moving but – it may be objected – how
can the Achuar feel real love when they have had no say in their
marriage unions, which are for the most part determined by the customary rules and the law of the strongest? The fact is that our Western
tendency to assume that the choice of sexual partners must result

solely from the freely expressed inclinations of the individuals involved makes it hard for many people to believe that conjugal love truly can flourish within the framework of an arranged marriage. Yet this situation which, not so long ago in Europe, prevailed both in the houses of nobility and in many peasant communities is, in truth, less constricting than it may appear.

In the first place, the obligation for men to take wives from the *waje* category – the children of their maternal uncles or their paternal aunts – is not absolutely binding. Some Achuar disregard it. Furthermore, families are so large that virtually everybody is bound to have at his disposal at least a dozen potential consorts in this category, many more if one also counts 'classificatory' *waje* – the progeny of brothers and sisters of the spouses of one's parents' siblings of the opposite sex. This swarm of male and female 'cousins' play together as children, when visits are paid, and develop likes and dislikes which, during adolescence, lead to more durable feelings of affection or antipathy. When boys tell their father or girls their mother about their tender feelings towards one of their cousins, this will probably lead without complications to a love-match. Secondly, the circle of relationships available to young Achuar is very limited. Given the extremely dispersed habitat, the hostility between many neighbouring groups and the resultant insecurity and the infrequent opportunities to bring together large numbers of boys and girls of the same age, everything conspires to limit choices of the heart without those involved being aware of the restriction, since this is as much taken for granted as is our own wide freedom of choice. It should also be added that both polygamy and repudiation offer men a chance of escaping from unhappy first unions, while women may find trickier solutions in divorce or adultery. Fundamentally then, the amorous life of the Achuar is not really so very different from that of the section of humanity which, on the face of things, appears to enjoy greater freedom.

The fact that Anne Christine and I constitute a couple certainly helps to make us seem less exotic in the eyes of the Indians. Day in day out, it projects the image of an emotional and social link which they find all the easier to recognize given that we both make a real effort in public to abide by the rules of matrimonial behaviour prescribed by etiquette. People are rather sorry for me for having only one wife, and several men have given me to understand that they would be happy to give me one of their daughters, a move that would be advantageous to them in view of my supposed wealth since, like all sons-in-law, I should then be subject to the guardianship of my father-in-law and obliged to live in his house. I have so far managed to extricate myself from this awkward situation by invoking the redoubtable figure of Anne Christine's father and how angry he would be if he discovered that I was avoiding my obligations towards him by passing into dependency upon another man. My companion's condition is regarded by the other women as less enviable. Although she quickly won their respect by mastering most of the skills befitting her sex, my persistent inability to provide her with game and my spindly appearance appear to make me a less than tempting conquest.

Although our monogamy no doubt lacks many of the attractions that the Achuar associate with marriage, it nevertheless renders us more human and makes it easier for them to fit us in. Celibacy is certainly considered an incongruity, even an object of ironical commiseration when, as in the case of the Salesian fathers, for example, it is attributed to some physical infirmity. When it results from temporary circumstances, however, it may equally arouse suspicion. An Italian colleague who visited the southern Achuar told me of the distrust with which he was surrounded whenever he arrived in one of their houses and the extreme precautions that he had to take when speaking to a woman, in order to avoid being suspected of seductive designs. An ostensible conjugal relationship, on the other hand, gives the Indians a chance to satisfy their curiosity as to our customs simply by watching us, and to some extent tempers the anxiety to which our foreignness gives rise. In this respect, confirmation of a somewhat comical nature was provided just a little while ago. While Anne Christine and I were washing our threadbare clothes in the muddy water of the Pastaza, surrounded by clouds of mosquitoes, exhausted by several days' march and physically weakened by several months of living in the forest, I allowed our last piece of soap to disappear downstream. This resulted in an acrimonious slanging match, a predictable enough consequence of our somewhat debilitated morale. At this point a canoe approached, filled with an Achuar family unknown to us. At first they manifested considerable alarm at the novel sight of this quarrel between Whites – possibly the first they had ever seen. However, once they realized that this was just a domestic wrangle, they moved on amid relieved but discreet laughter in which we eventually joined. News of this incident soon spread and for several days fuelled the indulgent irony of the people of Sasaïme.

For the Indians, the fact that we are couple, albeit a childless one, has the effect of making our respective individual personalities less visible, masked as they are behind the unsurprising configuration of a classifiable relationship. Our similar behaviour, whether conscious or unconscious, in the exceptional situation of shared isolation in which we find ourselves must also tend to obliterate our respective idiosyncrasies in our hosts' eyes. The strong emotional and cultural links that bind Anne Christine and me together and cause us to react to events in the same way, our use of a language that no other known being speaks, our common mastery of particular skills – writing, photography, surveying – and, finally, our possession of identical everyday objects unfamiliar to the Indians, from rangers-style boots to sleeping bags – all this has the effect of encouraging the Achuar to see the two of us as a generic category of humanity rather than as clearly distinct individuals. To readers surprised at not coming across Anne Christine more frequently in these pages, I must confess that the Achuar perception of us seems to have rubbed off on my own writing and that, although I am the only one actually writing this chronicle, it is in truth a means of expression for both of us, so indissolubly shared were our emotions, experiences and discoveries.

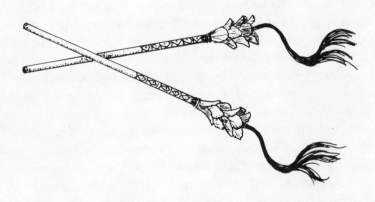

CHAPTER 13

Images from Without,
Images from Within

GREAT EXCITEMENT yesterday morning: the little Missionary Aviation Fellowship plane touched down at Capahuari, bringing us a North American preacher: Don Jaime, as he is known, is a large, squarely built blond fellow, sporting magnificent Elvis Presley sideburns, with the firm handshake and the intense, rather empty gaze of those with total faith. As well as his ice-boxes, camp bed and all the rest of the glittering equipment that he judges necessary for his comfort during his two-day visit, he has brought with him an electricity generator and a film projector to illustrate his biblical teaching with cinema shows. Chunji, who has been feeling unwell for several weeks, was intending to profit from the return flight to seek treatment in the evangelist hospital in Puyo. But upon discovering that the little Cessna is first to touch down on the landing-strip at Kunampentza, he has decided to disembark there instead, as it is the dwelling place of several highly reputed shamans. Unknown to the Christian *gringos*, who regard shamanism as work of the devil of a particularly abominable kind, the mission aeroplane is regularly used in this way as an ambulance flying clients to these native shamans, who have thus become the foremost beneficiaries of an air transport system set up by people bent on their elimination.

The preacher's arrival brings an unhoped-for chance of distraction. You cannot imagine the incommensurable boredom that sometimes assails us in Capahuari, this little village with no access to the outside world, where the same faces day after day bring us the same stories. The routines of our research work do help to dissipate the monotony of our existence somewhat by providing us with a systematic

201

occupation, but it is not very exciting: amid the welter of information that we are methodically accumulating there is very little to procure us the intellectual satisfaction of real discovery. Were it not for one or two incidents that bring home to us the exceptional nature of our situation – Anne Christine being stung by a scorpion that had made itself comfortable in her sleeping bag, or my distress when, having misguidedly gone off hunting on my own, I wandered in circles in the forest all day long until Wajari came to look for me at dusk – we might believe ourselves clerks in some little provincial office. The Indians seem to suffer from the boredom as much as we do – or possibly slightly less, given the diversion that our presence affords them – and I sometimes wonder whether the vendettas that punctuate their lives are not a means for them to escape from time to time from the everyday grey uniformity.

Unfortunately, the pastor's testimony to his faith did not come up to expectations. The afternoon dragged on with interminable sermons broken only by Don Jaime reading out passages from the New Testament translated into Jivaro by the missionaries of the Summer Institute of Linguistics and commenting on them without much inspiration before a large but inattentive audience. Despite his terrible Midwest accent, he spoke Shuar very correctly in the evangelists' standardized version of the language, to which the Achuar of Capahuari have eventually become accustomed from listening to the broadcasts of the missionary radio of Makuma on ancient transistors handed out by the mission. But if the Indians understood the words of his homily, its meaning most certainly escaped them for, in the first place, they were not concentrating. Amongst the Achuar, speech obeys strict rules of alternating dialogue and it is hard for them to show interest in discourse that is not directed towards a specific interlocutor. Even when traditional stories are being told, when a father recounts a myth to his children, for example, he addresses himself to one of them in particular and expects that one to respond in the course of the narration by interjecting exclamations of interest or requests for more details. Shuar and Achuar are, furthermore, strongly accentuated languages that the Indians play upon beautifully, modulating the phrases with expansive melodious variations punctuated by explosive exclamations and onomatopoeic expressions that retain the listener's interest. Don Jaime's monotonous sermon displayed none of these features. All that religious eloquence patiently acquired in a Bible School in Oklahoma City was as ineffective as a monologue without an addressee, amid the hum of private conversations.

The subjects of his sermons were also misjudged. Hoping to illustrate the power of Jesus by telling the story of the raising of Lazarus, he succeeded only in upsetting the Indians who, more than anything, fear the persistent obstinacy of the dead who try to return amongst the living. Told in the same evangelistic spirit, the story of Christ walking on the waters of the Lake of Tiberias was greeted by whispered speculations on the possible connection between Christ and Tsunki, the river spirit who is the ultimate master of shamanistic powers that the Son of God must surely also have possessed to work so many miraculous cures. As for Don Jaime's repeated exhortations to love one's enemies as one's brothers and not to take revenge for offences suffered, these were received with horrified incredulity by men and women brought up since childhood in the cult of the vendetta. The subject was all the more delicate in view of the fact that the assassination of Ikiam – known to the preacher – has not yet been resolved, since no definite murderer has been found. Our recent visit to Sasaïme has confirmed some of the Capahuari men in their belief in the guilt of Kawarunch, while others have doubts about the innocence of Washikta. Furthermore, Sumpaish, the man from the lower Kapawi who has married Ikiam's fugitive wife, is now again under suspicion despite the conclusions reached in the good-offices mission led by Kawarunch on behalf of Yaur – the victim's brother – conclusions which ruled him out as a suspect. According to Antunish, who has recently returned from a visit to relatives on the Copataza, Yaur has been told by Tukupi that Sumpaish has been boasting of having killed Ikiam. On a visit to the lower Kapawi Tukupi had apparently seen him bragging that he was not afraid of Yaur and, having killed one brother, would not hesitate to kill the other. The fact that the number of suspects has increased makes for an explosive situation, with every man choosing one camp or another on the basis of his own particular grudges from the past.

This dismaying session of piety was rounded off by two or three hymns that Don Jaime attempted without much success to get the children to drone. Pagans first, sinners next: after asking me whether I did not fear that the communists might soon take power in France and wipe out Christianity there, the missionary invited me to meditate upon a little pamphlet that he had brought along expressly for my edification. It took the form of a cartoon strip, produced in the United States but translated into Spanish. The story began in the lecture hall of a college. The front rows were occupied by an assortment of unwashed, hirsute hippies, hang-dog Blacks and sloppy hooligans with their feet up on the desks and cigarettes dangling from their lips. A short, greasy professor complete with the hooked nose and pendulous mouth favoured by anti-semitic tracts stood beneath a picture representing a monkey eating a banana, entitled 'Our Ancestor'. It was, of course, a lecture on the evolution of the species. The abject consensus of the impious students was soon upset by an immaculate young Aryan who rose from the back row haloed with light and brandishing a Bible. Despite the jeers of the other students and the threats of the professor, he patiently rejected the scientific bases of Darwinism, drawing his arguments from a literal interpretation of the account of the creation in Genesis and, as a counter-example, drawing attention to a number of palaeontological claims well known to be fraudulent. He was promptly ejected from the class but, before leaving, handed over his copy of the Bible to the professor who, scrupulous after all, ended up by becoming convinced of the truth of the creationist doctrine as he leafed through the sacred text in a moment of idle curiosity. With divine revelation progressively modifying his semitic features, the teacher then announced his new faith to the college administration and vowed never again to teach a false doctrine. The unfortunate man was sacked forthwith. By now as luminous and almost as Aryan-looking as the young man who had converted him, he was assassinated at the college gates by the furious mob of his former students. The last picture showed his apotheosis: a dazzling angel bearing the professor's soul away to a destiny of bliss while the instrument of his salvation looked on, contemplating the scene with beatitude. Duly edified but bearing no malice, I bought a New Testament in Jivaro from the delighted Don Jaime.

The evening session was slightly less dull. In a deserted house close to the landing-strip the missionary presented to a totally baffled audience several films produced by the Living Christ Series Inc. In a desert-and-cactus setting closer to Arizona than to Galilee, a handful of young, blond, blue-eyed athletes clad in kaftans and multicoloured mini-skirts endeavoured with plenty of conviction but not much talent to act out a few choice episodes from the Gospels. Despite Don Jaime's commentaries in Shuar, the Indians could make neither head nor tail of the episodes depicted but were quite interested in the landscape and the costumes. From time to time Mukuimp, sitting next to me, asked me ironical questions: 'Why do the *pankerista* [evangelists] want us to cut our hair and wear trousers when their own leaders have long hair and wear *itip*? Why do they ask us to give up drinking *nijiamanch* when Jesus multiplied the jars of *nijiamanch* at the wedding? Why can't we see Jesus walking on the water?' When, after close on two hours of projection, Don Jaime suggested running all the films through again and I quickly stole out with Anne Christine, Mukuimp was waiting for me at the door and whispered, 'Tomorrow, come and see *our* cinema!' Seeing my bewilderment, he added, 'Tomorrow we'll be drinking *natem* at your *amik*'s house.'

Now, daylight is rapidly fading and, while over there near the land-ing-strip Don Jaime is preparing for his second cinema show, we are gathered in Wajari's house, waiting for Mukuimp to bring the *natem*. *Natem* is the name that the Jivaro tribes give to a hallucinogenic beverage known throughout much of Amazonia by a variety of native names (*ayahuasca* in Ecuador and Peru, *caapi* along the middle reaches of the Amazon, *yagé* from Colombia to the Orinoco, etc.). It is concocted from certain wild lianas of the *Banisteriopsis* genus. The Achuar have acclimatized several species to their gardens and the two principal ones, *natem (Banisteriopsis caapi)* and *yaji* (probably *Banisteriopsis rusbyana*), are regularly used by shamans and others who, on particular occasions, wish to be transported to the part of the world that is ordinarily invisible. Its preparation is so simple that anyone could make it: the lianas are cut into several sections, pounded with a pestle and tidily arranged in the bottom of a large cooking pot. At this stage the *yaji* leaves are added, then covered with a second layer of *natem* stems. The whole thing must simmer for at least three hours until a viscous, brownish liquid is produced.

To tell the truth, Mukuimp's invitation is not entirely spontaneous. He is the only shaman in Capahuari, although he does not have the august appearance one would imagine to be associated with such a figure. He looks like an overgrown urchin and is slow in his move-ments to the point of clumsiness, but his eyes sparkle with irony and he always has a ready quip, possibly to disguise his secret sorrow: an eighth daughter has just been born to him and he still has no son. Mukuimp has been disinclined to talk to me about his function, partly on account of the virulent disapproval expressed on the subject of *natem* and shamanism by the evangelist missionaries, whose sentiments he naturally imagined to be shared by all Whites. To overcome his reluctance I thought it judicious to tell him that such practices were extremely common where I came from and that I myself was very familiar with them. Mukuimp then declared that, to learn of the powers that he possessed, I would have to 'become drunk on *natem*'. But he was worried that I might not be up to it, that it might prove too much for me and that 'my brother from France' would come to take revenge on him for my death. In order to plumb the mysteries of Achuar shamanism, I was thus led to compound my earlier bragging: already knowing something of the aims and effects of taking *natem* from my reading of ethnological literature, I went on to boast that I would come through the trial without difficulty. When Mukuimp asked me if I would be willing to sing during my trance, I said I would be happy to do so, despite my lack of musical talent; and this seemed to overcome his misgivings. Now the whole of Capahuari was buzzing with the rumour that this evening I was going 'to sing' in Wajari's house. Personally, I could not see what all the excitement was about.

At nightfall Mukuimp arrives with a pot of *natem* and a *tsayantar*, a kind of mouth bow made from a reed strung with opossum gut which one gets to vibrate in one's mouth, rather like a Jew's harp. With him is Piniantza with his *arawir*, a viol with two strings, played with a bow, which seems distantly inspired by the European violin. So they are not counting on my gifts alone to bring cheer to the evening!

Without standing on ceremony, Wajari, Mukuimp, Piniantza and I each drink about half a coffee-cupful of *natem*, then rinse out our mouths with hot water. A little way away, in the company of the other women, Anne Christine is in charge of the tape-recorder. For a minute or two I struggle against violent nausea, for the decoction is horribly bitter. The bitterness is said to be the sign of its strength, as with other substances classed as 'strong', such as curare, tobacco, fishing poison and stramonium.

We settle ourselves comfortably beneath the projecting roof of the house, overlooking the Kapawi from which a lazy mist is rising, just enough to blur the leafiness of the opposite bank, bathed in the light of the full moon. Mukuimp and Piniantza begin to play their respective instruments, not exactly keeping together, it seems to me, but with quite similar effects. The initial rather irritating impression of a colony of frantic hornets circling round and round inside a bottle to the accompaniment of a cheap fiddle eventually gives way to a more subtle harmony. Hanging on the music, time seems to be dilating in rhythm with some immense organism, as if the entire forest is peacefully breathing on a continuous bass note. Meanwhile my shuddering body gradually takes off on the wings of the drug in motionless yet ever-widening spirals. Independent of my limbs, which have become heavy and cumbersome, I open up to the world and pour myself into it. I am both the source and the receptacle of a thousand sensations at once piercing yet indistinct, my only memory of my physical identity expressed in an involuntary clenching of my jaws. On the crest of this extravagant magma, my spirit floats with total lucidity.

When Mukuimp invites me to sing, it is with no inhibitions at all and a comic gravity that I launch into a few couplets from Jacques Brel, followed by one or two blues that come to mind. The narcotics produce a miracle! My performance is greeted with appreciative comments and deemed to consist of true *natem* songs. But soon my intoxication takes a new turn. Against the serene glow of the night phosphorescent circles begin to whirl, then merge and separate, forming constantly changing kaleidoscopic designs. One after another all the symmetrical patterns invented by nature pass before me in a subtle continuum: lozenges first red, then yellow, then indigo, delicate traceries, crystalline prisms, iridescent scales, the eyes of butterfly wings, feline pelt markings, reticular carapaces. Animal forms of unrecognized species display their metamorphoses and transformations before my eyes: the water-marked skin of the anaconda merges into tortoise-shell scales that elongate into the stripes of an armadillo, then reshape into the crest of an iguana against the intense blue of the wings of a *Morpho* butterfly, then stretch into black stripes which immediately fragment into a constellation of haloes standing out against the silky fur of some large cat. Curiously enough, these unanchored visions do not obscure the still landscape that frames them. It is rather as though I were looking at them through the lens of a microscope operating as a window of variable dimensions set in the middle of my usual and unchanged field of vision.

I can hear everything going on around me with unaccustomed clarity yet cannot separate out the immediate background sounds: the murmur of the river, the continuous chirping of insects, the croaking of frogs and the conversation of my companions all hum in my ears with equal intensity. Mukuimp and Piniantza are animatedly discussing shamanistic darts, Iwianch spirits, *pasuk* and *supai*, but my wandering attention prevents me from registering more than a few disjointed words from their conversation. Mukuimp is panting noisily and continuously, smacking his lips as though blowing darts through an imaginary blowpipe. The detachment with which I am living through this experience is increased by my apparent sensation of a double consciousness of the world. I am a benevolent spectator watching my own delirium, observing the changes in my sensibilities with as much curiosity as external events. It is not so much a dissociation of the physical and the mental – if such a thing be possible outside Cartesian metaphysics – rather an agreeable fragmentation of the body, in which every element has become autonomous and seems to be endowed with an intelligence of its own, offering a series of different points of view on the dismembered composition from which it has emerged.

I am, as can be imagined, quite incapable of questioning Mukuimp as to the delicate points of doctrine that our shared trance is supposed to encourage him to reveal. Nevertheless, my mind is clear enough to meditate as it will upon the parallels between my second state and what I already know of the 'voyage' of shamans. It seems likely that the strange beings, monstrous spirits and animals in a perpetual state of metamorphosis that throng their visions – but have not yet visited me – appear to them like a succession of temporarily coagulated forms against a moving background composed of the geometric patterns whose strange beauty I am now experiencing. Rather like the figures used in *Gestalt* to demonstrate perceptive illusions, the brightly coloured hallucinations induced by *natem* lend themselves to the 'recognition' of animated beings with codified aspects, which must seem all the more realistic, their fantastic appearances notwithstanding, in that they borrow a vibrant uniform from the background against which they stand out. This explains how it is that the images

Woman and child,
Numpaïme

Jovial, but armed,
Apupentza

(above) A visitor in a
Surikentza house; he is
wearing very long *karis*
in his ears

(left) A visitor in a house
on the lower Kapawi; he is
wearing a *tawasap* crown
and *karis*

Opposite:

(above) Meeting in a garden,
fingers on triggers, lower
Kapawi

(below) A visitor pauses for
a moment's reflection before
entering a house, lower
Kapawi

A fine rocou make-up takes time, Mashumarentza

(above) Making a necklace with *nupir* beads, Ipiakentza | (opposite) A young boy tries out his new blowpipe, Capahuari

(above) A Wichim family. Hats and caps are becoming very fashionable for the men

(right) A little girl, Sasaïme

(left) A 'great man' often assumes an affable demeanour. Wichim

A Sasaïme couple

of iridescent scales, dappled fur or luminous filaments can, through a kind of visual metonymy, turn into frameworks that support incarnations of the animal spirits – the anaconda, the jaguar, the spider – that the shamans use as their assistants. The state of my body, shattered into a thousand pieces, and the persistent feeling of being a stranger to myself also meanwhile allow a few scraps of erudition to float to the surface of my memory: the voyage of the shaman's soul, which leaves behind its corporeal envelope in order to communicate unencumbered with the beings assisting it, is a feature of all forms of shamanism, even in the absence of hallucinogenics. I am now in a position to assess the extent to which their use facilitates this feat.

Mukuimp and Piniantza invite me for a bathe. I glide along to the Kapawi like a ghost in the moonlight, conscious of the infinite softness of the mud into which my bare feet are sinking. Light wisps of mist float on the surface of the river. The water is deliciously cool after the warmth of the night, but I do not feel as though I am passing from one element into another, for the water's immaterial fluidity is so much like the air. A whispering seems to rise from the Kapawi, now loud, now barely audible, now modulated, now indistinct. Gravely Mukuimp bids me, 'Listen to the fishes singing, and learn.' It is really the only lesson that the evening has taught me.

CHAPTER 14

Travelling Downstream

OUR AWAKENING IN Nayapi's house is somewhat bad-tempered. When we arrived yesterday, as night was falling, we were invited to sleep on a thin litter of banana leaves strewn directly on to the beaten earth floor, hardly protection against the potholes with which the ground is pitted. There *are* two beds in the *tankamash* but they are raised over two metres above the ground. The adolescents who constructed them are not keen on giving up their places there to visitors and know that, thanks to this stratagem, they will not have to do so: no one would ever risk offering a raised vantage point to strangers, who are always suspected of evil intentions. Furthermore, the anopheles, of which there was no sign at either Capahuari or Sasaïme, have made their appearance since we reached the low land downstream, forcing upon us a broken night divided between periods of sting-free sweating inside our sleeping bags and moments of mosquito-infested coolness without their protection. To make matters worse, around two o'clock Masurash, Nayapi's son-in-law, decided that he had slept enough. Taking possession of Tseremp's radio without so much as a by-your-leave, he treated us to the most discordant popular music that the Ecuadorian Andes can produce. The callow youth is convinced that the entire household, which he has thus awoken, admires his ability to do without much sleep, a virtue highly prized amongst the Achuar when paraded less ostentatiously. As nobody sees fit to grumble at the young man, we are obliged to put up with his demonstration of virility until at last Nayapi invites us to come and drink *wayus*.

We set off from Capahuari five days ago, on a long canoe expedition I had been planning ever since our brief stay in Puyo which was designed to allow us to spend several weeks exploring the lower

Kapawi, the lower Bobonaza and several of their minor tributaries, where many Achuar are living beyond all missionary influence. The season is right for the trip as the rivers are still high enough to eliminate the risk of becoming stranded on mudflats. On the other hand, there are frequent whirlpools which make manoeuvring particularly tricky, since our craft is weighed down by half a dozen drums of fuel flown into Capahuari in the mission plane. The water is almost level with the gunwales and the least ripple floods the floor, which we are constantly baling out with a gourd. Tseremp and his half-brother Tarir, who know the river well, have agreed to come along. After helping me to rearrange the layout of the canoe to accommodate the little outboard motor, they learned to handle it remarkably quickly. I do not regret having persuaded Tarir to accompany us. He is a tall, thin man of about thirty, with a rather diffident manner and a toneless way of talking, but he shows wisdom in his decisions and composure in his actions.

It is not just the climatic conditions that make this an opportune moment for our departure. After the *natem* session in Wajari's house it began to be rumoured in Capahuari that I was endowed with shamanistic powers since, under the influence of the drug, I had sung some particularly remarkable *anent*. Far from diminishing the supposed efficacy of my wretched couplets, the fact that they were incomprehensible to the Indians actually reinforced the credit that they afforded me. In truth, shamans themselves customarily mingle Quichua with Achuar in their songs to show that they derive their power and knowledge from sources that are all the more formidable for being so distant. Several times I was asked to assist Mukuimp in his sessions of shamanistic cures and several men, including Mukuimp himself, were insistent that I should spare them a few of my magic *tsentsak* darts, those invisible projectiles that shamans stockpile in their bodies and use either for putting spells on people or for curing them. Despite my embarrassed attempts to explain that the *tsentsak* of my country were of a quite different nature and would not work so far from their place of origin – so embroiled had I become in this seemingly innocent nonsense that I could no longer extricate myself – the stakes kept rising. At each of my refusals I was offered more and more precious objects: *tawasap* crowns, hunting dogs, even a rifle. The ultimate effect of all my disclaimers was to confirm the belief amongst the people of Capahuari that I was indeed a shaman, but probably of a particularly redoubtable kind since I was unwilling to negotiate over my *tsentsak* or to use them for the common good. It thus became urgent for me to get away for a while.

The journey downstream was difficult as the course of the Kapawi was regularly obstructed by huge trees torn from the banks in the floods. When only a small space remained between the tree-trunk and the surface of the water we had to unload the canoe and slip it under the obstacle, at the risk of submerging it. When the tree was partially submerged, Tseremp and Tarir took it in turns to hack their way through it to water level; then, taking a run at it with the engine turning over at full throttle, we would rush through the breach, making a violent impact. Our progress was very slow on that first day as the river meandered in countless loops, some of which practically met in a circle. Most of these bends looked very much the same: a rocky wall bounded them on one side, crowned with trees and lianas that cast their cool shade down on to a whirlpool of deep water, while the opposite bank, flat and frequently sandy, at times edged with little beaches, would be covered by an impenetrable but quite low thicket, dotted with the occasional tall silhouettes of palms and kapok trees.

Not a trace of any human presence along this winding, aquatic, interminably monotonous path! At one point we paused at the foot of a little terrace where Wajari had lived about ten years ago. Nothing remained to mark his stay there except perhaps two fine chonta palms and a few bushes of lonchocarpus submerged beneath the vegetation of fallow land that was already virtually indistinguishable from the neighbouring forest. With no human beings around to hunt them, the animals had the place to themselves: we could hear them going about their business, more or less unconcerned by our presence. A troop of woolly monkeys did not think it worth budging as they watched us pass and I had no difficulty in shooting one for our dinner. A little later a number of water hogs wallowing in the mud gazed at us, grunting placidly. On two occasions caymans sunning themselves on tree-trunks had quietly slipped into the water no more than an arm's stretch from the canoe.

Shortly before nightfall we set up a rudimentary camp on a high bank. Apparently not bothered in the slightest by the heavy rain that had started to fall, in a trice Tarir had lit a fire, using dead wood swollen with moisture and only one of my matches. Although we were surrounded by thousands of trees, we had to search far and wide for enough branches that were not too rotten; and Tseremp had stripped the bark from a standing tree, leaving it to die slowly and subsequently serve as fuel on some other occasion. It was one of the very rare actions betokening long-term forethought that I have ever seen an Achuar perform. All night long the rain never stopped. Just before dawn a sudden sense of increasing wetness roused us completely: during the night the river had risen at least three metres and water was gradually taking over our shelter. The canoe, which we had left immediately below us, attached to a very long liana, was now floating right alongside us.

Our second day's journey was almost identical to the first, perhaps rather more difficult on account of the tree-trunks which the swollen river was now sweeping relentlessly along, almost capsizing us on several occasions. The rain never let up, turning the canoe into a bath of filthy water that had to be continuously baled out. Towards evening the scenery began to change. After converging with the Ishpinkiu, the river had widened and become less sinuous and the current had slackened. The banks were less steep and sometimes parted for channels that led to huge swamps partially covered by vegetation. We had reached the part of their territory that the Achuar call *paka*, the 'flat lands' or, more simply, *tsumu*, 'downstream'.

After an uneventful night we set off once again down the now tranquil Kapawi, reaching Taish's house in the evening. He received us politely but without extravagant enthusiasm: his *amik* Tarir had not brought him anything. We moved on again in the afternoon of the following day and at nightfall came to a large fortified house standing at the top of a steep rise above the river and reached by an almost vertical staircase made from tree-trunk sections. This was the fortress inhabited, along with his two brothers, by Sumpaish, the man suspected of having killed Ikiam after marrying his fugitive wife, Pinik. Sumpaish was away visiting Nayapi, but Kajekui and Tsamarin offered us rather stiff hospitality for the night. A small boy stationed at the top of the rise stood sentry over the Kapawi all day long and when he came in at dusk the men barricaded the door in the palisade with a cross-bar. Via the circumlocutions of lengthy and ceremonious *aujmatin*, we were assured that Sumpaish had had nothing to do with Ikiam's murder and that he was, moreover, soon to pay Yaur *tumash*,

213

not as blood-money for his brother, whom he had not killed, but as legitimate compensation for Pinik, who would normally have fallen to Yaur according to the levirate custom, even though she had abandoned her husband and found herself another before all these other things happened. Tarir and Tseremp, whom Antunish had told of the 'Tukupi rumour' according to which Sumpaish had been bragging of having assassinated Ikiam, no longer knew what to believe.

Kajekui, Tsamarin and Sumpaish make up a rather unusual trio. It is normally rare for a group of married brothers to live for long under the same roof, as the Achuar hold the promiscuity of collective life in horror and fear the rows that it can cause, even between close relatives. Defensive needs sometimes lead to temporary regroupings, but this case is quite different, for the three brothers were already living together long before Sumpaish's life came under threat. Their social and geographical isolation seems quite deliberate: Kajekui is the widower of an orphan, Tsamarin took in a woman who had been abandoned by her husband, Sumpaish a fugitive. This situation certainly avoids subjection to a father-in-law but it also deprives them of the possibility of assistance from a network of relatives by marriage to strengthen this somewhat draughty association. Sumpaish and Tsamarin are *amik*, as are Pinchu and Tarir, although, like the latter, they do not get the chance to exchange many gifts. A middle-aged sister complements their fraternal isolation. This Nakaim, a woman with an easy manner and an uninhibited mode of speech, is the widow of a famous shaman. Now she looks after Kajekui's children, displaying considerable tender sympathy as she performs all the domestic duties of a wife. Malicious gossip (put about by Taish and his wives, as it happens) has it that Sumpaish is also very intimate with his sister's daughter, a charming adolescent called Week, and is keen to marry her. Although not actually prohibited – according to Achuar logic, Week is not a blood-relative since she is the daughter of Sumpaish's brother-in-law – the projected union is nevertheless considered most irregular. The old mother of the three brothers sheds her slightly senile benevolence over this pyramid of promiscuity.

Out of social indolence or a taste for tranquillity, possibly combined with real affection and a desire to return to the intimacy of a carefree childhood, some Achuar choose to retreat in this way into a Utopian togetherness, as close as can be to an impossible but secretly

dreamed-of incest. The situation is quasi-incestuous, for wives without relatives are considered almost consanguineous since there is nothing about them to recall the outside relationships that set the seal on marriages between different families: they are not the sisters of in-laws so, through marriage, become almost sisters. Likewise quasi-incestuous is this association of widows and widowers in which brothers and sisters, taught as children to play out together the roles prescribed for married couples, now at last, following the deaths of their respective spouses, rediscover the complicity for which they have been nostalgic their whole lives long. Also quasi-incestuous, finally, is the marriage projected between an uncle and a uterine niece, for it prevents the normal transmission of alliances from one generation to another, since a son is thereby deprived of the wife whom his father has appropriated for himself. The closing-in of a group upon itself in this way presupposes an abandonment of ambitions. It precludes any possibility of engaging upon the politics of affinity so as to become a man of consequence respected for his manipulation of his brothers-in-law. But this is the price that must be paid if it is security that one seeks: in retreats like this, well out of the way of rival factions, the echoes of warfare can be heard only dimly. It was only as a result of Sumpaish's whimsical love for a fugitive woman that the hostility of the outside world caught up with this family of timid misanthropes.

To live happily, live hidden. Marginal people such as Sumpaish and his brothers, and Taish too to a lesser degree, usually settle on the periphery of a region occupied by a network of relatives to whom they are connected genealogically rather than through solidarity. Several hours' or even a day's journey separates them from the main kernel of the habitat composed of perhaps six or seven households scattered within a radius of about a dozen kilometres, along a section of the same river or on the banks of its smaller tributaries. The inhabitants of such a neighbourhood are relatives who intermarry by preference and define themselves collectively by reference to the principal watercourse that provides for them and determines their travels. As we moved downstream we passed from the 'people of the Kapawi upstream' to the 'people of the Kapawi downstream', just as a few weeks ago, when we went to Sasaïme, we visited the 'people of the great river' (kanus). The social space of the Achuar can thus be seen as a network of houses/territories, quite dense at the heart of what might be called a 'neighbourhood', but looser on its outskirts, which eventually dissolve into vast, uninhabited expanses that separate them from other social entities, identical but potentially hostile. Immense as these 'neighbourhoods' are – in some cases close on a thousand square kilometres – they lack any substantial identity, since their geography depends solely upon the people living there at any particular time. They exist as expanses of forest made temporarily discontinuous simply because the people living there are accustomed to regard themselves as the natives or accepted inhabitants of this particular tiny portion of a gigantic hydrographic network. Apart from the very general distinction drawn between the downstream regions and the upstream ones, the Achuar 'neighbourhoods' are not distinguished from one another by marked ecological frontiers that would characterize each by a particular type of landscape. Nor do they even constitute homogeneous territorial units. They are simply as large as the sum of the individual hunting grounds of the men who live there; they do not coincide with an exclusive domain, managed as a communal property. Surrounded as they are, in the interests of security, by a vast no-man's-land, their boundaries remain vague and fluctuate according to the movements of families which greatly value solitude and live on their edges in order to avoid involvement in faction clashes.

But isolation does not always protect one from the ups and downs of politics; it can even turn out to be perilous. By living too far away from their kindred and begrudging it their support when conflicts arise, marginal people arouse suspicions and, like Kawarunch at Sasaïme, become the targets of cabals, usually at the instigation of the local *juunt*, who is not happy to see men from his entourage resisting his influence. In the last analysis a 'neighbourhood' means relatives, neighbours, affines, at the most twenty or thirty families disinclined to stray too far from a familiar network of rivers, for the most part maintaining a solidarity between them and prepared to band together in the event of a vendetta. It also means a 'great man' whose renown stretches beyond the frontiers of his own kindred and who regards the cohesion of this group, for which he regularly finds reinforcements when wars break out, as the best guarantee of perpetuating his own prestige and winning recognition as the incarnation of this little piece of the world that is pervaded by his influence.

* * *

There is nothing marginal about Nayapi. He is a solid, rather stout, cheery fellow, who tends to switch without warning from theatrical fury to the greatest joviality and who seems to have divided his life between warfare and affairs of the heart. As we take our *wayus* he gives us a most picaresque account of it, at my request.

'I was born on the Kusirentza, the other side of the Pastaza, downstream from here and really close to Peru. My mother died at my birth and my father Achayat then settled not far from there, on the Apupentza, where he was killed by Tiriruk, along with my two brothers, when I was just learning to walk. I remained alone with Shamich, my father's second wife. Ankuash, a great *kakaram*, wanted to marry Shamich. He was very insistent. *Juunt* Ankuash had assembled many relatives around him. He lived upstream from here, on the Sakeentza, in a fortified house with Kamijiu, Kayuye, Naanch and many others. They were at war with Pujupat and Taanchim. But Shamich was not interested in Ankuash, so we went off and took refuge with Washikta at Sasaïme, as he was a "branch" brother of Shamich. At Sasaïme Shamich married Tukupi and it was in his house that I grew to be a man. There I married Najur, Kawarunch's sister, but she gave me no children, so I left her. Kawarunch was angry with me for abandoning his sister, so I went off to stay with Timias, far away from Sasaïme on the Wayurentza, and I married his daughter, Anasat. However, one of Timias's wives, Kinintiur, was in love with me; she was always making advances, but I did not love her. And I tired of Anasat too: she was very young and didn't know a thing. I was in love with Nusiri, Timias's sister, who lived with him as she was a widow. She knew how to please a man, she did. Timias was jealous of me because of Kinintiur and kept telling everyone he was going to kill me. So I ran away with Nusiri, abandoning Anasat. I took refuge with Naanch, who was living on the Kapawi not far from here, and we went to war against Puanchir. Puanchir was very *kakaram*. He had been an ally of Tiriruk, and when the men of Sasaïme killed Tiriruk he decided to have done with all his enemies. As he was now all alone, he was very difficult to kill as he stayed inside his fortified house and only emerged to make surprise attacks. That was the way that he killed your brother Kayuye.'

'You're right,' says Tarir. 'After the death of my brother, I decided to finish off Puanchir once and for all, and I visited Naanch. Naanch agreed to help me and rallied his relatives around him: my brother Pinchu, my brothers-in-law Wajari and Titiar, Kuniach as well, and Entsakua, really a son of Tiriruk but also a "branch" brother of Naanch.'

'Yes, that's how it was,' says Nayapi, taking over again. 'Puanchir was also my "branch" brother, but I agreed to be a party to the affair so long as I would not have to shoot at him, as I wanted to avenge my father, killed by Tiriruk. So then Kuniach, who lived not far from Puanchir, went to visit him, accompanied by Entsakua. The rest of us were hidden in the forest at the edge of the garden. At one point a woman passed close by us, but she did not notice us. Entsakua asked Puanchir to tell him how he had killed Kayuye. He wanted to see his rifle, the one he had fired with. Puanchir suspected nothing: how could he have suspected a son of his ally Tiriruk? So he handed over the *akaru* that he was never without. Entsakua pretended to be aiming at a papaya tree to test the sights; then, swinging round, he fired on the disarmed Puanchir. But Puanchir did not die, for his *arutam* was powerful. All bleeding, he tried to grab the rifle from Entsakua's hands. So then Kuniach fired on him too, but still he did not die. Hearing the shots, we rushed into the house and everyone, except me, emptied his weapon into him. In the end he did die.'

'Absolutely,' adds Tarir, happily. 'He was such a mess, you couldn't recognize him.'

'When we left,' Nayapi goes on, 'we took Mirijiar, Puanchir's wife. Naanch had promised me I could take her if I joined the expedition. That is how it is that you see her here, my little wife, giving us our meal. With my two wives, Nusiri and Mirijiar, I then settled on the Kapawi, upstream from where Taish is living now. Later, I married Makatu, then Ampiur, both orphans. But Nusiri was jealous, she couldn't tolerate me having three new wives. So she found herself a lover. I was furious and I beat her a lot. Soon after, she committed suicide by taking *sunkipi*, a poison you can find in the forest. After that my brother Wisum was killed by Tumink, who lives on the other bank of the Pastaza. My brother was a shaman, it is true, but Tumink had no reason to kill him. That is why I moved down here, to prepare my vengeance. I was closer to Tumink here. Marching fast, you could get to him in two days. Then I arranged with Kamijiu, the one who lives on the Ishpinkiu, that he would join me to build our

219

fortifications. My brother Wisum was a neighbour of Kamijiu and they called each other "brother-in-law". But time passed and Kamijiu did not come; perhaps he was scared? Then I was told that Kamijiu wanted to marry my *waje* Kapair, my brother's widow. But she didn't want to: since Kamijiu and my brother called each other "brother-in-law", she was a sister to Kamijiu. I was the one she ought to marry; after all, we Achuar, should we not marry the wives of our brothers, our little *waje*? But I was very busy fortifying my house and working out how to take revenge on Tumink, so I didn't go and fetch my *waje* and bring her back here. That is how things were when I learned that Kamijiu had married my *waje* Kapair. I was furious and let Kamijiu know that we would have it out. How could I not kill him? But Kamijiu did not want war. A few months ago he sent me *tumash* for my *waje*, a *mayn akaru*. Tumink is dead now too. It is said that it was Chiriap who cast a spell on him. I have forgiven Kamijiu, since he did pay the *tumash*, but if ever I see my *waje* Kapair, I shall kill her. That is the way it is. At the moment we are living in peace.'

At daybreak the women serve us a manioc broth with a few fragments of emaciated trumpet-bird floating in it. Nayapi invites us to eat, then adds facetiously: 'But perhaps you are not in the habit of eating your own kind?' My companions laugh in a strained fashion, but Tarir's annoyed look shows that he is vexed by this remark, which a private aside with Tseremp soon allows me to work out. The people of the lower Kapawi like to scoff at some of the Capahuari men who, under the combined influence of the evangelist missionaries and the Quichuas, seem to have given up some of the traditional ornamentation that is the mark of true Achuar. That is clearly the case with Tarir and Tseremp: with their flowing locks shorn off and no feathered ornaments, face paintings, *shauk* or woven bracelets, they look as dowdy as the trumpet-bird, already partially tamed by the Whites, as the bird is by the Indians.

It may well be wondered what it is that is essential to an authentic Achuar. The dialect that he speaks? The way he dresses up? Customs that make him different from the other Jivaros? The question is not merely rhetorical and is one that arose as soon as we arrived in Capahuari. Anxious to make sure that we had truly arrived amongst the Achuar, we naively asked a number of people what they were. '*Shuaritjai*,' was their unanimous reply, 'I am *shuar*.' We were perplexed, as Shuar is the name that ethnologists customarily give to the neighbouring Jivaro tribe. Had we made a clumsy mistake in the choice of our area of research and could it be that our Achuar were not to be found in it? Yet the Quichuas of Montalvo called the people of Capahuari Achuar, the latter spoke a language noticeably different from the Shuar described by the Salesian missionaries, and a number of features in their culture were different from what was known of the Shuar. We ended up by thinking that the Indians of Capahuari constituted a kind of micro-tribe, neither Shuar nor Achuar, but influenced by both. This interpretation seemed to be confirmed by the fact that Wajari and the others called the inhabitants of the lower Kapawi and the opposite bank of the Pastaza 'Achuar', a fact that had in no small measure contributed to our desire to leave the place where we had first landed up and to stay amongst more clearly identifiable Indians. Our journey to Sasaïme dispelled our misconceptions, however, since there, as here on the lower Kapawi, it is on the contrary the people of Capahuari who are referred to as 'Achuar', whilst those who were represented to us as Achuar when we were in Capahuari were now declaring themselves to be *shuar* in exactly the same way as our first hosts had.

Our obsession with classifications, typical of apprentice ethnologists, had blinded us to something that we should have suspected much sooner: here, definitions of identity proceed from distinctive oppositions; the same ethnic adjective may thus switch from one referent to another depending on the context and the term with which it implicitly contrasts. The Jivaro cosmology is organized as a kind of arborescence, by progressively specifying antithetical pairs. The most encompassing category is that of 'persons', *aents*. This includes all beings with a soul (*wakan*), that is to say all those capable of communicating in that they are endowed with purpose and meaning and are susceptible to the messages aimed at them: human beings, of course, but also many plants and animals, the spirits of the forest and the river, and certain magic or profane objects. Language is not an indispensable attribute for *aents*, for information may equally be transmitted by decodable images or sounds. This is what happens, in particular, when spirits, ghosts or certain natural species appear in the course of dreams or visions induced by narcotics. *Shuar*, that is to say 'people', constitute one particular group of *aents* that is characterized by the faculty of speech: this corresponds more or less to what we understand by the human race. But as the universality of this category is meaningless to the Jivaros, they tend to use the term *shuar* in the restrictive sense of themselves, convinced as they are – like many other peoples – that they represent the perfect and exclusive incarnation of all the attributes of humanity.

Whatever the tribal label attributed to them, all Jivaro-speaking people thus describe themselves as *shuar*, in contrast to other ethnic groups whose members are also no doubt *shuar* in the abstract sense, but *shuar* to a lesser degree, by reason of the more or less great differences that their cultures manifest in comparison to the Jivaro norm. To emphasize this hierarchy, particular terms are used to refer to them. *Apach*, 'grandfather', covers the Quichuas and the *mestizos* and also includes a number of sub-groups such as *piruan*, Peruvians, *saasak*, the Salasaca Indians of the Andes, *suntar*, soldiers, and *napu*, the Quichuas of the Napo. *Kirinku*, 'gringo', covers all strangers with white skin, of whom there are several varieties, such as *pankerista*, the North American evangelists, *paati*, the Catholic missionaries, *pransis*, French (from the Spanish 'francés') – of recent origin, I take it – and *kumpania*, 'the company', the strange, highly mechanized tribe that from time to time comes foraging in the forest, cutting roads through it or counting trees. Some peoples are not associated with any larger group, either because their representatives are so few that it is impossible to decide with whom they should be connected – as in the case of the *nikru*, the Blacks from the Pacific coast sometimes glimpsed in the camps of petroleum prospectors – or, conversely because they live close enough to assume a familiar generic identity: *zapar*, the Zaparo, *kantuash*, the Candoshi, *kukam*, the Cocama, and *tawishiur*, the Waorani – also known as *misu aents*, 'those who go naked' – whom the Achuar consider to be savages who have barely emerged from animality.

As commonly used, then, *shuar* means the prototype of humanity constituted by the Jivaros, and it is purely through convention that the same term has come to apply to one particular tribe, the 'Shuar'. The Achuar refer to the latter by various names composed of the noun *shuar* and a geographical adjective – *muraya shuar*, 'the people of the hills', *makuma shuar*, 'the people of the Makuma', *mankusas shuar*, 'the people of the Mangosiza', etc. – expressions which thus refer to particular regional groups, not to the Shuar as a tribe. The only term that could be used for the latter is itself paradoxical: *shiwiar*, the Spanish version of which is probably at the origin of the word 'Jivaro', refers to all enemies who speak a different Jivaro dialect from one's own. The 'Shuar' as a whole are thus called *shiwiar* by the Achuar, but the Achuar themselves are similarly called *shiwiar* by the 'Shuar', who also refer to them using the descriptive expression *achuar*, a contraction of *achu shuar*, 'the people of the swamp palm' (*achu*), an epithet that evokes the many swamps with which their territory is scattered and in which this plant constitutes the principal ornament. The Achuar themselves refer to other neighbouring groups within their own tribe using various geographical descriptions – *kupatza shuar*, 'the people of the Copataza', *kanus shuar*, 'the people of the Pastaza', etc. – reserving the term *achuar* for potential or real enemies who are, however, related and so cannot be called *shiwiar* since they speak the same dialect. Hence our initial misunderstanding. Because of the uncertainty that it arouses, the Ikiam affair has upset the region's networks of alliance and that is why the people of Capahuari were referring to those of Sasaïme and the lower Pastaza as 'Achuar' and the latter were repaying them in exactly the same coin. Although it indicates a common ethnic origin, the use of this term paradoxically also expresses mutual distrust. My relief can therefore perhaps be imagined when Titiar, to emphasize the benefits that would come my way if I became his brother's *amik*, solemnly declared: 'We the Achuar [*achuartikia*] are accustomed to do thus!' Such statements are nevertheless rare: perhaps because their tribal identity rests not so much upon a self-conscious apprehension of the distinctiveness of their customs but rather upon a particular configuration of relationships with other people, the Achuar feel no need to be always reaffirming who they are and so leave this to their neighbours, both close and distant, ethnologists included.

The remarkable indifference that the Achuar display towards the past may help to explain why any idea of sharing a collective destiny remains alien to them. Self-declared individualists as they are, and amnesiac by vocation, they get along very well without a historical memory, all recall of events that affected earlier generations being carefully erased by their spontaneous forgetfulness.

Even their mythology has nothing to say about the origin of their

223

tribe and hardly more about the beginnings of the human race. The Indians of the north-western Amazon, whose myths obsessively retrace the slightest details concerning the genesis of the world, are at pains to find all kinds of significant circumstances to justify the hierarchy of peoples, the places where they live and their attributes. They strive to relate their present successes and failures to some founding act of a self-confident hero, and they are constantly inter-polating new episodes to account for the appearance of the latest gadget introduced by the Whites. In utter contrast to these people obsessed with total explanation, the Achuar make no effort at all to bestow upon the world a coherence that it manifestly lacks. Their mythology is loosely knit, composed of short fables which, with neither exhaustivity nor narrative continuity, evoke a limited number of events that led to the emergence of certain cultural arts, the estab-lishment of minimal organization in the cosmos, the appearance of two or three properties of human nature, or a plant's or animal's acquisition of its definitive form. Myths of this kind are by far the most numerous; they constitute various chapters in a natural history that traces the differentiation of the species, starting from the original stage when all beings were endowed with language and a human appearance. Taken literally, these stories do not make up a systematic chart of creation through a sequence of ordered stages, as may be found in Genesis in the Bible. The existence of most beings and things is presumed to date from all eternity, and nobody here ever wonders whether Humming-bird became a bird before Ipiak turned into a bush or whether, when Sun ascended into the sky, the Achuar already existed. These events certainly took place in another time, a confused period when distinctions of appearance and topography were not yet established in the universe, but a time still close enough to the present for the figures peopling it to continue to intervene in the daily life of today – as the myth of Nunkui had from the start suggested to me. The heroes of mythology are still living close to men, in the forest, beneath the waters or in the gardens. As for plants and animals, how could there be any doubt that they are still persons, whatever their new forms, since communication with them is still possible?

The immanence of mythical beings even to a large extent renders superfluous a knowledge of all the stories that record their exploits. And in this domain knowledge certainly varies widely, not because it

constitutes an esoteric treasury reserved for a few particular individuals, but because personal circumstances and dispositions dictate
that it should be so. The situation of Tukupi had recently illustrated
this point for me. His ostensible traditionalism had given me grounds
for hoping for a profusion of rich and original myths from him. However, I was disappointed when he confessed ignorance in this department. 'How could I possibly have learned the stories of the past, the
yaunchu aujmatsamu?' he asked me grumpily. 'When I was a child
my family was constantly engaged in wars. At the *wayus* hour we had
to keep quiet in the house, on the lookout for enemies. Do you think
that my parents had nothing else to bother about except telling us
stories about the olden days?' But such a lacuna is no great disadvan-
tage. The Achuar are pragmatic and, as they see it, their dealings with
the spirits and beings of nature do not depend upon a knowledge of
their mythical genesis, but rather upon a mastery of more concrete
techniques such as *anent*, the interpretation of dreams, magic charms,
and respect for taboos.

Mythology, of no use as practical knowledge, is generally told in
the imperfect rather than the past definite tense. The existence of its
protagonists is by no means over and continues to make itself felt
even today, rather like concentric waves on calm water. Nobody actually saw the stone fall but the ripples that it caused are still so clear
that, had one been there a moment earlier, one would have seen it.
Achuar myths do not operate with a linear duration such as obtains
in our subjective consciousness and for which the ageing of beings
and things day after day provides evidence. Nor do they introduce a
cyclical temporality, the old dream of an eternal return to origins
that was shared by the Mayas and the Stoics. The idea that identical
sequences of events may be repeated at regular intervals presupposes
that one has imposed an order on time by dividing it into periods,
the repetition of the past in the future being, as is well known, a belief
peculiar to peoples fascinated by astronomy and calendular science.
But my companions are totally unconcerned with time and how it is
computed. Their chronology is limited to the passing of a single year
whose unobtrusive recurrence is simply marked, in mid-June, by the
reappearance, just before dawn, of the Pleiades, which have been
absent from the nocturnal horizon for the past two months.

No, the time of the Achuar myths is more, as it were, dilated, as it is in contemporary physics, by a gravitational field. Just as the time–space curve produced by the relative densities of matter engenders different rhythms depending on different observation points, similarly the beings of myth disport themselves in a temporality that is parallel but sufficiently elastic for it occasionally to coincide with our own. The communication that is established with these figures in dreams, visions or *anent* perhaps presents some analogy with a passage through what some contemporary cosmologists call 'wormholes', those strange mathematical tunnels that connect extremely distant regions of the universe. The term *yaunchu*, 'once upon a time' or 'in the olden days', with which all myths begin and which even defines their narrative genre, should therefore not be taken literally. It does not so much mark a break between the present and a fabulous past as introduce a distance between two modalities of existence organized according to different time scales. Achuar mythology, neither contemporary nor from the remote past, is not a simulacrum of historical consciousness. Such a concept of becoming no doubt runs counter to our own fascination with history and to the idea that temporality rests upon an absolute distinction between what was and what will be, so that the present exists for us only thanks to the inexorable abolition of the past from which it proceeds, a past of mistakes and superstitions that patented specialists are charged with registering and reconstituting the better to keep it at a distance, safely confined to the collective memory. This concept of time as an irreversible arrow is in truth characteristic only of the modern period: it probably derives from the break that we established a few centuries ago between the world of nature and objects and the world of men, a break that all peoples before us had done without, just as they had had no need for the notion of progress that is its corollary.

The intemporality of Achuar myths makes room for one exception: a body of stories devoted to the evil deeds once committed by a race of cannibalistic giants, the Ajaimp, whom men eventually managed, not without difficulty, to eliminate. The Ajaimp, who are the only mythological beings to have been wiped off the face of the earth definitively, really are creatures of the ancient times; but even their reality is confirmed by evidence that is still tangible, for the Achuar attribute to them the creation of the axes of polished stone that they sometimes come across when clearing their gardens. Yet, if we are to believe the accounts of pre-war explorers, these 'Ajaimp axes' were in common use among the Jivaros no more than three generations ago. The invention of a fantastical prehistory thus took place at the cost of forgetting the more prosaic historical narratives woven at another level by some family memories.

A few weeks ago, in Capahuari, Naanch gave me his version of the end of the time of the Ajaimp.

Once upon a time, there were people like us, their name was Ajaimp. There were many more of them than there were of us. In the olden days we were not valiant: the Ajaimp used to eat us. The Ajaimp had thought up a ruse: they used to make gardens, like us, but they planted *kurikri* thorn bushes all around them, and whenever people passed that way they got caught on the thorns. Ajaimp came regularly to see if any animal had fallen into the trap. If it was a man, the Ajaimp killed him and carried him off in a sack to eat him. Nowadays we too set traps in our gardens to kill birds and agutis. That is what the Ajaimp did. Ajaimp said, 'The *kurikri* thorns have again caught someone.' He killed him with his spear, cut off his head and brought him home. Ajaimp had a big cooking pot; when he killed someone, he cooked him and ate him that very day. He was very greedy. With so many of us being eaten, we were on the point of disappearing altogether. It was then that people began to think of a way to get rid of the Ajaimp.

Basilisk [*sumpa*] was furious at Ajaimp and wanted to kill him. At that time he was learning to use the *tashimpiu* [a curved musical instrument played with a little bow]. Basilisk was stretched out on the ground playing his *tashimpiu*: *suniaa, suniaa*, he went with his instrument, to attract Ajaimp. Ajaimp heard those melodious sounds and they made him feel happy. He came up to Basilisk. 'What are you doing?' he asked. 'I want to learn too.'

So Basilisk showed him: 'You take the bow and you slide it towards you, like this. Here! Lie down, then you can go *suniaa, suniaa* too.' Ajaimp did as Basilisk bade him, but with a clumsy movement of the bow he pierced his belly and died. That was how the first Ajaimp was killed.

Cricket [*tinkishapi*] wanted to kill Ajaimp too. Cricket slept in the ashes and, upon waking, would sing *shir-shir*. One day he had the idea of changing his appearance. He went into the hot ashes and very soon his carapace peeled off completely. He found himself attired handsomely, like a person. Another day he did this again. Ajaimp, who could hear him singing, came up to him and asked what he was doing. Cricket explained to Ajaimp that he too could change his appearance if he wished to. Cricket advised Ajaimp to wrap himself in leaves and lie in the fire; then he said, 'Sing like me, *sasaaship-sasaaship*.' Ajaimp sang *sasaaship-sasaaship*, but his carapace caught fire and he was burned to death.

Sapajou Monkey [*tsere*] was also thinking of killing Ajaimp. He wandered around in the trees singing *krua-krua-krua*. At this time, to avoid the Ajaimp, people used to climb into the trees, but Ajaimp felled the trees with an axe and killed them all. One day, when Ajaimp was cutting down a tree close to the river, so as to catch the people who had taken refuge in it, Sapajou came up to him and offered to help: 'Give me your axe, little grandfather. I can handle it better than you.' Sapajou went at the tree, dealing it fearsome blows, but he had replaced the hard stone axe-blade with one of pumice. The people up the tree were terrified and said to each other, 'This fellow is going to cut our tree down,' but Sapajou gestured to them not to worry and rolled his eyes, whispering, 'No, no, do not fear! I am just pretending.' Ajaimp did not notice all this going on since, licking his lips, he could not take his eyes off the people in the tree. As he hacked at the tree with the pumice stone, Sapajou kept saying, 'Little grandfather, the trunk is well cut into now; it will fall in no time.' Then, with a sudden movement, Sapajou hurled Ajaimp's axe into the river, crying, '*Maj!* Little grandfather, the axe slipped from my grasp just when I was almost done; it has fallen in the river.'

'You did it on purpose,' shouted Ajaimp. 'Now go and fetch it!'

Sapajou pretended to be trying to catch hold of the axe under the water, but really he was all the time pushing it further away until it fell into a deep pool where many anacondas lived. Ajaimp realized that he would never be able to get his axe back and he was furious with Sapajou. When he returned to the tree, he saw that the people had made their escape. Wildly enraged, Ajaimp was about to kill Sapajou, when Sapajou said: 'Little grandfather, you can avenge yourself another way. Flatten my rod, instead.' So that is what Ajaimp did and Sapajou's rod became quite flat.

Another day, Sapajou was eating the fruits of the caimito tree. Ajaimp saw him and asked for some. 'Would you like some more, little grandfather?' asked Sapajou. 'I have planted several caimito trees over there, near the ravine. They are nice and ripe. Tomorrow, if you like, we can go with all your family to gather them.'

The next day, off they all went, Ajaimp accompanied by all his children. Sapajou climbed up to pick a fruit, then came down to give it to an Ajaimp, then climbed up again, and so on. But the Ajaimp were very greedy and grew impatient, wanting to fell the caimito trees so as to eat their fill. Sapajou said, 'If we fell the trees, we shall never have any more fruit; it would be better for you to climb up to pick them for yourselves.' Now, Sapajou had cut clefts in the trunks and when all the Ajaimp had climbed up into them, the caimito trees crashed down into the ravine under their weight. Advancing to the edge of the precipice, Sapajou called out, 'Little grandfather, are you alive?' Hearing nothing, he decided to go down to make sure, calling to the Ajaimp as he went. When he reached the bottom, Sapajou ironically lamented, 'Little grandfather, little grandfather! Not knowing that this is how it would end, my little grandfather was eating the fruit of the caimito tree! If he were alive, he would mock me; he would imitate my lamentations *apachiru see, apachiru see.*' So saying, Sapajou shook his rod, which was good and straight, like a dog wagging its tail. The Ajaimp had split their skulls and their brains were spilt all over the rocks. Still mocking them, Sapajou dipped his finger into the brains and licked it. That is how it is that Sapajou now has such a large brain. That is how the Ajaimp met their end.

Unlike other Achuar myths, this one tells of a disappearance, not of a transformation, for the death of the Ajaimp is not accompanied by the metamorphosis of the creatures that helped to bring it about with their cunning ruses. Basilisk, Cricket and Sapajou Monkey are indeed endowed with composite faculties. They still resemble men with their language and technical skills, but already also possess the features of their own species: a particular kind of song for each, the cricket's ability to moult, the monkey's cheekiness. This mixture of attributes is unique in Jivaro mythology. The loss of the use of speech and the acquisition of a stereotyped means of vocal expression is a feature of the mutation from human beings into animals, the circumstances of which provide the subject matter for most of the myths. It is as if here the indeterminacy of the other figures in the myth and the imprecision with which they fit into the time scale simply serve the better to underline the irreversibility of the Ajaimp's demise. In this one exceptional episode, the evocation of original events is obscured by a picture of the last moments of another age, and the mythical narrative is briefly converted into a legend.

*   *   *

The morning is already well advanced, but neither Nayapi nor my companions seem in a hurry to set about other occupations and are only too happy to sit around gossiping, emptying bowl after bowl of *nijiamanch*. Only Masurash does not join in. Lying on his *peak*, Nayapi's son-in-law is complaining of stomach pains and a bad headache, just retribution, it must be said, for the din that he inflicted on us in the night. As his state shows no improvement, eventually he is paid some attention. Masurash is apparently suffering from *kujamak*, an indisposition caused by the mocking thoughts projected at one by one's companions and the indefinable sense of shame that they provoke. The cure is quickly administered: each in turn, we take Masurash's head on our knees and disgorge into his mouth a bitter jet of green tobacco juice that he immediately draws into his sinuses. Then, as the green phlegm runs out of his nostrils, we blow on his head repeating, '*Kujamak tsuajai*,' 'I am curing the *kujamak*.' This rather unpleasant operation has to be repeated by every member of the household, since *kujamak* can only be properly cured by whoever was unwittingly responsible for it. Seeing the ardour with which each person present executes this obligation, I suspect that in the depths of their hearts they must all have harboured mocking thoughts about the young braggart's demonstration of his virility.

CHAPTER 15

To Each His Due

THIS MORNING it is one of Nayapi's wives who is unwell. Makatu is suffering from a sharp pain in her shoulder joint, identified as *tampunch*, the origin of which seems as bizarre as that of the *kujamak* of which Masurash was the target yesterday. You are in danger of contracting *tampunch* when you use an object that you have been lent or given. In Makatu's case the offending agent is a machete presented to her by Tseremp soon after our arrival, which she used yesterday in the garden. The *tampunch* must be cared for by the person who is unwittingly responsible for it; he or she carries it in a latent state, having earlier contracted it in identical circumstances but not necessarily from the same object. Each time it strikes a new carrier, the *tampunch* becomes virulent once again. At this point the person who passed it on must calm it, since his body is the familiar place where the pain had earlier become dormant. That is what Tseremp is now doing, blowing on Makatu's shoulder, beating it lightly with a stinging nettle and then massaging it with both hands under the attentive gaze of Nayapi. Passed from one person to the next as in a game of pass-the-parcel, the *tampunch* provides quite a good example, in the physical register, of the inextinguishable nature of the obligations that stem from even a derisory debt. Whether lent or given, the object causing the pain gives rise to a moral obligation in the beneficiary that can never be wiped out by giving a gift in exchange: a passing indisposition emphasizes the principle of insolvency more than it constitutes compensation.

Kujamak and *tampunch* are part of a vaster complex of organic disorders known as *iniaptin*, provoked fortuitously by the action of one member of the circle surrounding the victim, and therefore to be repaired by that particular person. This is also true of 'snake hair',

231

jintiash napiri, which is manifested by a high fever; its aetiology and treatment, however, are exactly the same as for *kujamak*. The incidence of these disorders appears to increase at a time of journeys – our recent trip to Sasaïme was studded with them – no doubt because the tension provoked by visits, during which all present are slightly concerned for their own safety, finds a handy outlet in these benign maladies.

The behaviour of someone close may also be the involuntary origin of decline in an infant. It is said that when a man takes a second wife whilst his first is still suckling her baby, the first wife finds her milk drying up or becoming thinner and the health of her child suffers. The phenomenon is called *nuwe pimpirwai*, 'his wife becomes exhausted', and this unfortunate effect of male lasciviousness probably has to do with the principle of the mechanism of humours, in which many peoples believe: the theory is that the lactation of women depends upon the quantity of sperm they receive. Given that the physiology of reproduction imposes limits upon the exercise of a man's virility, the remedy is more a matter of curing the result than of preventing the cause: the father must suck the baby's wrists with his mouth full of green tobacco juice.

Whatever the mode of its preparation, tobacco is believed by the Achuar to possess all kinds of extraordinary properties. Exhaled as smoke over afflicted parts, it cools and anaesthetizes them, at the same time serving as a vehicle for substances or immaterial principles that are thereby transferred from the healer to the sufferer. It plays exactly the same role when taken in an infusion, for the tobacco is believed to form an invisible covering that for a while protects the region of the body where it is applied from external infections. When swallowed in the form of pellets, it operates as an internal magnet, making it possible to suck out and neutralize certain pains. Finally, in all its forms, it sharpens the senses and increases lucidity. By blowing tobacco juice on to a child, the father transmits some of his own vital energy to it on the very spot where it is most likely to impart strength, since the wrists are not only joints that are fragile – and therefore weak points in a body always in danger of fragmenting – but also the seat of the pulse, the very spot where separation between the inside and the outside of the organism is abolished and communication between the two becomes possible.

The Achuar also appeal to accidental influence, but of a spirit this time, not a human being, to account for a whole succession of serious complaints that affect children. Children are believed to be vulnerable because their corporeal limits are not yet definitively fixed and this state of incompleteness somehow leaves them open to all kinds of influences from their environment. So it is with 'blowing', *nasemar*, a chill caused by contact with the freezing shade of a dead person, which is manifested mainly in a light-coloured diarrhoea. The treatment, so far as I could see from my observations in both Capahuari and Sasaïme, rests upon a well-worn but spectacular cure involving an annulment of contraries: heat must be applied to eliminate the cold. The person applying the remedy rubs his hands several times with glowing cinders without flinching, then for a long time strokes the patient's body before sweeping a brand over it. As for *tapimiur* and *pajum*, they apparently belong to another aetiological category, one present throughout indigenous America and even in Europe in past times: namely, 'sudden fright'. The source of the affliction is the same as for 'blowing', and again the method of cure is based upon bringing together opposed principles. A child contracts *pajum* when he suffers a bad fright, usually as a result of a brief, terrifying vision that he alone can see thanks to his imperfect separation from surroundings where all kinds of monstrous entities wander, although these cannot normally be seen by others. The image, of a quasi-material nature, imprints itself upon him like a photographic negative, provoking a high fever that must be banished by cooling his whole body with tobacco smoke. The person administering the cure moreover takes care to draw upon the cigarette the other way around, by placing the glowing tip inside his mouth, to hide the burning source of the desired cooling. *Tapimiur*, which is treated in exactly the same way, is also caused by an apparition reputed to be terrifying for the very small children who alone are subject to it and are moreover unable to understand what it is: namely, the soul of someone dead or dying, glimpsed close to the place of burial or perched at the bedside of the dying person. For the *wakan* abandons the body some time before clinical death and wanders first through the house, then around the tomb, before eventually disappearing in a series of metamorphoses. The vision gives rise to a sense of oppression that is manifested in respiratory difficulties.

233

Even more serious is the deliberate possession of a child by the *wakan* of someone dead, a kind of spiritual contamination known as *imimketin*. The Achuar's *wakan* corresponds well enough to what Western philosophy and Christian theology call the soul: it is a component of the person, endowed with an existence of its own and therefore able to separate itself from the body, temporarily in dreams and visionary trances, and definitively when physical decrepitude, disease or the destruction of the vital organs extinguish all desire to live. Just as the sleeper maintains himself in a vegetative state when his *wakan* goes forth on nocturnal voyages, similarly the organism of a dying person continues to run for a while under its own momentum, even when its conscious faculties have deserted it. Death is not something one is subjected to but somehow results from the *wakan*'s deliberate decision to abandon the now useless shell in which it has been lodged since soon after the conception of the foetus. That separation brings dire consequences for the *wakan*. The *wakan*'s relationship to the body is like that of a mirror image, as is suggested by the meanings of this term in other contexts where it can denote 'a cast shadow' or 'a reflection in the water'. By nature indissociable from what it represents, the soul is thus not so much a double or copy, but rather another side to the body or a projection of it. It is certainly able to detach itself, on occasion, from the body whose consciousness it forms; but it loses its *raison d'être* and all access to the world of senses when it is once and for all separated from the person it used to inhabit. That is why the dead are eternally dissatisfied. Blind and dumb, hungry and thirsty and sexually frustrated, they preserve as it were an imprint of the impulses of a sensibility that they no longer have the means to satisfy. In these circumstances a young child is a veritable boon to a *wakan*: its permeability to the influences surrounding it and the incompleteness of its own *wakan* make it just the kind of receptacle in which the soul of someone recently dead can reacquire a window on to the world. The cohabitation of the two *wakan* has a dramatic effect on the health of the possessed child, who is deeply disturbed and soon succumbs if not treated. He must be covered in warm ash, perhaps to reinforce with an extra layer the envelope provided by his own all too porous body. However, the cure does not always succeed. Many times, while trying to trace back a family's genealogy, I have been told of children who died in this way.

The spirits are responsible for many other disorders too, for which the mode of transmission is generally surrounded in mystery. The case of *panki* provides a good example. Although relatively rare, anacondas terrify the Achuar for a whole host of reasons, in particular because they are reputed to cause an illness that bears their name, *panki*, but whose propagation and transmission nobody has ever been able to explain to me. It is the fault of *panki*, and that is all there is to it. These great reptiles have an ambiguous status among the animal species because they are used as assistants by shamans, so you never quite know what you are dealing with – a real anaconda, a spirit in disguise, or even a temporary incarnation of the *wakan* of its master. The only thing you can be certain of where they are concerned is that they are malevolent. In the disorders mentioned earlier, the identification and therapeutic treatment depend on the form that the contamination takes, which is described literally if not always plausibly. In contrast, the origin of *panki* is largely metaphorical. It is the symptoms rather than the causes that point the finger at the anaconda. *Panki* takes the form of swelling either of the stomach or of the joints, suggesting an obvious analogy with the distended stomach of the snake digesting its prey. In consequence, the treatment makes no reference at all to the presumed agent of the disorder and sticks to the domain of well-tried recipes – plasters of manioc leaves and stramonium, chilli-pepper frictions and the eternal panacea, tobacco juice. If the anaconda is given the role of the villain here, even if nobody really believes it, it is because, with this ailment as with most other disorders of the body or the mind, it is essential to designate some responsible agent, however improbable. My companions have hardly any concept of there being 'natural causes' for pain or misfortune. Instead they usually consider them to stem from the actions of others, either involuntary or deliberate. This carefully managed determinism makes it unnecessary for them to pile mental torment on top of physical ills, since it protects them both from the sense of sin inculcated by religions of salvation and also from the feeling of unfairness experienced by more secular spirits when they are inexplicably struck down by sickness.

Several hours later Makatu's pain is no better. Nayapi now thinks that the initial diagnosis was wrong and that his wife is really suffering from a *tunchi*, a shamanistic spell. Our host is himself a bit of a shaman, sufficiently so, he claims, to be able to make out the coloured aura that surrounds his colleagues when they are under the influence of *natem*. So he sets about sucking out the *tsentsak*, the magic darts he believes to be stuck in Makatu's shoulder, having first absorbed a dose of tobacco juice through his nose. The operation is carried out with gusto but not with great conviction. Nayapi is well aware that he is not strong enough to take on a stubborn *tunchi*. His change of mind illustrates the elasticity of the classification of organic disorders and the pragmatism that governs it. My interlocutors without hesitation distinguish two major categories of ailments: *tunchi*, provoked and cured by shamans; and *sunkur*, that is to say all the rest. But the difference between the two depends upon the context and a cut and dried distinction between 'sorcery' and 'sickness' is never drawn. In practice, most *sunkur* in the last analysis result from the actions of a human being or a spirit and, like *tunchi*, can be traced to an external cause. Above all, any *sunkur* that does not respond rapidly to the appropriate treatment is reinterpreted as a *tunchi*. The Indians seek instant results and cannot accept that a remedy may need time to take effect. A similar example to Makatu's case had been provided in Capahuari, where a little girl who had scratched her eyelid on a branch had been declared the victim of a *tunchi* because her eye was still rather red the next morning despite the compress that had been applied to it. A *tunchi* is recognizable not from its symptoms but from its resistance to non-shamanistic techniques of healing, even when its accidental origin is clearly attested.

However, there is no lack of medicinal plants and knowledge of their properties is fairly widespread. As a conscientious ethnologist, I have embarked upon drawing up a list of these medicinal remedies and their uses, sometimes attempting to identify their botanical affiliation. At the present stage of my inventory I know that the Achuar pharmacopoeia comprises at least thirty or so species. About a dozen are cultivated in or acclimatized to their gardens and serve the most common needs. Among these garden species can be found certain plants such as ginger, recently obtained from the Shuar and very much in fashion for stomach aches, as well as the usual assortment grown by most Indians of the Andean foothills: the inevitable *piripiri*, the cyperus whose roots and leaves are used against snake-bites, dysentery, the diarrhoea of breast-feeding babies or as a tonic for women who have recently given birth; various species of graminaceous plants known as *chirichiri* and used as poultices or in infusions to treat headaches or intestinal infections; two plants of the amaranth family, *kantse* for swellings and *pirisuk* for painting the throat; *sesa*, a mallow reputed to be effective against worms; *yapaipa*, a verbena used against 'flu and stomach pains; the common stinging nettle, a sovereign cure when used to beat parts of the body affected by muscular pains and rheumatism; not to mention plants that are used for all kinds of purposes, such as stramonium (several species of *Datura* and *Brug-mansia*), commonly consumed for its hallucinogenic properties but also to cure wounds and gangrene and rubbed on the body to bring down swellings, and genipa which, apart from its cosmetic function, is frequently used as an astringent for cleaning wounds. The forest is even richer: leaves, bark, alburnum, roots, resin, latex, and fruits of a score or so of species can be beneficial used as decoctions, compresses, plasters or lotions to cure disorders of many kinds – malaria, aphtae, parasitism and tropical ulcers as well as snake-bites, bronchitis, uterine haemorrhages and yaws: in short, a whole treasury of plant remedies whose very real curative qualities would without doubt be revealed by pharmacological analyses but which I have seldom seen my hosts using on a day-to-day basis. Their knowledge in this field is mostly theoretical and is tinged with scepticism. Anyone can tell me the most common *tsuak* (remedies) but nobody would claim either to use them regularly or to place much faith in their therapeutic efficacy. In truth, the Achuar's attitude towards the *tsuak* that we bring them is very similar. We are constantly being asked for them but it is more on account of their attraction as novelties than as a result of any real belief in their beneficial effects, despite the spectacular cures that we have produced with infinitesimal doses of antibiotics or even with aspirin. In truth, the only *tsuak* that is in constant use for almost any complaint is tobacco.

The relative indifference of the Achuar towards their plant remedies – in total contrast, it is worth noting, to the mythical image of the Indians of Amazonia promoted by western enthusiasts of 'alternative medicine' – is nowhere more striking than in their treatment of dis-eases of the skin or parasite infestations. In appearance both kinds of affliction are typical *sunkur* since, in contrast to *tunchi*, which mainly affect the inside of the body, their manifestations are either superficial (eczema, scalp disease, ulcers, mycosis . . .) or can be blamed upon some visible animal (guinea worm, scabies, tapeworm). Each is named, its symptoms are known, and there is an appropriate *tsuak* in the local pharmacopoeia that corresponds to it. However, since most of these external pathologies take a long time to heal or are even impossible to cure, they are eventually considered to be caused instead by a particular kind of *tunchi* that primarily affects the surface of the body and that is provoked – as are more serious but less common diseases such as leishmaniosis or leprosy – by an inferior variety of shaman, 'spittle shamans' (*maen uwishin*).

The absence of a clear distinction between *sunkur* and *tunchi* probably stems from the fact that all therapeutic practices appear to be derived, to varying degrees, from the shamanistic model. Everybody tells me that this is based upon a very simple mechanism: a shaman operates from a distance by means of invisible projectiles, *tsentsak*, which another shaman will have the power to extract from the victim's body provided he possesses *tsentsak* of an identical type. The two principles that govern shamanistic operations are thus firstly, that the cause of the affliction is external, and secondly, that there is a homology between that cause and the agent of the cure. The treatment of *sunkur* rests upon a similar logic. Even if it is not caused by some malevolent intention, a sickness can always be ascribed, at some particular moment in its evolution, to the action of some clearly distinguishable individual; it must therefore be treated either by the individual responsible for setting it off or by someone who can be said to have acquired some affinity with that person, or even by someone sufficiently foreign to be seen as even more distant from the patient than the presumed source of his/her sufferings.

None of all this has been told to me in so many words by the men and women whose existence we are sharing. Having bombarded them with requests for explanations in our frenzy to learn during the first few months, we eventually realized that we should learn far more by listening to their day-to-day conversations than by constantly interrogating them. Despite my precautions, there is a risk that, through their very formulation or simply the ignorance that they reveal, the questions that I ask immediately condition the nature of the replies that I receive. A poignant example of this made me aware of the problem. During the first weeks of our stay in Capahuari I noticed a

238

long zigzag line burnt into the side of Pinchu's canoe, and I asked him if it was the image of an anaconda. It was not a random question, for in Upper Amazonia the anaconda is often represented by a broken line and furthermore many of the region's myths use this snake as a metaphor for a canoe. I accepted Pinchu's laconic 'Yes' with satisfaction and noted the information in my fieldwork journal. A little while ago I came to realize how mistaken I had been. In Achuar iconography – on pottery or on woven bracelets, for example, or in games making patterns with string – a zigzag in fact indicates the constellation of Orion, with two vertical lines and one diagonal linking together all the stars in the group, and the pattern can be extended indefinitely simply by repeating the same motif. As for the obscure relation that might link Orion with a canoe, there is a myth that provides the key to this. It relates how a group of orphans, the Musach, were fleeing on a raft to get away from their stepfather. Eventually they reached the spot where the river joins the vault of the heavens, which they proceeded to ascend. The Musach became the Pleiades and their raft became Orion. Their journey by water is repeated every year when, towards mid-April, the Pleiades disappear from the western horizon and plunge downstream on their raft, Orion, to reappear in the east during the month of June, at the end of their descent. How on earth could you explain to an obtuse stranger with very little grasp of your language all these subtle connections of which you might not, yourself, be all that aware? Pinchu seems to have preferred simply to answer 'Yes', and I cannot say that I blame him.

Like all intuitive work, ethnological interpretation stems from a multitude of tiny observations that accumulate in one's memory, where they lead an idle existence until such time as some new fact, not necessarily at all spectacular, makes it possible for some of them to form a critical mass. Suddenly order emerges of its own accord, its retrospective clarity illuminating some of the welter of data accumulated thus far. It is true that working as a partnership facilitates the process of discovery, for Anne Christine and I are constantly pooling our impressions and our doubts and can, when the moment seems right, try out our exegeses upon one another. It was in this way, not thanks to systematic information from a particularly good informant, that I came to form a general idea of the way the Achuar conceive sickness.

We had noticed that nobody in Capahuari ever treated their own infirmities, not even Mukuimp, the shaman. In the cases of both human beings and dogs it was always a man or a woman from another family who administered the *tsuak* or, more usually, the tobacco treatment. Furthermore, it was clear that some people were more in demand than others because they were credited with particular talents for curing such or such an affliction. The good offices of Naanch and Tsukanka were required for treating *pajum*, whereas Wajari's were used for *panki*. Although not shamans themselves, they had acquired their particular powers from some other, equally specialized, healer. Distance seemed to play an important role, for the first request made to Taish when he came from the lower Kapawi to visit Tarir was that he should work upon a cure for *pajum*, with the assistance of Tsukanka. The same thing had happened, but this time for *panki*, with Antikiu, a man from the Kurientza who had stayed with Titiar for a while.

Our trip to Sasaïme clarified these confused impressions of ours. The local people were constantly asking Tsukanka and Wajari to take a hand in curing a wide assortment of *sunkur*, and on several occasions I was persuaded to assist them. Mukuimp, for his part, took care of the ailments declared to be *tunchi*, for there is no shaman at Sasaïme. While I was there I also witnessed Tsukanka passing on his power to cure *pajum* to Tirinkias, Picham's young son-in-law, in return for two hens. Not that the ceremony was particularly impressive, although it was typical enough of all the hasty little rituals that are the daily fare of ethnology: while Tirinkias sat at Tsukanka's feet holding out his hands to him, the latter had arranged ten rolls of dried tobacco, eight small ones between his finger joints and two large ones on his palms. Then, taking each in turn, he had put them into the mouth of the young man, who had swallowed them. Tirinkias had then rubbed his own arms after passing his hands over Tsukanka's and, lastly, made each of the old man's joints crack by pulling on his fingers. Tsukanka's grudging commentary ran as follows: 'The tobacco drinks the *pajum* when you brush with your hands.' No wonder I usually abstain from asking for explanations! Mukuimp had added that this is also the procedure for the initiation of a shaman, except that pimento is sometimes used instead of tobacco.

The cures that we have observed have made use, to varying degrees, of what we – for want of a better word – should call 'magic' techniques that are by no means restricted to shamans: 'brushing' (*japirtin*) to dissipate or cool the illness, 'blowing' (*umpuntrutin*) air or tobacco over the patient's body or on to a liquid that he then drinks, 'sucking' (*mukuntratin*) the painful part to extract the pain or transmit strength, reciting stereotyped formulae, etc. Even the most ordinary *tsuak*, including those from our Western pharmacy, can only be administered if many precautions are observed. The recipient, but also and especially the person administering the cure, must be fasting and then for a while observe a special diet or even the particular eating taboos that go with each illness. There is nothing really purgative in these prescriptions, rather a belief that the efficacy of a therapy depends not so much upon the inherent properties of the remedy but rather upon the qualities of the person administering it and the conditions in which he does so. In short – as I am now reminded as I watch Nayapi drooling tobacco juice on to his wife's shoulder – almost all ailments are potential spells and must be treated as such. Treatments using 'herbal remedies' are no more than palliatives in this kind of medicine, which is more at home with psychosomatic procedures than with herbalist prescriptions.

Even epidemics are not beyond the power of malevolent influences. Admittedly, it is openly conceded that a shaman could hardly strike down a whole lot of people at the same time with his *tsentsak*: to do so, he would need far too many. Having learnt from plenty of dramatic experiences, my companions also recognize the principle of contagion, although they sometimes ascribe some surprising vectors to it. Since yesterday, for example, Tseremp and Tarir have been relentlessly complaining of the risks I am making them run by taking them to a region infested by *chukuch*, which is what they call malaria, despite our having taken the usual precautions and my giving them each a daily dose of Nivaquine. To them the idea of preventative treatment is absurd, and they feel helpless faced with a malady that they know to be incurable, having noted that even if *chukuch tsuak* – both their own and those of the Whites – can cure a high fever, they cannot prevent it from recurring. According to them, there used to be no *chukuch* in the lower Kapawi region; it was an Achuar from Peru who brought it to the Chirta, a tributary of the Huasaga, five or six days' march from here. Then Kamijiu, on a visit to an *amik* on the Chirta,

241

brought it back to his home on the Ishpinkiu, from where it travelled a bit further downstream from where we are now, carried there by Winchikiur, at whose home Nayapi himself caught it. The genealogy is impeccable and the human agents are carefully identified, but that is where any analogy stops. My mention of mosquitoes is received with general hilarity. The *Kirinku* certainly have fertile imaginations: everyone knows that *chukuch* is transmitted by food, in particular manioc beer, sugar cane and cultivated fruits. The interpretation of my hosts is no more improbable than the vague noxious emanations that were believed to be the source of malaria not so very long ago in Europe, but the coincidence between the presence of anopheles and that of malaria ought to be obvious to such attentive observers of the natural realm. What blinds them here is probably not a lack of observation but rather an inability to envisage the possibility of an insect, disagreeable to be sure but lacking any motives of its own, being the source of such a vast epidemic. Contagion from a shared meal fits in better with a philosophy that ascribes to mankind the responsibility for virtually all misfortunes.

Other infectious diseases – measles, chickenpox, whooping cough, 'flu – are also believed to be transmitted through commensality. As soon as a case occurs the news spreads fast and all visits are thereupon suspended even though, as the Achuar recognize, reorganizing the habitat into a village has made contagion inevitable. In fact this is the chief argument that Taish, Tsamarin and Nayapi put forward for not imitating the example of the people of Capahuari. Since the disappearance of smallpox (*keaku sunkur*, 'the red disease'), it has been 'flu (*penke sunkur*, 'the absolute disease') that has caused the most ravages; no doubt because of its particular virulence its outbreak is sometimes attributed to the action of a shaman. That is what I deduce from a story that Tarir told me just before our arrival at Taish's house, as we passed an old fallow at the edge of the Kapawi. Seven or eight years ago several men now living in Capahuari had built their house on this site; one of these was Tarir. Now, not far away there lived a powerful Quichua shaman by the name of Mukuchiwa who viewed this sudden competition on his hunting patch with a certain unease. He sent an invisible anaconda to install itself in the bank below the little village and to contaminate the new-comers with an implacable 'flu, hoping in this way to force them to flee immediately. The Achuar called in

Chalua, another Quichua shaman, who discovered the monster and chased it out in the course of a memorable trance. But the flight of the anaconda, attested by a sudden fall in the depth of the river water, solved nothing. The 'flu had become too well established and the survivors fled in disorder without even stopping to bury the dead. For my companions this crafty ploy served to reconcile their belief in the infinite power of shamans with their factual knowledge of the way in which epidemics are propagated.

Some *sunkur* considered to be contagious are totally beyond the scope of my modest medical knowledge: the very common 'paling' (*putsumar*), for example, a kind of anaemia which affects young and old alike and which, everybody swears, spreads as fast as lightning; and the 'mouldering' (*mamu*), which is particularly difficult to classify on account of the wide variety of its symptoms – an eruption of spots for a child in Capahuari, face ulcers for another, and what is probably cancer of the knee for Kawarunch's son at Sasaïme – but the transmission of which is traced back from one individual to another all the way to its source amongst the Shuar. Epidemics could definitely not be autochthonous: whether they come from Peru, the Quichuas, the Shuar or the Whites, the origin of the infection is always ascribed to others – not without historical vraisemblance. In such cases the Achuar are quick to recognize the efficacy of Western medicaments, since there is no better way of treating an illness than by whoever caused it. On the other hand, if the remedy is not successful they are convinced that their diagnosis was mistaken and the contagious *sunkur* is once again eventually classed as a disguised *tunchi*: fine and simple certainty in the face of the iniquity of physical suffering ... How comforting it would be to share their confidence!

Perhaps to console Makatu for the *tampunch* that turned out not to be one, but also, he says, because she is a distant 'branch' sister of his, Tseremp makes her a gift of an assortment of needles and thread that I myself had given his wife some weeks earlier. Ever since our arrival the toing and froing of presents has not let up for a moment between my Capahuari companions and Nayapi's household. Everyone is caught up in the binding circuit of gifts and counter-gifts. The list of them that I have noted down reads like the slate of some rural general store. Tseremp gives Nayapi a radio, a torch, a pair of swimming trunks, a harpoon tip and a length of cotton and gives Makatu a machete and a sewing-kit. Nayapi gives Tseremp a coil of *shauk* that Makatu was wearing; Tarir gives Nayapi his monkey-skin satchel, *uyun*, and Makatu a ball of strong fishing line; Makatu gives Tarir some woven bracelets, and so on. As can be seen, women are not excluded from these little deals, in which they can swap articles that they themselves have made. On the other hand, their glass bead ornaments and their dogs continue to belong to their husbands who therefore have the right to re-enter them into circulation on the implicit but imperative condition that they will quickly replace them with substitutes of the same value or kind: that is the price of house-hold peace.

This series of transactions stands in contrast to the total absence of present-giving when we stayed with Taish, despite the fact that he is an *amik* of Tarir's, and it reflects the particular interest that Tseremp and Tarir take in Nayapi. The reasons for this are eminently political. Taish is a marginal who loves his solitude, whereas Nayapi is estab-lished at the centre of a solid network of alliances that cover the whole of the lower Kapawi and could, if need be, provide valuable support in a conflict. The swapping of presents is simply a pretext to secure his support by weaving a network of mutual obligations in which the detail of what objects are exchanged counts for relatively little, as is suggested, for example, by the rapid switch in the kinship positions adopted towards one another. Given that all Achuar are ideally related, men of the same generation who are unable to determine their exact genealogical connections generally address one another as 'brother', a relationship that in these circumstances implies no particular obliga-tions. This was the solution chosen by Tarir and Tseremp *vis-à-vis* Nayapi upon our arrival. By the next day, however, they were calling him 'brother-in-law', thereby indicating that they wished to establish a relationship of symbolic affinity, that is to say one based upon reciprocal commitments of assistance identical to those that link close relationships by marriage. This overture was accepted by Nayapi, who responded in the same fashion, possibly as a prelude to the establish-ment of an *amik* link that would set a stricter seal upon the agreement thus suggested.

Because it frequently serves to set up or cement political alliances, the exchange of gifts does not solely concern ritual friends. Whoever the partners involved may be, the code for the transactions remains identical. It is always on the occasion of visits that gifts and counter-gifts are presented, in an apparently spontaneous fashion. Very seldom does one hear any precise request made. Similarly, thanks are neither given nor expected when an object changes hands, and the two part-ners hasten to continue their conversation as though nothing had happened. Furthermore, it would be in extremely bad taste to offer a gift in exchange immediately, as that would imply a desire to free oneself as soon as possible from the obligations that stem from any debt and so would constitute a tacit rejection of the relationship of mutual dependence that is instituted by a gift – in short, it would virtually amount to a declaration of hostility. Although this system of silent exchange takes place without any explicit negotiations or bargaining, it seems to satisfy most people's expectations. That is because everyone is apprised of the state of wealth and indebtedness of virtually everyone else. It is a subject never even raised with those immediately concerned but it does, on the other hand, constitute a choice morsel for discussion with their relatives and neighbours. Thus, when a man learns that one of his debtors has recently acquired or made an item that he covets – a rifle for example, or a canoe – he will let everyone know either that his life is endangered because he does not possess a rifle or that he cannot get about because he is without a canoe: news that will not take long to reach the ears of the party concerned. The transfer of goods can then take place on the occasion of a seemingly chance visit without any definite request having been made.

The rarity of the exchangeable goods, the differences in status amongst the creditors, and the intricate mesh of debts all combine to make the movement of gifts and counter-gifts more complex than it may seem, forcing each person involved to make choices between contradictory obligations. Tseremp's recent transactions provide a good illustration. A while ago he received from his wife's father, Tsukanka, a muzzle-loading gun the latter had received from his *amik* Washikta during the visit that we paid together to Sasaïme. Tsukanka had let it be known to Tseremp that he was in need of a good hunting dog, since Washikta had indirectly expressed his desire for one. Before setting out with us on our expedition to the lower Kapawi, Tseremp had been counting on obtaining this dog from Nayapi. He would then have given it to Tsukanka, who would have presented it to his *amik* Washikta to compensate for the rifle. Nayapi was in debt to Tseremp since the latter had sent him that very rifle via Taish, to pay off a debt dating from several years earlier and also, in all likelihood, to pave the way for a future alliance to be ratified when we passed through. However, the situation was complicated by the fact that Tseremp was hoping at the end of the journey to be taken on as casual labour by a petroleum company prospecting to the north of Montalvo. This meant that a long time would elapse before he would be able to bring the dog back to Capahuari. To resolve the problem Tseremp gave Tsukanka a radio that he had received from his *amik* Titiar, his sister's husband, who had obtained it from a Shuar *amik* who had bought it from an evangelist missionary. Having no use for a radio, since it was a dog that his *amik* wanted, Tsukanka had then suggested that Tseremp take back the radio, sell it in the petroleum company's camp, and send the money back in the company's little aeroplane to a Shuar *amik* of Tsukanka's. This *amik* would then buy a dog from the Shuar and Tsukanka would fetch it. This admirable plan collapsed, however, yesterday morning, when Tseremp gave the radio to Nayapi. The fact is that Tseremp covets a large canoe that Nayapi is just completing. He would return to pick it up in a few months' time, take it back to Capahuari and give it to Titiar in exchange for the radio. It would be pointless to seek for any economic rationality or any commercial motive in this ballet that bounces two articles from hand to hand along apparently endless paths and rivers in flood. No material gain is likely at the end, or rather the provisional end, of the chain of transactions, but through it Tseremp will have reinforced his links with a number of individuals from whom he hopes to win support – some very close to him, for example his brother-in-law Titiar, others very distant, to wit his new ally Nayapi. Admittedly, Tsukanka has for the moment been short-changed and Tseremp is once again in his debt. But there is no harm done, for a son-in-law is anyway eternally indebted to his father-in-law for the wife that he has received in marriage from him.

It would, no doubt, have been simpler for each person to transfer his debt and for Tseremp or Nayapi to reimburse Washikta directly, given that both know him. But nothing could be more alien to the Achuar philosophy of exchange than such a redeeming of debts. In market capitalism it is the movement of objects that generates contractual links between those involved, and relations between individuals are established through goods by reason of the profit that each stage in their circulation makes it possible to pocket. In contrast, the barter that my companions engage in rests upon a personal and exclusive relationship between two partners only, in which the exchange of goods is a means rather than an end. Such a relationship cannot be extended in either direction to any of those who have used or will use those same goods, so that they too could perpetuate a link of the same type. Quite apart from the fact that a system such as this in no way affects the value of the objects exchanged, a value that remains constant however many hands the articles pass through, it operates against the formation of truly commercial networks. The *amik* of my *amik* is not my *amik*; in fact he may well be my enemy.

The absence of any connection between the various pairs of trading partners means that the goods can circulate over considerable distances but the people involved cannot. As soon as an Achuar leaves the limit of the territory of the most distant of his *amik*, he finds himself on hostile terrain. This state of affairs considerably restricts the journeys that one can make and presents problems for those who wish to see more of the world. Hence Tseremp's and Tarir's interest in accompanying us. According to them, our presence is a guarantee of protection for them, for the soldiers of Montalvo have made it known to the Achuar that they will leave them free to make war on one another so long as they do not involve Whites. The extreme isolation of the Jivaros over several centuries was no doubt in part due to this limitation on their movements and the turning in on themselves to which this led. Unlike other Amazonian peoples, those of the Orinoco and the Ucayali in particular, who undertook canoe journeys of several hundred kilometres in order to exchange salt, curare or feathers, sometimes in market-places with truly extra-territorial status, no safe-conduct system has ever made it possible for commercial expeditions to travel through the Jivaro citadel. There is no trace here of the vast inter-ethnic confederations that have come into being elsewhere along the trading routes.

The afternoon brings a surprise and the key to a long-standing mystery. Tii has come to visit Nayapi as a neighbour and to entrust him with a mission. Yesterday Tii's brother-in-law, Yaur, arrived at his home from the lower Copataza to collect from Sumpaish the *tumash* owed to him as compensation for the widow of his brother Ikiam, and Tii is asking Nayapi to act as intermediary in the negotiation with Sumpaish. Yaur wants a rifle and two boxes of cartridges, and has a good chance of getting them since Tsamarin declared, while we were visiting him, that he would willingly give his rifle to his brother Sumpaish in the event of Yaur claiming the *tumash*. In the stilted style peculiar to this kind of conversation, in which each speaker comments interminably on the motives and justifications of each of the protagonists, the two men little by little reveal all the details of the 'Ikiam affair'.

It will be remembered that this whole affair began several months ago when Pinik, fed up with her husband's ill-treatment of her, ran away from him. Fleeing down the Pastaza in a canoe, she had landed up on the lower Kapawi, where Sumpaish had made her his wife. Determined to avenge this affront, Ikiam had set out with the intention of killing the illicit couple, but had soon disappeared without trace. It is now known that Sumpaish had nothing to do with his disappearance and that it was in truth Pinik's own father, a powerful shaman by the name of Ujukam, who had set it up. Sick of seeing his daughter beaten by his son-in-law under his very own roof, despite all his remonstrations, it was he in the first place who helped Pinik to flee by giving her a canoe. As Ikiam was announcing to all and sundry that he was about to go after the young woman and kill her, Ujukam had then secretly arranged with his brother-in-law Washikta, of Sasaïme, to have the man intercepted and prevented from doing further damage. It is said that Ujukam was acting not only out of paternal love but also in the interests of public fairness. Ikiam, also a shaman, had an execrable reputation and was accused of spreading *tunchi* on all sides and even casting spells on dogs out of pure malice. Given the credit that Ujukam enjoyed as a shaman, he was well placed to foster such allegations and was no doubt, at least in part, motivated by a desire to ruin the career of a rival. On the evening before Ikiam set out, Ujukam sent word to Washikta who, along with his brother-in-law Narankas, had by dawn taken up position on the bank of the main branch of the Pastaza. To look natural, they pretended to be fishing. When Ikiam appeared, proudly sporting his *tawasap* and war-paint, Washikta and Narankas hailed him from the bank, calling him over to talk. He explained his plans to them, lamenting the fact that his brother Yaur had refused to accompany him. The two accomplices expressed sympathy over his misfortune and offered to lend him a hand. As is customary on such occasions, when the coming fight is so to speak mimed out in advance, they then all took to brandishing their rifles and making excited threats. Hopping rhythmically from one foot to the other, they proclaimed their unity and boasted of their future exploits. When the excitement was at its peak Narankas fired a shot into the air and Ikiam followed suit. This was exactly what Washikta was waiting for and he promptly fired point-blank at the poor dupe, who was now defenceless. They then weighted his body with stones and flung it into the river.

When I look back over this story it seems to me to provide a perfect illustration of the tragi-comic way in which rumours, false news and trickery all combine in the weaving of a vendetta. Right from the start there were those who were in the know and those who were not, the former lying to the latter either actively or by omission, each for different reasons. Thus when Tayujin, on his return from Sasaïme, brought the news of Ikiam's disappearance to Capahuari, he must already have known who the guilty parties were since he had just spent several days staying with one of them, his own brother, Narankas. Yet it was Tayujin who had suggested to his father-in-law Tsukanka the two hypotheses that were thereafter fancied in Capahuari – the Sumpaish variant and the Kawarunch variant. Perhaps he was afraid of alienating Tsukanka if it became known that his brother Narankas had been involved in the assassination of the uncle of Auju, the mother of his own wife. On the occasion of our visit to Sasaïme Washikta had taken good care not to reveal his role in Ikiam's murder to the people from Capahuari, even carrying duplicity to the point of giving his *amik* Tsukanka the weapon he had used, the very rifle now in Nayapi's hands. Only Auju had been wary of Washikta, although without any evidence for her suspicions. But the real fool in this farce was the luckless Kawarunch: not only was he the only man at Sasaïme kept in the dark about what had really happened, but he had then found himself accused of the crime by the very man who had committed it and who took malicious pleasure in spreading that slander, with the active complicity of Tukupi and his relatives. No doubt in order to protect Washikta and Ujukam, Tukupi had spared himself no pains in the spreading of false rumours, particularly when he had told Yaur that Sumpaish had boasted in his presence of killing Yaur's brother. The height of ridicule for Kawarunch was when he went down the lower Kapawi with his brother-in-law Narankas to claim a rifle from Sumpaish on behalf of Yaur, as compensation for the murder of Ikiam. The people of the lower Kapawi, who had been put in the picture by Ujukam, knew perfectly well that Narankas had taken part in the affair, but nobody put Kawarunch straight. All they told him was that Sumpaish could not possibly have done what he was accused of. Narankas is said to have remained very quiet during these transactions, his eyes fixed on the ground. Yaur is the other dupe in the affair. Having been too pusillanimous to help his brother to avenge his honour, and being thereby responsible for allowing him to face a perilous situation all on his own, he had hung around Ujukam for months, discussing the chances of his obtaining from Sumpaish compensation for the very crime that his neighbour had himself instigated. Yaur now knows all that really happened, but he has no intention of taking revenge in the immediate future. The rifle he is claiming from Sumpaish in exchange for the widow of his brother is quite enough for his modest ambitions. Neither he nor Sumpaish want any trouble and the transaction should be completed quickly. However, the *tumash* that he would be justified in demanding from Washikta or even Ujukam for Ikiam's death is quite a different matter. If he claimed it, he would find himself on his own facing a group of dangerous, unified allies who have, furthermore, never admitted their guilt.

It may be found surprising that the Achuar equate the abduction of a woman with the death of a man and insist in both cases on compensation in the form of a rifle. But the fact is that reparation for infractions of the marriage code obeys the principle of a return to parity through payment of an indemnity. The principle involved is in every respect identical to that which governs vengeance for a murder. Deprived of a person who should by rights fall to him or over whom he exercises guardianship, a creditor considers himself authorized to compensate himself for his loss by eliminating the person who is responsible for it and who, on that account, owes him a life. The rifle that Yaur is claiming from Sumpaish is thus not the price that the latter must pay in order to keep Pinik, but a substitute for vengeance.

250

It liberates Yaur from the obligation to kill and buys back Sumpaish's life rather than his right to do what he will with the young woman.

There is nothing metaphorical about this vocabulary of debt. An exchange of goods, an exchange of women and an exchange of lives all belong to the same field of meanings and are designated by identical terms. Thus *yapajia* means 'to pay off a debt', 'to give in return' in the case of an exchange that is not completed on the spot, and also 'to avenge oneself'; and *tumash* is the strict equivalent of what we understand by 'debt', that is to say not only a moral commitment but also both what created that commitment and whatever is used to pay it off. However, the personal obligation introduced by a 'blood debt' (*numpa tumash*) differs from that created by a gift: the latter is binding upon the debtor, whereas the former above all concerns the creditor, who cannot rest until he has obtained satisfaction for the assassination of one of his relatives. Once this is done, he is again 'free' (*ankan*), no longer bound by any obligation, in exactly the same way as someone who has just paid off a debt by giving a gift in return. Unlike in other parts of the world where it used to be customary to exchange people for riches – slaves, for example, or wives bought from their parents – the payment of a rifle in return for a life does not imply that the value of a human being is commensurable with that of an object: not only is this the only situation in which such a transaction is possible, but the nature of the article claimed suggests a kind of commutative justice in which the taking of a life is paid for by the very instrument that will make a future murder possible. Substituting a life by the potentiality of a death thus creates new credit and perpetuates the cycle of exchange.

CHAPTER 16

Drinking Party

PULLED BY THE WOMEN and pushed by the men, the canoe moves a few metres forward amid a chorus of shouts, then grinds to a halt, askew. Nayapi and Tsamarin remove the logs on which the craft has just slid along and rearrange them in front of the prow; then everyone harnesses up once more. For over three hours now we have been dragging this burden along a straight path, opened up with machetes, from the little hill where Nayapi felled the huge trunk of *cedro* out of which he made his canoe. The Chundaykiu is only a few hundred metres away now but it will be some time before we can set the canoe afloat in this little tributary of the Kapawi. A whole crowd of people has gathered from round about for the *ipiakratatuin*, the invitation issued by Nayapi. As well as his wives, Makatu and Mirijiar, there are Taish and his sister Mamays, a sharp-tongued widow, Kajekui, Tsamarin and his wife, Tii and his wife Ishtik, two Achuar from further downstream, Winchikiur and Samik, accompanied by their wives, and even three Quichuas, Isango, Chango and Dahua, each accompanied by a wife. Nayapi asked us to stay on for a few days to help him finish his canoe, to the great satisfaction of Tseremp, who will now have a chance to check out its qualities and defects, as he is hoping that Nayapi will give it to him. My companion is also looking forward to the little party that the master of the house is to give this evening to thank his guests, and is hoping that it will bring some relief to his enforced celibacy.

Despite the hard work, the atmosphere is cheerful. Streaming with sweat beneath a hellish sun, in the physical excitement of common exertion men and women seem to have abandoned the rather stiff reserve that generally marks relations between the sexes in public. The laughter is punctuated by jokes, each going one better than the last.

252

'It is we, the little women, who do everything,' says Mamays. 'Here we are, pulling, pulling, and the men all fall into our net. Given that we are Tsunki women, how could they possibly resist us?'

'Poor Nayapi,' quips the Quichua Isango. 'He really needs his little Tsunki wife now, considering how long it has been since he's been able to fuck Makatu and Mirijiar!'

'You can talk,' retorts his wife. 'But you wouldn't mind having several wives, like the Achuar. Perhaps then you would pay less attention to the wives of others!'

The Quichuas have gone too far and an embarrassed silence immediately falls. Isango's joke is a rather heavy allusion to the self-imposed chastity of a man engaged in making a canoe, without which the boat would be unstable, like a couple rolling on a bed in each other's arms. The remark was too explicitly sexual and shocked the Achuar who are, in general, critical of the Quichuas' excessive liberty of tone and behaviour, always particularly noticeable in situations of collective labour.

Isango is a short man, aged about thirty, rather stooping but dry and muscular as an athlete and with bright, cunning eyes that testify to his cleverness as a go-between. He works as a *tambero* for a tiny detachment of soldiers stationed at the confluence of the Kapawi and the Pastaza known as Capitán Chiriboga, in honour of a hero of the 1941 war against Peru. A *tambero* is a kind of military road mender. Isango is responsible for keeping clear the path that leads, in a four- to five-day forced march, from this outpost to the Montalvo garrison. He took over this job from his father Etsa, a Shuar from the Makuma who moved to Canelos, where he married a Quichua woman, and who played a major role in the creation of this detachment a dozen or so years ago. Obsessed by the idea of guarding their border with Peru, an imaginary line running through an uninhabited forest, the Ecuadorian army has dotted around two or three squads in huts set up alongside the principal rivers leading to their powerful neighbour – maybe fifteen men at the most for the whole Achuar territory, to patrol about 150 kilometres of the frontier. The establishment of this altogether symbolic force was made possible by the collaboration of the Quichuas of Montalvo, who built the outposts and opened up the paths leading to them. They provide for all the needs of the wretched conscripts, who are too scared of getting lost in the forest or of being killed by the Achuar ever to stray from their quarters. The Quichuas, who are officially Christianized and more or less mono-gamous and who speak Spanish and are outwardly respectful to the authorities, constitute a splendid auxiliary force for the Ecuadorian army. The army is extremely distrustful of the Achuar, whom it con-siders to be savages with a repugnant way of life, speaking an incom-prehensible gibberish and all the more inclined to betray their nominal country given that so many of their kinsmen live in Peruvian territory. Each military detachment is looked after by two or three Quichua families, who maintain good relations with the neighbouring Achuar. Many of these Quichuas are cultural hybrids, as are Isango and his father, that is to say they are Indians of Shuar or Achuar origin who became 'civilized' two or three generations back, adopting the lan-guage and customs of the Quichuas. They speak the Jivaro language well and understand all its rhetorical subtleties, as Isango proved this morning when he took part in an orthodox *yaitias chicham* dialogue. Also like Isango many of them are shamans of considerable repute, for in this domain the Achuar credit the Quichuas, in particular those who work for the army, with powers far greater than their own.

Around mid-afternoon the canoe at last reaches the end of its overland journey. The women now simulate its launching, struggling to haul an imaginary weight to the little river into which they then all tumble, splashing one another. They are the daughters of Tsunki, the spirit of the waters, and their presence mollifies the new element in which the hollowed trunk is about to begin its second life. With much panting, the craft is then thrust into the Chundaykiu, where it floats, perfectly balanced, to the visible relief of its owner.

A visitor awaits us in Nayapi's house: a *regatón* from Montalvo by the name of Jaramillo, who has come to claim payment for a debt from the master of the house. Like all the river pedlars of the region, the man practises *enganche*, providing a kind of credit whereby manu-factured goods are advanced to the Indians to be paid for later in kind, generally with produce that they have gathered that has a far greater market value than the objects with which they were provided. A few months ago Nayapi took receipt of four or five pieces of cotton material from Jaramillo who, in return, had asked for a quintal of ivory palm fibres. This plant is very common in the region and its tough fibres are used in the Sierra to make brooms. A quintal is about the equivalent of 50 kilos, but here it is more a unit of volume than of weight, defined as a cube the side of which is measured by a standard length stick. Nayapi has not prepared even a third of the agreed quintal but does not seem particularly bothered. Nor is Jaramillo seriously put out. Possibly because he is too easy-going in business matters, Jaramillo presents a very scruffy spectacle. With his bare feet, a tattered shirt and an antediluvian pair of trousers, all that distinguishes him from the Indians is his slightly paler skin. His command of Quichua is good and he understands Achuar. His canoe has no motor and is poled along by a Quichua *péon* standing amid the jumble of bundles of fibres and heaps of peccary skins that he has collected from his debtors along the way. Weeks of effort, negotiation and trying weather, and all to bring a relatively meagre collection of booty back to Montalvo.

Surprised at meeting Whites in the heart of Achuar country and initially rather suspicious, Jaramillo eventually opens up and confides his story to us. Obliged to leave his native province, Loja, to escape from a murderous political vendetta, he took refuge in Montalvo one fine day in 1949, after several months' travelling through the Andes and the forest. Amazonia was at that time a sanctuary for outlaws and down-and-outs of many kinds: as in the French Foreign Legion, no indiscreet questions were put to the adventurers who arrived there in search of a new existence. The landing-strip had not yet been opened and Montalvo then amounted to no more than a handful of Whites who scraped a living trading with the Indians. Jaramillo had worked for one of these *regatones*, Jaime Cevallos, and soon married his daughter. He could not have made a better choice: Don Jaime, now extremely old, is a legendary figure throughout the region to the north of the Pastaza, held in high esteem not only by the few Whites living there but also by the Indians, virtually all of whom he knows personally. He is the last survivor of the three men who founded Montalvo during the First World War as a trading post for the collection of rubber, his two bosses, Juan Jerez and Angel Montalvo, having abandoned trafficking in balata during the thirties, when this trade became less profitable. Don Jaime had acted as their agent amongst the Indians and travelled everywhere in the forest, equally at ease with the Quichuas and the Achuar, whose language he mastered. He offered them hospitality in Montalvo and himself enjoyed theirs on his trips, becoming 'godfather' to a multitude of children whose parents are now linked to him by a web of mutual obligations.

In many regions of Upper Amazonia the rubber boom was a nightmarish episode for the Indians who, forced to work like slaves, fell victims in their thousands to the inhumane treatment meted out by the blood-thirsty militia of the rubber barons. But the Achuar and Quichuas of the Montalvo hinterland were spared the exactions of that sinister period. Don Jaime certainly practised *enganche* to obtain his bales of latex, but in exchange he gave the Indians objects hitherto unknown, in particular weapons and metal tools that were soon much in demand. In some Achuar houses you still come across dismantled Mannlicher rifles left over from the 1914–18 war and destined, through the Treaty of Versailles, to end their long and lethal existences amongst the Indians.

The 1941 conflict with Peru put a stop to this general prosperity by closing the waterways along which the rubber had been carried to Iquitos, whence it was exported via the Amazon to Europe and North America. Don Jaime fell back on the less lucrative products that the Indians could collect, sending them on by canoe from Montalvo to the Dominican mission at Canelos and thence, along rough mule tracks, into the Andes. Jaramillo now carries on the torch of what he claims to consider a civilizing mission rather than a commercial enterprise and, in truth, the life is a dream of his youth come true: a free and adventurous existence lived as a kind of soliloquy in the shelter of the jungle. A forest wanderer by vocation and a business man by necessity, this little cheap-jack trader is accepted with equanimity by the Achuar, perhaps because in him, as in his father-in-law, they detect all the signs of a moral scepticism too deep to be alienated by a taste for power or greed for riches.

After a short lecture delivered without conviction and received without anxiety, Jaramillo left empty-handed for Capitán Chiriboga. Now the *namper* can begin. With the party in view, Nayapi's wives have prepared vast quantities of manioc beer which they have left to ferment for several days, mixed with the juice of sugar cane to increase the alcoholic content. The men are seated in a semicircle on logs in the *tankamash*, while the women, based in the *ekent*, operate a constant ferrying service to keep them tanked up directly from their gourds. Unlike on visits, when you are offered a *pininkia* that you can then sip at your leisure, at a *namper* it is not possible to avoid getting drunk, as the women stick their receptacles between your lips with a sardonic delight, keeping them upturned until the entire contents have disappeared down your gullet. Anne Christine is taking mischievous pleasure in assisting our hostesses, to the amazement of the men, who are soon enchanted by this novelty. Pint after pint of this sourish beer is thus consumed in a state of semi-suffocation, not without damage to one's clothes, which are repeatedly drenched with the overflow. The purpose of the drinking session is not to savour the drink but, as with many beer-drinking peoples, to consume the maximum in the minimum length of time, so as to get drunk. This does not take long: the noisy conversation becomes more animated, words are enunciated less distinctly, a vague smile shines in blurred eyes, the jokes become broader, the laughter more emphatic.

Most of the guests have donned their gala gear. Many of the men are crowned with their *tawasap* and some of them are wearing coils of *shauk* or jaguar teeth as necklaces. Samik even sports a *kunch wearmu* worn crosswise, a wide woven band fringed with a mixture of *nupir* bells, the dried fruits of a kind of sapote tree, and ornaments made from coins hooked to pieces of toucan bone. With his every movement it tinkles in a most charming fashion. Several of the women are also wearing *nupir* bells and jangle, like bead curtains in southern France, as they walk. In contrast to the men, who wear their *shauk* quite loosely, the women have wound them in serried coils around their wrists and necks, like gaily coloured collars. Some of them have inserted labrets, fine ornamental sticks beneath their lower lips, which bounce on their chins and emphasize the shape of their mouths far better than any make-up. Those who have favoured this kind of adornment are well aware of its effects. Irarit, Winchikiur's very young wife, fiddles with her little stick in a deliciously provocative way, rolling it around, tapping it and pulling it out to suck it in an ingenuous fashion under the furtive but lustful eye of Tseremp.

Samik has begun to play the *tsayantar*, the mouth bow. Not only does the music go well with the *natem*-induced hallucinations but it also suits the euphoria produced by the alcohol, its thin, monotonous sound first lulling the drowsy mind, then from time to time jolting it with a discordant note. Urged on by his guests, Nayapi, in a firm voice, strikes up a *nampet*.

Cacique with a crest of vibrant yellow, I am the cacique from far away
On the path, on the path, all vibrant yellow, I met you
And what are you going to do to me? you asked me, you asked me
Ha hai! Ha ha hai!
That's what I was, just that I was
A cacique of the hills, I was going along, going towards distant lands
   and on the way I met you
Already I had been rejected, so alone, so alone
Having met you on the path, standing there, standing on the path, I
   sucked your breasts
So alone, so alone though, on the path, my gaze lingered over your
   body
Ha ha! Ha ha hai!
Cacique from the hills, cacique from the hills, on the path I met you
What are you going to do with all that yellow? you said to me
And I, carried away, swept away, transported, I gazed at the whole of
   you
Ha hai! Ha ha hai!
And you, returning to your land, to your land, are you not going to
   shoot at my nest?
Will you not do that, and me carried away, swept away, transported
Ha hai! Ha ha hai! Ha hai! Ha ha hai!

In the *ekent* the women are whispering and laughing and Mirijiar
comes forward to reply to Nayapi.

Round a bend in the path, there she was, weeping for me
Ha hai! Ha ha hai!
Woman from another river, leaning, leaning over the water, round a
   bend in the path, there she was weeping for me
Ha hai! Ha ha hai!
Woman lying on the surface of the waters, I will take you with me, I
   said to her lying, lying there, she was weeping for me
Ha hai! Ha ha hai!
Woman of another river, leaning, leaning over the water, lying there,
   she was weeping for me
Ha hai! Ha ha hai!
Woman lying on the surface of the waters, woman with provocative
   lips, lying there, she was weeping for me
Ha hai! Ha ha hai! Ha hai! Ha ha hai!

'*Ijiamprami! Ijiamprami!*' cry the men. 'Let's dance! Let's dance! It is our music that makes the women dance. All they can do is sing!' No doubt stung by this remark, pretty Irarit launches into a *nampet* with a faster rhythm than the last two.

> There where they all go to dance, I am only doing the same
> There where the armadillos go to dance, I am only doing as they
>   do
> There where the acouchis go to dance, I am only doing as they do
> There where the agoutis go to dance, I am only doing as they do
> There where the achira flowers, I am only doing the same
> *Ha hai! Ha ha hai!*
> There where the armadillos go to dance, I stay quite still
> There where the acouchis go to dance, I am still, like this
> There where the red deer go to dance, I am still, like this
> And I am what I do
> *Ha hai! Ha ha hai! Ha hai! Ha ha hai!*

In contrast to *anent*, monologues of the soul whose magic efficacy lies in a secret meaning, *nampet* are public, secular songs that exalt love and tell of its pains with the aid of allegorical figures as subtle and codified as those of courtly poetry. A chance meeting on a path, self-deprecation, the solitude of the traveller, bucolic images, lovers' melancholy, metaphors drawn from the lives of birds and the mystery of the river are among the most common tropes that a knowledgeable audience savours as so many evocations of the various registers of passionate love. *Nampet* shares the same root as *namper*, drinking party, but as can be seen it is no drinking song, rather a kind of madrigal, sometimes in part improvised. It is suited to a drinking party only because drink momentarily liberates men and women from the shyness that would normally inhibit them from giving public expression to such personal feelings.

Transported by Irarit's song, Nayapi seizes his drum and urges everyone to dance. Holding the instrument under his left arm, he pounds out a four-beat rhythm with a stick and begins to dance rhythmically around the main pillars of the house. After a slight hesitation, Tii follows suit, also with his drum. Soon he is joined by Samik, still playing his *tsayantar*, then by Winchikiur with his *pinkui*, a long, transverse, two-holed flute reserved for playing dancing music – as opposed to the short *peem* flute, which is kept for *anent*. Against the background of regular drumbeats, the two melodies intertwine harmoniously, the mouth bow chiming in with the flute and the latter from time to time taking off on its own with sudden, intense variations that shrilly soar above. One after another, all the men join in this somnambulic stomp. I imitate those who carry no musical instrument, tapping my rounded beer-belly in the same rhythm as the drummers. The women for their part unrelentingly continue to dispense their libations to whoever they can catch in passing.

Pointing an imperious drumstick at Makatu, Nayapi invites her to enter the men's area and dance with him in the middle of the house. To the accompaniment of fervent exclamations of '*Pai! pai!*' she launches into a series of jumping half turns, her legs together, her body bent slightly forward and her hands pressed flat against her thighs. At each of these little jumps the suddenly rejuvenated matron tosses her head back, sweeping her loosened hair through the air in a movement at once alluring and full of abandon. Nayapi is content simply to move around her in a rather pompous fashion, still beating his drum. Then another couple takes over, followed by another until the moment comes when Anne Christine and I can no longer avoid taking a turn about the floor in what is more of a tropical 'salsa' than an orthodox *ijiampramu* but is nevertheless greeted by a chorus of enthusiastic exclamations.

In the house dimly lit by the trembling flicker of the fires and the copal resin torches, fleeting glances, discreet finger-tip touches and secret, hasty whispers are beginning to add relish to the party. In a society where adultery may seal a wife's death warrant, the game of seduction and the behaviour of lovers in public demand considerable reserves of dissimulation and subtlety. The way in which a woman serves a man his bowl of beer, arranging to touch his hand as she does so, or addresses him quietly by his name instead of by the appropriate kinship title, a soft movement of the lips in his direction, the little presents that a man gives without her husband knowing, the way he belittles himself in conversation – all are the practically imperceptible signs of a yearning heart that those involved are quick to recognize. Discretion is essential, the more so given that in itself it constitutes a powerful force of attraction: a woman's modest and reserved demeanour is considered by a man as an erotic stimulus, perhaps by virtue of

the contrast that it presents with the thought of the pleasure that he is looking forward to giving her.

Both men and women go to considerable trouble to further the caprices of inclination with a whole arsenal of love philtres. These are classic ingredients in the love life of much of Upper Amazonia, where they are known by the Quichua name *pusanga*. The Achuar refer to them as *musap* or *semayuk*. The most widely used *musap* are the plants women use to perfume themselves so as to attract men or that they slip, in infinitesimal quantities, into their *pininkia* when offering manioc beer to a visitor. The most sought after are preparations made from birds: on the one hand the heart and brain of the grosbeak, a little sparrow with a red beak, considered to be unlucky, whose soft, tuneful whistle accounts for its Achuar name, *pees-a-pees*, and on the other the particularly prized long, thin, barbed tongue of the toucan that can be taken from it if it falls to earth upon its back with outstretched wings, provided it is then deeply buried in exactly the same position. In the hierarchy of perception, the statuses of these two birds are very different. The grosbeak is also called 'the evil spirit bird' (*iwianch chinki*) because it is one of the possible incarnations for the souls of the dead and is associated with their frenzied desire to seduce the living, which impels their various avatars to lure women and children to them to alleviate their desperate solitude. In contrast, the toucan, by reason of its attractive plumage and a love life reputed to be identical to that of human beings, is a symbol of triumphant virility. It is hardly surprising that when it lies with its great beak pointing skywards it possesses an immediate phallic symbolism for the Achuar.

However, my companions are not as keen on amulets and magic potions as their Quichua neighbours are. In Tseremp's opinion, one of the philtres considered by the Quichuas to be particularly effective for attracting women, the vulva of a freshwater dolphin worn as a bracelet, is nothing but a risible superstition. In truth, the Quichuas seem attached to a literal kind of homeopathic alchemy based on a direct derivation of the qualities of a substance, and in this they are more vitalist than the Achuar, for whom charms above all condense abstract relations and thereby, on a miniature scale, synthesize the relations that they desire to establish with particular people or animals.

The materialism of the Quichuas also goes hand in hand with a more extrovert sociability. Men and women alike, it is they who are the noisiest this evening, their jokes always salacious and their behaviour almost beyond the limits of flirtatiousness. When Isango seizes Tii's wife by the waist to dance with her, he oversteps the bounds of party behaviour and an angry quarrel breaks out between the two men. The contrast between their respective attitudes is striking. Isango, flushed with anger, is waving his fists about, restrained with difficulty by Chango and Dahua. Meanwhile Tii, very pale, stands stiffly with folded arms, pouring forth a loud monologue on the respect due to him and interspersing this from time to time with calls to the kind of war that real men know how to wage. The Achuar have a horror of the bare-fisted brawls that are common amongst the Quichuas and respond to provocation solely with promises of swift retribution, their cold determination all the more alarming because these are frequently followed up. As in most quarrels that flare up at drinking parties, an antagonism already existed between the two men even before the present, relatively harmless motive for the dispute. Tarir tells me that both Isango and Tii are shamans and are therefore professional rivals, and that the considerable reputation of the former puts the more mediocre successes of the latter in the shade. Contrary to the beliefs of the evangelist missionaries, who abominate this kind of festivity because they imagine that it provokes conflict and division, the drunkenness in this case simply reveals deeper tensions, which are not usually expressed because of the constraints of the social code. Suppressing these *namper*, as they would like to, would simply result in increasing the unexpectedness of assassinations that a public display of disagreement may up to a point help to prevent.

The fact is that relations between the Achuar and the Quichuas are marked by ambiguity. Their affinity is manifest, since the forest Quichuas are for the most part former Jivaros tempered over the past two centuries in the melting-pot of the Dominican missions, where they have learned the lingua franca that they now speak but meanwhile retain many elements of their original culture. As one result of this ethnic transmigration, in the eyes of the Quichuas the Jivaros continue to embody all the values that they themselves lost when they elected to seek from the Whites a knowledge of the big wide world – a knowledge that the Achuar now secretly envy them. The Quichuas admire the warrior virtues of the Achuar, the men's show of virility, their skills as huntsmen and their physical endurance – in short all the qualities of a free and proud people for which they are still nostalgic. On the other hand they condemn their duplicity and also their jealous, bloodthirsty nature – all the negative side of their still intact 'wildness'. Conversely, the Quichuas are regarded by the Achuar as good-for-nothings, drunkards and cowards, as slow and lymphatic as can be thanks to an undiscriminating diet, for these are people without principles who stoop so low – would you believe it? – as to eat slothful creatures such as opossums and great anteaters. On the other hand, they do recognize their considerable shamanistic powers, to such a point that little Achuar boys are sometimes even sent as apprentices to the Quichua *kumpa* of their fathers to learn the manners and language of these 'white' Indians in the hope that, by marrying the daughter of a shaman, they will one day inherit the knowledge of their father-in-law. The passage from the one culture to the other thus continues to be one-way, but its ease has no doubt protected the Achuar as a whole from changes of a too profound nature. Those who feel attracted to change need only travel a few dozen kilometres to find in already familiar Quichua country the by now well-tried apparatus for conversion.

It is long past midnight now and the hubbub has finally calmed down, leaving various individuals to nurse their resentment or their beer in the post-party disorder. Samik's *tsayantar* is still throbbing quietly amid snores and whispered conversations, while from the river below come the sounds of bathing and muffled laughter. Slumped on a banana leaf, Tseremp is brooding: he has had no luck this evening.

CHAPTER 17

The Art of Accommodating Enemies

ON THE MORNING AFTER the night before, Tseremp is in a gloomy mood and blocks all my arguments with a wall of blinkered obstinacy. For several days now I have been urging that we move on, for I am anxious to continue as soon as possible on a journey that is as yet hardly begun. But Tseremp finds it very comfortable here in Nayapi's home and jibs at venturing further, amongst people whom he does not know. Beyond Capitán Chiriboga we shall be entering territory unknown to my Capahuari companions and we shall have to ask for hospitality from potential enemies. Quite apart from his recurrent fear of malaria, Tseremp is now afraid of being assassinated by these distant Achuar, for no particular reason apart from the bloodthirsty disposition that he attributes to them. I try first persuasion, then flattery; I appeal to his self-esteem and his pride; I jeer at his cowardice and threaten to broadcast it everywhere; and I explain, without really believing it, that our presence guarantees his safety. Finally, I remind him that his brother-in-law Wajari has entrusted our safety to him. To my great exasperation, nothing does the trick. Then inspiration strikes me. One of the men I hope to visit is Nankiti, his father's assassin, who is believed to live in total isolation on a small tributary of the Corrientes. Now, as I have learnt from my discreet enquiries, not only has Tseremp never attempted to avenge himself, since at the time he was too young to do so, but furthermore he has never claimed *tumash* from Nankiti. So here is the needed spur. It is admittedly two-edged, for there is no reason why Nankiti should welcome this belated request. Nevertheless, as I have taken care to make my proposal before a large audience, Tseremp can no longer retreat without losing face.

Unlike Wajari, whom the description did not fit at all, Tseremp is in many respects typical of what ethnographic literature terms an informant. The role of a patented intermediary seems one to which his past life and temperament predestined him, yet it is one in which he has never found fulfilment, encumbered as he is with too calculating a character to inspire lasting friendship. Sly rather than intelligent, craving novelty and fascinated by foreigners, right from the start he tried to win our confidence, proffering his taste for gossip, his desire for dependence and the detached, even disillusioned attitude towards his own culture that has little by little been sharpened by the lack of respect his own people show him. Orphaned at a tender age, he was taken in by his 'godfather' Cevallos at Montalvo, where he learned to speak Quichua and picked up a few White manners, before returning, as an adolescent, to his half-brother Tarir. Cut off from his original life and deprived of his parents during the crucial years when young Achuar learn how to behave as adults, Tseremp is an unskilful hunter and an inferior orator, two educational handicaps that are impossible to overcome. Moreover, despite all his efforts, he has never managed to encounter *arutam*, the terrifying initiatory experience that all young people are expected to pass through and without which they cannot claim to be fully developed men.

Although conscious of not being a fully committed Achuar, Tseremp does not want to become Quichua and is thus left in the limbo of an evanescent identity that causes him intermittent dissatisfaction, fortunately tempered none the less by his jovial nature. The detachment that he affects towards a culture in which he has never found his place no doubt determined his wish to become my intermediary. But his knowledge is unfortunately too scrappy to be accepted with confidence, and I find his conniving insinuations extremely irritating on account of all that they presume in the way of shared prejudices and common condescension towards those whose interpreter he seeks to be. Yet that complicity of his is encouraged by our own impotence, forced as we are to rely upon his paid assistance in our journey, which none of our Capahuari companions, not even my *amik* Wajari, had judged it opportune to undertake with us. Already smarting somewhat from our cool reception of his overtures of good faith, Tseremp may now be beginning to feel positively resentful.

A visit from Tii introduces the timely diversion of a sensational piece of news. Kawarunch has just been killed by Narankas and his brother Nurinksa. This time, not the slightest doubt surrounds either the identity of the murderers or the circumstances of the drama, the pretext for which was once again a woman. A few weeks ago Iyun, no longer able to put up with the nasty character of her husband Narankas, took refuge with her father, Tuntuam, another deaf-mute, like Tukupi's brother. Furious at being deserted, Narankas went off to fetch his brother Nurinksa, on the Chinkianentza, to help him to kill his father-in-law, whom he considered responsible for his daughter's flight. The two brothers combed the region in search of Tuntuam, who had left home, even pushing as far south as the Surikentza, where this deaf-mute often went for treatment by the great shaman Chumpi. Frustrated in his desire for vengeance, Narankas one day unexpectedly came across Kawarunch, who was making a canoe in the forest. Now, Kawarunch was the maternal uncle of Narankas's wife and Narankas suspected him of having persuaded his niece to run away and of having set his sister and brother-in-law against him. Kawarunch was indeed well known to exert considerable influence over Tuntuam, his only remaining supporter since his clashes with the people of Sasaïme. According to Narankas, Kawarunch had it in for him partly because of the ridiculous role he had been made to play in the Ikiam affair but also on account of a secret desire to get his niece back and marry her himself. At any rate, the three men became so angry as they hurled unpleasant accusations at one another that Narankas ended up by firing at Kawarunch from point-blank range.

Now the entire region is simmering. According to Tii, Narankas and Nurinksa have holed up in a fortified house on the Chinkianentza, to which they have summoned their brothers Tayujin and Jempe from Capahuari, and also Yakum, a 'branch' brother living amongst the southern Achuar. Kawarunch's sons and relatives by marriage, Kunamp, Awiritiur, Tsuink, Yaur and Seum, have gathered at Tuntuam's house and are feeling out the lie of the land as regards alliances. They say they can count on the help of Wajari and Titiar in Capahuari. Tsukanka is talking of going to war again and says he will kill his son-in-law Tayujin. On the other hand, predictably enough, the people of Sasaïme do not seem keen to get involved, not even Tukupi, whose half-sister Kawarunch had married. The general view is that the murder was not justified: Narankas and Nurinksa are 'hot-heads' (*waumak*), excitable youths whose impulsive violence spreads trouble and who lack the self-control that is the mark of a *kakaram*, a truly valiant man.

Nayapi is himself beginning to get angry, shouting boastfully that he will avenge his brother-in-law Kawarunch, despite the fact that he had not been slow in repudiating the latter's sister. Tii is chiming in with him, whilst Tarir is pronouncing sententious words of blame to which nobody is listening. As soon as they heard the news, Nayapi's wives launched themselves into the ritual lamentations of mourning: 'Little father, little father, shall I never see-ee-ee you any more? Little father, little father, where have you go-o-one? Little father, little father, do not loo-oo-ook at me any more!' On and on they drone, albeit in a rather distracted manner, it seems to me, meanwhile going about their domestic chores and from time to time breaking off to exchange a few words in a perfectly collected fashion. Tseremp now remembers that I have a recording of Kawarunch and the chorus of lamentations and threats comes to an abrupt halt as soon as Nayapi asks if he can listen to it. As a relayer of messages, our tape-recorder plays a role that smooths the way to a welcome for us from Achuar whom we do not know. Wherever we go, we record news and salutations for distant relatives, along with injunctions to treat us well that have, so far, been effective. So making a dead man speak is simply a new facet to our role of magnetic postmen.

I had asked Kawarunch to tell me about the wars in which he used to fight against the Shuar before the latter had been made amenable by missionary 'pacification'. The events of which he speaks took place in the early fifties.

Ayu! Antuktaram! In the old days, before I was married, I used to accompany my father to make war on the *shiwiar*. In those days we had no rifles, only spears to fight with. To protect themselves the *shiwiar* used to make round shields, *tantar*, from the roots of *kamak*, a good, hard wood. And we, we did likewise. We waged war against Ampam, and against Uwa too. They used to say that Uwa could never be caught. Once, when we learned that this Uwa had assembled all his people to attack us, we took up our spears and our shields and went off to fight him. He lived on the Chiwias, far, far away, upstream. We had to march for five days without stopping; two women came with us.

['Why women?']

To carry the food. We only took shelled groundnuts and manioc paste to make beer. We suffered terribly from hunger. Uwa's house was very big, but it had no palisade. All his people were there, ready to march into battle with their spears and their shields. As for us, we arrived in single file, silently, and hid in the garden. My father Churuwia was the most *kakaram* of all. Before deploying us around the house, he had said, 'I shall attack from the front'; the others said, 'I shall attack from the side, I dreamed that was what I should do.' From where we were we could see clearly into the house.

The women were very cheerful, laughing their heads off, '*Ha, ha, hai*,' as they served the beer to the men. They were laughing away without thinking that they would soon have reason to shed tears of bereavement. There was a large gathering of men, all chattering away like a flight of birds alighting on a tree to eat the fruit. As we approached the house, keeping under cover, some hens took fright and ran off, clucking *kaa-ka, kaa-ka!* Seeing this, the women grew alarmed: 'The Achuar are coming, the Achuar are coming to kill us! Stir yourselves! Grab your spears!' One man was busy weaving; he leaped up to seize his spear that was propped alongside him but got it tangled up in his loom. The other men were plunged into confusion, rushing in all directions to find their weapons. Some were trying to flee and the shrieking women were scattering. As for us, we rushed at the house. Churuwia shouted, 'Each of you choose an enemy! Don't let him get away!' We fought face to face, seeking an opening to jab in a spear; but they knew how to dodge and parry the blows with their shields. My spear had a barbed point and my father Churuwia had taught me how to use it: '*Tsak!* You stick your spear into his foot and topple your enemy as you pull it out sharply; once he is down, how can he defend himself?' But the struggle was long and hard as they defended themselves well, even on their knees.

The man who had been weaving had taken refuge some way from the house, backed up against a big tree and there were several of us trying to strike him. But he was very strong and with a push of his shield he knocked us all over, *tupej!* All of us down! As we picked ourselves up all we could see was the shield left against the tree. The man had run off. Some of us threw our spears at the fleeing enemy, but they ran a great risk doing that as, if they missed their man, he could come back and kill them easily. For that reason, my father Churuwia had advised me only to fight hand to hand.

In that attack Uwa managed to escape. When Shirmachi succeeded in killing his son, he called out: '*Chut! chut! chut!*' We all scattered to meet up again at the agreed spot. There, Shirmachi was stamping his foot and brandishing his spear: 'I killed, I did, I killed!' The return journey was even longer, as Uwa was searching everywhere for us and we had to march through the forest, not knowing the way. The second day we saw a herd of peccaries moving eastwards and we followed them at a good distance. As they were very shy, they would have given the alarm if they had seen any men.

Some time later we were once again fighting the same enemies. An Achuar from the Kapawi, Taasham, had invited us to join the war, as the *shiwiar* had taken the head of his brother to make it into a *tsantsa*. We were a large band, armed with spears and shields and we set out to attack them. On the way we came across them on a shingle beach by the Pastaza. They too had set out to take us by surprise. In the old days we often used to fight on beaches and we fought hard, not as you do now, with rifles. *We* used to struggle in hand-to-hand fighting for days, under the terrible sun, with nothing to drink or eat. When an enemy felt he was weakening, he would plunge into the river to escape. There were several of us against Uweiti and suddenly he rushed into the river with his spear, abandoning his shield. He was swimming strongly downstream. Then Shirmachi said to me, '*Chuwa!* Give me your spear, brother-in-law! Why do you talk so much without doing anything? Give me your spear! It is shorter than mine.' From the bank, Shirmachi hurled the spear at Uweiti, who was getting away. *Tup!* It lodged in his shoulder. Then Shirmachi began to boast: 'Me, me, that's the way I am! *Hai! hai! hai!* I told you so!'

Uweiti, with the spear stuck in his shoulder, began to howl with pain, '*Ararau, ararau!*' He was close to drowning.

Then Shirmachi started to swim towards Uweiti. Halting a few strokes away from him, he jeered at him: 'That's the way I am! *Hai! Hai! Hai!* And that's the way I wanted to see you!'

But Uweiti had kept hold of his spear under the water and, *tuk*, he jabbed it into Shirmachi and said: 'That's the way Uweiti is too! *Hai! Hai! Hai!* And that's the way I wanted to see you too!'

Shirmachi could not get Uweiti's spear out of his thigh. But he had kept his own spear and tried to strike Uweiti with it. Uweiti managed to grab it by the tip and they struggled in the water, *tuntun, tuntun*, each one trying to wrest the spear from the other's grasp, each with a spear stuck in his body. Then Shirmachi began to shout: 'The *shiwiar* is taking his revenge on me!'

Meanwhile, Taasham was doing an *impikmartin*, roaring like a jaguar: '*Juum, juum, juum!*' He had just killed an enemy: 'That's the way I am! I told you so: that's the way I am Taasham! I am Taasham! I am Taasham!' He was surrounded by enemies who were throwing big stones at him to break his shield. But they were not throwing hard enough and the stones rolled through the sand to him. Then, in mockery, Taasham bent down and bit one of the stones: '*Jai! Jai! Jai!* That's what I do with your stones!' While he was bending, a *shiwiar* managed to wound him in the thigh, *paa!* The spear went right through his thigh and out the other side. Taasham crumbled to the ground like a jaguar falling. But he managed to pull out the spear and, grabbing his shield again, he went on fighting his enemy. After a long struggle the *shiwiar* managed to wound Taasham in the head, but he went on fighting as though nothing had happened, his head covered in blood. At last Taasham killed his opponent. He had riddled him with spear stabs all over his body. Then Taasham went off to take refuge in the forest, half-staggering, half-crawling, and there he fainted.

All this time the battle had been continuing in little scattered groups. And now we noticed two men fighting like maniacs in the river: it was Shirmachi and Uweiti, whom everyone had forgotten in the confusion. We said to ourselves: '*Chuwa!* Who is going to end up killing the other?' Then the last onslaught began and they killed four of our men – I'm including Taasham, who had disappeared. The rest of us killed three warriors, one of whom was Uweiti, who had suffered in vain, and also a younger man. The rest eventually fled, their shields smashed, by swimming across the river.

Shirmachi was wounded all over his body, in the legs, in the shoulder, the chest and the stomach. Although shuddering with pain, he kept telling us calmly: 'It's nothing, take me home. I'm not going to die this time round.'

We bore him home, taking it in turns to carry him on our backs. When we reached home, we had to break the news of Taasham's disappearance; no doubt the *shiwiar* had taken his head to make a *tsantsa*. His widows began to wail in heartrending fashion and they cut off their hair, as is customary. For five days they never ceased their lamentations.

Then, on the fifth day, Taasham turned up, dragging himself along, his wounds swarming with maggots, surrounded by a cloud of flies and looking terribly thin. He had remained unconscious for a long time. He had wounds on his thighs, his head, everywhere; but none of them was fatal and he had survived. He had made his way back slowly, leaning on a stick, following the bank of the Pastaza. His wives, who had mourned him so much, cared for him with great devotion; and then they organized

271

a *namper* to celebrate his return. That's how we did it, we Achuar, when we fought against the 'hill people'.

['Did you take their heads to make them into *tsantsa?*']

No, that is very bad! We used to leave the dead, without touching them. It was the *shiwiar* who used to come to collect our heads. We Achuar, we fought the *shiwiar* to avenge our dead; we never made *tsantsa*. My uncle Uyunkar and my uncle Shirap too, the *shiwiar* took their heads. They did that not so very long ago. The *shiwiar* are like the Ajaimp; they used to eat the Achuar so as to wipe us out.

This reply concerning the *tsantsa* is rather disappointing, but it confirms what other Achuar have told me. All the men I have questioned have emphatically declared that they never made shrunken heads and that this practice, which they themselves equated with cannibalism, was associated solely with the Shuar, who used to come amongst the Achuar for the express purpose of procuring heads. So the wars against the Shuar were simply reprisal expeditions, sometimes of considerable proportions but in which head-hunting was excluded. In this respect, the Achuar differ from the other Jivaro tribes, which continued to shrink the heads of their enemies until the Church and the military authorities persuaded them to desist, but not until quite recently in the case of the Shuar, who took the head of an Achuar no more than eight years ago. The good faith of my companions seems beyond doubt. It was borne out by their fascinated horror at a series of pictures that I showed them, selected from a collection published by the Salesian missionaries, which most realistically depicted the various stages in the production of a *tsantsa*. The way in which they pressed for details when the drawings were not sufficiently explicit showed that all they knew of the business was that they had been its victims, and the cooking process to which their relatives had been subjected was definitely news to them. There was no question of false modesty put on for our benefit. The Achuar are the last Jivaros still continuing their tradition of vendettas unhindered, and they have never disguised the passion involved nor hesitated to describe to us the most macabre details of their exploits. Scattered references to *tsantsa* in their war-songs nevertheless suggest that the Achuar did shrink heads a few generations back; but for reasons unknown they must have abandoned the custom well before the end of their wars against other tribes. No recollection of it now remains; it has been wiped out by the forgetfulness of this people without memory.

I myself know much more about head-hunting than any of the Achuar whom I questioned, largely thanks to the ethnographic zeal of the Salesian missionaries, who for decades have been collecting from the oldest Shuar precise descriptions of the *tsantsa* rituals in which they took part as young men. It has long been known that there was nothing mysterious in itself about the preparation of a head. Once killed, the enemy was immediately decapitated and his attackers would pull back to an agreed spot sufficiently distant from the theatre of war for the operations that followed to take place without too much danger to them. Here, the head was cut from the nape of the neck to the sinciput and the skull, jaw, nose cartilage and most of the muscles were extracted before boiling the rest in a cooking pot to get rid of the fat. What remained of the head was then filled with burning sand and began to contract and harden as the water evaporated from the tissues. Once this preliminary phase was completed, the warriors returned to their own territory as fast as possible and confined themselves to the strictest seclusion during which they continued to dry out the head, taking care to remodel the victim's features each time the skin shrank. The incision at the back of the head was then sewn up, the eyes and the mouth were stitched together and the interior of the *tsantsa* was stuffed with kapok.

The ritual that followed is more enigmatic but it constitutes our only clue for understanding this baffling practice, for which the Shuar themselves provide no explicit exegesis. It unfolds in two episodes, each lasting several days and separated by an interval of about a year. The first is known as 'his very blood' (*numpenk*), the second as 'the fulfilment' (*amiamu*). The ceremonies consist of a series of linked choreographic figures and regularly repeated choruses and are held first in the home of the great man who led the raid, then in that of the killer. The principal features are the *waimianch*, a song sung as a round at dusk, with the singers grouped about the *tsantsa*, followed by *ujaj*, sung in canon by the women from sunset until dawn, and the *ijianma*, a kind of procession to accompany the *tsantsa* on each of its ceremonial entries into a house, when it passes through a hedge of shields struck sharply by the men to simulate thunder. In addition to these strictly liturgical ceremonies men and women also like to dance and sing *namper* in the course of more secular celebrations involving copious refreshment in the shape of manioc beer, which take place during the afternoons when no ritual is planned.

The major protagonists in 'the great feast' are the *tsantsa* itself, referred to first as the 'profile' and later as the 'soft thing'; a trio comprising the killer, a close female blood-relative – his mother or sister – and a female relative by marriage, generally his wife, who are collectively known as 'the tobacco-sated ones' (*tsaankram*) by reason of the large quantities of green tobacco juice they ingest throughout the ritual; a master of ceremonies, the *wea*, a term ordinarily employed as a mark of respect when addressing a father-in-law which here turns this figure into the personification of affinity; the *wea*'s wife, whose task is to lead the chorus of feminine *ujaj* and who is known by that name; the '*ujaj*-carrrier' (*ujajan-ju*), a man who acts as intermediary between the *ujaj* on the one hand and the *wea* and 'the tobacco-sated ones' on the other – for this latter group must not, under any circumstances, communicate directly with the rest of the participants; and, finally, a whole series of ceremonial groups with minor roles, in particular the 'initiates' (*amikiu*), that is to say all those who have already taken part in the complete cycle of a 'great feast', and the *yaku*, the warriors whose job it is to imitate rumbles of thunder.

A multitude of other operations, intermingled with songs and dances, are carried out by various officiating figures. The *tsantsa* is instructed in the social and spatial characteristics of the territory to which it has been brought. It is decorated, then reboiled in a broth poetically known as 'water of the stars'. Women sprinkle it with metaphorical sperm. At first the killer is isolated like a wild, fetid animal, then, after going off into the forest in quest of an *arutam* vision under the influence of stramonium, he is purified and adorned with new body paintings. The *wea* and he sprinkle the insides of each other's thighs with the blood of a rooster to represent menstruation. He is subjected to the rituals of mourning – his hair being shorn and his face marked with genipa. He puts mould into a special manioc beer to make it ferment, thereby assuming the position of a woman, whose saliva performs the same function. Pigs are sacrificed and consumed as 'substitute' (*imiak*) enemies, etc. In short, a baroque kind of epiphany, lasting many days and nights, takes place, which is crammed

274

with esoteric allusions to death and rebirth, fecundity and childbirth, the savagery of cannibalism and the immemorial rules of social harmony.

What can be learned from this 'great feast', whose ceremonial and symbolic complexity is much admired even by the missionaries? In the first place, the *tsantsa* is no ordinary trophy. In contrast to what happens amongst other head-hunting peoples, the *tsantsa* is not a relic commemorating some exploit. At the end of the ritual it is simply discarded, without fuss. Nor is it a kind of amulet, a source of energy and power deemed capable of conciliating spirits, attracting game or increasing the fertility of gardens. Far removed from the robust vitalism of a fetish, this object without substance or content functions, rather, as a logical operator, an abstract mark of identity which, by virtue of its very abstraction, can be used to construct new identities. This is what gives the shrinking its *raison d'être*: whereas the 'ordinary' trophy heads captured by other Amazonian peoples rapidly dry up under the effect of the climate and thus lose their original physiognomy, a *tsantsa*, thanks to the treatment it has undergone, perpetuates the representation of a recognizable face. The miniaturization of the head is no more than an incidental effect – probably quite accidental – of a technique of conservation intended to preserve the features of the decapitated individual from the normal corruption of flesh.

This preoccupation with realism, shown in the careful preparation of the head, may seem paradoxical in view of the fact that the people from whom *tsantsa* are taken are generally total strangers. One immutable rule of head-hunting is that its victims must be Jivaros, but Jivaros of a different tribe with whom no known links of kinship exist, who speak a different dialect and whose patronyms are unknown – in short, generic enemies, not individual opponents, too distant to identify yet close enough not to be perceived as totally alien. A *tsantsa* therefore cannot be a condensed effigy of a particular person. It is, rather, a formal representation of one human existence, signifiable by any distinctive face, no matter which, provided it is that of an unrelated Jivaro. All Jivaros share the idea that the identity of an individual lies not so much in the features of his face but rather in certain social attributes of his person: his name, his manner of speech, his memory of shared experiences and the face-paintings associated with an experience of *arutam*. The first phase of the ritual consists in dissociating the *tsantsa* from any residual references that would prevent it from embodying a generic Jivaro identity: it is never called by the name – even if known – of the person from whom it was taken; its face is blackened to conceal the memory of the patterns that were traced there; all its orifices are sealed, thereby condemning its sensual organs to phenomenal amnesia in all eternity; finally, it is instructed as to its new social space, taken through the house to each of its cardinal points and made familiar, as the songs put it, with its 'land of adoption'.

The depersonalization to which a *tsantsa* is submitted may be likened to a forger's falsification of an identity document. The authenticity of the original document is attested by the permanence of the face, which proves the legitimate provenance of the identity document and is the physical equivalent of the official number given to each person by a Health Authority or an electoral register. The task of the ritual is progressively to alter that document without making it seem any different – for that would render it invalid – by using it as the basis for the gradual creation of a new identity. Throughout the 'great feast' the *tsantsa*, the *wea* and 'the tobacco-sated ones' change places, each in turn swapping sexes and relations of kinship, alternately without reciprocation and reciprocally, assuming either an antagonistic or a complementary new relationship, one that either reinforces the earlier one or is symmetrically opposed to it, all of these being symbolic expressions of a fictitious genealogy that has been elaborated episode by episode. By the end of this topological ballet the *tsantsa* has assumed all the social roles necessary in a symbolic procreation: the non-relative, the giver of a woman, the taker of a woman, the concubine of the killer, the lover of his wives, and finally the embryo with 'his little snout stuck into the belly of a woman', in the words of the songs that are addressed to him at the very end of the ritual. The very real fruit of this simulated alliance – a child to be born to kin of the murderer in the course of the coming year – thus presents the paradox of being a perfect relative by blood yet not incestuous. This virtual existence derived from people unknown yet not altogether alien owes its creation to the staging of an ideal affinity: the only kind totally satisfying for the Jivaros since it carries with it no obligation of reciprocity – in short a relationship of affinity that involves no affines.

On the face of it, head-hunting and vendettas appear to obey very different logics, and this might be thought to explain how it is that the former has disappeared amongst the Achuar without the latter being affected. The word that my companions use for vendetta, *meset* ('harm' or 'damage'), suggests that it is perceived as an inevitable deterioration of social relations between people who in other respects recognize one another as relatives, speak the same dialect, know one another personally and, in normal times, occasionally visit one another. The clashes are motivated by specific grudges, for the most part conflicts over a woman between her blood-relatives and her relatives by marriage, backed up or reinforced by mutual accusations of shamanistic aggression. Mechanisms of mediation make it possible to bring hostilities to a provisional end to stop them from spreading. They may lead to reversals in political alliances and temporary coalitions that allow former enemies to associate once again in a pretence of impossible peace that is sufficient for all concerned. The situation is quite different in a war between tribes. When the Achuar speak of their past battles against the Shuar, they use expressions with a more openly military ring – *maniakmu*, 'a killing', or *nanki jukimiau*, 'a raising of spears' – and they stress that there were no negotiated solutions to suspend hostilities or to compensate the relatives of a victim. Besides, for the Shuar, as for the Aguaruna and the Huambisa, the sole purpose of these wars was to capture heads in the course of long-distance raids amongst unknown Jivaros selected purely for their strategic convenience. Those who died in vendettas, in contrast, were never decapitated since they could not be used in the *tsantsa* ritual as emblems of otherness, on account of their kinship, albeit distant, with their murderers.

Yet although head-hunting and vendettas express hostility on two different registers, in the last analysis they are nevertheless tuned to the same pitch: the enemy is always seen as an affine. Conflicts within the same tribe break out between relatives by marriage, either real or 'branch' ones, occasionally within the same 'neighbourhood', but more often between two groups whose neighbourhoods border upon one another and whose members may be related by marriage. They are thus family matters, as the murders of Ikiam and Kawarunch show. In some cases, hostilities erupt between more distant kindred, but again because of problems over women: a wife fleeing a bad-tempered husband and finding herself a new one far away, or a widow who turns to a distant Achuar in contravention of levirate obligations. Given that relations between the two 'neighbourhoods' involved are virtually non-existent, a payment of *tumash* turns out to be almost impossible since no mediator is prepared to risk his life amongst quasi-strangers. Conflicts such as these sometimes escalate and turn into far more bloodthirsty wars than those between two different tribes, for the leaders of the opposed factions appeal to their marriage-alliance networks in neighbouring regions in order to form coalitions that tend to grow every time a new death triggers the duty to take revenge in kindred that are increasingly distant from the initial kernel of hostility. Despite the distance, both geographical and genealogical, between the two coalitions, it is clearly still affinity that defines the relationship between them. It may be an affinity more potential than instituted since it began with an irregular marriage and is perpetuated partly by reciprocal seizures of women and children. Nevertheless, in principle it is still an affinity, as is testified by the collective name given to the opponents, *nua suru*, 'the givers of women'. The real affinity of one's closest enemies, usually brothers-in-law, and the potential affinity of distant enemies differ only through an inversion: the one that distinguishes a marriage alliance consented to but not realized from a marriage alliance realized but not consented to.

With its strange morganatic union between a victorious community and a generic, unknown enemy, the *tsantsa* ritual constitutes the last word in variations on the theme of affinity: there is only a difference of degree, not one of nature, between carrying off women and children from potential relatives by marriage, whom a vendetta has excluded from the number of one's relatives, and stealing identities that can produce offspring from non-relatives with whom one simulates an ideal affinity. However, among the Achuar this last variation is lacking. No longer practising head-hunting, they seem simply to have applied to their wars against the Shuar the same philosophy of vengeance that governs the vendetta. In a culture that is in other respects so very much alive, the disappearance of head-hunting seems astonishing, but it may be that the void that it has left has been filled by a substitute yet to be discovered.

CHAPTER 18

Scenes in a House of War

IT IS A LITTLE BEFORE MIDDAY, just after fording the Yukunentza, when we come across the first sign of hostility: across the path leading to Nankiti's house a large branch stuck into the ground is festooned with twenty or so cartridge cases, their bright red colour standing out like bloodstains amid the forest shadows. The warning is aimed at the people of the Apupentza with whom Nankiti and his folk are at war. This is the point where the virtually closed path from the Apupentza meets the one leading from the Bobonaza, which we have been following since this morning. A couple of generations back, they used to arrange spears in a sheaf pointing in the direction from which the enemy would come, to convey a message that was easy to understand and that the modernization of weapons has not altered: you cross this barricade at your peril! Tseremp is on the verge of turning back, preferring to forgo the *tumash* he was hoping for from Nankiti for the murder of his father, rather than risk his own life in this dangerous region. Tarir is saying nothing, as he does not want to seem a coward, but I know that he is not happy about accompanying me on this visit. Fortunately, we are with Kayap, a 'branch' brother of Nankiti, who is acting as our guide and, we hope, our safe-conduct pass. His reassurances, coupled with my no more than half-convinced exhortations, eventually persuade Tseremp to press on. Anne Christine has remained in Kayap's house, on the Bobonaza, as the men deemed it unsuitable for her to go to a house of war.

It is now several weeks since we left Nayapi's house, passing down the Kapawi as far as the Pastaza, then exploring the banks and tributaries of the great river down as far as its confluence with the Bobonaza, which we followed upstream for two days before reaching Kayap's house. On the way we visited a dozen or so households, some of them in deeply isolated positions on little rivers, or in a maze of marshes and channels inaccessible except by canoe. We were well received, sometimes with a certain reticence, with some of the men unable to disguise their suspicious surprise faced with the first *kirinku* they had ever seen. As we push further into unknown country I find myself thinking of Capahuari more or less as my own native village and of its inhabitants as my lifelong companions, so distant does the rest of the world seem. For months now we have forgotten about even the most modest of the amenities of civilization: a cake of soap, new clothes, a mirror, a tube of toothpaste – they all seem as exotic as luxury goods in a society impoverished by war. Our clothes are threadbare, mended and patched many times over to make them last, and we are already practising walking barefoot, to prepare for the time when our shoes give out. This ascetic life has grown upon us with the passing of time and the depletion of our meagre reserves. We put up with it as a state that seems the more natural given that it is the common lot of the people whose life we are sharing; our aspirations are limited to eating our fill from time to time and being able to sleep sheltered from the weather. Our privations are more than compensated for by a sense of adventure very much in contrast to the monotony of our former village existence, for each day now brings a new harvest of discoveries and, occasionally, dangers: rare explorers' privileges that make our expedition seem an exploit.

Over the last few days we have learnt a little more about the vendetta between Nankiti and the people of the Apupentza. It grew out of the rivalry between two well-known shamans, Peas and Awananch, each a powerful *juunt* in his own region, the Apupentza for the one, the Chirta for the other, both of them small tributaries of the western side of the Bobonaza, about one day's march apart. A sick woman who had been to consult Awananch without success soon after went to be treated by Peas, who cured her on the spot. Peas had then boasted extravagantly of his superiority, causing Awananch to become furiously jealous. Awananch then spread the rumour that Peas's successes were easy to explain since it was he himself who put spells on people in the first place, which was why he had no difficulty at all in removing his own *tsentsak* from the bodies of his patients, thereby earning himself both riches and respect. Not content with making accusations of such gravity, Awananch had convinced

Nankiti, a 'branch' brother-in-law of his, to organize a raid to kill Peas.

Nankiti and his folk, whom the people here call *mayn shuar*, make up a small, extremely isolated group which, following trouble with the Peruvian military, found refuge on the Yutsuentza, a tributary of the Corrientes. They have virtually no contact with the Achuar of the region except for Awananch and his kindred with whom, over a generation, they have established a few links by marriage. But the complicity between Awananch and Nankiti is founded not so much upon the mutual obligations of somewhat distant kinship but rather upon a form of connivance typical of many political alliances formed between a powerful shaman and a great warrior: they protect each other, each in his own particular domain. Awananch defends Nankiti and his kindred from the *tsentsak* sent by other shamans, while Nankiti and his kin in exchange undertake to liquidate the enemies of their acolyte.

Awananch managed to convince Nankiti that Peas was responsible for various afflictions that had recently struck his group. About three months ago Nankiti accordingly went to see Peas on the pretext of needing treatment and, when the treatment was completed, stayed the night in Peas's house. The following day he was joined by Yank-uam, who asked Peas to treat his wife. While the shaman, with his head thrown back, was sniffing tobacco juice up his nose to prepare for the task, Yankuam fired point-blank at him, followed by Nankiti and other members of their faction, who had spent the night close by, in hiding. As Kayap described it, 'there were so many of them firing at Peas that no more than half of him was left'. The people of the Apupentza took this very badly indeed. Turipiur, the victim's brother and himself also a shaman, sent a declaration of war to Awananch and Nankiti, using a young messenger as an intermediary: 'You have killed my brother Peas *nankami* (to please yourselves). He was a shaman, but a *tsuakratin* (healing) shaman, not a *wawekratin* (sorceror) shaman. Perhaps you think we are not men! Well, let us measure up! Let us build *tanish* (palisades) and measure up! Let us fight and we shall see who is left!' Awananch's kindred had moved to the edge of the Bobonaza to get away from the theatre of operations, and had just finished building a fortified house there. At first Nankiti had said that he was ready to negotiate, claiming that he had performed a public service against a bad shaman but that it would be possible to come to an arrangement regarding a *tumash*. But this was really a ruse to gain time during which he finished converting his house into an entrenched camp where all his kindred then joined him.

We proceed cautiously, for fear of traps. Access to houses of war is defended by all kinds of mechanisms triggered by invisible lianas: a lath of flexible wood with sharp points may slice into the small of your back, or a pole innocently lying in the path may swing up between your legs, crushing your testicles; or it may be a matter of an ordinary rifle hidden behind a bush, the hammer of which operates at the least tension, or the classic pit filled with pointed staves, normally used to catch jaguars or ocelots that are too greedy for chickens. It is even said that shamans set up barrages of magic darts along the paths where their enemies need to pass, forcing them to make wide detours through the woods. Towards mid-afternoon we pass an abandoned house in a garden that is almost bare. Nearly all the furniture has disappeared; even the *peak* are dismantled. Soon after, another house presents the same desolate aspect. Kayap tells us that their inhabitants have taken refuge with Nankiti and return to their own homes only very occasionally, in armed columns preceded by dogs, to fetch manioc from their former gardens.

As we walk we make as much noise as possible, talking loudly and exchanging rather forced jokes, so as not to be mistaken for an enemy expedition advancing stealthily. Long before the fortified house comes into sight Kayap signals our arrival by blowing into the barrel of his rifle, as into a horn, then each of us utters the long cry that heralds a visit, thereby indicating how many we are. The palisade comes into view at the top of a well-cleared little hill. It is so high that, seen from below, only the top of the roof rises above it. A massive wooden door, ajar for the moment, provides access to this little fort, which is reinforced inside by another row of stakes designed to make the palisade more impenetrable and to prevent anyone from slipping the barrel of a rifle through from outside. The door faces the *tankamash*, where half a dozen men, seated on their *chimpui*, await us in silence. At the *ekent* end of the house another door opens on to a narrow passage leading down to the Yutsuentza between two walls of logs, the last of which are set in the water. Alongside each of the doors stand two little platforms reached by tree-trunks into which footholds have been cut, which serve as lookout posts, deserted at the moment except for a solitary rooster which looks us arrogantly up and down.

The welcome is glacial. Once our presence has been acknowledged by an invitation to enter, we are kept waiting half an hour without anything to drink while the men of the house converse together as though we were not there. The company consists of Nankiti and his 'branch' brother Supinanch, two elderly men with very long hair and stern expressions, Chinkim, Supinanch's son, Yankuam, his son-in-law, and Tentets, his nephew, as well as Kuji, a son-in-law of Nankiti's. Two other young men aged about twenty who are also Supinanch's nephews are not entitled to *chimpui*, which means they are still unmarried. All the faces of the men are painted with patterns of rocou, sometimes combined with black designs of genipa, and each holds a rifle on his knees or propped against his legs. Yankuam even sports a high-calibre lever-action rifle and a well-stocked cartridge belt worn crosswise. A dozen or so women are busy in the half-light of the *ekent*, surrounded by a swarm of children who fix us with fascinated eyes.

Nankiti is a well-built man with a snub nose and a square chin in a very pale face. His features are fearless but not the expression in his eyes, where arrogance appears to be vying with apprehension. Having presumably decided that we have been sufficiently humiliated by being made to wait so long, he orders that we be served with manioc beer and then addresses Kayap. The series of *aujmatin* then proceeds in order of age and genealogical proximity. Nankiti holds a dialogue first with Tarir and then with Tseremp, soon followed by Supinanch, who repeats the same cycle, after which the men address my companions in turn, by which time several *aujmatin* are unfolding simultaneously and inter-crossing. As is customary in these purely rhetorical exchanges, nothing is divulged about the purpose of our visit except for the bizarre desire of the *kirinku* to meet a man whose reputation for bravery is known the whole length of the lower Bobonaza, a tailor-made compliment that I myself repeat to Nankiti in a laborious *yaitias chicham*, the minor version of an *aujmatin* that I have eventually more or less managed to master. Impermeable to flattery, the man seems to regret having allowed us in, particularly since, having discovered Tseremp's identity, he must have guessed the real motive of our visit. Despite Kayap's presence, we had feared that he would purely and simply shut his door in our faces, treating us to an *atsanmartin*, the virulent monologue by which one refuses to accept an undesirable visit, at the very threshold of the house – an extremely rare manifestation of distrust and dislike to which only Tarir can remember ever having been subjected. The protocol of hospitality has thus been respected so far, which is reassuring for the time being although no commitment is thereby made as to our future safety.

By the time the *aujmatin* are concluded night has already fallen. Nankiti asks Kayap for news of Awananch and his kindred, but no conversation is started with the rest of us, despite the curiosity of the youngest members of the household concerning me and contrary to the Achuar's usual custom of tempering the aridity of the ceremonial dialogues by engaging in some freer conversational exchanges once they are over. The house is large but encumbered by dozens of *peak*, quantities of jars, cooking hearths and piles of manioc, a whole jumble of utensils, baskets and tools, not to mention swarms of dogs tethered in separate packs to all available pillars. Each of the six households now gathered within the shelter of the palisade retains its own autonomy, each wife cooking for her own family and each husband hunting for her, although this culinary independence is mitigated by the constant exchanges of food rendered necessary by the difficulties of maintaining adequate supplies in this climate of insecurity. We can judge the situation for ourselves from the meagre meal that we are served by Nankiti's wife: a few pieces of boiled manioc with a little pimento. Once dinner is out of the way, the doors are barricaded with cross-bars and the dogs are let loose within the enclosure while, in response to Nankiti's invitation – '*kanurtaram!*' – I try to find sleep, stretched out on the beaten earth floor, surrounded by the indistinct murmur of forty or so individuals of all ages.

Around three o'clock in the morning I awake with a start to an infernal din: the dogs are barking furiously at the foot of the palisade, accompanied by a chorus of shrill shrieks from the women: 'The Achuar are coming! The Achuar are coming!' The children are all crying and the men are rushing in all directions, rifles in hand, stumbling over jars and *chimpui* in the darkness and shouting threats and orders too confused to be understood. The alert was given by a suspicious noise outside and a young man is sent to the lookout post to scrutinize the surroundings. Almost immediately a shot rings out,

although I cannot make out whether it came from inside the house or from outside. The lookout scrambles down from his perch, unharmed, in the midst of the women's lamentations of 'They have killed him! They have killed him!' while several of the men fire shots into the air out in the enclosed precinct. In the glow of the fires, now stoked up, Nankiti strides to face the door and in loud, staccato tones begins to sound forth against the enemy, hopping from one foot to the other as he does so:

Shuaraiti! shuaraiti! shuaraiti!
watska! winiti, winiti, winiti, winiti!
shuar jintia tarutchik, shuar tarutchik!
turakuisha, jimiar apatuk! jimiar apatuk! jimiar apatuk! maniatatjai!
haa! ekentru pitiak urukan!
haa! paara suruitia! paara suruitia! paara suruitia! paara suruitia!
haa! aishmankchiru, yamai, yamai, watska! jintia jiistai! jintia jiistai!
    jintia jiistai!
kame! kame! niish, haa! niisha, niisha, kame! meseta ekematish, haa!
    jintia akaruka
ipiatrurarj awainkitai! awainkitai! awainkintai! awainkitai!
    awainkitai!
wisha, wisha! nu paarak takusa pujajai!
haa! yawa! yawa! yawa! yawa!
waurshi! waurshi! waurshi! waurshi! waurshia!
winin mesetan kuikmatish, haa! jimiar apatuk! jimiar apatuk! wisha
    wari mesetan
wakeruketja! nuni mesetnak! nu mesetnak! nu mesetnak! nu mesetnak!
    pujajai! pujajai! pujajai! pujajai! pujajaaai!

This is the *impikmartin*, a tirade of defiance and intimidation, an amazing snatch of bravura that momentarily allays my fears by creating the illusion that we are suddenly back in the heroic age:

People! people! people!
we'll see! let them come! let them come! let them come! let them
    come!
along the path, have people not come, have they not come!
right then, between us two! between us two! between us two! between
    us two!
I shall kill!

haa! woman! in my *pitiak*!

haa! bring me bullets! bring me bullets! bring me bullets! bring me
bullets!

haa! my little men! now, now, we'll see! let's examine the path! examine
the path! examine the path!

now then! now then! him, *haa!* and him and him, now then! even
though he's ready to attack, *haa!*

with a barrage of shots from our rifles on the path, let us stop him!
make him flee! make him flee! make him flee!

and me! and me! I am armed with this bullet!

haa! jaguar! jaguar! jaguar! jaguar!

haa! angry! angry! angry! angry!

although it was he who wanted war, *haa!* it's between us two! between
us two! and as for me

I can think only of fighting, now, immediately! in this war! in this war!
in this war! I'm in it! I'm in it!

I'm in it! I'm in i-i-i-t!

With no signs of hostility outside, the tumult at last calms down
and we crouch by the fires, in tense silence, waiting for dawn. At
daybreak the lookouts announce that there is nobody about and
Nankiti ventures out with a few men, having first let the dogs loose.
Everything seems peaceful, but for once I too am glad of my cumbersome shotgun. Soon a cry is heard: '*Shuar nawe! Shuar nawe! Irunui!*'
'Footprints! Footprints! Lots of them!' Nankiti promptly launches
into another passionate *impikmartin*. As soon as it is over he immediately calms down and even shoots a smile at me, the first I've glimpsed
on his face since our arrival. 'Come, *juuntur!*' he says to me. 'Let us
wait!'

A long day now begins in the fortified house. The women and
children go off together to answer a call of nature, protected from a
distance by an armed man. I follow suit with Tarir and Tseremp and
the door is closed once more, then opened a fraction for Tentets
and Yankuam, who are sent out as scouts to follow the tracks of
our nocturnal visitors. The children are strangely silent, and all the
members of the household busying themselves with small domestic
tasks, weaving a basket, delousing one another, sharpening darts, but
doing so with marked diligence as though these were tasks that could
not possibly be left until later. My Capahuari companions are torn

between their desire to flee immediately and their fear of falling into an ambush. Tseremp, moreover, is annoyed at not having had a chance to make his request to Nankiti as he hoped to do, before daybreak, over a bowl of *wayus*, during that moment of intimacy when you can discuss important matters without bothering about the rhetoric and etiquette that make visits so strained for most of the time. I have a long quiet talk with him and persuade him to stay for one more night so as to claim his *tumash* tomorrow morning at *wayus* time. Perhaps because we have come through what seems to have been an abortive attack with him, Nankiti is less harsh with us today. As if to set our minds at rest, he confidently declares that the enemies will not dare to return for a while. This appears to be confirmed by Tentets and Yankuam when they return from their mission around midday: half a dozen or so men certainly did come in the night and their tracks, after tacking about a lot, then lead straight towards the Apupentza, indicating that they are probably back in their own homes by now.

Collective life in a fortified house, sometimes for as long as two or three years, imposes upon the Achuar constraints that are hard to bear. By reason of the constant danger in which they find themselves, they cannot move about outside, except to go on raids, and the effect of this is temporarily to suspend exchanges and bartering at the time when they most need weapons and ammunition. Even ordinary supplies become a problem. Nankiti's people have extended his garden plot and have begun to plant manioc to build up their meagre reserves, but the cuttings will not mature for six months or so; they depend largely upon their own gardens, which cannot now be reached without peril. Besides, even when the new plantation begins to be productive, to judge by its size it will barely suffice to cover the needs of such a numerous community. Game, the symbol of any real meal, virtually disappears from daily fare, for the men cease to hunt regularly as soon as the animals desert the immediate neighbourhood of the house. Nankiti and his relatives do occasionally organize a nocturnal hunting expedition, but the chances of good results are poor since the animals have to be located by sound alone and, apart from nocturnal hoccos, all the species normally hunted are asleep. The alternative is fish, but the Yutsuentza, a very small river, can provide only a meagre quantity. A number of forest products indispensable to the domestic economy are also in short supply: kapok, clay for pottery, the plants for making curare, fibre for darts and chambira for plaiting string. To mount an expedition to go in search of them is to deplete the house's defences and expose the lives of the women and children. Even satisfying natural needs becomes a risky affair: I have heard so many stories of women seized and abducted as they go off on their own to relieve themselves at the edge of the garden. And once the doors are closed for the night, there can be no question of going out for a pee! The fortified corridor leading to the Yutsuentza at least allows one to wash, but only in the midst of the left-overs. As for the joys of the flesh, they have to be suspended for a time as the over-population of the house is hardly conducive to making love in peace and a forest tryst is too dangerous. Tseremp finds an evocative image to describe this slowed-down kind of life: 'They are like sloths which take two days to move from one branch to another and only crap at each new moon.' Possibly the virtues of continence upon which the Achuar set such high value are in truth an expression, in the form of a moral imperative, of the need to train oneself for the ascetic life that war regularly imposes upon everyone.

But the hardest thing for the Indians to bear in this besieged existence is promiscuity. Their horror of sharing the intimacy of their own hearth with others puts the fortified household under constant pressure, as they are obliged to submit their customary freedom of action to the demands of the common weal and to strive to prevent the frictions constantly provoked by their touchy sense of independence. As the example of Capahuari shows, learning to live in close village relationships is not easy. How much worse, then, must be the tensions engendered by enforced cohabitation in a tiny, enclosed space that is, furthermore, pervaded by constant fear of an attack? The children must be supervised to prevent their arguments degenerating into quarrels between parents ever prompt to take their own offspring's part; the women must share the cooking utensils and check waspish comments upon one another's skills, and the men, in principle all equal, are sensitive about any hint of superiority and stand on even more than customary ceremony in their daily relations. Meanwhile, motives for envy abound, as the exceptional circumstances encourage exploits of all kinds and emphasize natural disparities in courage, cunning, strength and skill. But it is above all jealousy that plays havoc, with all the men and women suspecting one another of infidelity, and the enforced constant intimacy within the confines of the fortress lending their suspicions an air of probability even if it does not afford many opportunities to succumb to them.

The house of war is a necessary evil, since in a vendetta nobody is spared. It is enough to be related to the murderer and to live close to him, or visibly to belong to the entourage of a great man with whom he is on good terms to be accounted a supporter of his actions and thus to become a target of indiscriminate vengeance. In times of adversity, that presumed complicity periodically tightens links that have slackened amongst kindred and leads the less bellicose to seek the security of collective defence as soon as the situation becomes dangerous. Yet a desire for protection is not in itself enough to bring together people who prefer to live on their own. The charisma of a great man is also needed to get relatives scattered over a neighbour-hood zone to coalesce into a veritable faction. It is he who takes the initiative to gather them all together in his house, to build fortifica-tions there at such time as he judges a serious clash to be inevitable, either because a first murder has already been committed, or because a grudge, justified or not, against men of another 'neighbourhood' is leading to a volatile situation. As in the case of Nankiti, the initial kernel of the faction is composed of direct dependants – sons, sons-in-law, younger brothers – together with a few other blood-relatives or relatives by marriage of proven loyalty, 'branch' brothers, or 'blood' brothers-in-law, that is to say the sons of his maternal uncle or his paternal aunt, a sister of whose he has married or who have married a sister of his. Because he is the 'master of the house' (*jea nurintin*) and the rest are his guests, and also because everybody relies on his recognized qualities of military leadership, the *juunt* is invested with a pre-eminent role. He becomes the *mesetan chicharu*, literally 'the war herald'. It is he who organizes the defence of the fortress, he who settles problems of organization within it, he who makes plans and organizes raids and, finally, he who seeks to enter into alliances with neighbouring great men or, if need be, tries to find a compromise with the enemy. The vendetta becomes to a large extent his own personal affair, even if the initial murder that caused it resulted from a conflict that did not concern him directly. Whether or not he fired the fatal shot, his opponents hold him directly responsible for every

290

death in their ranks, an imputation that helps to perpetuate the fame of figures who become almost legendary by virtue of the huge death tolls attributed to them. When I record genealogies, for example, I am always initially told that one out of four or five characters killed such or such a relative, although closer questioning often subsequently reveals that the actual murderer was a more obscure member of his faction. The great man's function as a catalyst is also underlined, on the other hand, by the fact that if he dies in battle, his group disbands as quickly as possible and takes refuge far away from the theatre of operations.

However, the ascendancy exercised by the *juunt* during the war is never converted into veritable domination over the members of his entourage. If he shows unmistakable signs of working solely for his own glory, becoming engaged for no valid reasons in constant clashes with new enemies, one by one his partisans will eventually desert him, wearying of the perpetual insecurity in which he forces them to live. There is one renowned case in the annals of the region, that of Pujupat, an old *juunt* of the south bank of the Pastaza who waged war against everyone indiscriminately and with his own hands – and in his case this is probably true – killed close on twenty people. My companions describe him as a 'mad killer', who stripped the women he killed and spread their legs to expose their sexual parts, without hesitation accepted 'contracts' to liquidate people unknown to him, and now lives as a recluse in his fortified house with only his sons for company, since they are the only men he can still trust to protect him and hunt for him.

It is not by disseminating terror that a great man wins lasting support, but through persuasion and example. He must impress others with his courage and strength of character and above all he must play skilfully on kinship, assuming towards his relatives a fatherly or elder brotherly manner, as the case may be, from which he derives authority of a kind with which they are already familiar. By calling his warriors 'my sons' and being himself frequently designated as 'the elder', through his behaviour he helps to efface the relations of affinity within the kindred gathered round him and to reinforce the idea that it derives its unity and even its substance from ideal bonds of consanguinity. Without clans and lineages to perpetuate through the years a corporate identity with clearly established social and territorial frontiers, the Achuar tend to think of the relations between the scattered inhabitants of the same 'neighbourhood' as though they were blood relationships, even if it is the marriages repeated within each generation which in reality structure their solidarity. The Utopian togetherness of these neighbourhood groups is thus periodically reaffirmed by living together in fortified houses, while the dangers and shared exploits give each person the illusion of daily rediscovering the community of a large family. Fathers-in-law, brothers-in-law and sons-in-law disappear from the field of social references to be transformed into chosen blood-relatives, while affinity, now lacking an effective basis, tends to be converted into an abstract relationship, making it possible to characterize enemies as 'givers of women'. This consubstantiality, founded upon a deliberate amnesia concerning the links established by marriage alliances, is expressed in a profound identification with the others whose fate one is sharing and who, on that account, can no longer be distinguished from oneself. Thus a man announcing the death of a relative killed in battle will say: 'So-and-so has killed me!' Each new loss among those who are close to me means that a part of me dies too, a part that I can only revive by fortifying myself with vengeance.

A great man who is the instrument of a family cohesion that, without him, would remain no more than a potentiality could not exist outside the codified context of kinship and this aspiration towards a fusion of consanguinity, the quintessence of which he, for the moment, expresses. His influence upon others and his possible ascendancy are thus strictly limited by the existing models of authority within a family, the authority of a father over his children, a husband over his wives and a father-in-law over his sons-in-law, for these are the only precedents that can bestow an appearance of legitimacy upon his temporary exercise of command. When he assumes a pre-eminent role in conditions of war, the *juunt* is not guided, like Cincinnatus, by any altruistic devotion. On the contrary, he is prompted by his ambition, but it is an ambition for prestige and admiration that is accepted by one and all because it is shared by each of them; it is not ambition for a limitless power which nobody would be disposed to concede to him; he himself would probably be quite incapable of imagining such a power. Far from possessing a special status – the term 'chief' is untranslatable into Jivaro – he has simply achieved full realization of the ideal of virility to which most Achuar men aspire. Famous and respected for his bravery, master of his destiny, reigning over many wives, vast gardens and sons-in-law who are indebted to him, skilful at sealing alliances and thereby extending his influence beyond the limits of the family, he is the very image of a success that is accessible to every man, rather than an insidious threat to the liberty of others.

Oscillating between the gentle anarchy of ordinary times and the factional solidarity fomented by one man whose authority remains limited by circumstances, the Achuar have established a form of political organization that safeguards each man's independence without bringing about a total dissolution of social links. It would be an exaggeration to define these libertarian coalitions as democracy, in the first place because women are excluded from the conduct of external affairs, but also because there simply is no ideal of a *res publica* or a common weal that might transcend individual interests, nor does there exist any indisputable authority capable of implementing such a project. Those are two conditions that would run counter to the maintenance of the sovereignty that each head of family is recognized to possess. Yet among the Achuar, as in modern democracies, it is certainly a declared individualism that provides the basis for the equality of statuses, an equality that is unquestionably more real amongst them than amongst us. That comparison may be found surprising. Political philosophy has popularized a rough opposition between, on the one hand, societies born in Western Europe from a union between capitalism and the Enlightenment ideology – in which the individual, the source of rights and the proprietor of his own person, is the touchstone upon which the collective edifice rests – and, on the other, pre-modern societies, totalities structured by immutable hierarchies – in which the individual is absent, or at least has meaning and existence only as an element in a greater whole that defines him entirely. But although societies founded upon the pre-eminence of the whole over the parts certainly covered much of the earth's surface before the triumph of parliaments, there are, in contrast, others, no less numerous but probably less well known, that have placed the very highest value of their social philosophy upon the realization of an individual's destiny, freely mastered and within the reach of every man. The Achuar belong to this latter category: unconcerned to present themselves as an organic community, forgetful of their past, and indifferent to their future, bending the language of kinship to the demands of their immediate interests, mindful of their personal reputation, and quick to desert those who seek too much commitment from others, the only thing that checks their self-exaltation is the absence of any public to applaud them.

Since I have been here Nankiti has given no orders, except when he asked his wife to serve the manioc beer. He spends the day conferring with 'his sons', apparently discussing a possible offensive, or else lying on his *peak*, meditating. In the late afternoon he suddenly leaves the house and takes but a few minutes to build a rudimentary shelter on the edge of the Yutsuentza, a few paces away from the palisade. The evening routine is then repeated, as on the previous day: a frugal meal, the dogs released into the enclosure, and everyone to bed at nightfall – except for Nankiti, who goes off to his little cabin with a gourd of tobacco juice, there, according to Tarir, to seek assistance and omens from his *arutam*.

The night is peaceful but short. At about three o'clock in the morning Nankiti knocks at the door for admittance and announces, without further ceremony, that his dreams were good. Tarir's, on the other hand, were not good at all – a jaguar got into his house – and he entreats me to take this bad omen seriously and to depart at dawn. So it is now or never for Tseremp to make his request. While each of us sips at his *wayus*, in a thin, plaintive voice he proceeds to give a circumstantial account of the wrongs that he has suffered, as if he himself did not really believe that the *tumash* that he is claiming is justified. Tseremp's father, Kirimint, used to live on the upper Kapawi, not far from a certain Sharian, whose sister he had married. Sharian, having been cuckolded by his own wife without her brothers showing the slightest concern, conceived a great resentment against his in-laws, abandoned the faithless woman and went off to settle far away on the lower Corrientes, where he married one of Nankiti's sisters. Now, Kirimint was in the habit of beating his wife, and this came to the ears of Sharian, who let his brother-in-law know that he ought to stop mistreating her. Tseremp's father took no notice of his remonstrances and, after a particularly violent beating, his wife fell sick and died. At about the same time a brother of Nankiti's, a certain Unupi, came to the upper Kapawi to consult Kirimint's brother, Mashinkiash, who was a famous shaman. But instead of recovering, Unupi died as soon as he got home and Mashinkiash was blamed for this. Nankiti and Sharian then organized a raid to kill Mashinkiash, thereby avenging the two losses that they had suffered. However, they were not successful as they were spotted before the attack. At this point Kirimint himself went to the Bobonaza for treatment from a shaman called Kantuash. Sharian learned of his presence, probably from Kantuash himself, and reactivated Nankiti's desire for revenge. It was in Kantuash's house that Nankiti killed Kirimint.

In support of his claim for compensation Tseremp uses two types of argument: first, the injustice of killing a man who had done Nankiti no direct wrong, since he was not himself a shaman and could not be held responsible for the actions of his shaman brother; and secondly, and above all, his own sad lot as an orphan pushed from house to house, eventually to be taken in by an *apach*, far from his native land. It is true that here orphans, especially those without mothers, do complain of their unhappy childhoods, not because they are unkindly treated or begrudged food but because, since nobody really cares about them, they do not receive the affection and attention that they need. Their solitude sometimes leads the younger ones to commit suicide by eating earth; as for adults, the memory of their orphaned childhood remains vividly painful and leaves them with a lasting rancour against those who deprived them of their parents. It is when painting a picture of his sad condition that Tseremp is at his most eloquent – all, it would appear, to no avail, since at no point in his pleas does Nankiti sympathize over his trials or even attempt to justify his own action, contenting himself with grunting the odd conventional formula to show that he is still listening. The hearing is over when Nankiti brings it to a close with an emphatic: 'Right! I have heard! We'll see!' All we can do now is await daybreak to find out whether we are to leave empty-handed.

At this point the household is seized by an orderly kind of excitement. The men are using genipa to paint large black circles around their mouths – 'the mouth of the jaguar', according to Tarir – and are taking off the woven bracelets that they wear round their wrists as a sign of their meeting with *arutam*, then tidying them away in their *pitiak*. Each man is cleaning his rifle with care and checking that it is in good order, while the women are busy packing provisions of fermented manioc paste into banana leaves. We are clearly not the only ones to be leaving. Pretending not to notice these preparations, we make our hasty farewells as soon as it is light enough and, just as we get up to leave, Nankiti also stands up and, with a very bad grace, hands his rifle to Tseremp, saying: 'Here! Take this for me! It is the *tumash*!'

As we move off as rapidly as possible, Tseremp barely restraining himself from running, a tumult from the house makes me look back. From where we are, half hidden by the manioc shrubs, we can see the open space in front of the palisade, where the men are now lined up facing each other in two rows of four, yelling at one another at the tops of their voices. Tarir has halted too and is watching the scene with me. The stentorian dialogue suddenly winds down in an abrupt decrescendo and the men in one of the rows begin to threaten their opposite numbers, brandishing their rifles and hopping as one from foot to foot, punctuating their gestures with rhythmic exclamations that I cannot understand, while the other row remains impassive, unblinking, arms folded and rifles cradled in the crooks of their arms, firmly responding: '*Hai*! It's true! *Pai, pai, pai*!' After three or four minutes everything stops, then starts up again with the roles reversed and the men who were submitted to the last assault now yelling even louder and brandishing their weapons with even greater savagery than their companions did a moment before. Women surround them, carrying bowls of beer which they relentlessly serve to the protagonists in this simulated combat that is growing increasingly excited at every change. Tarir seems as fascinated as I am by the spectacle of this martial frenzy. Perhaps he is nostalgic for the times when he too made war, and it is with regret that he drags me away to resume our return journey: 'It is the *anemat*, brother-in-law, they are preparing to seek out those of the Apupentza. It is better to be on our way.'

III

VISIONS

'We must try to penetrate their thoughts, not aim to make them think as we do.'

JOSEPH-MARIE DE GERANDO,
*Reflections on Methods Appropriate in
the Observation of Savages*

CHAPTER 19

Paths of Revelation

THE ALMOST NON-EXISTENT track at last widens out, opening on to a little glade cleared of bushes. Squatting in the middle, in a shelter constructed from palms, Pakunt wordlessly watches our approach. He is shivering, stark naked, his body crisscrossed with scratches and his hair entangled with the remains of plants. His pale face is expressionless, seeming enlarged by his dilated eyes that are fixed upon us yet appear not to see us. It is four days since Pakunt 'set off on the path', to use the time-honoured expression. Alone in the depths of the forest, neither eating nor drinking, he has been swallowing stramonium and tobacco juice without respite, so as to be visited by an *arutam* vision. The well-cleared entrances to the glade are very much part of the setting: *arutam* only appears to those who have cleared a wide, unimpeded approach for him, literally a 'path', next to which the supplicant, positioned in his 'resting place' (*ayamti*), awaits the arrival of the wandering ghost. I have come along with my host Tunki from his house two hours away, as he was beginning to worry about Pakunt's continuing absence. Trances induced by stramonium can be violent, leading a hallucinating subject to dash through the forest heedless of the perils lurking there: a bad fall or a drowning are not to be ruled out, even in the cases of those who, like Pakunt, have already several times undergone this ordeal successfully. Despite the grazes and the pair of shorts lying beside him in shreds, the young man seems to have emerged unharmed; and it is with a firm voice that he announces to Tunki: '*Pai! kanutrajai! waimiakjai!*' 'All is well! I had the vision! I met him!'

The reason why Pakunt 'set off on the path' is that he has just killed a man. On pain of being deserted by his vital forces at this critical moment, he therefore had to renew his vision of *arutam* as soon as possible. The murder was committed a few days after our arrival at the home of Tunki, who is a very great shaman and the brother of my Capahuari friend, Mukuimp, who had long been urging me to visit the Kunampentza to see this elder brother of his who taught him virtually all he knows about shamanery. It was a project that I had been putting off, since the Kunampentza lies on the northernmost edge of the Achuar territory a long way from our usual stamping grounds, where much work still remained to be done before embarking upon an enquiry in greater depth into shamanism.

Since the completion of our canoe expedition with Tseremp and Tarir more than eight months have elapsed, spent in long stays in places already familiar – Capahuari and Sasaïme – interspersed by short trips to more peripheral regions on the Copataza or the upper Pastaza. For almost two years we have been wandering amongst the northern Achuar and by now we are known virtually everywhere and nobody is surprised at our presence. This in itself entails certain problems: since everyone now believes that I have at last learned sense, they are all expecting me to take seriously the obligations of the fictitious kinship into which I have been fitted and to take sides with this or that faction when conflict arises between them. That is exactly what happened about two weeks ago when we landed from a small aircraft at Conambo, on our way to visit Tunki.

Conambo is situated on the middle reaches of the Kunampentza, 'the river of the squirrel'. It amounts to no more than a landing-strip built ten years ago or so, when a short-lived petroleum prospecting project was launched, around which a few Achuar and Quichua families recently settled. By the time we arrived most of the Achuar houses had been deserted as a result of a serious conflict between two groups linked by marriage. One faction had taken refuge on the Wayusentza, a minor tributary of the Pindo Yacu, two days' march away to the north, while the other, led by Tunki and Mukucham, had withdrawn to the banks of the Kunampentza, one day's canoe journey upstream from the village of Conambo. It is a well-chosen site since the river, which is easy to guard, is its sole path of access. Knowing of my friendship with Mukuimp and learning that I had come to see his brother, a relative of Tunki's who happened to be in Conambo on that day had taken us in his canoe to our host's house.

The conflict had, as usual, arisen over a conjugal problem: fed up with being ill-treated by her husband Chuchukia, Chayuk had abandoned him and taken refuge with her brothers. Several of her nephews and nieces had recently died and soon people were accusing Mashu, Chuchukia's father and a well-known shaman, of having 'eaten' them in revenge for his daughter-in-law's defection. At her mother's instigation Chayuk's daughter, who had married a 'branch' nephew of Chuchukia's, also left her husband, thereby severing the marriage links between these two groups of affines. Contrary to custom in such cases, moreover, the children had remained with their respective fathers, to the despair of their mothers, who had little hope of seeing them in the near future since visits were no longer possible between the two now deeply hostile groups. It was at this fraught point that Pakunt, a 'branch' son of Chayuk, had been afflicted by a semi-paralysis of the legs attributed to a shamanistic *tunchi*. Mukucham, his maternal uncle, had tried in vain to cure him and it was Tunki, related through his wives to Mukucham, who managed to effect a cure. When questioned by Pakunt, Tunki had prudently declared that he had not been able to glimpse the shaman responsible for the *tunchi*. However, hostility having escalated to such a degree that it was impossible to be content with this reply, it was eventually Chayuk, following a visionary trance produced by stramonium, who revealed that the guilt lay with Mashu. Such was the state of affairs when we arrived at Tunki's house. Chayuk, a big, strong woman, quite handsome in a mannish way and extremely free in her speech and manner for a person of her sex, had been persistently urging her relatives to avenge all this villainy, reproaching them almost openly for cowardice. Soon after, Pakunt had made the trip downstream to Conambo with his brother-in-law Shiki. When he returned a few days later we were not exactly surprised to learn that he had managed to kill Mashu the night before, making the most of the latter's brief visit to the village to collect some utensils from his former house.

Once back in Tunki's house, after a long bathe Pakunt is allowed his first meal since he 'set out on the path': a bowl of *tumpi*, a sort of purée of manioc and taro. For many long weeks he will continue to be limited to insipid dishes of this nature. As Tunki reminds him, up until the next new moon he must only eat small, spineless fishes, cooked by steaming, palm hearts, tubers from the garden and the boiled leaves of *jeep*, a wild arum, all of which are foods deemed to

301

be 'white', bloodless, tender and inactive, prepared without direct contact with the cooking fire and associated, as a group, with all that is most inert about vegetables. A mature and experienced man, probably Tunki himself, will eventually lift the prohibition against meat by placing a tiny morsel in Pakunt's mouth. But for several further months Pakunt will be obliged to eat nothing but tiny mammals with pale, non-fibrous flesh such as agoutis, acouchis, squirrels and marmosets, mammals that are considered virtually domesticated, given that they live close to human beings and find food in their gardens. Not until four or five months have elapsed from the time of his meeting with *arutam* will the young man be allowed to eat the strong 'black' meats of true game (peccaries, woolly monkeys, toucans, Penelope-birds and so on) and the flesh of the large cat-fish, the only fish endowed with a *wakan*, no doubt because it feeds partly on its own kind. This diet seems that of a convalescent: it will very gradually restore his upset body, provided he takes things gently. For the time being Pakunt must not go hunting, make any strenuous physical efforts or pay any long-distance visits. Even sexual activity is forbidden, as if he were still too fragile to allow himself to be spent by any procreative efforts.

What exactly is this mysterious *arutam*? That is a question that, following our predecessors amongst the Jivaros, we have been asking ourselves ever since our first days with them; and it is only now that I am beginning to see how to answer it, thanks to Pakunt's experience and the informed commentaries I have managed to elicit from Tunki, which are helping me to set in order the scattered information already collected. *Arutam* is first of all a vision produced by a consciousness affected by fasting, repeated ingestion of tobacco juice and, above all, the strong doses of scopolamine that are released by the stramonium preparation. However, pharmacology does not, on its own, explain either the nature of the hallucination or the meanings attributed to it. To judge from the accounts that I have been able to collect, the manifestations of *arutam* are very stereotyped. Prostrated by narcosis at the side of the path, his body weakened by lack of nourishment and his mind entirely directed towards the meeting to which he aspires, the supplicant suddenly becomes aware of echoes of a distant wind that swells into a hurricane and swoops violently upon the clearing at the precise moment when a strange or monstrous apparition gradually approaches him. It may be a gigantic jaguar with flaming eyes, a pair of huge, enlaced anacondas, an immense harpy-eagle, a troop of armed strangers laughing sarcastically, a truncated human body with limbs that crawl independently along the ground, or a great fiery head that falls from the sky and rolls convulsively towards him. Despite the terror that seizes the supplicant, he has to touch the apparition with his hand or with a stick. Thereupon it vanishes in a deafening explosion and the wind dies down as swiftly as it arose. In the sudden calm, an imposing old man then materializes. He is *arutam*, in other words 'the Ancient', the ghost of a valiant warrior who, after testing the supplicant's courage by adopting a terrifying avatar, now reveals himself in a benign form to deliver a brief message of hope, assistance and longevity. He then vanishes.

Although my companions agree about the sequence of events in meetings with *arutam*, they differ as to the tenor of his messages. Some claim that there are two kinds of *arutam*, each with a different kind of prediction. The one is concerned only with domestic happiness and tells of a long life full of down-to-earth satisfactions – plenty of wives, many respectful sons-in-law, richly productive gardens, and so on – while the other constitutes a guarantee of success in war, exemplary courage and, finally, a virtually absolute invincibility in battle. Some Achuar challenge that distinction, maintaining that you cannot dissociate the successes of a fulfilled life from the warrior exploits that a great strength of soul renders possible, since both types of success presuppose the perfect self-control and sense of one's own worth that can only be gained through an *arutam* meeting. This view, which certainly seems the more plausible, is even shared by men who, never having been privileged with such a revelation, feel themselves to be inferior to others in every domain of personal achievement. The quest for a vision is not always crowned with success, which would seem to confirm that the drug acts not so much as an automatic 'open Sesame', but rather as a catalyst of culturally determined aspirations. Tseremp has told me in confidence that he has never seen *arutam* despite many attempts to do so. He seems resigned to his lot and says it would be pointless for him to claim to have had the vision since the effects of *arutam* soon become manifest in a man in the way he behaves: he speaks out forcefully, particularly in ceremonial dialogues, is visibly at ease in all circumstances and can face danger and adversity with equanimity, all qualities that he himself admits to lacking. He is scornful of his brother-in-law Titiar, whom he suspects, on the basis of his demeanour, to be in the same predicament as himself yet who maintains, in the face of general disbelief, that he has met *arutam*.

The uncertainty surrounding the nature of the messages delivered by *arutam*, including the fact that it is possible to pretend to have received them, stems partly from the need to keep the revelation secret, on pain of forfeiting its benefits. The subject is such an intimate one that my companions will only speak of it with reticence, even when describing past visions whose personal relevance has now been superseded. The quest for an *arutam* needs to be repeated at regular intervals. It begins when a boy is ten or twelve years old, when it involves the supervision of a mentor, generally his father, on account of the dangers run in the undertaking. These first experiences constitute a kind of preparatory exercise in which the initiate learns to control his visions. The first real *arutam* meeting happens at the age of seventeen or eighteen, when the young man has acquired enough self-control to undertake the quest on his own. The social effects are immediately discernible: he tries to procure a rifle; he may take a wife; above all, he is now invited to take part in raids, usually by the father of his wife, under whose supervision he serves his warrior's apprenticeship. *Arutam* operates as a stimulus to valour and spurs a young man on to distinguish himself in battle. But the influence of *arutam* is dissipated once he has killed an enemy, and he then needs to 'set off on the path' for a new meeting. All the men who take part in a victorious expedition find themselves in the same position, since the killing of an enemy is a collective affair: as soon as a member of the troop has fired the fatal shot, all the others fire their own rifles at the fallen victim, becoming co-murderers through this act of solidarity which makes it possible for still inexperienced young men to start chalking up their warrior exploits at an early age.

My companions tell me that the effect of *arutam* disappears very promptly once you have killed, leaving you in a state of extreme languor, racked by insatiable hunger, all will annihilated except a desire to 'set off on the path'. It is important to go and seek *arutam* straight away at this point since one falls into this vulnerable state at the very moment when one is most exposed to reprisals on the part of the victim's relatives. Meeting with a new *arutam* seems not only to restore the strength of a victorious warrior, but also to increase it little by little, as he accumulates more visionary experiences, so that older men who have 'set off on the path' many times are reputed to be invincible. Old braves, such as Tsukanka and Naanch in Capahuari and Tukupi and Washikta at Sasaïme, do of course eventually die but, it is said, never of an accidental death or by physical violence. They manage to survive even when riddled with buck-shot and, if they do succumb in the end, it is not so much by reason of their wounds but because some shaman has weakened them by sending them a *tunchi*, the only way of getting rid of enemies so formidable that one is forced to give up the idea of killing them by more direct means. A series of tête-à-têtes with *arutam* as one sleeps in the 'resting place' results in a personal accumulation of power, which is the reason why great warriors are sometimes referred to as *kanuraur*, those who know how to sleep'.

Because its effects are gauged first and foremost in warfare, *arutam* is connected with the liberation of an internal force in acts of codified violence. But these are not always feats of arms. Tunki tells me that shamans sometimes experience a special kind of *arutam*, which they achieve by mixing their stramonium with a little *natem*, their own particular hallucinogenic beverage. This produces a meeting that consolidates their system of protection against enemy shamans, since it reinforces their own offensive powers. Just as an ordinary man, after seeing *arutam*, will yearn to test his reinforced bravery in battle, so a shaman visited by his special kind of *arutam* will be assailed by a desire to send off his invisible projectiles without necessarily bothering to control their destination.

However, the energy mobilized by the vision is not directed solely to exalting one's own supremacy. It may equally strengthen the day-to-day fulfilment of a long-lasting existence, as is clear from the benefits that women derive from their visionary experiences. It is less important for a woman 'to set off on the path' than it is for a man who must establish his glory on the field of battle and pick up the threads of his life anew every time he kills. So not all women submit themselves to this trial. It attracts above all the wives of men who are *kakaram*, or 'strong', that is to say those who have had many *arutam* meetings. What these women acquire, as well as longevity, is confidence in achieving perfection in their own areas of competence: skill in the cultivation and use of plants, pottery, weaving, raising dogs, and so on. Emulation no doubt has something to do with the desire of a wife to meet *arutam*, not so much so as to rival her husband in some improbable war between the sexes, but rather to establish a form of parity in their converging lives, whose complementarity will be guaranteed if both partners have received revelation. In the same way as the men, some women go regularly to the 'resting place' to take stramonium, usually with the assistance of their mother or an elder sister. Occasionally they also meet *arutam* in dreams, without taking any stimulants, in particular when they lose their husband or when his affection for them has been alienated by a violent misunderstanding. The temporary or definitive distancing of their husband seems to affect them as a murder affects a man. In both cases a singular event charged with passion has just taken place, bringing to a close the development of a period of life that a former *arutam* had outlined, and making it necessary to recast the destiny of the individual concerned under the auspices of a new prediction.

To give an account of the effects of *arutam*, as I have been attempting to do, is not enough to gain an understanding of its principles. A first question begs an answer: who is this 'Ancient' who brings a revelation? As a first approximation, he may be defined as an ancestor. He is someone who died relatively recently and whose memory for the moment lives on, as he himself ensures by declaring his name. In most cases he is a relative, sometimes a distant one but usually a native of the same 'neighbourhood' as the vision-seeker, someone respected in his lifetime, particularly for his longevity. Male ancestors manifest themselves to men, female ancestors to women, and shaman ancestors to shamans. In the absence of clearly defined lines of descent, these 'Ancients' are not always blood-relatives, although it is common for a father who died recently to reveal himself as *arutam* to his eldest son, having told him on his death-bed the places where he will be most likely to encounter him. Every *arutam* has thus existed in the recent past, and in many cases the vision-seeker has known him well, even loved him – which explains the benevolence that he displays once the fear occasioned by his initial form of apparition has been surmounted.

So is he a ghost? Not really, to judge from what Tunki tells me:

'The person [*aents*] that you see is not the real person. The real person has disappeared for ever. What you see is his *arutam*.'

Hmm! 'But', I say to him, '*arutam* is an Ancient, isn't he? – one of your dead relatives? So what is the *arutam* of this *arutam*?'

'The person that you see is an image [*wakan*] of *arutam*: the person no longer exists, but *arutam* exists for ever. *Arutam* sees with the eyes of that person, *arutam* speaks with the mouth of that person, because *arutam* is invisible. To make itself known, *arutam* makes itself like the person, but the person is dead.'

So this is an entity that seems to be eternal but very localized and that exists in the world only through its works: a complex idea, if ever there was one, and of a kind to stir my philosophical memories.

But let us, for now, leave aside questions of ontology and return to what the Achuar expect from a meeting with *arutam*. We know what the hoped-for benefits are, but how, precisely, do they come about? Here, as in so many other domains, the *anent* songs provide a precious key, though not one necessarily easy to use. To bring about the vision that he hopes for, the supplicant invokes *arutam* through an *anent* of a particular type, such as the following one, sung by Yaur at Copataza.

> My little grandfather, my little grandfather
> Plunged in distress, I awaken your compassion
> I myself am this one
> I, the son of the ocelot's paw
> Saying this, my ear alert
> You who cannot be surpassed by anyone
> Saying this, my ear alert
> My ancestors, where have they gone?
> My ancestors, where have you gone?
> Plunged in distress, I awaken your compassion
> Deep inside me all I ask is: 'Where have you gone?'
> I, the son of the ocelot's paw
> Saying this, my ear alert
> To you who declare: Like a ball of fire I usually go
> Plunged in distress, I awaken your compassion
> As you come like a ball of fire
> Fall, fall upon me! Shining like that, so brightly
> You who are my grandfather, you who are my grandfather

You who cannot be surpassed by anyone
I myself am the one who is here
Like the child carried by my mother, so I am
My grandfather who cannot be surpassed by anyone
Making me arise, all eager to go
All fragrant, making me all fragrant.

As in all *anent* of this type, *arutam* is invoked by an affectionate
term of relationship, 'little grandfather', which expresses the idea of
direct affiliation with earlier generations whose disappearance one
regrets, as is conveyed by the lamentation, 'My ancestors, where have
you gone?' The supplicant acts humbly, seeking to arouse the commiseration of *arutam* by stressing his abandoned, solitary state, beg-
ging for his protection and his reassuring touch, like an infant crying
for its mother. The presence of *arutam* manifests itself as a light that
is both moral and concrete, which the image of the ball of fire (*payar*)
appropriately conveys. Then the metamorphosis takes place: a new
personality spurts forth from the visionary experience ('Making me
arise, all eager to go'), as if purified by a lustral bath – the theme of
ablutions is common in these *anent* – and thus made 'all fragrant'.
An *anent* of Pinchu's helps to illuminate a few points:

My longed-for little grandfather
Simply unsurpassable
As the *uyun* of my little grandfather, flic-flac, swaying to and fro,
    flic-flac, swaying to and fro, I go
Listen to my jolting step! Listen to my jolting step!
Listen! Listen as I go! Listen! Listen!
As I wait in expectation, let him carry me off, as I wait in expectation,
    let him rearrange me
I am going to my grandfather
To the unsurpassable one, straight, straight I go
My distress arouses compassion
Humble and worthy of pity I go
Oh! Whence am I the son?
Plunged in affliction I go
My longed-for grandfather, speak to me! simply speak to me!
Going simply
As the *uyun* of my grandfather, as your swaying *uyun*, flic-flac I go
Longed-for grandfather, simply unsurpassable, alone I go

308

Straight ahead, straight ahead I go, longed-for grandfather
I cannot forgo gazing upon you
Swaying, swaying to and fro I go
Crackling I go, simply unsurpassable.

The metaphor of the *uyun*, the little string or leather pouch that men carry in the forest, throws some light upon the complex relationship that the supplicant is seeking to establish with *arutam*. By identifying himself with this object, he presents himself both as a vessel aspiring to be filled and also as an attribute indispensable to the ancestor but without any particular significance without his presence. The question, 'Whence am I the son?' expresses the confusion of the visionary seeking roots in a well-defined place and seems to invoke the comfort of a stable link with an ancestral territory that he hopes to obtain through *arutam*. Of particular significance, finally, is the exclamation, 'As I wait in expectation, let him carry me off [*juru-kuta*], as I wait in expectation, let him rearrange me [*iwiaitkuta*]': the effect of *arutam* is revealed here in two complementary modalities. The first evokes the adoption of a child and thus suggests the creation of a new social identity; the second indicates a metamorphosis in the course of which the supplicant discovers himself to be endowed with new characteristics. This is confirmed by Tunki who, in answer to the question, 'How does *arutam* act upon the visionary?' replied, '*Arutam* reorganizes [*iwiaitkawai*] the personality: it becomes a new personality.'

So could it be said that *arutam* is the 'soul' of an ancestor that returns to be reincarnated in a living person, in short, is this a simple metempsychosis, many examples of which are provided by the history of religions? Such an interpretation is dubious, given that the ancestor here is no more than an ephemeral apparition, the medium through which *arutam* can be recognized by an individual. No, all the indications are that *arutam* involves a more complex phenomenon in that it designates not only a relationship but also the term through which that relationship is established, a sought-for mystical link of dependence and at the same time the immaterial and unrepresentable principle with which the relationship is established. Although it has no identity of its own, this abstract entity is nevertheless individualized and attached to a particular territory, and this makes it possible for it to take on the appearance of a familiar dead person and thus appear cyclically to different men and women whose personalities it recomposes by predicting their destiny. The metamorphosis that results is expressed in tangible fashion through a transformation in behaviour, but this is not solely moral or psychological. The whole balance of a person's life is affected by the cycle of visionary experiences, so it must be supposed that *arutam* somehow or other becomes a part of those who have encountered it.

How do the Achuar represent this incorporation? A custom that I had noticed without attaching much importance to it, but on the subject of which Tunki has just provided me with more details throws new light upon this process. We already know that the effect of *arutam* is dissipated when a man kills an enemy. Foreseeing this loss that he knows to be inevitable, a warrior removes his bracelets just before setting out on a raid and only replaces them by new ones, woven by his wife, when he has met a new *arutam*, after returning from a victorious expedition. This is what Pakunt did before my very eyes, this morning. These long, multicoloured bands wrapped around the wrists are not emblems of valour, nor are they simply beguiling ornaments. Their function is to seal the pulse hermetically, for this is the necessary point of communication between the inside and the outside of the body and it so to speak constitutes the passageway for *arutam* which, depending on the circumstances, will either enter or depart through it. The weakness that assailed Pakunt as soon as he had killed Mashu and the quasi-convalescence to which he will now submit testify to the fact that the comings and goings of *arutam* provoke a profound perturbation that is felt by the entire body. Having been suddenly deserted by one of his essential components, the young man now finds himself restructured according to a new pattern that can only be stabilized with great difficulty and by dint of taking many precautions.

Arutam is more than an allegory of a destiny glimpsed whilst in a heightened state of consciousness, a stimulating experience that strengthens all the faculties. During a period of an individual's life, it accompanies him as an attentive double which, through either its presence or its absence, manifests itself in even the humblest actions of daily existence. For my companions, *arutam* is more than simply a mental projection. It is an eternal principle that is both multiple and

310

stable: multiple because every 'neighbourhood' possesses a stock of it, stable because that stock appears to be finite. In conformity with its vocation of eternity, *arutam* is neither created nor lost; always identical to itself, it is perpetuated down the generations in a multiplicity of individuals who yet are linked to one another through kinship and their place of residence.

So what is the explanation for the fact that successive acquisition of different *arutam* engenders a progressive accumulation of vital energy in an individual? Tunki, the proud possessor of a luxurious portable radio, tries to explain this to me using a physiochemical metaphor. '*Arutam* is like a radio battery that never dies. When *arutam* leaves a strong man, the battery is stronger than ever; when *arutam* leaves a weak man, it is weaker than before.' *Arutam* is thus more or less recharged or used up in accordance with the people with whom it is temporarily associated. This arrangement restores to each person the freedom to be whatever he is by virtue of his own temperament, and it prevents the cycle of visionary experiences from ever leading to the elevation of a man who is mediocre in the hierarchy of characters. No mechanical predestination is at work in these successive personality mutations. One always remains the product of what one does, even in respect of how much benefit one derives from *arutam*.

When a person whom it has been helping dies, *arutam* reverts to being a disembodied essence until such time as it reassumes the features of its former possessor in order to appear briefly to the new individual whose existence it will henceforth animate. The same thing happens when a man has killed, except that the *arutam* which deserts him adopts a different identity when it manifests itself to another supplicant. However, the parallelism between the two situations does raise the question: why does one have to be deserted by *arutam* when one has killed? It is true that every murder tends to close the cycle of a destiny partly defined by the very feat of arms which crowns its accomplishment. But there is more to it. Despite their fervour, the Achuar do not kill lightly, for by wiping out a life one puts one's own in danger. The state in which a murderer finds himself just before 'setting off on the path' presents many analogies with that of a dying man whose *wakan* leaves him some time before his last breath. Weak and helpless like the latter, he is, everyone agrees, destined for certain death unless he very soon meets a new *arutam*. Like the dead, he is

311

tortured by constant hunger, freezing with cold, and desperate to get back to his family, but this is forbidden him until such time as he has been strengthened by a new vision. While he is seeking *arutam*, his relatives must not look at him or even think of him, just as memories of the dead must be banished as soon as possible to prevent them from venting their resentment upon those still living. Far from one's strength increasing, each time one kills one dies a little oneself: a most dangerous condition, in which the desertion of *arutam* seems as much a symptom as a result.

Like so many symbols that tradition has sanctified to avoid elucidating them, *arutam* is a deliberately vague concept that makes it possible to accommodate, within a single term and a unique perceptive experience, a vast register of ideas, feelings, and desires that encapsulate some kind of Achuar concept of the human condition. The persuasive force of this symbol stems from the fact that it first manifests itself as a vision that is at once individual and held to be true by everyone; a vision that one can touch, hear, appropriate and retain in one's memory, yet never entirely control. Like the *anent*, whose form and function never change, the vision of *arutam* is a quasi-object. It is an immaterial entity yet its effects are real enough. It has unquestionably existed throughout all eternity and is granted to men and women on a temporary lease, so that they can continue to demonstrate its efficacy as they set it for a time at the very heart of their aspirations.

This figurative representation also allows one to glimpse the Achuars' own conception of causality. In its disembodied form, *arutam* is purely a possibility of destiny, a motivating principle aimed at no visible existence in particular. From time to time it becomes actualized through the succession of partial biographies it reveals. It is thus acted upon as much as activating, constantly revitalized by those whom it animates, always unique yet infinitely repeatable, a mystic patrimony over which nobody exercises control and whose perpetuation derives from the desire of every individual to draw upon it when his or her turn comes to do so. For a society indifferent to the past, it is an admirable device for annulling time: a present without depth is constantly renewed by this powerful mechanism of continuity which, ever since the deepest night of time, has guaranteed that each new generation shall share in the same *arutam* from which previous generations have already benefited. It thereby helps to perpetuate in fragments of discontinuous existence the unchanging collective basis of a shared identity.

According to the ethnographers' reports of other Jivaro tribes, the *arutam* of the Achuar seems to differ from the *arutam* of the Shuar, which itself differs from what the Aguarana call *ajutap*. These differences of interpretation do not result solely from the theoretical preconceptions or spontaneous philosophy that each of us injects into his/her descriptions. They also testify to the fundamental vagueness of this complex notion, the contents of which seem to have been impelled in different directions by each tribe to suit its own particular idiosyncrasies. All observers agree on the circumstances in which the Jivaros receive a revelation from the ghost of an ancestor. However, from one tribe to another there are many discrepancies in the consequences of these meetings and the characteristics ascribed to the ancestor in question. The Aguarana variant is expressed in a minor mode: *ajutap* is the transcendent instrument of a prediction of success in war. When this is recalled in public, before starting off on a raid, it stimulates the bravery of the beneficiary. However, the vision is not totally without substance as it is transformed into a new *ajutap* spirit at the death of the visionary. For the Shuar, the *arutam* vision makes it possible to acquire a new 'soul', donated by some unknown ancestor, the main effect of which is to arouse an irrepressible urge to kill. On the eve of an attack each warrior describes his own vision publicly, thereby causing his *arutam* soul to depart. The weakening that results is gradual, but all the same the man must seek a new *arutam*, for without this his life would be at risk. Finding a new *arutam* speedily will furthermore check the gradual dissipation of the power of the old *arutam* soul, thereby contributing to an accumulation of power that will increase with each consecutive acquisition. At his death, a warrior produces as many *arutam* souls as he has incorporated in his lifetime. All this is quite different from what prevails among the Achuar that I know, for with them the accumulation of energy takes place within the *arutam* itself, not in the bodies of those it visits. Furthermore, my companions insist that the number of existing *arutam* is finite, that they are connected with the territory of a particular local group, and that they reveal their former identity to the supplicant. In contrast to what happens in the other tribes, the same *arutam* are thus embodied generation after generation in the inhabitants of the

313

same 'neighbourhood' and in this way, despite the Achuars' genealogical amnesia, they contribute to the substantial perpetuation of the
distinctive identity of their respective kindred.

This transmission of *arutam* through a principle of continuous
descent, which seems to be peculiar to the Achuar alone, is possibly
their substitute for head-hunting. Both the capture of *tsantsa* and the
acquisition of *arutam* are designed, by means of warfare, to consolidate the imaginary consanguinity of neighbourhood groups, by reproducing in their midst as it were rough versions of persons who are
free of the stigma of affinity. The *tsantsa* ritual converts a non-related
enemy into a child related by blood; and a relationship of symbolic
affiliation with the same *arutam* 'grandfathers' turns all the members
of a kindred into a single group whose solidarity stems from the
ancestral principle that defines them as an ideal community. The
ingredients and the objectives are the same in both cases. All that is
different is the means used for achieving the latter: in the one case,
otherness produces 'selfness' by instituting an affinity without any real
affines; in the other, selfness reiterates selfness because one pretends to
be unaware of the affinity of real affines. The choice made between
these two alternatives no doubt depended upon historical contin-
gency. Having been for so long subjected to the constant attacks of
the Shuar, who far outnumbered them, the Achuar eventually withdrew into refuge zones, fleeing the dangerous proximity of their
neighbours. It was probably this withdrawal into themselves that led
to the permutation. Unable, for military reasons, to continue head-
hunting, they seem to have been forced to draw upon their own
resources, seeking from *arutam* the same service that used to be
performed by the *tsantsa* of their enemies: in short, *arutam* makes it
possible for them to remain identical to themselves without ever
owing anything to anyone else.

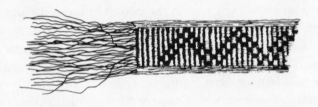

CHAPTER 20

The Shaman's Song

TUNKI'S VIBRATING TSAYANTAR, sharp and metallic, throbs in counterpoint to the continuous background of insect noises. There is no moon tonight and the semi-darkness of the house is barely affected by the fire glowing at the foot of the *chimpui* on which our host is seated. It is nearly half an hour since Tunki started 'drinking the *natem*', according to the formula for shamanistic cures. He has been playing his great mouth bow all the time, his gaze lost in serene meditation. His patient is sitting silently at his feet on a small *kutank*. He is a man from the village of Conambo, one Wisui, a 'branch' brother of Mukucham's, who has recently become Tunki's *amik*. Although not directly implicated in the vendetta against the people of Wayusentza, kinship and this elective friendship link him to Tunki's faction so, feeling ill, it is to Tunki that he has come. He arrived in his canoe this afternoon, his complexion waxy-white, his gait heavy, complaining of a persistent pain in his liver. He attributes it to a shamanistic *tunchi* because a short while ago he dreamed that little birds were pecking at his body and penetrating his side – a classic omen for an attack of *tsentsak*. In accordance with the custom that the patient provides the shaman with the instruments of his office, he has brought *natem* and tobacco along with him.

Both physically and morally, Tunki is quite different from his brother Mukuimp. However, he no more resembles the severe image one might have of a shaman than Mukuimp does. Tunki is a strapping, boastful man with rather a foppish face adorned by a small, sparse moustache, and short hair slicked with *kunkuk* oil, who affects a jovial manner that does not, however, succeed in concealing his sly temperament. I have declined his invitation to accompany him in his trance. It took me several months to dispel the false impression that

315

I unwittingly created by accepting Wajari's invitation to 'drink the *natem*' in his house, which caused me to move away from Capahuari for a time, to flee the reputation of shaman that this had instantly procured me. Even now I am not certain that I am believed when I deny that I am an *uwishin*, or shaman, but at least that disclaimer helps me to avert misunderstandings, even if not to prevent their arising or multiplying. When, on his brother's recommendation, I approached Tunki, I told him that I would like to learn how he proceeded before submitting myself to any initiation, that is to say before taking *natem* and acquiring a supply of *tsentsak* from him. He seemed doubtful as to whether one could learn anything at all about shamanism in such an abstract manner; but the information that he has been quite happy to give me over the last few days would be impossible to use without the tools to render it efficient, so we are both quite satisfied: flattered by my curiosity, Tunki is not unwilling to tell me the secrets of his profession, knowing that I would have to pay dearly for his *tsentsak* if I wanted to be able to use it; and meanwhile I am gathering precious information without too much risk of being given a hard time for practising sorcery.

Tunki has stopped playing and now goes down to the river where I soon hear him splashing about. The music of his *tsayantar* has enabled him to arouse the darts that he has stocked within his body, making them vibrate in unison, just as crystal will in response to certain notes played on a violin. This melodic excitation, presented as an operation designed to 'seduce' his own *tsentsak*, is addressed to a particular class of darts known as 'racoon darts' (*entsaya yawa tsentsakri*), which resonate with the music and song of the shaman and contribute to his internal harmony. To activate their response as successfully as possible, the *uwishin* must also be able to concentrate his mind at length upon images of vibration, such as humming-birds or dragonflies in stationary flight. In this way, all his senses combine in the experience of the trance so as to turn the whole body into one great, immobile vibration. Tunki is at present using his bathe to reinforce the 'cooling' process initiated by the *natem*. In the cool water he strives to control the organic quivering that turns him into a living carapace throbbing in silence. The river, furthermore, is the favourite haunt of the creatures that assist shamans, which he can summon without a single word simply by immersing himself in their original medium like a great, reverberating diapason producing concentric ripples.

After drying himself at the dying fire, Tunki begins to blow upon his patient's torso, enveloping him in the acrid smoke of a thick cigarette that Wisui has prepared by shredding a stick of tobacco into a dried banana leaf. He then seizes the *shinki-shinki*, a sheaf of rustling leaves made specially for the purpose, and sets about rhythmically brushing them over the painful part of the body. This first phase of the cure is designed to anaesthetize the harmful darts lodged in Wisui's body: doped by the smoke and cooled in the draught produced by the soporific movement of the *shinki-shinki*, they grow numb with cold, lose their virulence and will become easier to dislodge. In the silence of the house, the *tchak-tchak-tchak-tchak* of the sheaf of leaves has a calming effect that I too feel; it dilates time with its repetitive sound and induces an agreeable torpor. It is at this point, just as one's attention is beginning to wander, that Tunki begins to whistle a little tune through his teeth, keeping in time with his sweeping movements. He keeps this up for a few minutes then, maintaining the rhythm of the *shinki-shinki*, begins to sing in a barely audible voice, putting words to the melody he has been whistling:

> *Wi tsumai-tsum, tsumai-ai-ai-tsumai-ai-ai*
> *Tsumai, tsumai, tsumai-tsum*
> *Tsumai, tsumai, tsumai-tsum*
> *Tsumai, tsumai, wi, wi, wi, wi, wi, wi, wi*
> *Tsumai, tsumai, tsumai-tsum, tsumai, tsumai-tsum*
> *Wi, wi, wi, wi-nia um-pun-krun e-ken-tran-ku*
> *Wi, wi, wi, wi, wi, wi, wi e-ke-trait-ja . . .*

Now his voice swells, articulating with increasing precision and intensity.

> *Iwianch, iwianchi ji-irtan*
> *Wikia en-ket-ki-nia-ku nu-na-kun*
> *Wikia en-ket-ki-nia-ku nu-na-a-a-a*
> *Ajatke kurat, a-jat-ke ku-ra-ra-ra-rat*
> *Uratkinia um-puar-wit-jai*
> *Uratkinia um-puar-wit-jai-jai-jai-jai-jai*
> *Wi, wi, wi, wi, wi, wi, wi . . .*

As in more ordinary *anent*, the expression is allegorical and full of poetic images, but essentially the meaning remains accessible to the listeners, in particular to the sick man himself, who listens attentively to Tunki's words. There is no trace here of the enigmatic formulae and esoteric language that shamans employ in other regions of both North and South America, to arouse reverence in the profane and to conceal the secrets of their own mysterious art.

Me, *tsumai, tsumai* . . .
Me, me, me, me, me, me, me!
Tsumai, tsumai . . .
Me, me, me, while I make my projectile penetrate
Me, me, me, me, me, me, me, I am in harmony
Making my Iwianch spirits rise up
I make them pass through the barrier of darts
I make them penetrate the wall of little arrows
Giving them an immediate way out
Leaving them a free passage
In this way I blow, me, me, me . . .
Launching my blown projectile
Submerging everything, saturating everything
I am blowing, me, me, me . . .
Tarairira, tara, tariri-ri-ri-ri-ri
You, the extraordinary one
Tarairira, tara, tariri-ri-ri-ri-ri
As remarkable as you are, I am blowing
Tsunki, Tsunki, my spirits I am summoning you
Violently cleaving a path, I am blowing, I am blowing
Me, me, me, me, me, me, me!
Tsumai, tsumai . . .
Me, me, me . . .
Like a river carrying away its bank, I cover everything with my flood,
    I overflow everywhere
Unmoving on this very spot
Stretching into the depths, I am blowing
Me, me, me, me, me, me, me . . .
Even when they are embedded, out of reach, I unhook the *tsentsak*
    with a dry tap, blowing
Clearing a path for myself, I completely beguile the stranger who has
    invited himself into your body, by blowing, by blowing, me, me, me,
    me, me, me!

Tarairira, tara, tariri . . .

Tsumai, tsumai . . .

Making my breath penetrate, making it desirable, I work hard to make
them let go

I work to get rid of them completely, absolutely, by opening the exit

Me, me, me, me, me, me!

Tsumai, tsumai. . . me, me . . . *rari ri ri, rari ri ri* . . .

Supai, supai, supai, supai, supai, supai, me, me . . .

Like Tsunki himself, I know how to speak, me, me, me . . .

In your head that is so painful, in your painful head

However embedded the pain is, I unhook it with a dry tap

Leaving you perfectly well, I sing and I sing, I blow and I blow

Tarairira, tara, tariri, me, me . . . *ri ri ri ri*

The *pasuk* from the entrails of the earth, him too I call, me, me,
me

The death that I now ward off, I am brushing it away with my sheaf,
proudly

Me, me, me, me, me, me!

Like the *pasuk* of the great trees, like the *pasuk* all striped, I am in the
grip of *natem*

Unmoving, I wear the *pasuk* like a necklace and death itself I beguile,
carrying it far away, me, me, me, me

Tarairira, tara . . .

Tsumai, tsumai . . .

Relentlessly drawing the *pasuk* from the skies, all bleeding

Wearing it constantly around me like a necklace

Death itself I sweep away with my sheaf, that's what I do with the
death that inhabits you, that's what I do to the death to which I reveal
myself, me, me, me . . .

Superpowerful me, me . . . *tsumai* . . . *tarairira* . . .

With the *pasuk* from the entrails of the earth, with the multicoloured
pasuk I make myself a necklace

Unmoving, I pass you the necklace and, repairing your lack of appetite,
me, me, me, I leave you well recomposed, me, me, me

. . . *tsumai* . . . *tsumai* . . .

Pasuk from the entrails of the earth, it is you that I summon

Multicoloured one, it is you that I call

It is to you that I speak and I carry off with me all the creatures of
natem

That is what I do, me, me, me, me, me, me, me!

Tsumai, tsumai . . .

The one that is almost unreachable, that is the one I nevertheless wear as a necklace

Unmoving, I am here on the very spot where Tsunki is preparing to do his work, there where he will unleash the floods

My Iwianch spirits, I make them turn blue in my very soul, I make them turn blue

I make them come out quivering '*puririri!*', me, me, me!

Tsumai, tsumai . . .

The one called Tsunki, I make him come in the flood that roars '*shakaa!*'

Relentlessly I go, unleashing my flood in his very heart, the flood of my own river, ceaselessly summoning the flood, making the waters roar, I go paddling on

I have the power of rivers in flood, ceaselessly I call for the waters to overflow

Formidable I am, like the waves rolling on the pebbles, without respite ensuring my victory, all fragrant, all perfumed, I make Tsunki roll, me, me, me . . .

Tsumai, tsumai . . .

I become like a porcupine, wearing spines as a necklace, clothing myself in quills, I am covered with them

Your very death, I shall chain it up far away, confident in my fearlessness

Me, me, me, me, me, me!

Having summoned the soul that is here, I seize it and hold on to it firmly

In the golden ink I have spread myself

Imbued with my valour, I am proud of myself

All adorned with the necklace, all arrayed by the porcupine, I sweep away death with my sheaf of leaves, intrepid and confident

Me, me, me, me, me, me, me!

The one called the porcupine of the heavens, that is the one I seize to make a crown of darts and definitely make death draw back from your head

By the shivers I am seized, *tsumai, tsumai* . . .

To my call Tsunki has responded

In this golden pot where your soul was enclosed, boldly I make death flee

Dressing myself in new clothes, dressed all brand-new, brought by the *natem*, I adorn myself with them as with a necklace, me, me, me, me, me, me, me!

Tsumai, tsumai . . .

You are girded by the bow of Iwianch spirits

Twisting and turning without cease, I summon death and seize it
Me, me, me, me, me, me!
I summon the Iwianch spirits relentlessly and my voice makes them
  tremble
I make them come, brushing you with my sheaf of leaves so that they
  leave you in peace . . .

Tunki has been singing for almost an hour in a fine, rough, baritone
voice. Sometimes he pauses to whistle the melody again or to emit
strange sounds, deep sighs arising from his very guts, or ventriloquistic
grunts, as if some turbulent pack of animals is restless inside him and
must be disciplined by the movements of his diaphragm. Step by step,
the *anent* describes the metamorphoses that he is undergoing and
the powers that he is mobilizing. The song is at once an incantation
and a commentary and is addressed both to his own familiar
spirits and to Wisui, before whom, like some disembodied chorus, he
retraces the actions for which their two bodies constitute the theatre.

Under the effects of the *natem* the voyage has begun and Tunki's
soul is so to speak split or even dispersed in many interconnected
fragments. His firm, steady voice inducts and regulates the shield of
darts in his throat and chest that will transform his body into a fortress
from which to launch attacks against the auxiliaries of the enemy
shaman. His eyes scan the patient's body, determining, as if by radi-
oscopy, the exact positions of the *tsentsak* that are at the root of the
trouble. But his spirit is also moving through space at a prodigious
speed to gather together the creatures whose assistance he is seeking
and the spirits from which he draws his powers, while at the same
time, like a reconnaissance plane flying over enemy lines, he is spying
in the darkness on the movements of the adversary's henchmen,
who are flocking to tighten their evil hold upon the patient. Hence
the accumulation of discontinuous images in the *anent*, where they
testify to the many violent operations in which, despite his reassuring
immobility, Tunki is involved.

The two dominant refrains – 'tsumai, tsumai . . .' and 'tarairira,
tari-ri-ri . . .' are the only slightly esoteric allusions in the song. The
first refers to the *sumai*, the name given to a shaman by the Cocama
Indians, the Achuars' distant neighbours to the south, who enjoy an
excellent reputation for shamanery throughout the upper Amazon.

The term is also used by the Shipibo and Conibo Indians of the alluvial plains of the Ucayali, over 1,000 kilometres away, where it designates their own shamans' ability to move about at great speed beneath the waters, an enviable exploit that ensures fame for them amongst other shamans far beyond the frontiers of Peru. As for '*tari-ri-ri*', this is a classic formula used in the shamanistic songs of the Quichua Indians of the Napo, from whom Tunki is supposed to have acquired some of his *tsentsak*. It is a stylized invocation addressed to the spirit Jurijri, who is one of the 'mothers of game' responsible for watching over the animals and also one of the most loyal of the *uwishin*'s servants. The role of these overlapping citations, incomprehensible to the profane, is rather like that of the kitchen Latin used by ancient quack healers: not really so much an artifice to bamboozle people, as a reaffirmation of the shaman's membership of a vaster community, united despite rivalries by a common commitment to the initiatory knowledge of this great body. Even if he has not travelled much physically, a shaman is by nature a cosmopolitan creature. Constantly on the lookout for new ideas and metaphysical fashions, he strives to break out of his ethnic and linguistic isolation by making extensive use of metaphors and images that he gleans from chance encounters during his travels, not always aware of their origins or full meaning, but with a confused sense of sharing some kind of basic stock with the distant cultures from which they come. This probably accounts for the obsessive presence of the watery world in the trappings of Amazonian shamanery. In the solitude of his own little segment of the river, each shaman feels linked with his many unknown fellows by a river network that covers millions of square kilometres, through which he and his spirit helpers can move about as if using a private telephone network.

Tunki's *anent* presents many illustrations of this preponderance of water. One is the powerful allegory of the flood that rushes, roaring, through the song, like a metonymy of the *sumai*; another is the reference to the Tsunki spirits, the beings who resemble humans and, beneath the surface of the rivers, lead an existence in every way identical to theirs. The Tsunki, it seems, are depositories of shamanistic powers and guarantors of their lasting efficacy. We have already several times been told the story of the man who led a double life with a beautiful Tsunki woman and had children by her, dividing his hunting spoils equally between his earthly family and his aquatic one, and who showed his father-in-law of the depths great respect mingled with gratitude. The story is invariably about an *uwishin*, sometimes rather green, as in the case of Nayapi, but always identifiable as a shaman from his particular relationship with the water spirits. A myth that Wajari told us presents an almost canonical version of this complicit relationship:

Once upon a time the woman Sua lived on the shores of a lake. One night she dreamed of a very handsome man and in the morning her heart ached with the desire to see him again. This man was Tsunki. Eventually, he carried off the woman Sua and took her to the bottom of the lake. There, it is said, Tsunki seated her on a cayman. The woman Sua was frightened as the cayman kept gnashing its teeth, so Tsunki gave her a stick with which to tap it on the nose every time it opened its jaws. Seeing that the cayman was becoming annoyed, Tsunki then seated the woman Sua on a *charapa* tortoise, where she felt much better. From there, she could watch everything at her leisure. She could see all the animals that lived with Tsunki, the 'midnight-blue anacondas' in compact coils, the black jaguars tethered to the posts with chains: all these animals were sniffing at the woman Sua and showing their teeth, but Tsunki kept talking to them, telling them not to try to eat her. The woman Sua lived with Tsunki for a long time. Meanwhile, her mother was searching for her everywhere, weeping. She thought her daughter had been eaten by an anaconda. But after a while Sua came back. She told her mother, 'Tsunki carried me off; now he has bidden me visit my family.' She described how, under the waters, in the depths, there were great towns built of stone and how people moved around in canoes as swift as aeroplanes. The news of this spread but no one would believe her. Then she invited her relatives to accompany her to the lakeside where she declared, 'Now I am going away to drink maize beer.' Back she went into the lake, without getting wet. Just as the top of her head was about to disappear, she asked for the door to be opened. Everyone heard the creak of the door opening and even the dogs barking in the depths of the lake. So they were all persuaded she had told the truth. Much later she re-emerged from the lake, drunk on maize beer but not at all wet. Then she began to vomit maize beer, and that is how we came to discover maize; before that, there was no maize, and it was the woman Sua who brought it from the depths of the waters. As she was a very powerful *uwishin*, one day the people said, 'We must kill the woman Sua, for she is a sorceress, *wawekratin*.' At that she said, 'If that's the way it is, I shall go away for ever, back to my husband Tsunki,' and she disappeared into the lake, never to return.

Except for the change in the sexes of the protagonists, this myth differs very little from the stories we have so often been recounted, just as if they had really taken place in the parallel space of dreams. Admittedly, women shamans are rare in reality. They are usually widows, or have remained old maids out of devotion to their calling, but they compensate for a happily assumed celibacy in this world by a union with Tsunki that is more exclusive than the double lives that their male fellows share with the river creatures. The world of dreams is not far distant from the world of myths, with which it shares certain structural rules. But, contrary to the assumptions of scholars of the last century, who regarded the latter as a reflection of the former, here it is probably the converse that is true and it is the journey of the woman Sua to the town beneath the waters that most likely provides the material for all the oneiric adventures of concubinage with Tsunki that these *uwishin* like to recount. In fact the faithful assistants of shamans are today still the aquatic creatures which Tsunki has around him in the myth and which the heroine, with some trepidation, tames: the black jaguar, that rare, magnificent cat with its silky black coat and, above all, the 'midnight-blue anaconda' – *kintia panki*, which naturalists call the 'rainbow boa' – a reptile of an iridescent blue so deep that it seems to spread darkness around it, in the same way as a flame emits light. It is following this example that Tunki 'makes his soul become blue', that is to say camouflages it in darkness so that the enemy shaman can no longer make out what it is doing, for the ordinary darkness that surrounds us is not deep enough to hide anything from an *uwishin*'s eyes sharpened by *natem*. Tunki's *anent* constitutes an infinitely extendable lexicon of dissimulation and the 'golden ink' that our host pours into his patient is simply a modernist metaphor for the gleaming blackness that is so characteristic of the great anaconda.

Although part of the Amazonian bestiary, the black jaguar and the midnight-blue anaconda are invisible to the profane and bear allegiance only to shamans, who treat them as though they were domesticated animals. Every *uwishin* has his own anaconda installed in an underwater cave beneath his home. Meanwhile, the even more powerful black jaguar is an attribute of only top-ranking shamans. The anaconda is a vector of contamination, aided in this respect by its ability to carry a protective darkness around with it. It is also a vehicle in which the shaman's soul can be temporarily embodied in order to spy out what effects his operations are having. It seems immortal or at least quite exceptionally long-lived. Wajari one day pointed out to me a cliff overlooking a deep bend in the Kapawi, reputed to be the dwelling place of the anaconda of his father, a very famous *uwishin* who died ten or so years ago. An anaconda's subjection to its master is not automatic, however, and can only be perpetuated by constant beguilement, which a more powerful rival will not hesitate to overcome if possible. That is exactly what happened to Awananch, the shaman of the lower Bobonaza, whose faithless anaconda went off with a visiting colleague, causing the collapse of its den, together with that of the river bank this supported and also part of its former master's house, which was carried away in the landslide. The other river creatures – water hogs, freshwater dolphins, crabs, caymans, raccoons and otters – play the parts merely of extras to the anaconda and the jaguar, which from time to time delegate small tasks to these helpers. These creatures provide the *uwishin* with a fund of figurative attributes – features of their morphology or behaviour – that he can use to designate his various types of magic dart.

The Tsunki and their domesticated animals represent only a fraction of the creatures that make up this cohort of spirit helpers that the shamans call their *pasuk*. Although all covered by the same generic term, not all *pasuk* have equal status. On the one hand there are 'spirits of the forest', daunting genies who maintain an alliance with the *uwishin* but are not their vassals, on the other a mixed band of subordinate servants entirely subjected to the will of their masters, whose orders they carry out in the manner of zombies. Apart from Tsunki, the first group comprises the spirits that watch over the destiny of animals, the famous 'mothers of game' whose intercession is so vital to hunters: Amasank, the hunter of toucans, who moves around in the tree tops, passing from one to another on a bridge of blowpipes; Jurijri, the polyglot conquistador, bearded and troglodyte, whose second mouth, concealed by his hair, devours disrespectful hunters;

and Shaam, the misty monster of the marshes, whose palpitating heart is exposed to the elements. All these *pasuk* are themselves shamans, skilled at caring for the animals wounded by human beings, and Tunki regards them not so much as ordinary helpers but rather as eminent colleagues whose collaboration he seeks to gain. He does not enjoy any particular benefits from them when he goes on hunting expeditions, quite frequently returning empty-handed. The *uwishin* receive help from the 'mothers of game' only in professional matters: it is a wise limitation placed upon their already considerable power to act upon others; constant hunting successes would render this power intolerable to the mass of other people, who are denied the same advantages.

In contrast, no restrictions limit the use of the second-rank *pasuk*, beings that vary greatly in appearance but all faithfully accomplish the bidding of those who control them. Two of these are particularly feared: the Titipiur and the Nikru Iwianch. The former is visible only to shamans, to whom he appears as a man wearing a white robe: no doubt a fantastical extrapolation from one of the Dominican missionaries who have for several centuries been striving in vain to make some headway with the Achuar. The Titipiur prowls around houses at nightfall, easily recognizable from his melancholic cry, '*Piia-piia-piia!*' which spreads an intolerable anxiety in the hearts of all who hear him. If no fire is alight to keep him at a distance, he comes in when everyone is sleeping to devour the livers of the victims designated by his master, attracting no more attention than a vampire bat sucking at a sleeper's blood. Sometimes too, he constructs invisible traps on the paths close to the house, traps that fill those who fall into them with magic darts. Either way, death soon follows. The Nikru Iwianch is just as terrible but less discreet in his killing methods: he is a Herculean Black, wielding a huge sword and wearing enormous boots, who takes his prey by surprise when they are alone, batters them unconscious with his fists, then removes their clothes and seals all their bodily orifices, pinning them shut with small pointed sticks. It seems that they too die swiftly.

Nikru Iwianch is but one rather unusual variety of the Iwianch race; these are anthropoid beings, dark in colour, in whom, in certain circumstances, the souls of the dead become embodied. Vaguely hostile to the living but not evil by nature, they delight in frightening

327

women and children whom they sometimes carry off, or else amuse themselves by causing objects to fall and breaking dishes. Major shamans exercise considerable influence over these poltergeists and sometimes use it to suggest to them people whom they would like to see bothered in this fashion: between them, they combine to produce mischief rather than deliberately plot evil. Because the term designates a vague but on the whole malicious entity, '*iwianch*' is commonly used as a semantic cloak to cover a whole range of realities beneath a disturbing veil. Thus the arsenal of magic darts at the disposal of every *uwishin* is often referred to as *iwianch*, as are the spells cast and the animals whose function it is to make sure that these find their mark. Among these animal helpers are several species of birds – particularly owls and grosbeaks, the latter known as *iwianch chinki* or 'Iwianch birds' – spider-monkeys, white-headed saki monkeys, porcupines and spiders, a whole assortment of creatures, some of which are long-legged and black, others the possessors of sad or imperious countenances or hooked beaks or claws, others covered in quills – in short, creatures whose bizarre appearance suggests the mysterious malevolent power of which they are the instruments. It sometimes happens that the natural dispositions of particular species – ocelots prone to eat chickens, or snakes prone to inject venom – are guided by shamans to do harm to their enemies. As for the omnipotent anacondas, some *uwishin* are not above using them to capsize the odd canoe, drown a swimmer or – however improbable it may seem – uproot a tree so that it crushes an unsuspecting traveller.

But a *pasuk* may equally be a kind of intellectual tool with no figurative representation. It then becomes the active principle behind darts, something that gives them cohesion and a common goal, like a shepherd driving his flock, sometimes described, for the sake of a convenient image, as a homunculus linked to the shaman by something resembling filial piety. From this point of view, the *pasuk* seems a synthetic means for classifying the various categories of magic darts according to the motivating force that imparts unity to the way that they behave, a kind of ideal prototype similar to the *amana*, the exemplary individual who is a synthesis, as well as a standard exemplar, of the physical and moral characteristics of each animal species.

Tunki's *anent* is not only designed to summon his major and minor *pasuk* and to activate his *tsentsak* so that they set up a protective shield around his patient. His unfaltering, dominating voice, the exaltation of his own power, constantly repeated in the arrogant refrain 'me, me, me, . . .', the humiliation of his opponent, whose magic darts he is able to overcome by beguiling them, and even the calming soft brushing of the *shinki-shinki* – all these help to reassure Wisui, persuading him that he is in good hands, inducing the beginnings of a sense of relief and soon, perhaps, of healing.

Having rounded off his song with a series of loud and impressive expirations, Tunki turns to Wisui's wife. In a calm tone of voice, a complete contrast to the mystical exaltation by which he was carried away a moment ago, he sets about questioning her as to the symptoms of her husband. This whole exercise resembles what doctors sometimes call an anamnesis. Since when has he been suffering? In what precise circumstances did he begin to feel ill? What had he done or said just before? What has he dreamed since? What has he taken to relieve the pain? Shamans do not invariably undertake this kind of enquiry, but whenever I have witnessed one, the questions were addressed to those close to the patient, not to the patient himself. That is because replies given by Wisui could be fallacious, suggested by the enemy shaman who, having taken over his body, might already be imposing his own will upon Wisui's mind. In Copataza I was told the story of a young woman whom a *uwishin* had managed to take over completely. Having first struck her down with the mysterious 'evening melancholy', from which Naanch's son-in-law was suffering in Capahuari, he dictated despairing *anent* to her, which she sang at sunset and in which she ascribed the responsibility for her distress to a rival of her tormentor. Emboldened by this success, and after a third shaman had proved powerless to cure the unfortunate woman's attacks of neurasthenia, the *uwishin* had no compunction about making his victim sing in public *anent* of derision that ridiculed his rival and unreservedly exalted his own powers of sorcery.

The information that Tunki conscientiously elicits from Wisui's wife serves not so much to establish his diagnosis as to confirm it. While singing, he has located in Wisui's liver wads of darts the nature and origin of which he must ascertain. Eventually he comes to his conclusion: these are *tsentsak* of the *tseas* ('curare') type, the effects of which resemble poisoning, and there can be no doubt that they come from Chuchukia, the son of the shaman Mashu recently killed by Pakunt. Chuchukia is assumed to have taken over his father's Iwianch in order to take revenge upon Wisui, a marginal ally of the coalition of assassins who is inadequately protected against shamanistic attacks since he does not live in the immediate neighbourhood of Tunki. The dates correspond, as does the 'signature' of Mashu's *tsentsak* – their shape and way of reacting – with which Tunki has already had to grapple in the past. It is almost with relief that everyone greets this predictable verdict.

It is rare for a shaman not to confirm the presentiments of his patient. If someone does come to consult him it means that the relief expected from the native pharmacopoeia has been unforthcoming, a sure indication that the ailment is a *tunchi*, a spell, not a *sunkur* or ordinary illness. The distinction between the two categories is so elastic that it sometimes disappears. In Conambo, and equally in Copataza, even the most benign complaints are regarded from the outset as *tunchi*: migraine, indigestion, toothache – all are treated by shamanistic methods, the use of herbal remedies having virtually disappeared. There are so many shamans in these two localities – and in Conambo the discord is so pronounced – that the Achuar tendency to regard every *sunkur* as a potential *tunchi* is converted into a refusal to continue to believe in the existence of 'ordinary illnesses'. Even the recent death of Mukucham's little daughter, which resulted from whooping cough – a perfectly ordinary *sunkur*, after all – was in the end attributed to a *tunchi* sent by Mashu, who was believed to have aggravated the action of the illness, increasing its virulence so much that it proved fatal.

The likelihood of a shaman recognizing signs of a *sunkur* in his patient, rather than a *tunchi*, depends to a large extent upon both the social and the geographical distance between them. The more 'neutral' the shaman as regards the networks of alliance and conflict of the person consulting him, the less he will feel obliged to confirm the latter's fears. Tayujin, from Capahuari, who has for several years been suffering from stomach pains – probably an ulcer – and who has consulted several great Quichua shamans on the Bobonaza on the matter, was told by them that he was the victim of a perfectly ordinary *sunkur* against which they had no power. *Uwishin* claim that it is easy to distinguish an illness from a spell: whereas *tsentsak* are visible in the patient's body in the form of little bundles whose colour and luminosity vary according to the type of darts, *sunkur* have the appear-

330

ance of a bronze vapour emanating from the organ that is affected. But theory can be a far cry from practice. If the circumstances so dictate and provided it suits all parties concerned, the slightest ambiguity in the manner in which the symptoms present themselves will be enough to make the shaman pronounce a verdict of *tunchi* without, however, feeling that he is guilty of charlatanism.

The decision to pronounce on the identity of whoever is responsible for a *tunchi* is an even more delicate matter, and this likewise depends on the degree of the shaman's involvement in his patient's affairs. Technically, pronouncing such an allegation presents no difficulties. *Tsentsak* are connected by very long silvery threads to those who despatch them and can thus continue to direct them from a distance. These threads can only be seen by *uwishin* who have taken *natem*, who compare them to the iridescent filaments of a spider's web catching the light. By following the threads back to their distant source and also identifying the *pasuk* enemies charged with guarding these lines of telecommand, experienced shamans in principle possess the means for discovering the aggressor. But taking responsibility for revealing his name is quite another matter. Unless, as in Tunki's case, he is directly involved in a conflict that he can aggravate at will by unmasking the suspected culprit the shaman treating the patient runs the risk of incurring the mortal enmity of whoever he names, upon whom the relatives of his patient will seek to avenge themselves. That is why shamans with a wide clientele generally decline to render this service or, if forced to do so, demand high payment for it.

Now that he knows what he is dealing with, Tunki embarks upon the crucial stage of the treatment. Taking a stick of tobacco that has been soaking in a bowl of water, he squeezes the juice into his mouth and then swallows a number of large draughts, an operation that – as I know from experience – requires a strong stomach. He then imbibes another draught of tobacco juice, which he retains in his mouth, and sets about sucking at Wisui's side. He continues this for some time, then, with a noisy gargle, spits out the liquid and blows into his cupped hand. Having repeated this operation ten or so times, Tunki pronounces a satisfied '*Pai!*' and displays the contents of his hand to his audience: half a dozen small pieces of glass, opaque with age. Finally he blows repeatedly on the patient's stomach, then declares the treatment completed.

Tunki had previously given me a detailed description of this whole procedure, which has lasted no more than five minutes. By absorbing tobacco juice, he has formed a kind of viscous carapace inside his mouth and throat, thereby preventing the *tsentsak* that he sucks out of Wisui's body from slipping down into his own chest and stomach, from which position it could be very difficult to extract them and where they could do grave damage or even cause his death. The extraction of the darts is a very dangerous operation, during which the shaman risks himself becoming a victim of the harmful projectiles at which he is sucking. This explains all the care taken to get them into a favourable condition in the course of his song. Actually, it is not so much a matter of suction but of a kind of magnetic attraction. As Tunki himself possesses *tsentsak* of the *tseas* type, identical to those he has discovered in Wisui, which he usually stores in his own neck and stomach, he can despatch his own darts to adhere to enemy ones, making them seize upon the latter as if magnetically. He then brings them back into his own mouth. Protected behind a circular wall of *tsentsak*, he opens this no more than a crack in order to despatch his own darts and later to recover them, once their mission is accomplished. An operation such as this is only possible because the attacking *tsentsak* have been benumbed and disoriented by the earlier treatment, the threads that used to connect them to their master have been cut by Tunki's *tsentsak*, and the *pasuk* that were guarding them have been dispersed by his own *pasuk*. But the most important thing in all this sympathetic medicine is to be in possession of *tsentsak* of the same kind as those that are causing the pain, for it is solely on account of this perfect homology that the latter accompany those that resemble them, are deceived by their identical appearance and seek, without distrust, to unite with them. A shaman can thus only attain full mastery of his art if he is capable of mobilizing a sufficient variety of types of *tsentsak* to cope with the full diversity of the items that he will be called upon to extract.

There remains the matter of the regurgitation of the *tsentsak* that the shaman then displays publicly. In truth, this is simply a conjuring trick, for as Tunki has explained to me in a perfectly ingenuous fashion, he had secretly placed the pieces of glass in his mouth earlier. He gave me his reasons for doing so in a tone of paternal connivance befitting a master revealing the little secrets of his craft to his apprentice. For all that, they did him no discredit. Just as some Western doctors tell their patients as little as possible, either simply through laziness or because they resent bringing their knowledge down to the level of people they deem incapable of understanding their explanations, a shaman prefers a harmless mystification to the alternative of a fastidious lecture on how *tsentsak* work. For these 'darts' that Tunki extracted were not really spat out into his hand but were blown into his wrist, where he will keep them for his own use, together with a few of his own *tsentsak* to guard them. With these intercepted *tsentsak* he will, if he so desires, be able to cast a spell on his enemies. It would not be tactful to explain this to a patient and it is much simpler to produce a few small objects – insects, fragments of a blade, sometimes used batteries – whose material presence, now rendered inoffensive, is far more reassuring than any words.

If Tunki resorts to little deceptions, his chief reason for doing so is that the good old words of ordinary language can only give metaphorical expression to the combination of physical and mental experiences through which a shaman passes in the course of a cure: a combination of visions fragmented into constant metamorphoses, pulsing vibrations more or less in rhythm with the cadences of the song and exceptionally vivid impressions of being split and travelling through space. Initially, of course, these heightened perceptions are produced by the drug, but little by little, in the course of a shaman's initiation and the many sessions that follow it, he manages to domesticate them in such a way that they end up by fitting the mould of words and images traditionally used in this culture to codify shamanistic skills. The *tsentsak*, for example, are not real 'darts' or even invisible ones. They are animated principles or incorporeal automata that are as impossible to represent as the mysterious *entelecheia* ('actualities') of classical philosophy. In default of a more abstract concept capable of conveying them they are, by way of an analogy, given the very concrete name of something to which they can be compared in some of their effects. Similarly, *tunchi* is simply the word for a little spider that is clever at getting in everywhere, dragging its guiding thread with it. It is thus an excellent means of signifying the ability of shamans to despatch their spells without their victims realizing it and then to continue to control them from a distance. The material apparatus of a shaman is described using ordinary, everyday vocabulary that conveys actions, properties, behaviours and the interplaying forces for which nature or human techniques provide a model. But that apparatus has a literal existence only for the profane, who do not understand its subtleties and who, to spare the shaman long explanations, are allowed to believe that the formulae used to describe its mechanisms do faithfully depict the way in which they function. There can be no doubt, I think, that, under the combined effects of *natem* and their own apprenticeships, shamans do perceive a set of interconnected phenomena too complex to be wholly described in words. So it is not charlatanism that prompts them to resort to little tricks or to simplify the operations that they perform in comprehensible metaphors. Rather, it is because there is too much meaning in the total experience of the trance for ordinary speech to render adequately. Hence the insistence of Mukuimp and Tunki that I should take *natem* in order to 'see' the unsayable part of shamanism, which my séance of hallucinations in Wajari's house, futile though it seemed to me at the time, did help to illuminate, at least a little.

CHAPTER 21

Craftsmen of the Imaginary

WISUI WENT OFF TO Conambo yesterday, clearly much cheered and not forgetting to present Tunki with a blowpipe in payment for his good offices. Another 'client' took his place this afternoon, a Quichua by the name of Sampico, who lives a three-day canoe journey away upstream. Sampico is small but with the build of a weight-lifter, and is also a shaman. He has come to stock up with *tsentsak* from our host, whose *compadre* he is. The two men accordingly drank *natem* at nightfall, Tsunki played his *tsayantar* for a while and then they went off together to bathe in the river.

The respective *tsentsak* of the Achuar, the Shuar and the Quichuas are, in principle, all different and can only be extracted by shamans of the 'tribe' from which they come, which is the reason why people sometimes turn to the services of a stranger in order to lay a spell on a close enemy, thereby ensuring that it will not be possible for any local shaman to cure him. However, the general mechanisms of shamanism are identical in the three cultures and there is nothing to stop an enterprising practitioner from extending his scope by acquiring exotic *tsentsak* that will open up a new clientele for him beyond the frontiers of his own group.

Quite clearly, Tunki and Sampico regularly swap *tsentsak* and *supai*, their Quichua equivalents – an operation that presents virtually infinite possibilities, given the large number of categories that exist. My host claims he possesses a collection comprising forty-odd kinds, each of which he designates metaphorically by the name of an animal, a plant, or an object or by a quality exhibited in some form, by analogy, in each of them. Amongst those that he uses the most, I have noticed the following: the electric eel type, for its powerful electric charge; the *candirú* type, named after the tiny barbed fish reputed to lodge

335

itself in the natural orifices of bathers; the ray type, for its redoubtable sting; the spider-monkey type, for the strength of its prehensile tail; the humming-bird type, for its pointed beak and its swift movement; the harpy-eagle type, for the power of its talons; the toucan type, for its huge beak; the leech type (for obvious reasons); the chonta type, for the long thorns of this species of palm; the *kuichip* type, called after a plant with very sharp leaves; the stramonium type, because the drug 'brings on madness'; the mirror type, because of the brilliance of its refracted light; the cold type that freezes one's bones; the yellow type, for the vibrancy of this colour; and the *makina* type, a term used for the throbbing electric generators which the missionaries use with such mastery, much to the Achuar's admiration. Some *tsentsak* have special functions: as tonic, in the case of those that one injects into the lungs of men who complain of insufficient breath for their blowpipes; as deterrent – such as those that are despatched into enemy territory, to salt licks where animals gather, or to the wallowing holes of peccaries, to scare the animals off and make them desert that region.

Each type of *tsentsak* exists in its own 'mother-saliva' (*maen*), a sticky substance in which they develop as a foetus does in its amniotic fluid, which a shaman can draw up from his chest into his mouth when he needs to. This exercise requires a measure of expertise. During his apprenticeship a novice will spend a lot of time mastering the regurgitation of *tsentsak* saliva which his initiator has injected into him with the aid of generous libations of a mixture of manioc beer and tobacco juice. There are also types of saliva without *tsentsak*, reserved for minor shamans, 'spittle shamans'. They use these to provoke or cure external lesions which, though sometimes very painful and quite spectacular – breast abscesses, ulcers, leprosy, leishmaniosis, and so on – occupy a relatively low position in the hierarchy of *tunchi*, as they do not lead to rapid death. As in the case of fully formed *tsentsak*, each of these subsidiary types of spittle can only be neutralized by saliva of the same type. It is also said that the saliva of shamans is a powerful love philtre, which they deposit in the jars of beer without the knowledge of the women whose favours they seek to obtain. To judge by the recriminations voiced in confidence to Anne Christine by Tunki's wives, he certainly seems to make the most of this.

The transmission of *tsentsak* to Sampico does not take long.

(above) The ethno-
logist is often a pain!
Panintza

(right) Pottery:
painting a *pininkia*
bowl with mineral
pigments, Capahuari:
the woman is sitting
on an upturned
manioc mortar

Previous page:
Inter-ethnic relations
and acculturation.
A young Shuar
converses with an
Achuar wearing
his full battery of
ornaments,
Mashumarentza

(left) Spinning cotton with a spindle, Situch

(below) Making a *chankin* basket, Situch

(main picture) Cutting manioc slips, Numpaïme

(bottom far left) Returning from the garden with a hod of manioc, Numpaïme

(below) Preparing manioc beer in a mortar, Capahuari

(bottom) Back from the garden: now the manioc must be washed in the river, Numpaïme

(left) Blowpipe hunting starts as a game, Apupentza

(below) An empty-handed return from blowpipe hunting

Opposite:
(above) Fishing with poison in the Kusutka: the asphyxiated fish are collected in a basket

(below) Barrage for fishing with poison in the Kusutka, seen from downstream; the over-flow shoot is in the middle

Writing, forever writing

Holding the head of his *kumpa*, Tunki blows tobacco smoke on to the crown of his head and then into his mouth. He is giving him darts of the 'lightning' type, used like mortar shells, to make the invisible casemate of the enemy *uwishin* explode or to destroy recalcitrant *tsentsak* in the patient's body. Tunki, in liberal mood, decides for good measure to throw in the *namur* corresponding to these *tsentsak*, which up until this point has been soaking in a bowlful of tobacco juice. It is a black, almost round pebble with a hole in the middle through which one can blow to direct the missiles with greater accuracy. A little while ago Tunki showed me his collection of shamanistic *namur*, pebbles with unusual shapes and mineral ores whose function is similar to that of the *namur* used in hunting. Each one is appropriate for a particular type of *tsentsak*, whose powers it concentrates and activates when left to soak in tobacco juice during a shamanistic session.

If the transmission of *tsentsak* to Sampico is soon completed, that is because Sampico is already a confirmed shaman who is well versed in the techniques for controlling the darts and preventing them from promptly returning to their former owner. A first initiation is a quite different matter, however, a lengthy affair of uncertain outcome that calls for much self-denial and a steely will on the part of the novice, as I learned yesterday evening, when Tunki told me of his early experiences.

I decided to become a *uwishin* after my marriage. My father-in-law had died from a spell, followed by my brother-in-law. Then my son died too, while still a suckling babe. A bad *uwishin* had sent *tsentsak* into the breasts of my wife Najari, and the baby died very quickly from suckling at the *tsentsak*. What could I do? I was powerless before the *tunchi*. Do you really think that I should have waited for us all to be exterminated? So off I went to Sharian so that I too could learn. The first night I drank *natem* with Sharian and we took tobacco juice through our noses. He blew *tsentsak* on to the top of my head and on to my shoulders and between my fingers. Then he passed on his saliva to me, into my mouth, and he told me the names of the different kinds: 'Take the saliva of the anaconda! Take the saliva of the rainbow! Take the saliva of iron!' I felt sick and wanted to vomit it all. Then we stayed awake and all night long we played the *tsayantar*, to please the *tsentsak*. The first night you must not sleep, or the *tsentsak* think that you are a corpse and they go back to the person who gave them to you. The next day I ate nothing and drank nothing. I couldn't speak, for the *tsentsak* would have escaped if I had opened my mouth. I didn't sleep either. It was very tough. We drank *natem* again and Sharian sang all his *anent*; I whistled them, to learn them. I remained sitting up all night long and kept sticking a chonta thorn into my thigh, so as not to fall asleep. The next day again I ate and drank nothing. I was very weak and I remained lying down all day, smoking all the time. In the evening we drank *natem* again and I began to learn Sharian's *anent*. That night I was able to sleep, as the *tsentsak* were by then used to me. The next day I again fasted. I spent the day lying on a *peak*, as I had lost all my strength. I smoked and I slept. On the last day Sharian gave me manioc beer to drink, mixed with tobacco juice, and then I had to eat pimentoes, little *yantana* pimentoes, the strongest ones. My stomach heaved and all the saliva rose into my mouth. I almost spat everything out, but managed to swallow it down. Then Sharian told me that now I would be able to blow my *tsentsak*. His wife served me plantain bananas and some tiny boiled fish. I had eaten nothing for several days. After that I went for a bathe, as I had not washed either. I was stinking like an opossum. I stayed on for a while with Sharian and he blew me some other *tsentsak*. Then I went home. ['How much did you pay for all that?'] A lot, for Sharian was a very famous shaman. I gave him a *tawasap* and a blowpipe. You have to be careful, as if you don't give enough to whoever passes his *tsentsak* on to you, he may take them back. Some even send *tunchi*, to take their revenge. ['And did you immediately start to cure people?'] No, not immediately. First the *tsentsak* had to get properly used to me. For over a month I stayed at home without so much as budging, like an armadillo. I didn't go hunting. I took tobacco water nearly every day. Sharian had told me not to drink manioc beer and all I ate were little fish. For several moons I was unable to make love. My little wife, Najari, was furious; and on top of that, she had no meat to eat. It was very tough, but as I wanted to be one of those who know, I stuck it out!

A shaman's apprenticeship involves a change in the ecology of his physical system, the creation of a new internal *milieu* to receive its new whimsical residents: the *tsentsak*. This is something that can only be achieved by adhering to a strict ascetic discipline. The very term for an initiation, *ijiarmak*, is derived from the word for 'to fast', *ijiarma*, to which the suffix '-k' is added, a marker indicating that an action has been completed following a whole series of operations. In other words, to become a shaman is to achieve a state of equilibrium or accommodation with the *tsentsak* through a gradual purging of the body. To reach this state, one must not only endure privations but also follow a strict diet that is defined down to the last detail. In a culture in which undertaking even the most commonplace action – sowing maize, making curare, administering a cure to a dog – means avoiding certain foods, it is not surprising to find shamans, even more than other people, subjected to a diet of Byzantine complexity.

Certain foods that are eaten by the profane are banned for ever for them: small, agile over-active creatures such as the sapajou monkey, the squirrel or the moustached tamarin, whose agitated movements might upset cohabitation with the *tsentsak*, unstable even at the best of times. Other creatures, such as the armadillo or the *wampi* fish, are forbidden because they sport a hard carapace that might make it difficult to reach the *tsentsak* embedded in the bodies of their patients. Others, with sharp teeth, such as *kusea* fish, are banned because they might sever the *tsentsaks'* tele-guiding threads. Some animals, such as the white-headed saki monkey with its sad, almost human countenance, are themselves said to be shamans, so eating them would be a kind of cannibalism. Also forbidden at the time of initiation and thereafter for a period of up to five months, is all 'black'-fleshed game – peccaries, woolly monkeys, toucans, howler monkeys, etc. – the same creatures from which you abstain after an *arutam* vision, for the shaman's apprenticeship upsets the essential equilibrium of his personality; a period of convalescence is therefore necessary, during which strong meats should not be eaten. Salt, pimento and fruits are proscribed for similar reasons, for the savour of sweet fruits and condiments threatens the neutral ambience that *tsentsak* need if they are to thrive. Finally, a whole series of animals is prohibited for more specific reasons: the macaw because it flies very high, as it were beyond the reach of *tsentsak*; the *yawa aikiam*, a large, spotted cat-fish, because it evokes the pelt of the jaguar, always associated with shamans; and palm-tree grubs that make holes in rotten wood, because *tsentsak* similarly perforate the bodies of human beings.

The resulting diet is dauntingly dull, its basis being plantains (from which the pips must be removed) and boiled palm hearts, sometimes accompanied by small fish, all to be eaten – for some reason that nobody has been able to explain to me – with the aid of little sticks, direct contact with the fingers being considered harmful. As for prolonged chastity – the greatest deterrent to those thinking of taking up the profession, most people tell me – it is, in a way, the equivalent of fasting since, in this culture as in many others, 'consummation' with a woman is likened to the consumption of food. My already shaky resolution cracked, I must confess, in the face of the formidable initiatory apparatus described to me by Tunki. At the end of his account I declared that I did not feel ready to become a *uwishin*.

Even more than in the other situations where they are imposed, the shaman's dietary prohibitions are a means of establishing a difference of status in a more or less durable fashion. Each taboo is, in itself, relatively arbitrary: such or such an animal deemed to possess a particular quality could quite well be replaced by another that exhibits the same quality or might, through its appearance or behaviour, even serve to typify a quality in contradiction to that first one. The motivation of the link established between an animal and the baleful disposition it is believed to induce is not as important as the collection of animals (each time different ones) used to signify negatively a state that is antithetical to them. However irrational they may seem, taboos may be regarded as an effect produced by classificatory thinking. Because they draw attention to a system of concrete properties signified by a limited collection of natural species – properties that make the point that no person is exactly like any other in that the flesh of these species is proscribed for him or her personally either temporarily or permanently – taboos testify to a desire to confer order upon the chaos of the social and natural world, purely on the basis of the categories of physical experience. In a culture marked by a remarkable uniformity of social status, the avoidance of certain foods thus makes it possible to institute between individuals those small differences that are indispensable to social life, without, however, compromising the equality of conditions by any exaggerated distinctions.

Despite their special powers and their different diet, *uwishin* are not individuals set apart. They come to their vocation not as the result of a sign that they are chosen or some revelation, but because of a moral crisis triggered by their terrible sense of impotence when faced by a cascade of deaths amongst those close to them or when they are themselves struck down in their youth by some long malady, which a shaman eventually manages to cure. Of course, curiosity also plays a role, as does the desire to ensure oneself a measure of power over others – very human sentiments that certainly do not constitute evidence of a pathological personality for whom the practice of shamanism would provide an outlet recognized and accepted by society.

It is true that the craft of shamanism is sometimes passed on in a quasi-hereditary fashion. Some *uwishin* start supplying their sons with *tsentsak* at a very early age, even while they are still suckling, by blowing darts into the breasts of the mother, who passes them on to her baby with the milk. A little while ago Tunki began passing *tsentsak* to his twelve-year-old son Sunti because he fears that he himself may die of a *tunchi* in his battle against the shamans of the Wayusentza and hopes in this way to ensure that his family will continue to benefit from some protection even in the event of his death. The most powerful *uwishin* certainly are those who began in childhood to accumulate *tsentsak* and who, thanks to this long-standing familiarity with the tools of their trade, are more expert than others at controlling their sometimes unforeseeable behaviour. That is why some Achuar send their little sons or even daughters to serve an apprenticeship under famous Quichua shamans, generally their own *kumpa*. The 'placed' children often become the sons-in-law of their masters in shamanery and thereby acquire not only an envied skill but also the language, kinship and culture of one of these *apach* Indians, who are said to be more skilled at sharing in the world of the Whites.

Where shamanism is concerned, nothing can ever be taken for granted. Initiation at a tender age proves useless unless it is followed up by constant further supplies of *tsentsak* from suppliers as diverse as possible. My *amik* Wajari, whose father was probably the most powerful Achuar shaman north of the Pastaza, was gradually deserted by all the *tsentsak* blown into him by his father in the past, because at adolescence Wajari chose not to pursue the career that his family had favoured for him. To become an ordinary *uwishin* it is necessary to visit five or six different suppliers of *tsentsak* after one's initial apprenticeship, and many more if one aspires to rise in the hierarchy. The undertaking is very costly, leading to a kind of selection through wealth. Minor shamans, who receive poor payment from their patients, are unable to amass enough possessions to be able to obtain from their more prestigious colleagues the *tsentsak* that are precisely what they need if they are to become famous. As one's reputation grows, one has to spend more and more on rare and precious *tsentsak* that will constitute as it were the choicest pieces of all in one's panoply. For example, Tunki, who has travelled all the way to the Napo, more than 300 kilometres away, to obtain *tsentsak* from a great Quichua shaman, had to give him a gourdful of curare, a *tawasap* crown of feathers, a blowpipe, a hunting dog, and a breech-loading shotgun – in short, a small fortune for an Achuar. The value of *tsentsak* is more or less standard, according to their category, and Chalua, a Quichua shaman of the Bobonaza, required those same items from our host in return for very special darts that originated from the Antuas of Peru. Tunki has still not paid off this last purchase and I can see he is struggling with the logic of expansion through debt, which is certainly familiar to us but is quite surprising to encounter here. A shaman from the Copataza told me that he renewed his supplies of *tsentsak* in his dreams, often taking tobacco juice just before going to bed. He was visited in his sleep by *uwishin* now deceased but known personally to him, who supplied him, free of charge, with what others were ruining themselves for by paying very high prices. However, as his reputation was extremely modest, I concluded that he had discovered this solution in default of sufficient means to continue his function.

The price and presumed efficacy of *tsentsak* increase in proportion to the distance of their origin, and to such a point that some Quichua shamans on the Bobonaza are reputed nowadays to travel as far as the Indians of Otalvo in the northern Andes in order to obtain new supplies. Whatever can be the ultimate source of these *tsentsak* that are in such perpetual flux? The Tsunki water spirits, no doubt, but they are their creators rather than their purveyors. Given that the Tsunki are supposed to exist all over the place, there is no reason why they should have given more *tsentsak* to the Achuar than to any of the many other peoples who live along the river banks. So do they perhaps come from immediately neighbouring ethnic groups, in particular the Quichuas, whose 'darts' seem to be so highly rated by the Achuar? But then, where do the Quichuas themselves procure them? That is a question that I put to a Quichua Indian from the Napo, whom I met one day in Puyo and whose father was a well-known shaman. His reply took the form of an anecdote. One day when he was still just a little boy and was out hunting with his father, a violent storm broke and they suddenly found themselves surrounded by many animals. Delighted with this unhoped-for stroke of luck, the father fired at the animals, but when his son went to collect them up, they suddenly disappeared. At this juncture a group of blond white men dressed as missionaries of the order of Saint Joseph arrived upon the scene and carried off the father. He was away for more than a month and everyone had written him off as dead when, one fine day, he returned, declaring that he had drunk *ayahuasca* every day with his kidnappers and had now become a great shaman.

So the most powerful shamanistic powers definitely do come from the Whites, from those masters of writing with pale hair, the most exotic of all strangers. This is why my companions were so insistent that I should hand over my own hypothetical *tsentsak* or, failing this, that I should assist Mukuimp in his cures. Tunki has explicitly confirmed this, adding a bizarre detail. There are two reasons for our immunity to Achuar *tsentsak*: one is that our *tsentsak* are stronger than theirs; the other, that we are eaters of onions: the native darts are as allergic to this modest bulb as the vampires of the Carpathians are to cloves of garlic.

If the Quichuas serve as intermediaries in the chain of shamanistic supplies, that is because in this domain as in others, the Achuar regard them as substitute Whites, so to speak. There can be no doubt about this, given that the best-known of the Quichua shamans of the Bobonaza are almost all employed by the Ecuadorian army. As *tamberos* or professional non-commissioned officers, unknown to their superiors they lead a double life on the edges of the army camp. Attentive and efficient soldiers during the day, at night they receive a clientele that has journeyed far to see them, attracted as much by the aura of power associated with the military machine as by their own personal reputations for excellence. Thanks to their pay and the low prices in the special army stores, they are in a position to amass consumer goods of the most ostentatious nature, but at the same time do not disdain the more traditional goods, which they continue to receive as remuneration for their cures. Similarly, it is the proximity of the *kirinku*, from whom they are supposed to receive some of their powers, that accounts for the great success of the Shuar shamans of Makuma, the location of the large mission of the North American evangelists. Fascinated by their cosmopolitan skills, the Achuar of Capahuari cannot resist visiting these outstanding *uwishin*, taking care to conceal their true motives under pretexts of piety, in the hope of obtaining free transport in the missionaries' aeroplane. Thanks to their strategic position on the edge of the Whites' world, these interloper shamans thus operate as turntables in the extensive trafficking of objects both material and immaterial. This is a very far cry from the stereotyped image of the Indian shaman acting as the strongest possible protective bulwark for tradition and cultural conservatism against the assaults of modernity, for these days it is, on the contrary, from his imagined relations with the Western world that he derives much of his prestige.

Provided they learn Quichua and leave their native community, the Achuar can also play this game, as I discovered a few months ago when I met a shaman of Achuar origin answering to the name of Rufeo, who has also become a corporal in the small military detachment of Cabo Pozo on the lower Bobonaza. Rufeo is a *panku*, one of the only three or four in the whole province of Pastaza.

The *panku* constitute a special class of *uwishin*, the *non plus ultra* of the profession, for not only can they diagnose the nature of a *tunchi* with certainty and reveal who is reponsible for it, but they can also give an infallible prognosis of how the malady will develop. They receive this power from the souls of the dead, who become embodied in them when they drink *natem* and who speak through their mouths 'like on the radio', to quote Wajari, whose father was himself a *panku*. People also turn to them when they require a kind of mediumistic autopsy, during which the *panku* embodies the *wakan* of someone recently deceased so that he can name whoever was responsible for the spell cast upon him. Here, the *panku* is the subject of a veritable possession, a very different matter from a classic shamanistic cure. *Panku* are believed to possess *tsentsak* that are invisible to ordinary practitioners and are particularly to be feared because they obtain them directly from the dead. However, their reputation rests first and foremost on their divinatory faculty. The institution may be of Quichua origin, for in the Quichua language the word *panku* designates what the Achuar call a *kutank*, that is to say the little bench reserved for visitors: the *panku* would thus become the 'seat' of the souls of the dead.

Rufeo's trance was not as spectacular as I had hoped. No more than a few paces away from the building where the second lieutenant was sleeping with the half-dozen conscripts who made up the entire detachment, the *panku* had installed himself in a dark shanty to drink *natem* at the request of Tentets, a 'nephew' of Nankiti of the Yutsu-entza, in whose house we were a few days later to pass a very disturbed night. Against a background of *pasillos* emitted by a radio in the neighbouring barracks, a nasal voice had soon made itself heard, with-out Rufeo appearing to open his mouth: probably a ventriloquist's trick which would explain why a *panku*'s apprenticeship may last a whole year. 'I come from the depths of the Tungurahua volcano,' declared this sepulchral voice, 'to see the *tsentsak* hidden in your body. Nothing escapes my clairvoyance, for I am blind in the light and exist only in the darkness. I see metal *tsentsak* that gleam like the surface of the water. I see many *tsentsak* in your legs . . .' The diagnosis continued for some time, in very repetitive vein, before finally letting slip the name of the guilty party: as was to be expected, it was Turipiur, the shaman of the Apupentza with whom Nankiti's people were at war and a man particularly prone to 'sorcery'. For this little scene alone, without even having attempted a cure, our corporal had required payment in the form of a splendid *tawasap* feathered crown.

All the *uwishin* whom I have met maintain most emphatically that they are *tsuakratin* (healers), not *wawekratin* (sorcerors), but it is a distinction that seems more circumstantial than technical. Tunki claims that every *uwishin* possesses both *tsentsak* 'for healing' and *tsentsak* 'for spells', distinguished not so much by their nature as by the circumstances in which they are used. The darts used for spells are those that the shaman extracts from his patients and accumulates in his wrists. The ravages they have already begun to wreak have given them a taste for human flesh and a vague kind of malignity that impels them to escape from the control of the shaman who has captured them and go off hunting on their own. A *uwishin* is a healer if he is capable of maintaining control over these subproducts of his activity by sending them from time to time to gather nectar from flowers to satisfy their insatiable appetite. On the other hand, a sorceror *uwishin*, taken over by the *tsentsak* that he has sucked out and unable to control them, is a source of danger for everyone, including those closest to him, since *tsentsak* such as these will attack all human beings indis-criminately. Given that a healer shaman has at his disposal a stock of darts that, in principle, he keeps well disciplined, he can, on occasion, use these to attack an enemy: a purpose for which he should never use his own personal *tsentsak*. If he did succumb to the temptation to do so, another shaman could acquire them by sucking them out of the body of his victim and could then promptly return them to him, thereby causing his speedy death. Constantly shuttling to and fro in this way, the fatal *tsentsak* disposed of by each shaman as he will render all those protestations of exclusive devotion to other people's health somewhat suspect and make the distinction between sorcerors and healers quite illusory. This equivocation is a constitutive element of shamanism, as is attested by the following little myth that I was told by Mamays. It tells how a bad choice made between two *uwishin* was at the origin of definitive death.

It is said that long ago Nettle was a *uwishin*. When people fell ill, he cured them. Those who were suffering from the spells of the 'people-of-stone' [*kaya aents*] were cured by him; he restored life to them. There was also another *uwishin*, Amaran [a tiny ant with a painful sting]. He, in contrast, was very much a sorceror. In the olden days, when men died, their bodies were placed in a little hut, specially constructed at the top of a high tree. The dead man was seated there on his *chimpui*, in all his finery, wearing his *tawasap* crown. After a while like this, the dead man began to live again. His widow, who was left alone in the house, would weep as she swept, singing, 'My man, my man, where have you go-o-o-one?' When the widow went to see her husband after a few days, she would find him in fine fettle, saying, 'Now I am cured.' The man would go home and explain that he had been fishing, and his wife would serve him the manioc beer that she had prepared for the occasion. In the past, that is what we used to do with our husbands. Now, a man fell sick and the *uwishin* were sent for. They went to fetch Amaran and they went to fetch Nettle and they even sent Sesenk [a coleoptera] to fetch the people-of-stone. Amaran was the one who arrived first, but the man was already dead. In those days, when people died, their hearts continued to beat. Amaran felt his chest and saw that the heart was beating very slowly. Then he plunged his spear into the heart and that is how definitive death came about, for all that Amaran knew how to deliver was death. After this Nettle arrived, but it was too late. Nettle said, 'If you had come to fetch me first, I could have "blown" on the body so that you would never know definitive death, but now it is too late.' With that he presented his nettle as a gift and 'blew' on it. That is why we now use the nettle for healing.

Nowadays, the distinction between good and bad *uwishin* is made more pragmatically. The closest shamans, those linked to you by kinship, are supposed to set their talents at the service of the community and reserve their *tunchi* for harming common enemies. These, in return, ask their own *uwishin* to attack you. Only the greatest shamans of all are capable of attracting a clientele from beyond the limits of their immediate kindred, as their widely proclaimed neutrality makes it possible for them either to treat or to cast a spell on anybody at all, so long as the right price is paid. However, even within a neighbourhood, the slightest tension is enough to cast suspicion upon a *uwishin* if he is in any way identified with one of its contentious factions. The Mashu affair provides a good illustration, for this was a man who had for a long time enjoyed an honourable reputation amongst his closest affines, yet was then killed by them for his sorcery. Being recognized as a *uwishin* actually depends more upon the whims of public opinion than upon any acknowledged status or upon a famous practice.

Time and again I have heard it said, on the lower Kapawi, that my *amik* Wajari is a *uwishin*, since his father was one and Wajari received *tsentsak* from him as a child. Naanch also had this reputation amongst the people of the Copataza, although I never could make out any objective evidence for this. I had myself been suspected of being one simply because I had drunk *natem*. As will be understood, openly embracing the career of a shaman exposes one to deadly danger, as all practitioners are very much aware. The murder of a shaman reputed to be a sorceror is considered legitimate by just about everybody – including his closest relatives, who fatalistically accept that this is more or less the destiny to be expected by anyone in this dangerous profession.

Exposed as they are to all these dangers, *uwishin* devote much of their energy and resources to contracting defensive alliances. They usually have a greater than average number of *amik*, for this assures them of a more dense and far-reaching network of protectors and also affords them the moral satisfaction that accompanies their expectation of being avenged in the event of a premature demise. Major *uwishin* have no trouble in finding ritual friends, who regard such a link as a guarantee that they themselves and those close to them will obtain prompt help from him when in need of it, and – they hope – at a cut price. They also gain from their shaman *amik*'s tacit undertaking to reject any 'contract' to cast spells on them on behalf of one of their enemies. Equally, it is in the interest of the *uwishin* to commit himself to active complicity with a 'great man', an arrangement frequently formalized by an exchange of sisters. The two brothers-in-law thereafter offer each other mutual protection in their own respective spheres, as did Awananch and Nankiti in their war against the people of the Apupentza. The *uwishin*, who become so to speak warriors in the invisible world, devote their powers to supporting the military strategy of their faction. Or, in the rare cases where they themselves are at the same time 'great men', they conduct the action from a distance, without themselves leading the raids, a role delegated to young, well-tried warriors.

In order to consolidate these protective alliances, a shaman must display a calculated generosity towards his potential defenders, agreeing to deals which are unfavourable to himself and make considerable inroads into the riches accumulated as payment for his services. From this point of view, there is a great disparity between the small neighbourhood *uwishin* and the most highly thought of shamans. People go to consult the latter when driven to despair by the failure of the smaller *uwishin* to help them; and costs mount in proportion to the *uwishin*'s renown and the desperation of the patients. But great shamans such as these are rare and relatively marginal. Living in the shadow of the Whites and enjoying as it were extra-territorial privileges, they are already so cut off from their native communities that they do not usually deign to use their wealth in order to acquire an eminent position in the interplay of local coalitions. In contrast, *uwishin* without reputations are not marked out from the common crowd in any way. Like Mukuimp, they may even be more disadvantaged than most since they are periodically bound to invest their own meagre earnings in the costly purchase of new *tsentsak*. Committed to an ascetic existence, forced to redistribute their goods in order to win respect and security, constantly faced with high expenses to renew the tools of their profession, relentlessly exposed to the threat of summary execution, and engaged in permanent competition if not open warfare with one another – all in all, shamans pay dearly for the privilege of being recognized as the arbiters of the misfortunes of others. Although all these constraints have not as yet dried up the number of would-be shamans, they have at least prevented the *uwishin* from exploiting their function to acquire the kind of political and economic power that would have set them above other men.

The extreme social control that this anarchic society delegates to each of its members prevents the shamans from becoming despots over all the rest; nor are they charlatans whom a secret dissatisfaction has prompted to exploit the credulity of the profane. Their initial sense of vocation is sincere and, under the effect of *natem*, they clearly do 'see' all the entities that they have been taught to recognize and whose actions they believe they can control. But is conviction enough to make them healers? Well, if it is shared by their patients, how could it fail to do so, sometimes at least?

Often enough, the ills that affect a shaman's client are imaginary or psychosomatic. I have several times seen people virtually on the point of death, who had renounced all desire to live, so convinced were they that nothing could lift the spell cast upon them, yet who, I would have wagered, actually enjoyed perfect health, since they appeared to manifest no alarming symptoms. Having been dragged by a close family member to some famous *uwishin* whose abode they could reach only with great difficulty, they would return home a few days later with a lively step and a blooming look, delivered from a torment that probably never did have an organic origin. Because they calm the fears of those who consult them and deliver them from their terrible sense of alienation in the face of pain and the unknown, shamans even manage to produce a temporary improvement in people who truly are ill. Any subsequent deterioration in their condition is regarded not so much as a sign of failure on the part of the shaman, but rather as the indication of a new spell being cast upon them, one that is totally unconnected with the first. Contrary to the Catholic missionaries' rather naive belief that the present mercantile attitude of the Jivaro shamans results from a distressing degradation of former values, it really does seem that the comfort afforded by a cure is proportional to its cost. Everyone knows that a cure is the more rapid the more you pay for it, for the shamans are aware of what psychoanalysts discovered later, namely that a patient must literally 'bear the cost' if a situation of dependence is to be converted into the condition of his or her salvation.

CHAPTER 22

Holy Writ

TO ANYBODY BEHOLDING HIM for the first time, Father Albo presents a very curious contrast. He has the face of a cleric. His clear, ingenuous eyes behind his patched-up glasses, his untidy blond beard, his slight stoop, his serious expression and the pallor of his face all evoke long night hours spent poring over texts, along with the serene transparency of perfect faith. So it is surprising to find superimposed upon this benign appearance the customary, distinctive signs of the Achuar warrior: the feathered crown that partially covers his long hair, the rocou patterns on his cheekbones, a fine *itip* loincloth worn with instinctive grace, wide bands wound about his wrists – all of these not merely ornaments, but attributes that normally magnify and project the personality of bronzed, muscular men and that, arrayed on the somewhat frail person of this Salesian priest, have the air of pieces of finery assembled in a game of dressing-up. Only the rifle is lacking in this virile panoply, its place being taken by a discreet cross slung around his neck. But any sense of incongruity evaporates as soon as Father Albo starts to speak. The slightly croaking voice of this Italian missionary pronounces the Jivaro staccatos perfectly and is as firm and assured as that of a great man, making you forget his slender aspect. His gait, with its short, hurried steps, his gestures, his manner of drinking manioc beer – all show that he has inured to the forest customs a body that has long since forgotten the modest comforts of the seminary. We have known him by reputation for a long while. Meeting him could not fail to be quite an event.

It is two days since Father Albo, or rather Ankuaji, his self-chosen Indian name, arrived in Sasaïme. He came in the company of Kaniras, a man from Pumpuentza, who is here to negotiate *tumash* for the assassination of Kawarunch by Narankas, Nurinksa and Kuunt a few

350

months ago. Pumpuentza, two days' march to the south-east, is a village of recent foundation, of the same type as Capahuari but formed under the auspices of the Salesians, Father Albo being the first of their number to settle amongst the Achuar of the south. Like most northern Achuar, the people of Sasaïme, for their part, are more inclined to favour the Protestant missionaries of Makuma. Furthermore, they have for decades been at war with the people of Pumpuentza and tend to extend to the Salesian *paati* the same mistrust as they feel for their traditional enemies. However, the moral authority of Father Ankuaji reaches far beyond the region of his pastoral activities, six or seven days' march south of here; and it is as much to guarantee the safety of Kaniras as to prevent the eruption of a vendetta between his own flock and the men of Sasaïme that he has decided to mediate. The people of Pumpuentza are themselves merely intermediaries in this complicated affair, which yet again underlines the crucial role played by splits between blood-relatives and affines in the construction of factions. The three brothers who murdered Kawarunch came from a little river to the north of Pumpuentza and are related to the inhabi- tants of the village, but they found their wives a long way from home, in Sasaïme and Capahuari. After assassinating Kawarunch, Narankas, Nurinksa and Kuunt naturally enough fled from their 'land' of adop- tion to seek refuge amongst their 'branch' uncles and cousins in Pumpuentza, counting on solidarity from them in the event of their affines seeking to avenge themselves. But that solidarity was grudg- ingly given. According to Father Ankuaji, the people of Pumpuentza greeted the three men with great reticence for, by general consent, their crime was gratuitous and threatened to lead to a war with the northern Achuar that nobody desired. It was thus with many mis- givings that Kaniras complied with the Salesian missionary's pleas that he should help to play the role of mediator.

Over the past few months Father Ankuaji has twice been to Sasaïme, and on his last visit even brought a rifle as *tumash* payment. Kawa- runch's eldest son was prepared to accept this compensation, but his 'branch' brother would have none of it, declaring himself ready for war. So the present attempt at reconciliation may well present the last hope of avoiding a conflict. Unfortunately, the chances do not look too good: yesterday's discussion was broken off because the Sasaïme people were seeking to raise the stakes by making quite unreasonable demands. This morning Kaniras left for Pumpuentza unexpectedly and in disgust, but not before telling Picham, with whom he was staying, of his exasperation with the ill-will of his interlocutors and his desire to have no more to do with them. When Picham, who had accompanied him for a way to ensure his safety, returned with this news, it was interpreted as a declaration of hostility. Tukupi and Washikta began to proclaim loudly that they were not afraid to wage war, enumerating all the allies upon whom they could count. Through the intermediary of Picham, whom Father Ankuaji already knew, the priest has ever since been endeavouring to smother the glowing embers of a possible conflagration. He has also asked us to explain to Tukupi, with whom we have been staying for several days, that Kaniras's decision was a purely personal one that did not reflect the attitude of the inhabitants of Pumpuentza: some of his family had in the past been killed by people from Sasaïme and Copataza and his flight was prompted by an impulse of panic.

Most of the men of Sasaïme have behaved with a singular lack of good faith in this matter. When alive, Kawarunch had suffered from the full weight of their ostracism. He had been slandered by Washikta, who accused him of the murder that he had himself committed, and had been ridiculed by Narankas, his future assassin, with the complicity of Tukupi, his brother-in-law; and it is hard to see how his death can have caused his detractors anything but a secret satisfaction. His son Kunamp is relegated very much to the margins of the community because of his acute kleptomania. This compulsion of his, very uncommon among the Achuar, which everybody agrees is a kind of madness for which he is not really responsible, makes him quite disliked by those who have had to suffer his petty larcenies. So Tukupi, Washikta and their circle could not care less about avenging Kawarunch, yet are content to foster the threat of war in order to profit from the favourable balance of forces that the circumstances happen to have afforded them and also, no doubt, because they derive a sardonic satisfaction from putting the Salesian missionary in an embarrassing situation.

Although Father Ankuaji has been civil with us, since yesterday he has not sought us out, possibly because he unconsciously aligns us with the enemy faction. His reservations also stem from the chasm that, despite a superficial similarity, separates our respective vocations.

This man has devoted his life to the Achuar as much as to God and, while he has made their destiny his personal concern and has passionately striven to protect them from Westernization, his purpose in doing so has been the better to guide them along the path to the Christian Utopia that is his dream for them. He finds it hard to concede that, despite the affection that ties us to some of our companions and despite the admiration that we feel for certain aspects of their culture, we do not feel ourselves to be invested with a prophetic mission, as he does. No doubt he is conscious of these feelings of reticence without fully understanding them. Some of his remarks imply that he considers us as cold-hearted people, incapable of feeling for the Achuar the immense abstract love that he himself bears each one of them. I nevertheless did explain the local situation to him, to reassure him, and he did ask me to tell Tukupi that he would visit him to take part in an *aujmatin.*

A little before the time agreed upon for this conversation, a number of men arrived at Tukupi's house, as if on a casual visit. The atmosphere is cheerful, with everyone anticipating a spectacle quite out of the usual run. Tukupi wore an ironical smile when I told him of the *paati*'s wish: how could a White possibly succeed in this ceremonial dialogue for which young Achuar boys train assiduously for years and which many young men still manage badly? Nevertheless, Father Ankuaji's performance turns out to be brilliant. Faultlessly, he produces a series of rhythmic sentences brimming with syntactical virtuosity. There is not a single hesitation, not a stammer, not a repetition, despite the almost continuous barrage of interpolations from Tukupi. At one point Tukupi even seems out of his depth, unable to produce any rejoinder except a relentless repetition of his own name. Admittedly, the missionary is not improvising but reading an *aujmatin* that he has composed in advance for this kind of occasion. However, he does this in the manner of a consummate actor, without really seeming to refer to his notes. The style is, as always, extremely rhetorical and repetitive, but the message is conveyed in an original fashion, with the evangelical theme embroidered upon the habitual background of warlike news: 'I am here to tell you that my little father of past times is dead; the wicked killed him; he died for you . . .' In response to this Tukupi professes flaccid contrition: 'I have killed enemies in the past, but now I no longer make war – or only in self-defence . . .'

353

An extremely long silence follows this dialogue. The *aujmatin* is a formidable contest, a clash of characters and abilities. From this one, Father Ankuaji emerges as the indisputable victor.

A few days have passed. Father Ankuaji left after persuading Picham to go to negotiate the *tumash* at Pumpuentza. Now the monotony of daily life has resumed. However, Tukupi seems ill at ease, worried and glum. He hardly leaves his house and alternates between periods of black gloom, when he retreats into grumpy silence, and quasi-paternal impulses of affection, when he comes and sits beside me and asks extremely personal questions, something that he never did before; up until now he has manifested supreme indifference with regard to the world from which we have come. It is above all my fieldwork journal that fascinates him, and he asks me to translate it to him, page by page. In the evening, by the light of a torch gripped in the hollow of my shoulder, I note down whatever I have learned during the day. Tukupi watches me carefully and thoughtfully, from time to time asking me to read out what I have written. Little by little, as he confides in me and questions me, I begin to understand the reason for his behaviour. Father Ankuaji has provoked in Tukupi a serious crisis of identity, no doubt already latent for some time but now suddenly brought to the surface by the rhetorical mastery of his interlocutor.

With great intelligence, Tukupi had soon realized that it would be pointless to oppose the missionaries whose activities were becoming more and more noticeable on the edges of his domain. Two years ago he eventually accepted the advances of the North American missionaries from Makuma and agreed to their sending a Shuar preacher, who made great efforts to set up a school. His decision, purely tactical, had enabled him to use this external support to consolidate the legitimacy of a position that he had acquired by his own merits, bringing into play the entire gamut of qualities expected from a great man. For him, nothing had changed; and he continued, as before, to manipulate others with consummate skill, as attested by the murders of Ikiam and Kawarunch, which could not have been undertaken without his knowledge and the second of which, at least, was probably committed at his instigation. Despite the formidable technical apparatus of the Whites and despite their control of clearly infinite riches, Tukupi was convinced that his own pre-eminence in the traditional political system could not be challenged by these intruders who were so ignorant of his culture. He placed his confidence in his glorious past, his tried and tested charisma and above all the persuasive power of his eloquence. And now this little *paati* with his scrap of paper had bested him in an art in which he had prided himself on being unrivalled!

This bitter experience is now forcing our host to reconsider the assured confidence that has so far ruled his life: the Achuar possess the virtuosity of speech dictated by the inspiration of *arutam*, and this reveals character and acts as a powerful lever on the souls of others. The Whites, for their part, have at their disposal the aid of writing, a process that has certainly made it possible for them to recount in Jivaro the only myth they seem to possess, one that had seemed to him of no use for anything except setting down in the only book he knew of – and in very simplified language – a most esoteric message that meant absolutely nothing to him. But the recent *aujma-tin* contest has upset that reassuring equilibrium. Tukupi now realizes that writing can spill over from the covers of the Book within which it has so far been confined, and that it may even be about to invade his own particular domain, undermining the long-established bases of his own authority through its instrumental power. The *arutam* vision, that fleeting, secret revelation in which speech used to be fortified, might now lose its justification. It might soon be supplanted by the 'vision' of a piece of paper, a more effective operation since it could be repeated in any circumstances and was available to any green-horn that happened along. Let us be clear about this: it is not that Tukupi sees anything profane in Father Ankuaji's remarkable *aujmatin*; rather it presents a disturbing parallel to the conditions in which he himself exercises his eloquence. Because he is incapable of conceiving that the complex counterpoint of the ceremonial dialogue might truly be encoded by writing, he regards that sheet of paper as a kind of talisman endowed with its own autonomy. The text, just like *arutam*, seems to him to constitute a very personal illumination, not an ancillary support for inspiration that in fact pre-existed it.

The paradox of this terrible, upsetting discovery is that its effect is quite the reverse of what Father Ankuaji has always hoped for. In adopting the costume and customs of the Achuar and expressing himself in their language and in accordance with the canons of traditional rhetoric, his purpose is not only to win their confidence but also publicly to celebrate their culture and their institutions in this delicate phase of early contacts, during which many peoples give way to depression and self-deprecation. However, far from dissipating Tukupi's potential sense of alienation, this White, by competing with him in what Tukupi still believed to be a speciality of the Indians, has in effect suddenly brought home to him the full extent of his impotence. Even when inspired by the best of intentions, evangelization constantly produces misunderstandings of this kind, and it is naive to believe otherwise. The understanding of the uniqueness of others to which ethnologists, and many missionaries too, aspire sits uneasily with a desire to make those people share your beliefs.

Despite his desire not to upset the life and culture of the Achuar, and despite his low score of conversions, Father Ankuaji is probably undermining the traditional values of the four or five communities in which he carries out his pastoral mission far more than the North American fundamentalists. In contrast to the Protestants, in the first place he lives permanently amongst his parishioners. Like a country parish priest, he intervenes constantly to settle their quarrels and influence their decisions, arguing now against a projected polygamous marriage, now against a resolution in favour of vengeance; and he thereby constitutes an effective, if discreet, obstacle to the free interplay of social institutions and faction politics. Despite serious misgivings on the part of the Salesian hierarchy, he has set about adapting the Catholic cult and theology to the needs of his ministry. The celebration of mass with native ornaments and substances, the use of *anent* and *nampet* for liturgical purposes, the bold parallels drawn between certain Jivaro rituals and festivals of the Roman calendar, the transformation of heroes of Achuar mythology into hypostases of the attributes of the Holy Trinity – all are well-intentioned innovations that seek to demonstrate the prefiguration of a divine presence in the Achuar's autochthonous religion. But the effect of this deliberately constructed syncretism is to dispossess the Achuar of all the unique, original elements in their relationship with the supernatural far more surely than biblical orthodoxy would.

In the eyes of the Protestant preachers, such practices border on

356

idolatry. Impervious to the doubts that occasionally assail the Salesian missionaries and convinced that the totality of the Christian message lies in the literalness of the Holy Gospels, their sole aspiration is to deliver the Achuar from the power of the Devil by certain simple, well-tried means: that is to say by categorically condemning most of the features of the Achuar culture which, they believe, testify to the Devil's presence, and by imposing upon them the precepts and way of life that they believe they have discovered in the Bible. By reason of its very immoderation, such a project would seem doomed to failure. A Jivaro warrior cannot be changed overnight into a faithful Bible-belt fundamentalist. Deculturization on such a scale is made all the more unlikely by the fact that the Evangelist pastors visit their flock only very occasionally and are consequently incapable of exerting any lasting influence upon them, let alone understanding that the show of piety put on for their benefit is the Achuar's very best guarantee of being able to return to their 'Satanic' existence as soon as the fundamentalists have departed.

The Achuar's attitude is only half prompted by a deliberate desire to deceive and they do sometimes openly reject conversion with true sincerity, as I discovered at Conambo in the course of an astonishing episode of cultural misunderstanding. During the last days of our stay with Tunki an American missionary had arranged for a great collective baptism, probably to exorcize the influence of the Devil by which Mashu's assassination was clearly marked. On the appointed day the rival factions met in the village, sizing each other up like paired china dogs positioned on either side of the landing-strip where the missionary was due to touch down, their rifles out of sight but to hand. To the great disappointment of the pastor, despite his vigorous exhortations, only a few young women accompanied him to the river to be baptized. But the reasons that the men gave me for not becoming *yus shuar* ('people of God') indicated precisely that they took the consequences of such a sacrament very seriously indeed. They told me that if they became Christians they would have to do without the help of shamanism and the advantages of polygamy, abstain from smoking and drinking manioc beer and, above all, renounce vendettas which, in the present circumstances, seemed to them totally unthinkable. Logically enough, they reckoned that the eternal punishment with which the missionary threatened them only affected believers who sinned, and that if they themselves rejected baptism they could with impunity continue to infringe the many interdictions laid upon them.

Such rigorous reasoning is relatively rare, however. The few Achuar who claim to be *yus shuar* came to their new religion not so much through the grace of revelation but because it was in their interest to do so. That is the case of Tseremp, whose failure to meet with *arutam* and whose lack of prestige amongst his fellows led him to seek from the evangelists the sign of election that his own culture denied him. Being convinced that he now enjoys the special protection of the Lord God, he treats his fellows with the same pitying condescension as they bestow upon him, an attitude that does nothing to improve his reputation, particularly since his profound ignorance of theology prevents him from engaging upon any effective proselytizing. Other converts, the majority in fact, are attracted by the economic advantages they expect from the Protestant missionaries. It is not that the latter are all that generous, but they like to foster an entrepreneurial attitude amongst the Indians, encouraging them to grow saleable crops or to engage in the collection of products for which there is a market demand and which, thanks to their small aircraft, can then be set on a commercial footing. In exchange they sell the Achuar the manufactured goods that they need at cost price, thereby short-circuiting the *regatones'* network and incurring the resentment of the latter.

Practical initiation into the mechanisms of free enterprise has so far affected only a tiny minority and has produced patterns of behaviour that are more inspired by magic than by economics. In Copataza, the village most open to the missionaries' trading, the obsessive question that recurs in every conversation is, 'What must one do in order to benefit from "God's riches" [*yus kuit*]?' The evident abundance of material goods at the disposal of the North American preachers must, it is thought, proceed from the very special link that they have with this mysterious deity. So, clearly, the thing to do is likewise to get closer to Him, in order to benefit from the same advantages. The missionaries recommend direct dialogue with God through the medium of prayer so there should, in principle, be nothing to stop Him making his benefits rain down upon the Indians with just the same liberality. In consequence, in several houses in Copataza where we have stayed, the master of the house would embark at nightfall upon an exercise in piety by which he set great store. With his eyes closed and his brow furrowed in concentration, he would send up to heaven an interminable litany of demands: '*Yus*, give me cows! *Yus*, give me a rifle! *Yus*, give me remedies! *Yus*, give me glass beads!' Requests of this type, upon which part of the fundamentalists' success rests even in America itself, are reminiscent of the 'Cargo cult' adopted by certain Melanesian societies. These engage in a prophetic ritual designed to lure to their villages the ships and aeroplanes filled with goods that the Whites have so far managed to monopolize for their own benefit. However, whereas in Oceania the ancestors remain deaf to these pleas, and the storehouses optimistically built to receive the cargoes remain depressingly empty, in Copataza the light aircraft of the Protestant mission do sometimes touch down and unload merchandise. Admittedly, you still have to pay for it, but their very arrival does, after all, testify to the fact that the Indians' prayers are beginning to prove effective.

Copataza's supplies from heaven fit in well enough with a little myth related by Mukuimp, which accounts for the present inequality between the Whites and the Achuar in the distribution of riches: 'In olden times, the ancestors of the Whites and those of the Achuar were identical. One day an aeroplane came. The ancestors of the Achuar were afraid to enter the aeroplane. Those who did go off in it became Whites. They learned to make everything with machines, while the Achuar had to do everything the hard way, using their hands.' The airy brevity of this myth, the only one that I know of with such a theme, testifies to the Achuar's singular lack of interest in the origins of the differences between peoples and also, more generally, to their indifference to retrospective historical explanations. It is probably of recent origin, for the term *wapur*, used by Mukuimp and his companions to designate the aeroplane, is the same one used to refer to the small steamers which, at the end of the last century, began to make their way from the warehouses of the Marañon up the southernmost rivers in Jivaro country – incidental vehicles of trade by barter that were accepted then as fatalistically as the light aircraft of the Evangelists are by the Achuar of today. The moral of the story conveys no bitterness: the Indians of today are not trying to become Whites when they accept the facilities of transport by air and try to channel its advantages towards themselves through their repeated prayers.

Now that they have been offered a second chance, they are simply trying to correct in some small measure the consequences of their initial unfortunate choice.

In the eyes of the Achuar, some of the attractions of prayer must stem from its obvious affinities with the *arutam* vision. As in the latter, a mystical and personal link is established with a protective principle, a link periodically reactivated through direct communication, the effects of which make themselves felt in the ostensible success of profane actions. The resemblance between these two pleas for intercession thus supports the Salesian thesis, according to which the *arutam* vision is central to Jivaro religiosity. However, that is not, as they believe, because it prefigures the experience of divine revelation, but rather because it makes a literal and self-interested interpretation of piety acceptable.

Even the sessions of worship organized by the Protestant missionaries are exploited by the Achuar with a view to realizing ambitions of the most down-to-earth kind. The North American preachers do not engage in itinerant pastoral work as Father Ankuaji does, but instead favour periodical meetings, which they hold in one of the villages under their control, ferrying any *yus shuar* who ask to go in their light aircraft, free of charge. These 'evangelical conferences' offer a splendid opportunity to find new *amik* easily, enter into any number of bartering deals, negotiate marriages, arrange political alliances, exchange news or consult a famous shaman. Although the pastors are probably aware of all this, they choose to turn a blind eye. Perhaps they even profit from the situation by allowing these periodical congregations to help cement networks of solidarity far wider than those that result from the normal interplay of neighbourly and kinship relations – networks in which they then become the principal mediators. The complicities that are cemented in this fashion are all the more effective given that they are founded upon the old adage which says that the enemies of my enemies must be my friends: they bring together men hailing from far distant localities, quasi strangers who are usually kept apart by factions of common enemies against whom, precisely because of the distances involved, they could not until now even envisage forming a coalition. Hence the intricate mosaic-like geography of the respective influences of the Catholics and the Protestants. It is not on the basis of their personal beliefs that the Achuar choose between the two rival religions, nor is it by comparing the respective material advantages that each may offer them. Rather, their choice is dictated by the tendencies of traditional enmities. Since yesterday's enemies – let alone today's – could not conceivably countenance being brought together under the authority of the same missionary organization, religious affiliation takes on an automatic and ineluctable character. As in Tukupi's case, the fact that hereditary enemies on the Pumpuentza have passed under the aegis of the Salesians will be enough to ensure success for the solicitations of the evangelists. The missionaries' own lack of ecumenism combines with the partiality of the Indians to extend, at tribal level and in the guise of a new kind of religious war, the mechanisms of secular hostility between neighbouring groups that are definitely averse to any kind of cohabitation.

Because the influence of evangelization is far from all-pervasive and, above all, because it is confused by all these reinterpretations which distort its meaning and implications, its strength should not be overestimated. The truth is that none of the institutions deplored by the missionaries – the vendettas, the shamanism, the polygamy, the quest for *arutam* – seem threatened, even in the few villages that have been subjected to intermittent proselytizing over the past three or four years. Furthermore, whatever influence does exist proves to be reversible – a sign of the unquestionable good health of the social body. So much is certainly suggested by the example of certain young Shuar preachers whom the Protestants sent into Achuar country with the task of eradicating those customs they consider to be the most perverse. Far from accomplishing this mission, nearly all these young men chose to abandon it and instead take a wife on the spot – in fact, some of them have by now taken several – at the same time adopting the traditional values of their new affines, the very values that they had been taught to despise. Despite being extremely westernized in both appearance and behaviour when they started out, these exemplary products of missionary brainwashing slipped with disconcerting ease into the ancient customs that their own fathers had progressively been persuaded to renounce. It was a back-to-front acculturation, no doubt facilitated by some strong yet unacknowledged residual nostalgia.

Such a reversal in the march of history is probably temporary. It nevertheless suggests that the schematic manner in which the imposition of 'White peace' upon tribal minorities is still sometimes considered needs modification. Acculturation rarely amounts to westernization except in its most superficial aspects: speaking a European language, wearing a shirt and a pair of trousers, and using techniques perfected in industrialized countries have not converted the Shuar to the value systems and modes of life common to the modern nations of Europe and North America. The model with which they are presented is not that of 'Western culture' – if such an abstraction exists – but that of the popular culture of their co-citizens in the small third-world country of which they have long been members without realizing it. The new references for the Shuar converts are the current customs of the rural populations of Ecuador; what they aspire to identify with are those populations' music and dances, their eating habits, their characteristic way of talking, in which Spanish is mixed with Quichua, their community systems and the social morality that governs them – in short a whole network of typical codes and points of reference that are as unfamiliar to a Westerner as the Jivaro culture itself. Variations in degrees of exoticism such as this certainly do not exonerate us from our collective responsibility for the destruction, over the centuries, of thousands of societies, each of which in its own particular way used to contribute to the indispensable diversity of human expression. However, there is perhaps still consolation in the thought that in truth our planet has not yet become a village, only at the very most a kind of tentacular town where, over the ruins of the hamlets that used to populate its periphery, there arise each day new quarters with increasingly diverse personalities.

CHAPTER 23

The Dead and the Living

WELL BEFORE DAWN I am awakened by a sudden explosion of heart-rending lamentations from the women of the household: '*Nuku-chiru! nukuchirua! jaka-yi-i-i-i, nukuchiru! nukuchirua! yamaikia jarutka-yi-i-i-i!*' Old Mayanch has just died. She has been ill for a long time and when we went to bed everyone had a feeling that the end was near. Turipiur sat up with her for most of the night. Each time I surfaced from my fitful sleep I could see him seated on his *chimpui*, listening to the whistling breaths of his dying sister. May-anch, who was about fifty years old, had been taken in by Turipiur two or three years ago, when she was widowed, and had won the affection of the entire household. Since my arrival in Turipiur's house, nearly a month ago, she had hardly left her *peak*, daily growing weaker. I had not been asked to cure her and did not try: she displayed all the signs of advanced tuberculosis against which an injection of antibiotics would have had no lasting effects. I should, moreover, have run the risk of finding myself accused of killing her, as often happens to shamans consulted at the last moment whose patients die soon after being treated. When this happens their impotence is considered to indicate complicity with the shaman who is the aggressor, which is why experienced practitioners tend to abstain from treating hopeless cases. The risk in this instance was all the greater since Mayanch had been treated solely by her brother Turipiur, who is a well-known *uwishin*. Despite our apparently good relations, he might well, with-out hesitation, have shifted all the weight of his own failure on to me.

Turipiur, who is the brother of the shaman Peas, assassinated a while ago by Yankuam, is a phlegmatic man of about forty, tall and dry as a stick, with thoughtful eyes and measured gestures. It was he who led the abortive expedition for reprisals that I had witnessed

363

while staying with Nankiti, and it was against him that Nankiti was planning to launch the raid being prepared when I had somewhat precipitately left his house about a year ago. I have since learned that there was no follow-up to that last episode in the vendetta. Nankiti and his warriors had been halted by the flooding of the Apupentza river, which flows by about 100 metres from here and which they had planned to ford. Having taken the precaution of making a wide detour upstream, the little band had set about felling a large tree on the bank to use as a bridge. The sound of hacking had been noticed by a relative of Turipiur's, who happened to be on the opposite bank. He had taken a pot shot at the enemy and then raised the alarm. Having lost the advantage of surprise, Nankiti had retreated. It was to a large extent because I myself had only narrowly escaped being attacked by him that I had decided to visit Turipiur. Impelled by a rather perverse curiosity, I was keen to make the most of a chance that was denied to the Achuar themselves, and to take a look at the other side of the picture. As I had no guarantee as to the welcome I might receive, I had come alone, while Anne Christine remained in Capahuari with our friend Wajari.

Turipiur had turned out to be a charming and attentive host, considerably more sympathetic than his enemy Nankiti, and I had come round to embracing his cause, particularly since in this whole business it was certainly he who was the victim. When I explained the reasons that had led me to his enemy at the time of the attack, he became retrospectively very perturbed, perhaps less on account of the danger he had put me in than through fear of the reprisals that the army is said to be ready to exact in the event of a White being killed. Turipiur's faction is, in truth, more consistent than Nankiti's. He is the eldest of five brothers, and his group also includes a number of sons-in-law and brothers-in-law as well as several adult sons, making up a force of about fifteen well-armed warriors, whose weapons include a number of high-calibre repeating rifles. Each brother lives in a fortified house within earshot of the rest. Turipiur's, larger than most, and particularly well defended, functions rather in the manner of the keep of a medieval castle. Despite the state of war and Mayanch's illness, the atmosphere in Turipiur's house has been agreeable, rendering my solitude less irksome. So, once I had learned how to observe the precautions necessary in this embattled kind of life (less Draconian ones, it must be said, than those that obtained in Nankiti's house), after a few days my awareness of the exceptional circumstances in which I found myself became less oppressive.

All the same, over the past week the mood in the house has become more sombre at the manifest deterioration in Mayanch's state of health. Those nursing her had certainly not improved it: because the old lady was feverish, the women regularly took her to a nearby stream, usually in the pouring rain, to soak her in the cold water so as to 'cool her fever'. The poor thing would return shivering in every limb, increasingly pitiful after each bathe, until she became so weak that the useless ordeal was discontinued. My horrified remonstrations were greeted with polite indifference: had this not always been the way to cool fever? By yesterday morning the women had already begun their lamentations, treating the old woman as though she had already expired. 'You are dead, little grandmother, you are dead,' they said to her sadly, even as she continued to talk and ask for food. Admittedly, for the Achuar dying is a cumulative, almost deliberate action. 'To be ill', *jaawai*, and 'to be dead', *jakayi*, are formed from the same root, the transition from the one state to the other being expressed through a series of adverbs and suffixes that mark successive degrees in the progression towards the extinction of life. One is already a bit dead before being deceased, for a sick person is considered as a potential dead one and a dead person as a fully sick one.

It was already known, from a number of unequivocal signs, that Mayanch had begun to decompose, not yet in her body but in her personality, the various attributes of which were gradually recovering their independence. Two days ago one of Turipiur's nephews found the corpse of a little owl a few steps from the house. '*Mese ajakratin!*' Turipiur immediately exclaimed. This was a bad omen foretelling the approaching end, for an owl is one of the avatars in which the souls of the dead become embodied. Everyone knew that Mayanch's *wakan* had already left her body to become an Iwianch whose presence, although invisible, could be felt every day. Sometimes it would be a matter of the sound of running feet outside the house or a few knocks at the door of the palisade in the middle of the night; sometimes a cooking pot that tipped over on the fire for no good reason, or a bowl that fell from a high shelf. Although Mayanch seemed still to retain most of her faculties, for those close to her she was now no more than an automaton deprived of thought and emotive sensitivity. Even her desire for food was interpreted as confirmation of this spiritual dispossession, for one of the principal characteristics of an Iwianch is precisely its insatiable appetite. Several days before the cessation of her vital functions the escape of her soul and its clumsy manifestations around the house told them all that the old woman had joined the world of the dead.

The Achuar profess many different opinions as to the true nature of this transmutation and also as to the more general fate of the soul after death, as I have ascertained during the last few days by asking Turipiur's household what will become of Mayanch. My companions' uncertainty regarding the mechanisms of a person's decomposition simply reflects their total indifference regarding its constitution. Men and women are, it is true, in agreement on the general principles according to which a child is made: the father deposits in the uterus of the mother a tiny 'egg', contained in his seed, an egg that he must feed and fortify throughout its gestation, particularly during the last months, by regular contributions of sperm. The woman plays no more than a subsidiary role in the process, that of a passive receptacle. Yet she it is who is blamed where there is sterility, for this is supposed to result from an inability to provide the 'egg' with an environment propitious to its development. It is accepted that the embryo is endowed with a *wakan* as soon as it is conceived, but nobody seems to know where this soul comes from or bothers in the slightest about the matter. And such a lack of interest is comprehensible, given the lack of any notion of descent in this society: parents transmit to their children no prerogatives except a name – generally that of a grand-parent – and occasionally a pattern tattooed on the face, but these are marks of individualization rather than symbols of continuity with preceding generations. In contrast to what happens in many pre-modern societies, amongst the Achuar birth does not qualify one to be incorporated into a clan or lineage with clearly defined interests; it does not confer any rights to any responsibilities or titles, nor does it impose any particular duties towards any local deity or domestic altar. It is simply the initial impulse given to an incipient existence that will owe everything to its own efforts. An elaborate theory of formative substances and principles would accordingly be superfluous. Since the father and the mother represent only themselves, not groups eager to establish rights over their descendants, there is no need to sort out who does what in the genesis of a child.

At birth the *wakan* is fluid and plastic. It develops along with the body, as dictated by the experiences that little by little produce an individual idiosyncrasy in which the particular person's character is expressed. A baby's *wakan* gives it no individuality, at the very most a promise of the faculties that characterize beings with a language. It does not contain the child's potential identity, far less its destiny. Identity and destiny are forged in the course of successive meetings with *arutam*, an impersonal and abstract motor that produces temporary effects but is never definitively embodied, for its apparitions are unpredictable and it never belongs to anybody in particular. Generation after generation, *arutam* makes it possible for personalities to develop and for the human condition to define itself, without any predetermination on the part of the *wakan*, that little glimmer of consciousness and affectivity that amounts to no more than a predicate of life. The avatars of the *wakan* after death are therefore not of great importance; its function was to accompany an existence, but when that existence comes to an end, its role lapses.

According to the most generally accepted interpretation, the *wakan* leaves the body shortly before death and is changed into an Iwianch, which haunts the house until the body of the deceased has totally decomposed. At this point the Iwianch-*wakan* undergoes a metamorphosis and becomes an animal. The *wakan* has no precise seat in the human body, so the species whose form it takes depends on the part of the body where it was residing immediately before its departure: it will be an owl if it was residing in the liver, a grosbeak for the heart, a morpho butterfly for the auricules – some say for the lungs – a red deer for the 'flesh' or sometimes for the shadow cast by that body. The shadow is an essential part of the person, as is his or her reflection in the water; and both are, moreover, designated by the term *wakan*, for which they somehow provide a figurative form. The *wakan* of men become embodied in the males of the species, the *wakan* of women in the females. However, some people believe that the *wakan* returns to the placenta of the dead person buried close to the house in which he or she was born and there, throughout all eternity, leads the vegetative life of a foetus, while the various parts of the body become autonomous and change into animals according to the same rules as those mentioned above. As for Iwianch, in their humanoid guise at least, they are believed to be put together in the forest by the grosbeaks. Other Achuar maintain that the *wakan* is swallowed up by the Sangay volcano – a belief transmitted by the Shuar and probably originated by the missionaries – and it is the liver that changes into an Iwianch, either in the shape of a tall, furry, very thin being with a monkey-like head, or in that of one of the animals already mentioned. It is also said that a *wakan* likes to become embodied in an owl or a grosbeak so as to recover the faculty of sight, for it is reputed to become blind as soon as it leaves the body. These birds are believed to lend their eyes to the dead and it is quite common for an Achuar, hearing a grosbeak whistle its characteristic *pees-a-pees*, to grumble with lowered head, 'Go off and bother whoever put a spell on you!' Finally, some Achuar confess to knowing nothing at all about the soul after death and press me to enlighten them on this question. In short, it would seem that each individual embroiders as he or she feels inspired upon a common canvas, this being more of an exercise of the imagination to while away the time than an agonizing questioning requiring some orthodox and socially acceptable resolution.

Of all the figures from beyond the grave, that of Iwianch is the most unusual. Its ontological frontiers are very vague, since Iwianch is used both generically and individually. It refers to the various manifestations, most of them animal, of the souls of the dead – the red brocket deer is known as the 'Iwianch deer', the grosbeak as the 'Iwianch sparrow' – and also to all the harmful creatures in the magic arsenal of shamans. Iwianch may also be a specific, vaguely humanoid being whose not particularly alarming malevolence probably accounts for the other baleful meanings that are attached to the term. With unerring ethnographical flair, the missionaries have translated Iwianch as 'demon', echoing the semantic vagueness of the Jivaro concept in this analogy.

In its humanoid avatar, Iwianch presents a number of paradoxical features. In the first place, whatever the differences of interpretation with regard to the mechanisms that produce it, nobody at all seems to doubt its existence. Yet this phantom is usually invisible, its presence mainly identifiable from the effects that it produces: it is blind and so moves in an erratic fashion about the house, bumping into things; it is famished and steals food; it is sexually frustrated and gropes at

sleeping women in the night; and it is terribly lonely and steals dogs
for company. Even in the forest, it manifests itself chiefly through its
typical cry of *chikiur-chikiur*, or by the sound of a twig cracking
underfoot, as if this timid dead thing is loath to reveal the horror of
its face to the living. It is true that it sometimes appears to women
and to children, but without them at first realizing what they are faced
with. Children see it simply as a friendly looking stranger. Attracted
as they are by whatever is forbidden, they allow themselves to be lured
by this new playmate into long walks in the forest, plunging their
parents into panic-stricken anxiety. The young absconders whom I
questioned retained only a very vague memory of their experience,
which proved much less traumatic for them than for those who cared
for them.

A myth told me by Wajari captures the more or less affectionate
camaraderie that exists between the dead and children:

It is said that in the old days, in a house where the parents had gone
out, a dead grandfather came to visit his grandchildren. He took meat
from the larder and prepared a stew; then he called his grandchildren:
'Come and eat!' After eating, he invited them to play with him. The
children took blowpipe darts, lit them at the fire and set fire to his
pees-a-pees [grosbeak] head. While his head was burning like a torch, he
kept on singing, 'Grandchildren, I still exist, I still exist!' The children
had a fine time and at last, when they were tired out, they went to sleep.

Seizing his chance, the grandfather devoured all the stores of meat in
the house.

When their parents returned, the children said, 'Don't you know what
happened? Grandfather came and gave us stew to eat.'

'What grandfather are you talking about? Your grandfather died years
ago,' replied the parents.

The children insisted that the grandfather had told them, 'You are
my grandchildren.'

'What nonsense! Your grandfather disappeared long ago; it was an
Iwianch who came to see you.'

The father was worried and decided to hide on a high shelf to see
what went on in his absence. An old man with shaggy hair arrived, and
set about making a stew and telling the children to eat. While they were
all eating, the grandfather took out one of his eyes and put it in the stew
to salt it. After a moment he removed it and set it on one of the logs
by the fire to dry. Seeing this, the father said to himself, 'So this is the

one who is stealing our food stocks!' He had equipped himself with a long stick and managed to reach the eye without anyone noticing. He pushed the eye into the fire, where it burst.

'*Chaa!* What was that?' exclaimed the grandfather. 'Perhaps it was a lump of moss that caught fire; it gave me a fright.' After eating, the grandfather wanted his eye again, but he could not find it. Very worried, he searched for it everywhere. Then, as he could hear the members of the household returning, he took leave of the children and went away, saying, '*Wee, wee* [salt, salt].'

In answer to the parents' questions, the children said that the grandfather had gone away for good. As time passed, the episode was eventually forgotten.

One day an old woman who was in the garden with her daughters was caught in a heavy shower. She decided to go home to get dry, while her daughters remained in the garden to peel and wash the manioc roots. Shivering with cold, the old woman arrived home and there found a man lying on a bed in front of a good fire. 'Who are you?' she asked, but the man did not reply. In terror, the old woman seized a firebrand, but at that moment the man flung himself upon her, rolled her over on the floor and pulled out an eye, which he then placed in his own empty socket. Then he went off, satisfied, leaving the old woman lifeless.

Everyone soon understood that it was the dead man who had come to seize an eye from the old woman. The father was surprised. 'It is probably my father. Can he be alive?' They then decided that they would kill him, and the father resumed his position on the high shelf.

Not long after, the dead man returned, prepared a stew and bade the children eat. He again salted the food with his eye, but put it straight back in his socket. As instructed by their father, the children clustered round the grandfather and, pressing closer and closer without him noticing, they pushed him nearer and nearer to the hearth until he caught fire. Then the children said, 'Grandfather, grandfather, you are burning!'

'No, no, children, I am just swaying to and fro.' But as he spoke he noticed that his body was indeed slowly beginning to burn, so he decided to leave: 'Grandchildren, I bid you farewell. Take care of yourselves, for I am leaving for ever.' He went away, burning up little by little, until he reached the deepest part of the forest, where his burning body set fire to the vegetation and then disintegrated into ashes.

As the myth indicates, women receive less sympathetic treatment than children do from the Iwianch. The women's encounters with ghosts usually seem to take place at night, taking the form of an intimate or a brutal physical, non-visual contact. Whilst in Sasaïme, we were the perplexed witnesses to one such confrontation. Towards midnight the whole of Picham's household, where we were guests, was awoken by the pitiful whimpers of Asamat, Tukupi's brother, a deaf-mute from birth. He seemed to be asking for cigarettes, as was confirmed by Picham who, like all the inhabitants of Sasaïme, was used to the sign language that made it possible to communicate with Asamat and his wife, also a deaf-mute. As deaf-mutism has long been a hereditary affliction in Sasaïme, this sign language was by now codified into an elementary means of communication, perpetuated and enriched from generation to generation. Asamat's wife, who had gone out to relieve herself, had apparently been assaulted by an Iwianch who, having grabbed her from behind, had then hit her a couple of times and disappeared. As usually happens in such cases, the unfortunate woman had fainted as soon as she began to describe her adventure to her husband, in sign language. The stupor into which she had fallen could only be dissipated by blowing smoke on to her head, and Asamat happened to be without any tobacco. We immediately provided him with some and his wife soon regained consciousness.

This event plunged us into deep speculation. How could beings deprived from birth of all verbal communication represent to themselves other beings that were generally invisible and dumb? What concept did the deaf-mute Asamat and his wife have of a ghost whose attributes could be communicated only imperfectly by the rudimentary code, thanks to which some features at least of the Achuar culture had been transmitted to them? Rather in the manner of hieroglyphs, their language is based on a mimetic principle, each signifying entity being expressed by an analogous image schematically conveyed by two or three gestures. The image thus derived its pertinence and evocative power from the fact that the referent which it indicated was always observable in the immediate social and natural environment. So, given that Asamat's wife had lost consciousness barely a couple of seconds after returning to him, how had Asamat managed to guess what she had just experienced? Short of sharing our hosts' belief in the existence of the Iwianch – which did not seem to present a problem for some of the Protestant missionaries – it had to be admitted that the Achuar's relations with these visitors from the beyond were

371

structured by a type of communication that did not depend very much on verbal expression.

It is principally through a subtle interplay between seeing and not seeing, and by exploiting the gamut of possible incompatibilities between various types of sensation, that interactions between the living and the dead seem to be judged to be either illusory or real. The dead, who are deprived of sight, are determined to see the living by using the eyes of the animals in which they are embodied. Failing this, they take advantage of the nocturnal darkness to try to touch women without themselves being seen yet at the same time without attempting to disguise their nature, which is revealed by their behaviour. Their attitude to children, on the other hand, is quite the reverse: to them they appear in visible form but do not reveal their identity. As for the living, their behaviour is the reverse of that of the dead, for they take very good care to avoid seeing them: they avert their eyes when they come across an Iwianch-animal; and they shrink from any situation that puts them into communication with ghosts.

However, not everyone is equally successful in this game of hide-and-seek, in which you must avoid being seen by those who aspire to see and, at the same time, avoid seeing those who wish to be seen. Possibly because of their superior mastery of discourse, men can usually manage to forestall any exchange of glances with the Iwianch by promptly demonstrating the superiority of sound over vision: as soon as a telltale noise heard in the forest warns of the proximity of a ghost, a hunter makes a sudden report – by snapping a branch or firing his rifle – deliberately seizing the initiative by responding to one sound with another so as to avoid slipping into a hypnotic fascination. He generally then adds, 'For my part, I am a man, I am!' thereby affirming the irreducible difference in status between the living and the dead and, through speech, re-establishing the necessary distance which a visual illusion might have for a moment threatened to abolish. Forestalled by a register of communication that it is not skilled at controlling, the Iwianch thereupon disappears without revealing itself.

With women, the Iwianch adopt a different tactic, on the contrary making the most of the nocturnal darkness that renders them invisible, and manifesting themselves through physical rather than visual contact. The warmth of women attracts them, but the fierce heat of the fire repulses them, which is why it is imprudent to wander too far from the fire during the night, particularly when camping in the forest. By fastening upon the bodies of women, the ghosts draw them into an interaction that they cannot avoid. For a brief moment they force them across the threshold leading to the world of the dead, in which an ambiguity of senses and a confusion of sentiments prevail. The aberrant relationship in which they have allowed themselves to be trapped for a while cuts these women off from the community of the living and it is only when they see their fellows around them again that the chimaera is dissipated. But it leaves them prostrate, unable to express themselves, their ability to enter into normal communication through speech and looks annulled by the fondling to which they have been subjected. Hence the importance of the tobacco, which clarifies the mind and fosters concentration. To a body rendered vulnerable by imperfect control it restores the domination of the *wakan*, the source of sight and language.

Children are even more vulnerable than women when faced with Iwianch. The as yet incomplete state of their *wakan* renders them porous to the influences of the environment and prone to be overwhelmed by perceived images, incapable of discriminating between the different sensations that assail them. It is only to them that the ghosts can appear in visible form, for to the children's unprejudiced eyes their appearance will seem nothing out of the ordinary; and it is only with them that Iwianch can engage in a dialogue, for they will not detect its absurdity. The youngest children run the greatest risk, since their unformed sensual perceptions encourage a lack of distinction between souls. The ultimate consequence of this may be that the child comes to incorporate the *wakan* of the deceased. If this happens, the deceased gains temporary access to the real world and to the marvellous range of an innocent sensibility, at least until such time as this impossible coexistence eventually brings about the child's death, whereupon the ghost is once again expelled into the twilight world of will o' the wisps.

All these different kinds of interaction between the living and the dead seem to be organized around a series of oppositions between the continuity of the visual field and the discontinuity of sonorous and tactile sensations. The fallacious existence of the ghosts is strengthened or weakened depending upon whether there is a continuity or a break in the field of communication that they seek to establish. Men prevent the establishment of a visual continuity with them by introducing a discontinuity of sound; meanwhile the Iwianch, for their part, are trying to produce in women, through their touch, a sudden discontinuity in perception; this makes it for a while impossible for their victims to tolerate the continuous gaze of the living. As for children, they are inevitably the best interlocutors for the ghosts: because they are not fully developed, they are incapable of gauging discontinuities and, in this respect, resemble these incorporeal beings who are partially oblivious to sensory distinctions.

It will now be understood why it is pointless to ask questions, as I at first did, about the precise circumstances in which someone or other claimed to have encountered an Iwianch, hoping that positive facts would reveal concrete explanations for the illusion. The anxiety in which my hosts are plunged when faced with the secretive actions of a dead person who is still alive cannot be interpreted in terms of truth or error unless we attribute to the Achuar a theory of objective knowledge identical to our own. Now, it seems increasingly clear to me that, for them, matter and beings have no existence in themselves apart from the representations that the mind can form of them through the senses. Unlike the rationalist philosophies that have made possible the rise of positive sciences in the West by establishing a radical separation between words and things and between the abstract ideas of our understanding and the realities that they apprehend, the Achuar do not conceive the *wakan*'s task to be to give form to a world of substances that pre-existed it. They are probably closer to the immaterialism of a thinker such as Berkeley in this respect, for they appear to found the existence of cognizant entities and the elements of their environment more or less entirely upon the act of perception. To paraphrase the famous formula of that Irish bishop, it is the perceptive qualities that, in a single movement, constitute at once things themselves and the subject who perceives them. Given that they lack full sensation, Iwianch are slightly less real than the living, who can only seize upon certain of their aspects and are themselves imperfectly discerned by the dead. Iwianch exist at certain moments for certain people and this intermittent and subjective mode of being makes it possible for every individual to believe in ghosts, even if they have never experienced their presence.

The whole of Achuar cosmology stems from this relational concept of belief. In it, the hierarchy of animate and inanimate beings is founded, not upon the degree of perfection of Being or upon a gradual accumulation of intrinsic properties, but upon the various modes of communication that are made possible by the apprehension of perceptive qualities that are unequally distributed. Contrary to the naive Platonism sometimes imputed to the Jivaros, in which the true world of essences, accessible through dreams and hallucinogenic visions, is opposed to the illusory world of daily existence, it seems to me that the Achuar structure their world on the basis of the type of exchange that they can establish with all its diverse inhabitants, each of which is invested with a greater or lesser existential reality according to the kind of perception to which it lends itself and with which it is in return credited.

Because the category of beings with language includes spirits, plants and animals, all endowed with *wakan*, this cosmology does not discriminate between humans and non-humans. It introduces distinctions of order only according to levels of communication. At the top of the pyramid are the Achuar: they see each other and speak to each other in the same language. Reciprocal interlocution also takes place between the various Jivaro tribes but in dialects which, although more or less intelligible to them all, are nevertheless all different and sometimes give rise to equivocation, either accidental or deliberate. With the *apach* – Whites or Quichuas – it is also possible to see and speak to one another simultaneously, so long as a common language exists – Achuar, Spanish or Quichua – but an imperfect mastery of that language on the part of one of the interlocutors sometimes makes it difficult for feelings and wishes to be totally understood, and this introduces a measure of doubt concerning the correspondence of faculties that testifies to the existence of two beings on the same level of reality. The further one moves from the domain of 'complete people', the more accentuated the distinctions between perceptive fields become. Thus, human beings can see plants and animals, which are themselves believed to be able to see human beings if they possess a *wakan*. But although the Achuar can speak to them, thanks to their *anent* incantations, they do not obtain any immediate reply, for this can only be communicated through dreams. The same applies to spirits and certain mythological heroes: these listen to what is said to them but, since they are for the most part invisible in their original form, they can only be fully apprehended in dreams or in visionary trances. Finally, some elements in the natural landscape – most insects and fish, grasses and brackens, pebbles, etc. – are visible to everybody but communicate with nobody since they possess no *wakan* of their own. For the Achuar, these, with their inconsequential and generic existence, probably correspond to what we should call nature.

That is all very well, you may say, but what is the source of this cosmological exegesis? Did some native sage suggest it? Is it transmitted through the oral tradition? Clearly not. My companions are no more likely to produce a considered theory concerning their modes of knowledge than we ourselves are conscious of using the principle of non-contradiction or the excluded middle in most of our judgements. But given that the common sense of some cultures is not the same as that of others, ethnologists must perforce sometimes make use of philosophers' instruments when they are out hunting in territory where the latter do not venture.

As soon as the day dawns the women begin to prepare the body. Mayanch's hair is carefully combed, she is dressed in her finest *tarach*, her favourite coil of yellow *shauk* is fastened round her neck, and her sister-in-law, using rocou, draws on her face the patterns of the Pleiades and Orion: two clusters of little dots on each cheekbone, edged by two bands containing a dotted line that follows the outer contour of her cheeks, mouth and temples. The dead woman is then laid out on her *peak*, flat on her back, with her legs together and her arms arranged close to her body. The body is then covered with a blanket that serves as a shroud. At this point most of the women scatter, lamenting, through the gardens to visit the places that Mayanch used to haunt – her little plot of manioc, the bank where she went to wash the roots, the path she took in the evenings, bent under her hod: all these revive painful memories that prompt a crescendo of laments. Muted and refracted by the mist that covers the landscape this morning, this concert of voices, husky with sorrow, seems poignantly unreal.

Turipiur, his gaze fixed and his expression shaken, has remained in the house in the company of his two sons-in-law. From time to time he speaks to them of his childhood with Mayanch, but despite his efforts his voice soon becomes choked and tears that he makes no attempt to brush aside flow down his cheeks. The sight is particularly moving as Turipiur usually preserves an imperturbable sangfroid. Like all great men, he exerts assiduous control over his passions and up until now nothing has ever seemed to have the power to affect his smiling equanimity. He even told me a little while ago, with obvious sincerity, that he was quite indifferent to dying in a clash with Nankiti's band and that, given that he had killed several men himself, his own turn would surely come one day. Actually, it is probably because he is so sure of his strength of soul that Turipiur can manifest his sorrow with no false shame. Unassailed by the slightest doubt of his own virility and with no need to furnish further proof of his moral fortitude, he is not afraid that his tears will be seen as a sign of weakness. I have several times seen men express their emotion in this unabashed way. A few weeks ago, for example, a visitor from the Kurientza came to tell Turipiur that his wife had just left him and run off with a lover, leaving him to cope with three young children on his own. He described his distress in the most pathetic terms, his voice breaking under the onrush of tears, held back with the greatest difficulty. It occurred to no one to ridicule him and when he had left and they were commenting on his misfortune, they did so with true pity, not the perverted kind in which commiseration is mixed with condescension, but the truly spontaneous sense of identification with another which Rousseau regarded as the most solid basis of the social virtues.

Once relatives begin to foregather, however, the tone changes altogether. For each one, the corpse is uncovered for a moment, at which the women immediately break into loud lamentations while the men stare in silence. Brothers, brothers-in-law, sons-in-law and nephews gradually gather around the master of the house to reflect on what has happened. Turipiur's grief now changes to anger and he openly accuses Awananch of having cast a spell upon his sister. 'How could she have died? Her *arutam* was too strong for her to die. Did she not meet *arutam* after the death of her husband? She was eaten away by *tsentsak*! I, Turipiur, saw them!' His listeners all agree

emphatically, each assuring Turipiur of his support: 'A crime as gratuitous as this cannot be allowed to go unpunished, especially as it has
followed hard upon the murder of Peas. These people want to liquidate the lot of us; but we are not afraid to go to war either . . .'

The women, listening to the men's words even as they keep up a
continuous counterpoint of laments, now join in. Turipiur's wife
launches into a kind of imprecatory chant in which a grief-stricken
evocation of the dead woman soon turns into a string of anathema
pronounced against the shameless shaman who has been mocking her
pain from a safe distance. By now the whole house resounds with
recriminations. Sharing their grief but not their animosity, I find
myself almost envying my companions their ability to transfer the
culpability of mourning to a scapegoat. This seems an admirable move
on the part of people without the consolation of any belief in eternal
life. Its price, however, is a state of permanent civil war in which death
ends up by assuming more importance than life.

Towards the end of the morning the visitors disperse. Kaitian and
Kashpa go off to fell a *shimiut*, a soft-wood tree, which they will
hollow out to make a coffin. Mashiant, Yakum and I set about digging
a grave at the very spot hitherto occupied by Mayanch's *peak*, which
we now dismantle. It is hard work, as we have only machetes with
which to loosen the beaten floor of the house and only the planks
from the bed to use as spades for lifting out the earth. Turipiur wants
a deep grave and it takes us three hours of hard labour to get down
even to chest level.

Women and children are simply buried a few feet below the *peak*
where they used to sleep, the only space in the communal dwelling
that, in life as in death, belongs to them in particular. For a man it is
different. The whole house is his domain; he is its origin and its master
and bestows upon it its identity and its moral substance. It accordingly
becomes his solitary sepulchre when, having buried his body between
the central pillars, the rest of the family abandons the place and is
dispersed to the four corners of the kinship group. In order that the
link between the house and the man who founded it be made more
tangibly manifest, the deceased is sometimes arranged in the posture
of a host receiving visitors. Seated on his *chimpui* at the bottom of a
little circular pit protected by a wall of posts, with his elbows resting
on his knees and his head on his hands, wearing his *tawasap* and his

cross-belt, he will maintain his macabre vigil until such time as the roof collapses on to his whitened bones and, under the all-conquering advance of the vegetation, all traces of the site over which he used to rule begin to disappear.

Kaitian and Kashpa appear, bearing the coffin on their shoulders. It is made like a little canoe and is indeed called a *kanu*. They are followed, in some disorder, by other relatives who are returning for the burial. Even Senkuan is here, although he lives four or five hours' march away: having heard a loud explosion in the middle of the night, a sign that *arutam* is departing from the body of a dying person, he set off at dawn to discover the news. Mayanch is wrapped in her blanket, secured by lianas at the feet, the neck and the waist, then laid in the *kanu*, which is covered with the bark of the *shimiut*, held in place by chonta thorns that serve as nails. Two men lower it into the grave, the feet pointing eastwards and the coffin resting on small logs so as to avoid all contact with the earth. At the bottom of the hole they place a plate of plantains, a small gourd of peanuts and a bowl of manioc beer. The planks from the *peak* are then placed on top of three cross-bars that are forced into the tomb walls, forming a kind of platform above the *kanu*. Turipiur gives the signal for the burial by throwing a handful of earth into the grave. Each of those present then follows suit in order that, through this gesture, 'our *wakan* will not join the *wakan* of the dead woman, in the tomb'. We fill in the hole; the ground is trodden flat, then swept. Apart from the different shade of the newly turned soil, no indication now remains of the presence of Mayanch in this world. Everything about the burial seems designed so that the dead woman should not remain for all eternity in her underground abode. Provided with a few provisions of food and protected from being crushed in her little funerary chamber, her body is left unencumbered so that her departure will be the easier.

Now, led by Metekash, Turipiur's wife, all present make their way to a little beach bordering the Apupentza. Metekash is an active woman of about forty who, with great charm, combines a peaceful face with the lively, eager movements of a girl. She begins by rubbing each of us on the back and chest with handfuls of *chirichiri* grass, first the men, then the women. The children are rubbed all over. Then we process into the river, in which we all remain immersed for a few moments, including the babies who, upon emerging from this enforced bathe, set up a chorus of bawling. Each individual then washes his or her clothes in summary fashion, wringing them out over the water. Metekash stuffs the handfuls of *chirichiri* she has used into a large gourd, which she then allows to float into the middle of the Apupentza, where it is soon borne away by the current. This purification has rid us of the *pausak* contamination from the corpse, a vague notion that covers the harmful influences emanating from the corpse itself as well as the virulent entities which caused her death – possibly *sunkur*, but more probably *tsentsak* – and are now liberated from that morbid task, eager to cause new harm. It is quite possible, although nobody has confirmed this idea, that the canoe-shaped coffin may enable the dead woman to make a mystical journey downstream in the course of which the contaminating body fuses with the *pausak* released on the current as it makes its leisurely way along. On the path by which we return from the river, Menekash has set an old basket filled with dry palm leaves to which she now sets fire. In single file, we jump over the thick white smoke, thereby preventing May-anch's *wakan* from following us to the house. The soul of the dead woman is much more to be feared than the corpse's *pausak*, and the rest of the funerary rite is but an attempt to make it depart.

Dressed again in our dried clothes, we all gather in Turipiur's house. Two banana leaves are arranged on a manioc mortar to receive the locks of hair that Metekash is about to cut from our heads. The role of mistress of ceremonies falls to her, partly because she is the sister-in-law of the deceased, but mainly because, having already reached a mature age, her longevity guarantees her good protection against the risks attendant upon the direction of the funerary rites. She begins with Turipiur, setting into the back of his head a comb which he uses to run through his hair and select a thick lock, which his wife proceeds to hack off with a knife. Each of the other men then receives the same treatment, with me last in line. Then it is the turn of the women and children. One of Turipiur's sisters-in-law does the same for Metekash. I am told that this gesture represents a kind of appeal 'to get death to move away from us'. Next, Metekash takes a gulp from a gourd in which green tobacco is soaking, then spits it out into the eyes of her husband. To my consternation, she then proceeds to repeat this action in the same order as before, forcing open the eyes of those who are recalcitrant and sparing none but the youngest of the children, on to whose heads she instead blows the tobacco water. It is very painful at first, but after a few moments the sensation of burning and blindness passes in a gush of tears. This disagreeable little ritual is not really designed to provoke the tears of grieving relatives. Rather, its purpose is to stimulate their lucidity so that in the coming night they do not allow themselves to be dragged into bad *mesekramprar* dreams foretelling their own deaths or, more baleful still, giving the dead woman a chance to reappear. For the poor thing's *wakan* is avid for company and, to protect oneself from it, Mayanch's image must be banished for ever, as must her memory. To emphasize this ostracism, Metekash collects up the banana leaves with their pile of hair and goes to throw the whole lot into the river, together with the comb and the gourd of tobacco.

Despite all this, the meal that follows is not a gloomy one. It consists entirely of palm hearts, a symbol of abundance and longevity. However, salt is proscribed, as its friable consistency suggests ephemerality and decomposition. From time to time, one of the diners throws a handful of food over his shoulder, to feed Mayanch's famished *wakan*, rather as one might toss a morsel to a dog. We talk of everything but the dead woman and at nightfall the guests all return home as if nothing special had happened. Turipiur then splashes a few black streaks of genipa on to the cheeks of each member of the household. This is no sign of mourning, but a camouflage to trick the Iwianch by making us as black as them. Then comes the somewhat dreaded bedtime. Many people must, silently, be singing to themselves those *anent* of which Mukuimp once told me: pathetic injunctions addressed to the deceased, with refrains that express repulsion in all its forms: 'Do not call me son (or sister, or father . . .) any more! You are lost! Now you have gone for good! Do not look at me! Do not take my soul away! Above all, do not take my soul away!'

To us, imbued as we are with the cult of memory and the ceaseless homage we pay to the dead, such an attitude may seem shocking. But we should not interpret this expulsion of the dead from the memories of the living as indifference. It simply reflects the notion that the living cannot be truly living unless the dead are completely dead. The frontier that separates them is not always clearly marked, nor is transition instantaneous from one state to the other: it comes about gradually in the course of a dangerous in-between period, during which those close to the quasi-departed one are under threat of sharing his or her fate and are constantly assailed by invitations to do so. They have to dissolve the deceased in a willed oblivion so that, by fading from their thoughts, he or she is able to complete the process of his/her own extinction. Far from being a faculty to be cultivated, memory here is a regrettable inevitability to which one is subjected, an excitation of the mind triggered by another being. Accordingly, the funeral rites are expressly designed to prevent the deceased from seeking to stimulate memories, and most emphatically not to commemorate him/her. It is not the case that all remembrance can be wiped out in this way, but what the Achuar remember is not so much the person and the feelings they had for him/her, but rather what it was that linked him/her to them, his/her position amongst kindred, the immediate obligations and rights that his/her death produced, such as the duty of vengeance or levirate marriage. As a result of this quashing of emotions, the deceased soon becomes a pure abstraction, thereby paving the way for the collective amnesia that, within a few decades, wipes out all earlier generations. Just as they are given no tombs in their own names, they are allowed no memorials in the minds of those who survive them.

This is no doubt why my questions as to what becomes of the *wakan* produce contradictory replies or assertions of ignorance. For my companions, the dead are dangerous because they are radically different. No continuity links their ghostly and asocial existence to that of the living; no hope of reward or fear of punishment throws a bridge between the beyond and the here and now; there is no destiny to be had as an ancestor, no privilege to transmit in order to perpetuate a name and a lineage, no consolation to be expected from impossible reunions. Many cultures speculate in one way or another upon the permanence of a part of the self and are concerned to work out what survives in accordance with the condition and accomplishments of each individual. But among the Achuar, the break between life and death is total. It is accordingly not really important to know what happens in that negative world, unless it be to protect oneself from those who have landed up in it just for a short while, until such time as they fade away for ever. The Achuar's fatalism in the face of the idea of their own deaths is on that account all the more remarkable.

Against the beckoning nothingness, which the Iwianch purgatory cannot palliate, in the last analysis they have nothing to set except the satisfaction of having lived well and – in the case of the men, at least – of having killed well too.

CHAPTER 24

Dénouement

LIVING WITH THE Achuar for over two years has taught me to decipher the premonitory signs of their collective actions, so it has not been hard for me to guess to what Mayanch's death would lead. Over the week that has passed since we buried Turipiur's sister, excitement has been mounting. The men pay one another visits at all hours of the day for long confabulations from which although excluded, I sometimes catch loud bursts of talk. In my host's house, on the other hand, all is quiet. Because my presence in his house must embarrass him at this time, Turipiur receives virtually no visitors but instead spends his time hurrying between the houses of the other men. Furthermore, each night he retires 'to dream' – clearly consulting his *arutam* – in a shelter on the bank of the Apupentza. Meanwhile, his wives are preparing large quantities of *namuk*, an extremely alcoholic kind of manioc liqueur, distilled from a fermented paste that accumulates, drip by drip, at the bottom of the *muits*. I know that this constitutes the essential ingredient of *anemat*, the ritual for any departure for war. Yesterday the pace of events quickened. Turipiur announced to me that he would probably be going away for a few days, adding in level tones and as if he had only just had the idea that he would very much like to borrow my rifle. It is a fine double-barrelled weapon, the object of constant admiration on the part of the men. However, on the pretext that I myself only have it on loan from my wife's father, I have from the start declared that there can be no question of allowing it to enter the circuit of exchanges. Guessing what Turipiur wants to use it for, I politely refused his request, pointing out that I needed my rifle myself to go hunting; after all, if he is going away, who else is there to keep the household well supplied? Turipiur accepted this with a good grace, but he is no more duped by me than I am by him. We both know that no one could be a worse or less eager hunter than I. In the evening a small band of men came to stay the night: Yakum and Mashiant, Turipiur's sons-in-law, Kaitian and Kukush, his 'branch' brothers, and Pikiur, his brother-in-law. Turipiur himself went off to his 'dreaming hut', equipped with a gourd of tobacco juice.

At three in the morning we are awakened by Turipiur knocking on the palisade for admittance. He immediately announces loudly, '*Paant karampratjai,*' 'I have dreamed clearly.' I extricate myself from my sleeping bag very crossly indeed. We have slept very little: the other men talked together in low, excited voices well into the night. I neither tried to catch what they were saying nor wished to join them. Over the last few months my curiosity has become much less keen. Despite what is in the offing, I cannot shake off a disenchanted lassitude, a sense of *déja-vu*, even irritation at the all too predictable behaviour of these people who now try hard to continue to astonish me, as if it were their fault that they have no more surprises for me, rather than mine for inviting myself into their homes. Anne Christine's absence and the consequent lack of an alter ego in whom I can confide certainly have a lot to do with my disenchantment, but the main trouble is that my desire to understand has been eroded and it is this, more than my research schedule, that is tolling the hour for my fieldwork to come to an end. It is not the first time that I have felt discouraged over the past two years. Time and again I have asked myself what on earth I am doing, wasting my life here on this obscure stage, accumulating thousands of notes that are of no use to anyone. Yet never until today have I had such a jaded feeling of having landed up here more or less out of duty rather than through a passion for knowledge. Dissipated in day-to-day banalities, the exotic has lost the fresh appeal of its mystery. It is time to pack my bags.

Very much at odds with my morose mood, a surge of excitement seizes the household. The women stoke up the fires, light torches and go off to draw water from the river. The men unwind the woven bands from their wrists, don their *tawasap* and paint their faces red and black, exchanging pleasantries that are mostly to do with the great massacre of peccaries on which they are about to embark. Soon a loud babble of voices from outside the fortified precinct can be heard, followed by the long boom of a visitor blowing down his rifle to announce his arrival. The door is opened to reveal a small group of warlike men. The wavering light of the torches catches metallic glints on their weapons and enhances the red and yellow of their feathered crowns, pulled down to their eyebrows like shimmering helmets. Mayaproa is there, with Chuint, Kashpa and Nayash, Turipiur's four brothers, Utitiaj, Mayaproa's son-in-law, and his son Irarat, still unmarried and not yet twenty years old. In the background an indistinct cluster of women carrying flaming brands waits in silence.

Inside the palisade the men of the house line up to greet the visitors as they enter, one by one, led by Mayaproa. He is a short man with a face set sternly but vibrant with contained energy. The newcomers and their hosts fall into position facing one another in two lines of six, their arms crossed on their chests and their rifles lodged in the crooks of their elbows. In a loud voice, Mayaproa addresses Turipiur, opposite him: 'I come, I come, I come, I come, I come!'

'I am here, I am here, I am here, I am here!' replies his brother. It is the beginning of the *anemat*. Both men shout at the tops of their voices, in short rhythmic bursts, staring fixedly at each other. Mayaproa announces the reason for his coming:

'A man has killed me, my brother! A man has killed me! We'll see! For your help, to make blood flow, that is why I have come! I have come! I have come! My brother, a man has killed me! For your help, I come to you! So that you will come to my aid, I am going, I am going, I am going! And so that I will be comforted, I am going! And to unleash war in your company, I come! I come! I come! I come! I come! *Haa!* So it must be! *Haa!* Why did they do that to me, to me who am a *juunt*? Why did they do that to me? That is what I have come here to declare! We'll see! You too, help me! We'll see! So be it! So be it, I say!'

Turipiur meanwhile embroiders a counterpoint over this monologue:

'We'll see! That goes without saying! Have you not come here to see me? Right! We'll see! I'm here! I'm here! I'm here! I'm here! Has a man not killed me too? Right! I say I am with you! And them! Why did they do that? Little brother, I have left my *natem*! We'll see! Now I shall test my strength! We'll see! Now I shall seize my spear!'

This exchange continues for some time; then, as at the end of an *aujmatin*, the voices of the two men intermingle and conclude.

'So be it, I say!'

'We'll see! Now you have come!'

'If that is how it is, later we shall speak again!'

'Having done what had to be done! Having spoken well! Now let us go!'

'Agreed! Agreed!'

As one man, the visitors brandish their rifles and start hopping rhythmically one pace forward, one pace back, making as if to strike their rifles across the faces of their impassive partners. They punctuate these passes with fierce two-beat exclamations, the second beat strongly stressed every time their bodies and rifles are thrust forward: '*Tai-haa! Ta-tar! Tai-hi! Iis-ti! Is-ta! Warish-tai! Warishtai!* . . .'

In the face of this fierce ballet, Turipiur and his companions remain unmoved, their arms crossed, responding to the simulated aggression with a string of approving and encouraging interjections interspersed with clicks of the tongue: 'Hey, hey!' . . . 'You are right!' . . . 'Now then, now then, now then!' . . . '*Juut maj!*' 'So be it!' . . . '*Huum!*' . . .

The tumult is indescribable, each man striving to shout louder than the next, with the women meantime urging them on: 'Be strong! Do not weaken!' After three or four minutes of this, the visitors suddenly bring their exhibition to a close with a '*Hey, hey, hey!* I come!'; '*Hey, hey, hey!* I am here!' is the immediate rejoinder from the men of the house who, in their turn, thereupon set about brandishing their own weapons aggressively and yelling rhythmically even louder than the men facing them. The women begin to move amongst the protagonists, doling out great draughts of *namuk*. Soon the visitors resume their first role, then the men of the house take over; and so it continues at regular intervals amid rising excitement fuelled by the continuous flow of alcohol.

This well-synchronized performance goes on for about an hour. Then comes the third phase, which is closer to a classic ceremonial dialogue in structure and inspiration. Bobbing from one foot to the other on the spot, with his rifle gripped under his arm, Mayaproa launches into a lively, jerky harangue consisting of successive bursts of short phrases of four or five words, his voice dropping sharply on the last syllable of each burst:

So! Brother! I am! On the watch!
So! Me! I am! On the alert!
My brother! Go! Has spoken!
So! Me! I'll go!
Go! Visit! The relatives!
So! Elder brother! Has asked!
My elder! Has asked! To carry! The news!
To make them! Suffer greatly! I come!
With! This rifle! Truly! Captain!
But me! Like those! Of olden days!
But me! Like them! I do!
My brother! War! Has taught me!
With him! The paths! I've followed!
And me! Clearly! Having spoken!
Knowing! Running! The paths!
To! Bring! War!
So! Brother! I come!

Throughout this declaration of allegiance Turipiur and his companions respond to Mayaproa with the customary words of approval: 'I too am here!' ... 'Hey!' ... 'Right, right!' ... 'Let's drink!' ... 'Now then!' ... 'Try us!' ... 'You are right! Right! Right! Right!' ... 'So be it!' ...

Turipiur then takes over, with the same stacccato delivery as Mayaproa, but on a slightly higher note:

And me! Brother! As well! I am here!
Me! Being! The elder! Along the paths! I go!
Me! You'll see! Along the paths! I'll lead you!
Me too! Brother! My ancestors! Are valiant!
Thus said! Me too! Alert! I am!
My words! Mine! Are full! Of vigour!
Let war! Be! Thus! I say! ...

The dialogue goes on and on, sometimes barely comprehensible through the torrent of interjections from the row of men listening to it. Turipiur and Mayaproa each take two turns at this, then end off in the appropriate manner. 'Having spoken well, later we shall converse at leisure.' 'Now that you have come to me, let us go!' 'Right! Right!' 'Right! Right!' As the last words die away, all the men

discharge their rifles in a deafening salvo, the culmination of this simulated combat and the prelude to the real confrontation.

The *anemat* is many things: a ceremonial conversation, a choreographic show of arms in preparation for hand-to-hand fighting, a joust of wills demonstrating each warrior's worth. But it is also one of the rare collective rites that this individualistic society has devised for itself, a rite of confrontation in which the celebration of a temporary unity seems possible only at the expense of a common enemy. For the Achuar, being together means first and foremost being together in one small group ranged against another, in a fleeting coagulation of the social link, a rare gathering occasioned solely by a thirst for revenge and the lure of a chance to perform an exploit. The *anemat* expresses all these things, cementing them together in a performance in three stages, which constitutes a mimetic enaction of the various phases of a real conflict. The first part brings together two groups of men determined to wage war together, between whom solidarity is gradually constructed in the course of a dialogue setting out the motives for seeking vengeance and underlining the identical points of view and common interests of the two groups. This is immediately followed by a disjunctive phase, the most spectacular of the three, in which each group in turn adopts the position of the aggressors or that of the victims under attack in a controlled enaction of a real battle. The last phase returns to the theme of togetherness, exalting the two groups' refound unity and announcing the fate to be inflicted upon their enemies.

The *anemat* no doubt works upon the raw material of emotion. By arousing the men both physically and mentally and also compelling them to remain impassive in the face of threats, the rite is a useful preparation for battle. It also probably helps to stimulate each warrior's *arutam* by building up towards the paroxysmic explosion of the kill that at once proves its efficiency and heralds its subsequent disappearance. Above all, though, it is a formidable mechanism of illusion, in that it compounds all kinds of disparate and confused individual feelings and appears to resolve them in a homogeneous fashion. Hatred, self-interest, the hope of victory, grief, fear, and the desire to perform gloriously, all – to different degrees – present in each of the protagonists, are controlled by the extreme fragmentation of words and ritual gestures tirelessly repeated with tiny variations.

When transposed into a sequence of separate actions, each one imperceptibly leading into the next like a succession of images in a film, and each with its own particular place in the order of the *anemat*, these contradictory emotions lose their heterogeneity and their personal implications and are poured unstintingly into a common determination to emerge victorious.

Dawn is fast approaching and the *namuk* is still flowing. 'Drink up! Drink up!' Turipiur keeps saying, setting an example, while the warriors, still standing, down draught after draught amid cries of joy. It is considered bad luck for such an expedition to set out without having exhausted the total supply of manioc liquor. The jars will be empty by dawn. The youngest men load up with bundles of fermented manioc wrapped in banana leaves, securing them on their backs in a porter's sling. They carry enough to make beer for two or three days, this being the only nourishment the warriors will take until their return. Turipiur turns to me to tell me that he will soon be back. 'I am leaving you my son Ushpa [a boy of sixteen or seventeen]; take good care of the house and the women.' He then gives the signal for departure and the slightly tipsy warriors disappear into the last of the night. As they walk, no doubt each one of them is singing to himself one of the *anent* that lift a man's courage before battle, possibly the following one that Chunji taught me a while ago:

> The chattering, chattering anaconda, the one that talks and talks
> On the road, alert, awaits me
> Stretched out on the ground, he makes the earth tremble, all stretched
> out
> 'Tell your enemy that you are the jaguar Seet!' he tells me now
> That is how the anaconda knows how to speak to my soul
> I am a young anaconda without shame
> '*Put!*' my soul rang out, exploding
> And I became foam
> For my little wife. I put it all inside her.

Not particularly martial, perhaps. But Chunji's *anent* is that of a young man setting off to war for the first time. In the prime of his youth and full of swagger, he uses a transparent metaphor to establish a link between the kill and his own orgasm, just as there is a link between the wife he received from his father-in-law and the exploits

391

towards which the latter is now leading him. The *anent* for seasoned warriors, for whom vengeance is a duty, are less carefree and more fierce in tone. Here is an example that Yaur sang for me at Copataza.

> That one, that very one, brother! Little brother!
> He tries to bind me with slander
> But that is something that nobody repeats to me
> I don't allow it to be repeated, not to me
> I don't allow them to repeat it to me
> Going to visit Vulture in his house, I am like Vulture
> I go, blowing the wind
> So how could anyone harm me?
> Those who are my enemies I shall kill forthwith
> Whatever they say about it
> For I don't allow that to be told to me, not I
> I go bringing war
> I go bringing speech that cannot be shaken off
> I am going to kill my enemies
> And whatever they say, nobody can harm me
> Brother! Little brother! When you writhed in agony
> You said to me, 'A man has killed me'
> 'I am going to bring war,' you keep telling me
> Myself, myself, I am that very one, little brother!
> 'A Tsenku-Tsenku jaguar, watching for me from above, leapt on to my
>   neck,' you told me
> 'That is how a man killed me,' you said
> 'I am going to bring war,' you keep telling me
> Being a carnivorous jaguar, tracking from hill to hill
> Little brother! I too leapt upon him to bite him!

Whether comparing himself to the vulture, an eater of rotten flesh and, in Amerindian culture, the symbol of an anti-culture that rejects the civilizing fire for cooking, or identifying with the anaconda and the jaguar, great predators that are not averse to finding human beings on their menu, in his *anent* this warrior does not hesitate to place himself at the level of the wildest animality. In his jubilant liberation of the desire for destruction that lies hidden deep within us all, he reconnects with the instinctive violence of a nature unencumbered with moral judgements. The polite euphemisms used to address hunted animals are not appropriate for the enemy, for the latter is prey pure and simple, prey to be killed pitilessly, to satisfy a need for revenge, just as wild beasts attack their victims to satisfy their need to eat. And even though, for classificatory convenience, every enemy tends to be conceived as a metaphorical affine, the impulse to kill that leads the warrior to confront a foe temporarily abolishes even that abstract relationship. All that remains is a pair of men cut off from their humanity, whom hatred has stripped of the ordinary attributes of social existence.

All day long we remain immured indoors, without eating. After preparing large quantities of manioc beer, Metekash and her daughters delouse the children, chatting the while. Most unusually, they take a long siesta during the heat of the day, while Ushpa and his brother Katip, who is two or three years younger, stretch out on the lookout platform, keeping watch. I am rather surprised that Turipiur did not wait until my imminent departure before launching his raid against Nankiti and also that he felt no qualms about leaving me with the women. I have probably become transparent to my hosts. This might be interpreted as a privilege granted to an ethnologist of great skill, but I fear it is rather an effect of my growing detachment from the Achuar. The relative indifference that nowadays stops me asking too many questions, my greater integration into the household as a result of my temporary celibacy, the ease with which I appear to fall in with local customs, and the mask of affable comprehension that has become second nature to me – all this combines to make my presence extremely self-effacing and my position as a witness unthreatening.

Towards evening Mayaproa's wives pay us a visit, followed by the wives of Chuint and Kashpa and others too. Soon all the adult women of the neighbourhood are gathered in our house, about fifteen of them in all, attractively adorned by their *shauk* necklaces and wearing their finest *tarach*. Some wear *shakap* dancing belts with *nupir* bells that tinkle at every movement. Despite the circumstances, the mood is not gloomy. All these ladies chatter away, downing a fair quantity of manioc beer. It is not long before the effect of the alcohol on empty stomachs begins to be felt and a number of jokes soon follow, received with loud bursts of laughter. Untsumak, Peas's widow, eventually remonstrates, reminding her companions of their duty to be modest in my presence. She is a stern-faced woman of about fifty who clearly wields considerable influence over the others.

Night has already fallen when, led by Untsumak, the women arrange themselves in a circle, holding hands, in the middle of the house. The widow then strikes up with the opening words of a *ujaj* song, and the other women gradually join in, singing a kind of round for many voices.

> Like the Tsenku-Tsenku jaguar, like him
> So it is, son, my son
> Bewitching the woolly monkey, encircling him completely, he came
> He bit his young and forced him to lick their blood
> All of a sudden, he came to me
> His face bloodless, he came to me.

Then comes a refrain in which they all join, a series of deep, perfectly synchronized pants emerging from deep in the chest, a continuous, almost animal vibration in which only the last syllables are articulated:

> *Ouheu-heu-heu! Ouheu! Ouheu-hai!*
> *A-haa! A-hou! Ahou-hai!*
> *Ahaa! Hou-hou-hai!*

The main theme then takes over, again sung as a round:

> Like the Tsenku-Tsenku jaguar, like him
> Circling round the obstacle, he came
> Tearing the little ones apart, he came to me
> My son came to me, infinitely multiplied
> All of a sudden, he came to me, his face bloodless.

The refrain is repeated, a ground-swell submerging the house, its emotive force comparable to the strident '*you-you*' cries of Arab women. The circle breaks up to form a line of farandole dancers with Ushpa and Katip, the two adolescents, at either end. Amid indescribable tumult, the line moves quickly to the left and to the right, pulled along by Ushpa, who yells, '*Jeesti! Jeesti! Jeesti!*' ('Let him be off!'), while his brother at the other end echoes him with '*Au! Au! Au!*' ('That one!'). Their duet beats out the time for the continuous background chorus of women: '*Ha-houheu-heu-heu! Ha-houheu!*

Houheu-houheu! Ha-houheu-heu-heu! . . .' For a moment the farandole pauses, then sets off again in the opposite direction, now led by
Katip, continuously yelling '*Jeesti! Jeesti!*' in his turn. After a number
of changes of direction, they all stop to catch their breath. Then the
women again form a cirle for a new *ujaj*:

> The duck-spear is coming
> Dodge it nimbly!
> Those of the low lands, those of the low lands have strewn death in
>   their wake
> *Ouheu! Ouheu! Ou-hahai!*
> *Ouheu-heu-heu! Ouheu! Ouheu-hai!*
> My little brother, my own little brother, dodge aside nimbly!
> The duck-spear is coming
> My little brother of the low lands, he is clearly coming for me
> Dodge out of the way nimbly, dodge out of the way!
> *Ouheu! Ouheu! Ou-hahai!*
> *Ouheu-heu-heu! Ouheu! Ouheu-hai!*

The farandole starts up again, but this time Metekash asks me to
take Katip's place. In the red glow of the torches, attached to a line
of frenetic females and in rhythm with their powerful chorus, I begin
to gallop this way and that, yelling with a will, fleetingly struck by the
irony of the fact that it has taken me so many years of studious
preparation to end up here, so far from the austere halls of the *Ecole
Normale*, taking the part of a kid in a Jivaro ritual from which men
are generally excluded.

The *ujaj* is a kind of feminine equivalent of the *anemat*, a collective
ritual in which the wives and mothers of the warriors express their
solidarity in the current venture in a continuous chorus lasting from
dusk to dawn, during the nights when their men are out on the
warpath. Identifying themselves with the objectives of war and seeking
to guide its progress, the women keep up a series of allegorical incantations aimed at warning the fighters of the dangers that threaten them
and protecting them. It is an exercise in magic prophylaxis, as is
testified by the tirelessly repeated refrain of '*ujajai!*' (I warn you, I
advise you'). Far from tempering the violence of the warriors, their
women seek to stimulate it, making use of the same brutal images
as the masculine *anent*, and sometimes rendering them even more

bloodthirsty. The men are compared to jaguars, anacondas, predators, lying in wait like wild beasts, tearing their prey to pieces with their teeth, feeding on their flesh and relishing their blood. But the most common *ujaj* are those that urge the fighters to beware of the death that seeks to entrap them. Death is always designated by the same metaphors, *anku nanki* or 'spear of twilight', *waa nanki* or 'hollow spear' (rifle), 'duck-spear' (a fishing harpoon with a lozenge-shaped tip), to the accompaniment of the constantly repeated injunction, 'Dodge it nimbly!' While crude terms may be acceptable to describe the death in store for one's foes, references to the risk run by those close to one can only be made allusively: the women can thus ward off what they all fear without daring to say so.

With no respite, the sequence of *ujaj* continues, constructing a protective barrier against the death-bearing spears.

> Woman that I am, swallow-woman that I am
> I cleave through the ranks of the shrimps
> Woman that I am, swallow-woman that I am
> I cleave through the ranks of the shrimps
> We both have plumage bronzed in the light
> *Ouheu-heu-heu! Ouheu! Ouheu-hai!*
> *Ahaa! A-hou! Ahou-hai! Ahaa! Hou-hou-hai!*
> Woman that I am, swallow-woman that I am
> We are both nimble at dodging
> Our plumages are bronzed in the light
> *Ouheu-heu-heu! Ouheu! Ouheu-hai!*
> *A-haa! A-hou! Ahou-hai!*
> *Ahaa! Hou-hou-hai!*

Another purpose of the *ujaj* is to afford protection against a different danger, more subtle than a rifle-shot and seldom named: the *emesak*, the spectre of vengeance that emanates from the slain enemy and comes to harass his killer and his family. Like the acrobatic swallow whose plumage reflects the light, the woman and her victorious husband dodge the *emesak*, deflecting it into the distance, mercifully preserved from the doom-laden consequences of the killing. Even more than *arutam* or Iwianch, *emesak*, 'that which is harmful', is a concept that is – no doubt deliberately – ill-defined, and its powerful evocation of doom is greatly enhanced by the very imprecision with which the Achuar describe its nature and its effects. *Emesak* emanates from the victim's *wakan* as a frenzied desire for revenge, a kind of vindictive intention that is initially devoid of any material form but is sometimes capable of injecting its ill-will into various agents: snakes, poisonous insects or even a tree that falls for no obvious reason upon the killer or a member of his family. Above all, the *emesak* haunts the sleep of the murderer. By tormenting the object of its resentment night after night with ill-omened dreams, it becomes a dangerous weakening agent, exposing its victim to contamination from *sunkur* and making him an easy target for sorcery. In that it forestalls a loss of energy, sexual abstinence after a murder to some extent guards against *emesak* attacks. It also stabilizes the newly acquired *arutam*: little by little this becomes the best antidote against the harmful *emesak*, which will then be frustrated in its designs by a force stronger than itself and, once its *raison d'être* has disappeared, will be forced to return to nothingness.

The voices are growing hoarse, the farandoles more sluggish, but the succession of *ujaj* is unflagging, a refrain repeated over and over again yet with words that are always changing. Around midnight the women begin to take it in turns, so that there are always seven or eight singers in the circle, while the others take a rest. From time to time Untsumak blows tobacco juice into their noses to keep them awake and to stimulate their concentration. We are awash in a whirlpool of allegories, fleeting images and mysterious allusions to a humanized bestiary that seems to embody the entire gamut of properties both desirable and harmful. My mind, numbed by the effort of staying awake and the repetitive refrains, here and there catches fleeting phrases, scraps of a bizarre fable introduced with neither prologue nor follow-up: 'Show us the slain sloth! Is it not time to rejoice?' . . . 'Spilt on to the ground, barely quivering, my brother has become a midnight-blue anaconda' . . . 'Swallow-woman, I am waiting with my few companions' . . . 'Vanishing into the depths to avoid the poison fishing, the *wampi* fish has fired his rifle' . . . 'Convulsively opening and closing his talons, my brother the kite falls upon his nephew' . . . 'Here I go with a firm step, striking the ground with the feet of a thrush' . . . Making the most of a moment's respite that Untsumak is allowing herself and seized, despite my weariness, by a renewed curiosity, I seek enlightenment from her: Why the sloth? Why does the kite-brother carry off his own nephew? Why is the *wampi* fish called father-in-law? What does the thrush represent? And, above all, who are these songs addressed to? Unlike in the *anent*, whole strings of kinship terms appear in the greatest confusion, mixing up affines and blood-relatives in obscure actions in which it is hard to make out who is doing what. But she does not know. She learned the *ujaj* from her mother, exactly as *tushimp*, the golden-collared woodpecker, once taught them to men so that they would remain beyond the reach of *emesak*, like the anaconda, safe under the waters in its lair.

In fact, thanks to a vain triumph of writing over memory, I probably know more than Untsumak does about the meaning and origin of the rite that she is directing. In the protective songs these women have been repeating for hours without really understanding their contents, I recognize the principal themes of the *ujaj* used by the Shuar in the *tsantsa* ritual, for these were carefully noted down by a Salesian missionary and I had a chance to study them not long ago. Each category of animal is associated with particular figures that take part in the ritual. The sloth symbolizes the shrunken head and the *emesak* that emanates from it; the predators, swallows and thrushes represent the group of 'the tobacco-sated ones', the pivot of which is the murderer; the anaconda, the feline creatures and the *wampi* symbolize *arutam* mounting guard to keep the *emesak* at bay. The various kinship terms designate the positions occupied by the actors in the rite, each in turn, in this long exercise designed to achieve a metamorphosis of identities that will lead to the birth of a perfectly consanguineous child. It is in that ceremonial context that the *ujaj* take on their full significance, as ordered sequences in a vast liturgy to which they help to give meaning and whose efficacy they in part ensure. But the Achuar have lost even the memory of the great *tsantsa* festival that they must have practised in bygone days. All they have retained from that grandiose edifice are a few remnants faithfully handed down from one generation to the next and fervently pieced together again each time circumstances require the revival of a function whose full original significance has vanished. For them, as for me, all that remains is the thrill of thinking focused entirely in the present moment, obstinately refusing to call things by their names lest over-insistence should either wither them or make them last for ever. This is thinking that touches lightly upon things, reflects them, picks up their vibrations, thinking that is forged in a viscous world in flux, in which even death must be decked in the gleams of the setting sun if it is to confront the continuity of time:

> The spear of twilight is coming, son, my son
> Quick, dodge it!
> The hollow spear is coming, son, my son
> My son, Sun, the spear of twilight is coming for you
> Quick, dodge it!
> The *emesak*, as it is called
> Let it not lie in wait for you, son, my son
> Let it not behold you with the clear vision of *natem* trances
> As they gradually bear you away
> Let each of your steps be disguised as a chonta palm.

Epilogue

'What is truth? Conformity between our judgements
and beings.'

DENIS DIDEROT,
Discussions on the Natural Son

BETWEEN THIS MOMENT, as I near the end of the chronicle that I
have been writing intermittently over a whole decade, and the beginning of the experiences that it relates, just over sixteen years have
passed. That alone would be enough to turn it into a kind of fiction.
To be sure, the time of narrative is never that of action, but the reason
why I chose to evoke the past in the present tense was partly to help
the reader to sense the freshness of an astonishment whose novelty is
by now no more than a memory for me, and partly also to convince
myself that I truly did once feel it. It is true that my field journal has
constantly guided me into enclaves of my memory, bringing back to
me, as though it were yesterday, my initial wide-eyed naivety, my
infinitely slow advances in understanding, and the occasional joys of
suddenly seeing how things fitted together. But the man writing these
pages is no longer quite the one who came upon the Achuar all those
years ago, and fiction is also born of that slippage in time. Like all
those who try their hands at autobiography, I have been unable to
avoid superimposing upon the emotions and judgements that my
journal delivered up to me in all their ingenuousness the feelings and
ideas that happen to have stemmed from my subsequent existence. I
would like to think that these interpolations are not so much retrospective embellishments but rather plausible expansions of what I
might have written at the time. But the fact remains that they were
thought and written later, as are all ethnological monographs. That
is the main reason why this book has something in common with a
novel. Ethnologists are creators as well as chroniclers, and although
the *mores* and remarks of the people whose lives they have shared

401

are in general accurately reported and, so far as possible, correctly translated, the way in which they present and interpret them is a personal matter. By giving free rein to our own particular talents, imagination, prejudices, doctrinal orientation and temperament, the accounts that we produce of one and the same culture are sometimes so sharply contrasted that they are barely recognizable as stemming from the same source. Ethnologists, who must construct a representation of a society by writing alone, cannot possibly deliver a faithful copy of the reality observed. Rather, they offer as it were a scale model, a likeness of the salient features of the prototype, which may never be fully described.

But rest assured: I have not imagined the events and characters that provide the material of this story. Each scene truly did take place in the chronological order in which I have narrated it, in the place where I situate it, and with the protagonists whose behaviour I have described. Only their names have been changed so as not to embarrass their descendants in case, with predictable advances in the spread of literacy, they might one day happen to read my book. But on to that measure of truth are grafted two literary effects that ethnologists are bound to exploit, even if they are sometimes loath to admit it: that of composition, which selects from the continuity of lived experience particular clips of action which are reckoned to be more significant than others; and that of generalization, which invests these fragments of individual behaviour with a meaning that can in principle be extended to the entire culture under consideration.

From the thousands of pages of my field notebooks – which were themselves already filtered out from all that I had witnessed and, besides, only reflect the situations in which I happened, by chance, to find myself – I have had to select particular scenes, particular conversations and particular characters. And that has meant eliminating others that a different observer might have thought more significant. I have had to break the linear thread of time and draw on opportune memories to juxtapose a whole mass of disparate facts that should, perhaps, have been kept separate. Such procedures of composition were also used by novelists of the naturalistic school. Like them, an ethnologist profoundly reworks the basic material of his investigations, lifting from their context certain statements, events and aspects of behaviour which he proceeds to present as examples of a particular social situation or belief and which, in his book, acquire a life that is almost as independent of their original context as if they had been used to give substance to a novel. Nevertheless, the technique I have adopted certainly respects the process of acquiring understanding rather better than most scholarly works. The latter tend to present long, abstract analyses of particular cultural phenomena, sometimes appending an example – an expository device that avoids recognizing that the illustration is in truth both the starting point and the legitimization of the analysis. I, on the other hand, have been careful not to embark upon general comments until I had described the case that provided the matter for reflection. The chance unfolding of your fieldwork experience entirely commands the progress you make. During the first months, before you have mastered the language, you are deaf and dumb, reduced to observing attitudes, how space is used, techniques, and the ritualization of daily life, ever alert to sounds and smells in an unfamiliar environment, obliged to adapt physically to new customs, precautions, and forms of sensibility. Only as snatches of conversation at last become comprehensible do you gradually emerge from this immersion in material life. It is a process of revelation comparable to the sudden appearance of subtitles in a foreign film, the development of which you had until then only been able to piece together from the expressiveness of the acting. At this point it becomes possible to glimpse the full complexity of social life – not, initially, as to the rules that govern it, but the interplay of individual strategies, conflicts of interest, and contrary ambitions, and the expression of passions and the dialectics of feelings. Finally, much later, once you have some command of the language and the strangeness of certain beliefs and rituals has been dissipated through repetition, you can begin to speak more profoundly about them, almost with an illusion of being part of them. Then, and only then, does it become possible to return to the winding ways of thought. In the studies of earlier times these necessary different stages in the ethnographic enquiry were clearly identifiable in the conventional division of the work into three parts; these covered the economy, the society, and the religion. Naive and clumsy though this approach may have been when it came to interpreting a culture as an indivisible totality, it nevertheless did respect an implicit correspondence between the ways of understanding and the ways of presenting the results of that understanding. So it should not be surprising if traces of that method are detectable in the present work.

Literary composition means reorganizing reality to make it more accessible, and sometimes more worthy of interest, but it does not alter the substance of the facts. Interpretation, however, when it endeavours to reveal the significance of those facts, does give them a new dimension. Interpretation operates through invention, and there are no real guarantees to prevent it spilling over into the imaginary. Unlike a sociologist, an ethnologist analysing a culture cannot rely upon a statistical apparatus capable of predicting the norm on the basis of the frequency of particular occurrences. Instead, he must rely on his own inferences, intuitively constructed from a cloud of partial observations and fragments of the discourse of a handful of individuals. Consequently, in this book, as in any such work, the singular constantly serves as a springboard for the universal. How is it possible to pass, without excessive fraudulence, from a part to the whole – from the statement, 'Wajari told me that . . .' to the proposition, 'The Achuar think that . . .' and then from that proposition to the explanation, 'The Achuar think this for such or such a reason'? In the first place, by checking that the interpretation that I saw fit to draw from what Wajari told me is supported by Naanch or Tsukanka, or at least is not explicitly called into question by them. But also, and above all, by testing its validity by comparison. Interpreting a cultural phenomenon involves comparing it to other phenomena of the same nature that have already been described in neighbouring populations and also gauging how much it differs from what we ourselves know of the way it is expressed in our own culture. The perception of time, the union of a man and a woman, power struggles, and the concept of death are all part of a patrimony that is common to all peoples, and it is the distance perceived between on the one hand our own way of coping with all the little challenges that beset us and, on the other, what we manage to apprehend of it amongst other peoples that constitutes the true motivating force of ethnology. A long stay in an exotic society almost automatically prompts a kind of self-reassessment, with paradoxical results. When we step back from the life and institutions that have formed us, we soon realize how relative they are; and this renewed sense that our own way of looking at things is conditioned by very particular underlying cultural influences prevents us from adopting a condescending attitude towards the equal relativity of the values of the people we profess to be observing. To evoke this self-reflexive experience that all ethnologists live through is not to suggest that subjectivity is the best mode of learning. Rather, it is a way of emphasizing the obvious enough fact that the judgements we pass on the *mores* of others are largely determined, in life generally as well as in scholarship, by our own individual histories. Like the Achuar, who discriminate between levels of reality according to the fields of perception and the types of communication peculiar to them, an ethnologist does not believe in immutable correspondences between words and things. His work cannot dissociate description from invention and, even if the latter does not necessarily imply falsity, what it produces is closer to likeness than to truth.

Does this reduce ethnology to no more than a hermeneutics of cultures that turns out to be incapable of producing any general propositions on human beings in society? I do not think so, for it is probably the very subjectivity of our discipline that assures its wider import. The exercise of decentralizing oneself makes it possible to acquire a few basic convictions born of the manifest mismatch between what we are gradually discovering and what hitherto we had, more or less unconsciously, held to be universal. These convictions are all the stronger because they proceed from our own lived experience of otherness and from the strong sense of naturalness we feel when we identify with the way of being in the world that is temporarily dominant for us. And they are all the more legitimate given that others, before ourselves, in other regions of the world, have already felt them equally strongly. When I assess the personal lessons that my life among the Achuar has taught me, I realize that they almost all have an anthropological value that transcends the particularity of the circumstances in which they were formulated.

The first of those lessons, and perhaps the most important, is that nature is not something that exists everywhere and always; or, to be more precise, that the radical separation so long established by the West between the world of nature and the world of human beings does not have much meaning for other peoples who, for their part, confer the attributes of social life upon plants and animals, regarding these as subjects rather than objects, and who could therefore not possibly expel them into an autonomous sphere upon which science and technology gradually come to impose their mathematical laws and control. To say that the Indians are 'close to nature' is a kind of nonsense for, since they confer upon the beings that people it a dignity equal to their own, their behaviour towards them is not significantly different from their behaviour towards one another. In order for anyone to be close to nature, nature must exist; and it is only the moderns who have proved capable of conceiving its existence, a fact that probably renders our cosmology more enigmatic and less sympathetic than the cosmologies of all the cultures that have preceded us.

The Achuar have also taught me that it is possible to live out one's personal destiny without the aid of either divine or historical transcendence, those two branched alternatives that we have been arguing about for over a century. For them, an individual, in all his uniqueness, is not determined by any superior or exterior principle, is not activated by any vast, long-term collective moments of which he is not aware, nor is he defined by his place in a complex social hierarchy which will give his life meaning in accordance with the position into which he has happened to be born. For them, neither predestination, nor the messianism of mass movements, nor the pre-eminence of the whole over its parts plays the role that goes to each person's ability to affirm his identity by his actions, according to a scale of desirable goals that is shared by all. But, unlike the individualism of modern societies, which is a product of the few who have passed beyond a condition that was once common to all, the Achuar individualism is to some extent a quite original variety. It is not based upon any claim to social or economic equality, since it has not been preceded by any inegalitarian system. Nor does it regard the individual as the source of all values and the motivating force behind all innovations, since the Achuar's common subscription to a code of behaviour reputed to be eternal rules out the possibility of anyone setting himself apart from it or establishing new rules of conduct. Just like that 'spear of twilight' that from time to time threatens those who have acquired renown by killing an enemy, each person's destiny is thus immanent in his works yet is in a way identical for all.

Because the idea of progress is so very much a product of our own age, perhaps the hardest thing for me to accept was that it is possible to regard time as non-cumulative. Of course I knew that the concept of oriented time is not universal and that faith in a historical becoming is a very recent invention. But despite my knowledge, and despite the scepticism that it had aroused in me with respect to the mirages of contemporary ideology, I found it extremely difficult to understand, other than on an abstract level, the system of multiple temporalities that governs the life of the Achuar. The fact is that at this point I had reached the limit in my ability to identify with others: of all the atavisms that we receive from our culture, our way of measuring time is the one that most rapidly becomes indivisible from our ability to know things. Even the way in which the Achuar represented their relations to whatever is perceptible or intelligible was less difficult for me to understand – if, that is, I have not in fact got it all wrong – since philosophy had taught me to think about the relativity of theories of knowledge. This critical baggage of mine was a great help to me when it came to passing beyond the evidence of common sense and discovering among the Achuar a new, if not entirely original way of reconciling the needs of their understanding and the properties of matter. I discovered with pleasure that beliefs that appeared irrational turned out to pay subtle attention to relations between different categories of sensibility, the facts of language and the scale of beings, in a system of thought daily put into action by living men – however exotic and however few – rather than imagined by some past thinker. This provided me with a comforting alternative to the depressing dualism in which a certain line of modern thought has sought to confine us.

Another encouraging lesson I learned was from the way in which the Achuar live out their collective identity without encumbering themselves with a national consciousness. In Europe from the end of the eighteenth century onwards, the historical and ideological movement for the emancipation of peoples has sought to base claims for political autonomy solely upon a shared cultural or linguistic tradition. In contrast, the Jivaros do not conceive of their ethnicity as a catalogue of distinctive characteristics that might confer substance and eternity upon a shared destiny. Their common existence does not derive its meaning from their language, their religion or their past, nor even from a mystical attachment to a territory believed to embody all the values upon which their individuality rests. Instead, it is sustained by a common way of experiencing social links and relations with neighbouring peoples – relations that are, it is true, sometimes expressed in a bloody fashion – not by consigning others to a non-human status, but by fostering an acute consciousness that they are, be they friends or enemies, necessary for the perpetuation of their own identity. The Achuar offered to me a contrary demonstration that ethnic nationalisms, in all the barbarity of some of their manifestations, are not so much a heritage from pre-modern societies, but rather result from ancient styles of organization becoming contaminated by modern doctrines of State hegemony. What history has done it may undo, proving that the tribalism of contemporary nations is not inevitable and that our present way of signifying difference by exclusion might one day give way to a more fraternal sociability.

These lessons, together with a number of others that I will leave my readers to work out for themselves, emerge from the toing and froing between identification and a sense of otherness occasioned by an ethnographic experience: identification with sentiments, moral questioning, ambitions, and frames of mind that you think you recognize in others since you have experienced them yourself, yet upon which types of expression that are at first sight strange immediately confer a kind of objective externality. It is this revelation that then, in return, affects our own cultural frameworks, suddenly and by analogy illuminating the particular point of view that they convey. So is ethnology really just a relativist aesthetic that offers, as it were, a retrospective and disenchanted counterbalance to the positivist values of our modern world? That is certainly a criticism frequently levelled at it. Time and again we ethnologists have been reproached for promoting the dissolution of the great principles whose universality the contemporary Western world is always praising, purely on the grounds that we refuse to establish an assured hierarchy arranging in order of merit all the different ways of living out the human condition. When we declare that science provides no criteria to justify claims that such and such a culture is inferior or superior to another, our critics conclude that we are bent upon insidiously undermining the idea of liberty, respect for human individuals, equal rights, the demands of reason and even the great works of art and intelligence of which our civilization may legitimately be proud. We are judged to have been carried away by our admiration for the peoples we study and to have become incapable of discrimination, convinced that where artistic expression, social rules and personal ethics are concerned there is nothing to choose between one type and another, and all deserve to be defended equally.

But such a judgement misunderstands the nature of our endeavour. The ambition of ethnology is to shed some light upon the reasons that account for the distribution of cultural differences, and this rules out setting up as timeless norms particular forms of behaviour, modes of thought, and institutions which, for all that they are widely accepted, represent but one of the many possible combinations that make up a universe of social existence. However, this methodological relativism does not necessarily imply moral relativism; it may even prove to be its best antidote. What better way of sifting out what is essential from what is not in all that fashions your social personality than to be suddenly transplanted into an exotic tribe where you are out of your depth in everything except yourself? In these circumstances, you are bound to ponder on what makes up your identity, on what impels you to action and on what repels it, on what justifies your attachment to certain values of your native community and leads you to reject others. You are bound to dwell upon the basic reasons that cause you to love a particular view or book, a piece of music or a picture, the lack of which sharpens your memory of it; and you are bound even to consider, more carefully than those never deprived of them, the charm of the little familiar pleasures that you never imagined you would miss so much and that weave the inconspicuous web of your own particular cultural identity. Far from leading me to an improbable adoption of beliefs and modes of life so very distant from those that formed my sensibility and judgements, my few years living amongst the Achuar on the contrary brought home to me the virtues of the critical eye that our civilization has lately cast upon the world and upon itself, in a new attempt, possibly unprecedented in history, to found an understanding of others upon the revelation of one's own illusions. We have turned the ethnocentricity that is common to all peoples to our own advantage and any hope we may entertain of giving meaning to all the myriad customs and institutions to be found on our planet must depend upon our recognizing our debt to those that make us distinctive, for they have afforded us the unique ability to consider them all as legitimate manifestations of the human condition that we share.

These are fine lessons in philosophy, you may say, but they are not really relevant to the most urgent problems faced by our contemporary world. That is no doubt true, if – that is – we persist in regarding the human sciences as no more than a depository of techniques of secondary importance which enable us to diagnose the cleavages in modern society. Clearly, the Achuar do not offer any solutions to the problems of unemployment, the imbalance between North and South, or mass migration. But, for anyone willing to reflect without prejudice upon our immediate future, some of the questions that they have tried to resolve in their own way nevertheless do provide a full-scale thought experiment. The ability to rise above our frenetic attempts to dominate nature, to wipe out our blind nationalisms, to encourage the autonomy of different peoples while retaining a combination of self-awareness and respect for cultural diversity, to adopt new ways of coming to terms with the proliferation of hybrid objects that have become extensions of our own bodies: all this is what is at stake in our modern life, and it could be profitable to consider it by analogy with the concepts of the world that peoples such as the Achuar have forged for themselves. To be sure, no historical experience is transposable and the vocation of ethnology is not to offer alternative ways of life. But it does provide a means of stepping back from a present all too often conceived to be eternal by, for example, pointing out the wide variety of the paths open to us in the future. A few thousand Indians dotted about in a distant jungle are certainly worth as much attention as any volume of dubious futurology, and even if their present tribulations evoke nothing but indifference on the part of human beings too impatient to feel love for themselves in different guises, let us at least acknowledge that in their destiny, which has for so long been different from our own, we may perhaps glimpse a fate that is in store for ourselves.

Spelling

Jivaro is an isolated language, traditionally oral rather than written, of an agglutinate nature, that is to say its words are formed from radicals to which chains of suffixes are added, constituting so many indications of syntactical functions or specifications of mode, aspect, result, etc. Missionary publications and the didactic material used to promote literacy currently use a standard mode of transcribing Jivaro that is based on Spanish phonology. Although this transcription is not very rigorous phonetically, I have adopted it in this book so as to conform with common usage. Let me simply mention the vowels and consonants whose Spanish pronunciation is different from English:

'u' is pronounced 'oo'
'n' is pronounced 'oon'
'in' is pronounced 'een'
'ea' is pronounced 'e-a' (separating the two vowels)
'j' is pronounced as an aspirated 'h' (as in the Spanish *jota*)
'sh' is pronounced 'ch', and 'ch' is pronounced 'tch'.

Glossaries

achira
: *Renealmia alpinia*, a cultivated plant of the Zingiberaceae family (*kumpia* in Achuar).

acouchi
: *Myoprocta sp.*, a rodent similar to the agouti but smaller (*shaak* in Achuar).

affine
: relative by marriage or marriageable.

affinity
: real or potential link by marriage between two affines.

agami
: trumpet-bird (*Psophia crepitans*), (*chiwia*, in Achuar).

agouti
: *Dasyprocta sp.*, rodent the size of a rabbit, with succulent flesh (the Achuar distinguish two species: *kayuk* and *yunkits*).

aguaje
: swamp palm (*Mauritia flexuosa*), edible fruits, typical swamp vegetation (*achu* in Achuar).

Aguaruna
: Jivaro tribe of Peru.

Antuas
: Indians of the Andoas region on the Pastaza in Peru.

arrowroot
: *Maranta ruiziana*, cultivated plant (*chiki* in Achuar).

ayahuasca
: hallucinogenic beverage made from the *Banisteriopsis* liana, a term of Quichua origin used in Ecuador and Peru.

balata
: a type of natural rubber of quality inferior to that of *Hevea* rubber.

barbasco
: generic name for fish poison in Upper Amazonia.

cabiai or water hog
: also called capybara; a very large rodent, the size of a pig, living in herds along the river banks.

cacique
: *Psarocolius decumanus*, black bird with a yellow tail belonging to the Icteridae (oriole), family (*chuwi* in Achuar).

caimito
: *Pouteria caimito*, a Sapotacea cultivated for its fruits (*yaas* in Achuar).

Candoshi
: tribe speaking the Candoa language, culturally close to the Jivaros, lower Pastaza region, Peru.

Canelos	Indians speaking the Quichua language, from the upper Bobonaza region in Ecuador.
candirú	*Vandellia wieneri*, a tiny parasitic fish (*kanir* in Achuar).
canna	*Heliconia sp.*, wild species of Musaceae.
cedro	*Cedrela sp.*, tree used for making canoes.
chambira	*Astrocarym chambira* palm; the fruits are edible and the fibres are used for making thin ropes (*mata* in Achuar).
chonta	*Bactris gasipaes*, palm tree cultivated for its fruits (*uwi* in Achuar).
clibadium	*Clibadium sp.*, cultivated plant used as fishing poison (*masu* in Achuar).
coati	*Nasua nasua*, small carnivore with grey-brown fur and a tail ringed with black-and-white bands (*kushi* in Achuar).
Cocama	tribe speaking the Tupi language, on the lower Ucayali in Peru.
compadrazgo	link of spiritual kinship established at the baptism of a child.
compadre	mutual term of address used by men linked by *compadrazgo*.
cross-cousins	for a man or a woman, all the children of the father's sister and of the mother's brother.
enganche	the advance, on credit, of manufactured objects, allowed to Indians by *regatones* in exchange for natural products that they have gathered. Exorbitant taxes make the debt virtually unredeemable.
genipa	*Genipa americana*, cultivated plant used to make a black dye (*sua* in Achuar).
granadilla	a species of *Passiflora*, tree with edible fruits (*munchij* in Achuar).
grosbeak	*Pitylus grossus*, dark grey bird with a red beak, the size of a blackbird.
hoazin	*Opisthocomus hoazin*, bird that nests in trees growing beside rivers (*sasa* in Achuar).
hog-nosed skunk	*Conepatus sp.*, a kind of large badger living along the river banks (*juicham* in Achuar)
Huambisa	Jivaro tribe in Peru.
inga	a genera of leguminous plant, both wild and cultivated, with edible fruits.
ishpingo	*Nectandra cinnamonoides*, the fruits of this wild species, the taste of which is close to cinnamon, are one of the

	principal products in the bartering trade of central Ecuadorian Amazonia.
ivory palm	see Llarina.
labret	ornamental stick fixed into a small aperture pierced under the lower lip.
lagotrix	woolly monkey; *Lagothrix cana*, large monkey with russet fur and a black face (*chuu* in Achuar).
Lamistas	tribe speaking the Quichua language, mid Huallaga region, Peru.
levirate	the duty of a man to marry the widows of his brothers.
llarina	ivory palm, *Phytelephas sp.*; the inner fibres of the stem are used to make broom heads and the kernel of the fruits provides a vegetable type of ivory; important in the bartering trade of Upper Amazonia and on the Pacific coast (*chaapi* in Achuar).
lonchocarp	*Lonchocarpus sp.*, a cultivated leguminous plant, used as a poison for catching fish (*timiu* in Achuar).
Mayn	Jivaro tribe of Peru, also called Maynas.
morpho	large butterfly with blue-and-black wings, common throughout Upper Amazonia.
naranjilla	*Solanum coconilla*, cultivated species with edible fruits, typical of the tropical regions of Ecuador (*kukuch* in Achuar).
paca	*Cuniculus paca*, rodent resembling a very large guinea pig, russet fur with white spots (*kashai* in Achuar).
parallel cousins	for a man or a woman, all the children of sisters of the mother or brothers of the father.
pasillo	popular music typical of the Andes of Ecuador.
Penelope-bird	bird the size of a pheasant (*aunts* in Achuar).
Pishtaco	a Quichua term for certain Whites reputed to kill Indians to extract their fat (Ecuador, Peru, Bolivia).
pongo	deep gulch containing whirlpools, in the narrows of a river-bed passing through a gorge.
pusanga	love philtre, a Quichua term used in Ecuador and Peru.
Quichua (or Quechua):	the language spoken by several million Indians of the Andes and the Amazonian plains of Ecuador, Peru and Bolivia.
regatón	a river pedlar engaged in barter with the Indians (see also *enganche*).
rocou	*Bixa orellana*, cultivated plant used for red dye.

saïmiri	squirrel monkey, small monkey with grey-russet fur and a long tail (*tsenkush* in Achuar).
saki	*Pithecia monachus*, monkey with long brown-black fur and a white head (*sepur* in Achuar).
Shuar	Jivaro tribe in Ecuador.
stramonium	common name for several species of cultivated *Datura*.
supai	spirit in Quichua; denotes in particular magic 'darts' and the spirits that assist shamans.
swamp palm	see *aguaje*.
sweetsop, or chirimoya	*Anona squamosa*, tree cultivated for its delicious fruits (*keach* in Achuar).
swidden	plot of land cleared in the forest and cultivated for a few years before being abandoned.
tamandua	*Tamandua tetradactyla*, a species of anteater.
tamarin (or marmoset)	*Saguinus illigeri*, small, black monkey with a white moustache (*tsepi* in Achuar).
tambero	native employed by the army to keep paths clear.
tayra	*Tayra barbara*, a very aggressive species of mustelidae, the size of a large polecat (*amich* in Achuar).
trumpet-bird	see *agami*.
Waorani	a tribe with an isolated language, better known by the name Auca ('wild' in Quichua); central Ecuadorian Amazonia.
woolly monkey	see lagotrix.
Zaparo	a tribe with an isolated language, now extinct; only a few individuals married to Quichuas survive; central Ecuadorian Amazonia.

JIVARO (ACHUAR) VOCABULARY

achu	swamp palm or *aguaje*.
aents	'person'; any entity endowed with a *wakan*, soul, and reputed to be capable of communication and understanding; includes human beings, plants, animals and objects.
ajaimp	mythological character; a race of cannibalistic giants, now vanished.
ajutap	the Aguaruna equivalent of *arutam*.
akaru	rifle, from the Spanish *arcabuz*.
amana	individual representing the prototype of each species of hunted animals and responsible for watching over his fellows. A hunter must win his favour.
amaran	species of venomous ant; mythological figure responsible for the coming of definitive death.
amasank	one of the spirits who are 'mothers of hunted animals', responsible in particular for watching over toucans.
amik	ceremonial friend.
anemat	ritual before setting out for war.
anent	sung incantation, used in all circumstances, whether ordinary or ritual, to obtain some desirable result or win the favour of the addressee.
apach	generic term used to designate Quichuas and Spanish-speaking Whites.
arawir	a viol with two strings, probably copied from the European violin.
arutam	an immaterial principle embodied in the ghost of an ancestor during a trance induced by hallucinogenics, which confers strength and protection upon the recipient of the revelation.

atsanmartin	ceremonial monologue in which the master of a house refuses admittance to a visitor.
aujmatin	'conversation'; grand ceremonial dialogue with visitors.
charapa	large water turtle (*Podocnemis expansa*).
chimpui	sculpted stool of the master of the house.
chirichiri	cyperus; various species of Graminaceae used in the pharmacopoeia.
chukuch	malaria.
ekent	the women's part of the house.
emesak	'the harmful one'; an immaterial principle emanating from an enemy killed in war that returns to harass the killer.
ijiampramu	a dance, only danced during drinking parties.
imimketin	a grave disorder provoked by the soul of a dead person becoming embodied in a child.
impikmartin	ceremonial monologue used as an invective against an enemy during a battle or to let an enemy know that his presence has been detected.
iniayua	the *Maximiliana regia* palm tree; used in particular to make darts for blowpipes.
ipiakratatuin	'invitation'; collective work concluded by a drinking party offered by the beneficiary of the neighbourly help.
itip	cotton loincloth worn by men.
iwianch	spirits of the dead embodied in animals or in anthropoid ghosts; a generic term designating certain harmful manifestations of the supernatural world or of shamanistic practices.
jurijri	one of the 'mothers of hunted animals', a cannibalistic, bearded, troglodyte spirit, responsible in particular for watching over monkeys.
juunt	'great man'; a term of respect for great warriors who are faction leaders.
kakaram	man of valour.
kamak	type of tree used to make *tantar* shields.
kampanak	*Hyospatha sp.*, small palm tree used to make roof coverings.

kantse	a cultivated Amaranthacea used in the pharmacopoeia.
karamprar	a dream of communication with a being spatially or ontologically distant.
karis	ornamental tubes worn by men in their ear lobes.
kirinku	a White who does not speak Spanish; from the Spanish *gringo*.
kujamak	indisposition provoked in someone by the mocking thoughts of those around.
kumpa	from the Spanish *compadre*.
kunkuk	*Jessenia weberbaueri*; palm tree with edible fruits.
kuntuknar	a dream of favourable omen for hunting.
kusea	fish of the *Brycon* (Characidae) genus.
kutank	little wooden bench reserved for visitors.
machap	a liana of the *Phoebe* genus, used for making curare.
maen	spittle or mucus containing a shaman's magic 'darts'.
mamu	'mouldering'; a lesion reputed to be contagious, characterized by necrosis and ulcers.
mesekramprar	dream of ill omen.
muits	fermentation jar for manioc beer.
musach	the Pleiades constellation and mythological characters.
musap	love philtre.
namper	a party.
nampet	a party drinking song.
namuk	very fermented beer consumed during the ritual *anemat* before setting out for war.
namur	a stone concretion found in the bodies of certain animals, which serves as a charm for hunting or fishing.
nantar	a magic stone used as a charm for gardening.
nasemar	'blowing'; a chill caused in a child by contact with a shade of the dead.
natem	hallucinogenic beverage for shamans, made from the *Banisteriopsis* liana.
nijiamanch	manioc beer.

421

nunkui	a mythological figure, the creator and mistress of cultivated plants.
nupir	a Sapotacea, the fruits of which are used as little bells.
paati	Salesian missionaries; from the Spanish *padre*.
pajum	'sudden fright'; an organic disorder caused in a child by a terrifying vision, usually of some supernatural entity.
pankerista	Protestant missionaries; from the Spanish *evangelista*.
panki	anaconda.
panku	a type of particularly rare and famous shaman, capable of being possessed by the spirits of the dead.
pasuk	a generic term used to designate a shaman's helpers.
pasun	qualifies an event believed to be of ill omen.
pausak	'contamination' emanating from a dead person.
peak	a bed made from palm or bamboo slats.
peem	a short flute for playing *anent*.
pininkia	a decorated earthenware bowl used for drinking manioc beer.
pinkui	a transverse flute for playing dance music.
piripiri	several species of cultivated Piperaceae used in the pharmacopoeia.
pirisuk	*Althernanthera lanceolata*, an Amaranthacea used in the pharmacopoeia.
pitiak	a basket with a lid in which men keep their personal possessions.
pransis	'French', from the Spanish *francés*.
putsumar	'paling', a kind of anaemia reputed to be contagious.
shaam	a spirit, one of the 'mothers of hunted animals'; lives in marshes and manifests itself mainly by whimpering sounds heard through the mists.
shakaim	master spirit of the forest; the creator and tender of wild plants.
shakap	belt adorned with bells worn by women at parties.
shauk	glass beads.
shimiut	*Apeiba membranacea*, a tree of the Tiliaceae family.

shinki-shinki	the sheaf of leaves used by a shaman, made from a wild Piperacea of the same name.
shiwiar	a Jivaro tribal enemy: designates any Jivaro speaking a different dialect and with whom no link of kinship is recognized.
sunkipi	a poisonous wild Aracea, sometimes consumed by women to commit suicide.
sunkur	'sickness'; any organic disorder not directly attributable to a shaman.
tachau	a black-coated varnished earthenware plate.
tampunch	an indisposition produced by the use of an object that has been lent or given.
tanish	protective palisade of palm trees constructed around the houses of those at war.
tankamash	the men's part of a house.
tantar	a round shield.
tapimiur	'sudden fright'; an organic disorder provoked in a child by a vision of a dead person's soul.
tarach	a piece of cotton cloth used to make a loincloth for a woman (*pampaynia*).
tarimiat	first wife.
tashimpiu	musical instrument played with a bow.
taun	*Aspidosperma megalocarpon*, an Apocynacea with a thin, straight trunk that is used for rods and poles.
tawasap	a crown made from the black, red, and yellow feathers of the toucan; a masculine ornament.
titipiur	a spirit that works for shamans, devouring the liver of his victims as they sleep.
tsantsa	the shrunken head of an enemy; the principal element in the *juunt namper* ('great festival') ritual.
tsayantar	mouth bow, a musical instrument one end of which is placed in the mouth, which acts as a resounding chamber.
tseas	curare.
tsentsak	a blowpipe dart; and also the magic 'darts' of shamans.
tsuak	'remedy'.
tsuakratin	a 'healer' shaman.

tsunki	river spirits; creators and holders of shamanistic powers.
tumash	'debt'; used in the context of a deferred exchange, as in a case of vengeance.
tunchi	'sorcery' or spell; designates all organic or psychic disorders provoked by shamans.
tuntui	large drum made from a hollowed-out tree-trunk; it is positioned in the *tankamash* and serves as a means of communication between houses and also for summoning *arutam*.
turuji	*Hyospatha tessmannii*, a small palm tree used for roof coverings.
ujaj	the ritual for protecting and encouraging warriors carried out by their wives during all the nights when the men are away at war; also a song sung in canon peculiar to this ritual.
uwishin	shaman.
uyun	small pouch made of string or leather carried slung across the body by men out hunting or at war.
uyush	a species of sloth (*Choloepus hoffmanni capitalis*); Nunkui's daughter, in mythology.
waje	a potential marriage partner for a man or a woman; this category includes cross-cousins of both sexes (the children of the sisters of fathers and of the brothers of mothers) and also, for a man, the wives of a brother and, for a woman, the brothers of her husband.
wakan	'soul'; a spiritual principle possessed by all 'persons', which makes communication, understanding, and meaning possible; a faculty attributed to human beings but also to plants, animals, and objects.
wampi	a fish of the *Brycon* genus.
waumak	mad, crazy; a person of unpredictable and unseemly behaviour.
wawekratin	qualifies a 'sorceror' shaman.
wayus	a cultivated species of *Ilex*; an infusion made from the leaves and drunk in the early hours of the morning.
wea	the master of ceremonies in the *tsantsa* (shrunken head) ritual amongst the Shuar Jivaros.

424

winchu	canna.
yaitias chicham	'slow talk'; short ritual conversation with visitors.
yakuch	*Hyeronima alchorneoides,* a Euphorbiacea, the fruits of which are a favourite food of toucans.
yanas	the term a man uses to address the wife of a ceremonial friend and a woman uses to address the wife of her husband's ceremonial friend.
yapaipa	a species of cultivated *Verbena* used in the pharmacopoeia.
yaunchu aujmatsamu	'discourse of the olden days'; myth.
yawa	jaguar; the generic term for various species of cats; domesticated dog.
yawa aikiam	a large, blotchy cat-fish (Pimelodidae).
yus	God, from the Spanish *dios.*

Bibliographical Outline

This book is aimed at readers of many kinds and I hope that all will find something of interest in it. To make it accessible to a non-specialist public, I have deliberately kept the text free from notes, bibliographical references, scholarly argument, technical terms, and diagrams – in short, all the scholarly apparatus that can so often intimidate and alienate the lay reader tackling the more conventional ethnological works. The short guide that follows is designed to redress that offhandedness to some extent, and to provide a list of complementary works for those who would like more information. The references mentioned are given chapter by chapter, in the order in which their subject matter arises.

Prologue

There is an abundant literature on the myths that arose in the West as a result of the discovery of the Indians of America. Jean-Pierre Duviols's *L'Amérique espagnole vue et rêvée: les livres de voyage de Christophe Colomb à Bougainville* (Paris, Promodis, 1986) and Tzvetan Todorov's *The Conquest of America: the Question of the Other*, translated by Richard Howard (New York, Harper and Row, 1984) are good introductions to this field. Two major works by Antonello Gerbi are without question the most useful works of reference on the subject: *Nature in the New World: from Christopher Columbus to Gonzalo Fernàndez de Oviedo* (Pittsburgh, 1985), and *The Dispute of the New World: the History of a Polemic, 1750–1900*, translated by J. Moyle, (Pittsburgh, 1973). G. Chinard's work, published in 1913, is still relevant: *L'Amérique et le rêve exotique dans la littérature française du XVIIe et XVIIIe siècles* (Paris, Hachette). On how the sixteenth-century French perceived the Indians of Brazil, a useful work to consult is that by Bernadette Bucher, *La sauvage aux seins pendants* (Paris, Hermann, 1977), as is Frank Lestringant's *L'Atelier du cosmographe, ou l'image du monde à la Renaissance* (Paris, Albin Michel, 1991). Alain Gheerbrant's short work, *L'Amazone, un géant blessé* (Paris, Découvertes Gallimard, 1988), will suit readers in a hurry. Alexander von Humboldt, the pioneering geographer, naturalist, and ethnologist, is probably the first

426

scholar to have presented a modern, scholarly view of the Indians of South America, in the late eighteenth century, and his *Voyage dans l'Amérique équinoxiale* (Paris, Maspero, 1980) is extremely interesting. Although von Humboldt's many books on America met with great success throughout Europe, Hegel does not seem to have made the most of them. The negative, totally imaginary image that he presented of the Amerindians in his course of lectures on the philosophy of history (published in English as *Lectures on the Philosophy of World History. Introduction: Reason in History*, translated by H. B. Nisbit (Cambridge, Cambridge University Press, 1975)), no doubt owed much to the legacy of Buffon (*De l'homme*, Paris, Maspero, 1971), who was, in his turn, influenced by the tendentious accounts of the Jesuits in Paraguay.

On the town of Puyo and the Quichua-speaking Canelos Indians who live in the surrounding neighbourhood, see the two ethnological monographs by Norman Whitten: *Sacha Runa. Ethnicity and Adaptation of Ecuadorian Jungle Quichua* (Urbana, University of Illinois Press, 1976) and *Sicuanga Runa. The Other Side of Development in Amazonian Ecuador* (Urbana, University of Illinois Press, 1985).

The literature on the Jivaros is vast. A bibliography published in 1978 lists over 1,300 titles of articles and short works, to which another fifty that have appeared more recently should be added. Most are accounts of abortive expeditions of exploration, administrative or missionary documents, or idle speculations on shrunken heads written by retired military doctors. There are many reasons for the fascination of these scribblers: the shrunken heads, of course, but also the Jivaros' victorious resistance over more than four centuries to the presence of Whites in a territory as big as Portugal, yet very close to the large towns of the Andes. This wild isolation made them the subject of works of intellectual speculation seemingly made the more verbose in proportion to the Jivaros' inaccessibility. On top of all this, there is the demographic factor, for with a population of around 70,000 they still constitute the largest culturally homogeneous group in Amazonia.

On the image of the Jivaros in the Hispano-American world and in Europe, see the article by Anne Christine Taylor, ' "Cette atroce république de la forêt" . . . Les origines du paradigme jivaro' (*Gradhiva*, 3, 1987). Ethnology on the Jivaros falls into two periods. The first begins with Rafael Karsten's monograph, *The Head-Hunters of Western Amazonas: the Life and Culture of the Jibaro Indians of Eastern Ecuador and Peru* (Helsinki, Societas Scientarum Fennica, 1935). It continues with Matthew Stirling's *Historical and Ethnographical Notes on the Jivaro Indians* (Washington,

Smithsonian Institution Press, 1938), and ends with Michael Harner's *The Jivaros, People of the Sacred Waterfalls* (Garden City, Natural History Press, 1972; the original American edition is dated 1972, but the ethnographic enquiry was conducted essentially in the late fifties). The second period starts in the seventies with a sudden flood of ethnologists of many nationalities, very few of whom, however, have published monographs. Among those that have appeared, see Michael Brown, *Tsewa's Gift, Magic and Meaning in an Amazonian Society* (Washington, Smithsonian Institution Press, 1985) and *Una paz incierta* (Lima, CAAP, n.d.) on the Aguaruna Jivaros; Philippe Descola, *In the Society of Nature. A Native Ecology in Amazonia*, translated by N. Scott (Cambridge, Cambridge University Press, 1994), on the use and concepts of nature among the Achuar Jivaros; and Charlotte Seymour-Smith, *Shiwiar, Identidad étnica y cambio en el rio Corrientes* (Quito-Lima, Abya-Yala-CAAP co-publication, 1988) on the Jivaros of the Corrientes in Peru. It was also in the late seventies that missionaries, Salesians in Ecuador and Jesuits in Peru, began systematically to publish in Spanish the ethnographic material collected during their ministries. It is particularly rich in the field of mythology and ritual, and I shall be referring to it several times in the course of this bibliographical note.

Abbé François Pierre published an account of his adventures on the Bobonaza in his *Voyage d'exploration chez les tribus sauvages de l'Équateur* (Paris, Bureaux de l'année dominicaine, 1889). A descent of the same Bobonaza river is described by Bertrand Flornoy in his *Jivaro: Among the Headshrinkers of the Amazon* (London, Elek, 1953). As for the misfortunes of Isabelle Godin des Odonnais, these are related by her husband Louis in a long letter incorporated into a book by Charles-Marie de La Condamine, *Relation abrégée d'un voyage fait dans l'intérieur de l'Amérique méridionale . . .* (Paris, Veuve Pissot, 1745). Florence Trystram has recently produced a vivid account of Doña Isabelle's journey in a book devoted to the expedition of the French Academicians, *Le Procès des étoiles* (Paris, Seghers, 1979), which I warmly recommend. A selection of texts by La Condamine gives some idea of his travels on the Rio Marañon and the Amazon: *Voyage sur l'Amazone* (Paris, Maspero, 1981). Finally, there could be no better invitation to travel in Ecuador than the journal written by Henri Michaux after his visit there in 1921, *Ecuador. Journal de Voyage*.

Chapters 1, 2, and 3

I have devoted lengthy analyses to the symbolism of the Achuar house and to the techniques of its construction in *In the Society of Nature*, op. cit., chapter 4. On the sociological and ecological effects brought about by switching from a scattered habitat to artificially nucleated settlements, see Philippe Descola, 'Ethnicité et développement économique' in *Indianité, ethnocide, indigénisme en Amérique latine* (Toulouse and Paris, Éditions du CNRS, 1982), and 'From scattered to nucleated settlements: a process of socio-economic change among the Achuar' in Norman Whitten (ed.), *Cultural Transformations and Ethnicity in Modern Ecuador* (Urbana, University of Illinois Press, 1981).

The Jivaro kinship system derives from a type that ethnologists label 'Dravidian', because it was first described in southern India, but it is also to be found in other parts of the world, particularly in much of Amazonia. It is based upon a system of classifying relatives that distinguishes between parallel cousins (children of the brother of the father and of the sister of the mother), who are equated with brothers and sisters and are treated as blood-relatives, and cross-cousins (children of the sister of the father, and of the brother of the mother), who are considered as affines, that is to say as relatives by marriage with whom marriage is possible. On the basis of this central relationship, all persons linked genealogically to any individual can be classified by him into two categories: relatives by blood and affines. Thus, a paternal uncle will be related by blood, but a maternal uncle will be an affine. The wife of a paternal uncle will be a blood-relative, while the husband of a paternal aunt will be an affine, and so on. Among the Achuar, marriage is prescribed between cross-cousins and this results in perpetuating, generation after generation, cycles of alliance within a single kinship kernel (or kindred). Residence after marriage is known as uxorical; that is to say, a son-in-law must establish himself in the house of his wife's parents. On Dravidian kinship systems in general, see Louis Dumont, 'The Dravidian Kinship Terminology as an Expression of Marriage' (*Man* LIII (54) 1953), and *Hierarchy and Marriage Alliance in South Indian Kinship* (Occasional Papers of the Royal Anthropological Institute, No. 12, 1957). The Achuar kinship system is analysed by Philippe Descola, 'Territorial adjustments among the Achuar of Ecuador' (*Social Sciences Information*, 21 (1), 1982), and Anne Christine Taylor, 'The marriage alliance and its structural variations in Jivaroan societies' (*Social Sciences Information* 22 (3), 1983).

Chapter 4

The importance of chromatism in Amerindian thought has been illuminated by Claude Lévi-Strauss in the four volumes of his *Mythologiques* (Paris, Plon, 1964, 1966, 1968 and 1971), particularly in Vol. 1, *Le cru et le cuit* (1964); *A Science of Mythology*, Vols I, II and III, translated by J. and D. Weightman (London, Jonathan Cape, 1970); Vol. I, *The Raw and the Cooked*.

Chapter 5

The exchange of goods plays a central role in a number of pre-modern societies, but not always with a directly economic purpose. The first to draw attention to this was Marcel Mauss, in his famous *The Gift*, translated by W. D. Halls, with an introduction by Mary Douglas (London, Routledge, 1954). See also K. Polanyi, C. Arensberg *et alia*, *Trade and Market in the Early Empires, Economies in History and Theory* (Glencoe, The Free Press, 1957); Marshall Sahlins, *Stone Age Economics* (Chicago, University of Chicago Press, 1972); Maurice Godelier, *Perspectives in Marxist Anthropology*, translated by R. Brain (Cambridge, Cambridge University Press, 1977), chapter 4; Arjun Appadurai (ed.), *The Social Life of Things: Commodities in a Cultural Perspective* (Cambridge, Cambridge University Press, 1986), and Caroline Humphrey and S. Hugh-Jones (eds.), *Barter, Exchange and Value. An Anthropological Approach* (Cambridge, Cambridge University Press, 1992).

On the procedures of classifying natural objects used in societies without writing, see Claude Lévi-Strauss, *The Savage Mind* (London, Nature of Human Society Series, 1974). I devoted a lengthy study to Achuar classification systems for plants and animals in *In the Society of Nature*, op. cit., chapter 3. See the analyses of magic *anent* songs in Anne Christine Taylor, 'Jivaroan magical songs: Achuar *anent* of connubial love' (*Amerindia* 8, Paris, 1983), and P. Descola, *In the Society of Nature*, op. cit., *passim*, for the Achuar Jivaros, and Michael Brown, *Tsewa's Gift*, op. cit., *passim*, for the Aguaruna Jivaros.

Chapter 6

For a technical study of slash and burn cultivation, the treatment of cultivated plants, and garden symbolism among the Achuar, see P. Descola, *In the Society of Nature*, op. cit., chapter 5. The passage on Nunkui, the mythical mistress of gardens, stresses, against the theories of the transcendence of primitive religions – see, for example, Marcel Gauchet, *Le désenchantement du monde. Une histoire politique de la religion* (Paris, Gallimard, 1985), but also the Salesian missionaries – that the heroes of Jivaro mythology are immanent in the world, and that they are not very different from human beings and neither superior nor external to them. This is a feature that is probably characteristic of all polytheisms, as is suggested by Marc Augé in his *Génie du paganisme* (Paris, Gallimard, 1982).

Chapter 7

Ethnology very early on recognized the crucial importance that pre-modern societies attach to dreams and their interpretation. The first ethnological theorists even tried to use oneiric activity to explain not only primitive religion – for example, Edward Tylor, *Primitive Culture* (London [1871], 1929) – but also mythology – Karl Abraham, 'Dreams and Myths, a Study in Folk Psychology' (1909), reprinted in *Clinical Papers and Essays in Psychoanalysis* (New York, Basic Books, 1955). The literature on this question is abundant and expresses points of view that are frequently irreconcilable. Echoes of it are to be found in two recent works: Michel Perrin, *Les praticiens du rêve. Un exemple de chamanisme* (Paris, PUF, 1992), and B. Tedlock (ed.), *Dreaming. Anthropological and Psychological Interpretations* (Cambridge, Cambridge University Press, 1987). My analysis of the Achuar system of interpreting dreams is inspired by the structural method of analysis of myths developed by Claude Lévi-Strauss (*Mythologiques*, op. cit); it is also in line with Lévi-Strauss – *The Jealous Potter*, translated by Bénédicte Chorier (Chicago, University of Chicago Press, 1988) in his critique of the Freudian perspective – Sigmund Freud, *The Interpretation of Dreams* (1899), translated and edited by J. Strachey (Pelican, Harmondsworth, 1976).

Chapter 8

I devoted a long study to Achuar hunting techniques and the symbolism of the hunter's relationship to the hunted animals in *In the Society of Nature*, op. cit., chapter 6. On the cultural reasons that prevented the domestication of animals by the Indians of Amazonia, see Philippe Erikson, 'De l'apprivoisement à l'apprivosionnement: chasse, alliance et familiarisation en Amazonie amérindienne' (*Techniques et Culture* 9, 1987), and Philippe

Descola, 'Généalogie des objets et anthropologie de l'objectivation' in B. Latour (ed.) *et alia, L'intelligence des techniques* (Paris, La Découverte, 1993). The figure of a Master of Animals is common from Siberia – see, for example, Roberte Hamayon, *La chasse à l'âme. Esquisse d'une théorie du chamanisme sibérien* (Paris, Société d'ethnologie, 1990) – to Tierra del Fuego. A study of the phenomenon in South America may be found in Otto Zerries, 'Wild und Bushgeister in Südamerika' (*Studien zur Kulturkunde* 2, XI), and an attempt at a comparative ordering in P. Descola, 'Societies of nature and the nature of society' in A. Kuper (ed.), *Conceptualizing Society* (London, Routledge, 1992); see also, for a masterly case study in North-Western Amazonia, Gerardo Reichel-Dolmatoff, *Amazonian Cosmos. The Sexual and Religious Symbolism of the Tukano Indians* (Chicago, University of Chicago Press, 1971; original edition in Spanish, 1968).

Chapter 9

For complementary information on fishing techniques and river symbolism, see Philippe Descola, *In the Society of Nature*, op. cit., chapter 7; on seasonal cycles and the climatic calendar, ibid., chapter 2. A special number of *Bulletin de l'Institut français d'études andines* (Vol. XX (1), 1991) presents a very full panorama of *pishtaco* in the Andes; see also Nathan Wachtel, *Gods and Vampires. Return to Chipaya*, translated by Carol Volk (Chicago, University of Chicago Press, 1944).

Chapter 10

On the *amik* (or *amigri*) relationship among the Shuar Jivaros, see M. Harner, *The Jivaros*, op. cit., chapter 3. Studies of ceremonial friendship among the Indians of central Brazil can be found in David Maybury-Lewis (ed.), *Dialectical Societies. The Gê and Bororo of Central Brazil* (Cambridge, Mass., Harvard University Press, 1979), and among the Tupi Indians in Eduardo Viveiros de Castro, *From the Enemy's Point of View. Humanity and Divinity in an Amazonian Society* (Chicago, University of Chicago Press, 1992). Claude Lévi-Strauss was probably the first to draw attention to the extreme overlapping of relations of hostility and bartering relations in 'Guerre et commerce chez les Indiens d'Amérique du Sud' (*Renaissance* 1 (1–2), 1943).

Chapter 11

The Achuar 'great man' differs in several respects from the classic image of the Amerindian 'chief without power' presented by Pierre Clastres in *Society against the State. Essays in political anthropology*, translated by R. Hurley in collaboration with A. Stein (New York, Zone Books, 1987); for a critical discussion, see Philippe Descola, 'La chefferie amérindienne dans l'anthropologie politique' (*Revue française de science politique* 38 (5), 1988). On the Achuar kinship system, see the references above (chapters 1, 2, and 3).

Chapter 12

Anthropology of gender has been going strong for about fifteen years, spurred on in particular by feminist movements: see, for example, Nicole-Claude Mathieu (ed.), *L'arraisonnement des femmes. Essais en anthropologie des sexes* (Paris, Éditions de l'EHESS, 1985). In contrast, anthropology of the emotions is still in its infancy, at least so far as its non-psychoanalytic variants are concerned. On the role played by *anent* in conjugal love, see Anne Christine Taylor, 'Jivaroan magical songs: Achuar *anent* of connubial love', op. cit. The Jivaros' extremely puritanical view of extra-conjugal sexuality is by no means the norm in Amazonia, as two examples demonstrate: Thomas Gregor, *Mehinaku. The Drama of Daily Life in a Brazilian Indian Village* (Chicago, University of Chicago Press, 1977), and E. Viveiros de Castro, *From the Enemy's Point of View*, op. cit.

Chapter 13

The literature on the traditional uses of hallucinogenics is considerable. By way of introduction, see L. Lewin, *Phantastica. Narcotic and stimulating drugs* (London, Routledge and Kegan Paul, 1931); Patrick Allain, *Hallucinogènes et société. Cannabis et peyotl* (Paris, Payot, 1973); Peter Furst (ed.), *Flesh of the Gods: the ritual use of hallucinogenics* (London, George Allen and Unwin, 1972); and R. Shultes and A. Hofmann, *Plants of the God: origins of hallucinogenic use* (London, Hutchinson, 1980). On the ritual use of hallucinogenics of the *ayahuasca* type in the eastern foothills of the Andes, see Marlène Dobkin de Rios, *Visionary Vine. Psychedelic Healing in the Peruvian Amazon* (San Francisco, Chandler Publishing Company, 1972); Michael Harner, *Hallucinogens and Shamanism* (New York, Oxford

University Press, 1973), and Gerardo Reichel-Dolmatoff, *The Shaman and the Jaguar. A Study of Narcotic Drugs among the Indians of Colombia* (Philadelphia, Temple University Press, 1975). The monographs of M. Harner and M. Brown, already cited, contain passages on the use of hallucinogenics among the Shuar Jivaros and the Aguaruna Jivaros. Finally, on the relations between music and trance, see Gilbert Rouget, *La musique et la transe. Esquisse d'une théorie générale des relations entre la musique et la possession* (Paris, Gallimard, 1980).

Chapter 14

The pioneering book edited by Frederik Barth – *Social Groups and Boundaries. The Social Organization of Culture Differences* (London, George Allen and Unwin, 1969) – was responsible for stimulating new anthropological perspectives on ethnicity. In it, ethnic identity was no longer considered as a substantive category with characteristics fixed for all time, but as a system for codifying cultural differences between neighbouring groups. Among the many works stimulated by this theoretical adjustment, see: Jean-Loup Amselle and E. M'Bokolo (eds.), *Au coeur de l'ethnie. Ethnies, tribalisme et état en Afrique* (Paris, La Découverte, 1985), and *Indianité, ethnocide, indigénisme en Amérique latine*, op. cit. (in particular the article by Anne Christine Taylor, 'Relations interethniques et formes de résistance culturelle chez les Achuar de l'Équateur'); on Jivaro ethnic classifications, see also A. C. Taylor, 'L'Art de la réduction. La guerre et les mécanismes de la différenciation tribale dans la culture jivaro' (*Journal de la Société des Américanistes LXXI*, 1985), and C. Seymour-Smith, *Shiwiar*, op. cit.

On the general question of representations of the passing of time, see Henri Hubert and M. Mauss, 'Étude sommaire de la représentation du temps dans la religion et la magie' in *Mélanges d'histoire des religions* (Paris, Alcan, 1909); and, for Mesoamerica, Jacques Soustelle, *La pensée cosmogonique des anciens Mexicains* (Paris, Hermann, 1940). The relations between myth and history have given rise to many debates, echoes of which are to be found in: *Histoire et structure*, special issue of *Annales* (26 (3–4), 1971), and *Le mythe et ses métamorphoses*, special issue of *L'Homme* (106–7, 1988); the latter volume contains several articles on the treatment of history in Amerindian mythologies. France-Marie Renard-Casevitz's book, *Le banquet masqué. Une mythologie de l'étranger* (Paris, Lierre et Coudrier, 1991), has a particularly original way of tackling representations of history and temporality in the myths of the Arawak of Peru. On the early history of the Jivaros, in particular the Achuar, much still remains to be done. The work of reference on this question is France-Marie Renard-Casevitz, Thierry Saignes and Anne Christine Taylor, *L'Inca, l'Espagnol et les Sauvages. Rapports entre les sociétés amazoniennes et andines du XVe au XVIIe siècle* (Paris, Éditions Recherche sur les civilisations, 1986). On more recent periods, see Anne Christine Taylor, 'L'évolution démographique des populations indigènes de Haute-Amazonie du XVe au XXe siècle' in *Équateur 1986*, Vol. 1 (Paris, Éditions de L'ORSTOM, 1989).

Chapter 15

Concepts of health and sickness and, more generally, how misfortune is treated in traditional societies have, over the past twenty years, become a specialized branch of anthropology, sometimes called 'ethno-medicine'. Two publications convey a good overall idea of this field of research: Marc Augé and Claudine Herzlich (eds.), *Le sens du mal* (Paris, Éditions des Archives contemporaines, 1984), and the special issue of *L'Ethnographie* (96-7) entitled *Causes, origines et agents de la maladie chez les peuples sans écriture* (1985). On the Amerindian field, see Jean-Pierre Chaumeil, *Voir, savoir, pouvoir. Le chamanisme chez les Yagua du Nord-Est péruvien* (Paris, Éditions de l'EHESS, 1983), and Michel Perrin, *Les praticiens du rêve*, op. cit.

The Jivaro system of bartering partners is different from the large-scale trading expeditions characteristic of Peruvian central Amazonia – F.-M. Renard-Casevitz, 'Guerre, violence et identité à partir des sociétés du piémont amazonien des Andes centrales' (*Cahiers ORSTOM* [Human sciences series] 21 [1], 1985) – and the Orinoco Basin – Simone Dreyfus, 'Les réseaux politiques indigènes en Guyane occidentale et leurs transformations aux XVIIe et XVIIIe siècles' (*L'Homme* 122-4, 1992). On the very common association of debt and vengeance, see the articles collected by Raymond Verdier in *La vengeance. Études d'ethnologie, d'histoire et de philosophie* (Paris, Éditions Cujas, 4 vols, 1980-84).

Chapter 16

On the Quichuas' view of the Achuar, see the two monographs by N. Whitten.

435

Chapters 17 and 18

The internal wars waged by the Indians of South America against one another have always exerted an ambiguous fascination upon Western observers. From the earliest chroniclers of the conquest down to contemporary ethnologists, they all manifest a similar perplexity faced with the intensity of these clashes, their apparent lack of motives, and the macabre rituals by which they are often accompanied. Confronted by this apparent logical – or, to some, moral – scandal, modern ethnology has sought reasonable explanations mainly in the reputedly positive functions that warfare is believed to fulfil even without those practising it being aware of them. It has thus been suggested that Amerindian warfare provides a means of adapting to the constraints of the environment, in particular to the supposed rarity of game – for a synthesis of the debates on the ecological theories of warfare, see Brian Ferguson, 'Game Wars? Ecology and conflicts in Amazonia' (*Journal of Anthropological Research* 45, 1989); the elements of a critical refutation may be found in P. Descola, *In the Society of Nature*, op. cit., 'Le déterminisme famélique' in A. Cadoret (ed.), *Chasser le naturel* (Paris, Éditions de l'EHESS, 1988), and 'L'explication causale' in P. Descola *et alia*, *Les idées de l'anthropologie* (Paris, Armand Colin, 1988). For Pierre Clastres, in contrast, Amerindian warfare is a subtle mechanism of internal dissociation, which he believes prevents the emergence of the State – see his *Recherches d'anthropologie politique* (Paris, Le Seuil, 1980). Some authors even consider the Amerindian wars to be an instrument for the capitalization of the genetic patrimony of the greatest warriors – for example, Napoléon Chagnon, 'Life histories, blood revenge and warfare in a tribal population' (*Science* 239, 1988). Despite the incompatibility of the points of view that these explanations reflect, they are all characterized by a desire to reduce Amerindian warfare to a mere function, and thus to a single cause, without ever taking into account the extreme diversity of the sociological and cultural contexts of these armed clashes. Rather than taking Amerindian warfare to be a homogeneous set of phenomena that can be explained by a single hidden function, I myself consider it preferable to regard it as the manifestation of a particular type of social relations that are a means of constantly negotiating and reproducing the collective identity, ethnic frontiers and statutory positions. Violence is probably a constant element in human nature. So it does not, 'in itself', have to be explained. But what does deserve an ethnologist's attention is the way in which each society codifies, according to its own criteria, the individual and collective expression of violence, considering certain forms of it to be legitimate and others to be socially unacceptable. That codification constitutes a powerful indicator of the social philosophy of a particular culture. So for me, the cause, motives and results of Jivaro warfare are less significant than the way in which it marks out, within the social field, relations of alliance and of hostility; these are indicators that can help us to understand the criteria defining identity and otherness and at the same time establishing the limits and overlaps of the inter-tribal networks of exchange and the regional political systems. On this theme, see my article, 'Les affinités sélectives: alliance, guerre et prédation dans l'ensemble jivaro' (*L'Homme* 126–8, 1993).

The question of Jivaro head-hunting is tackled by R. Karsten and M. Harner in their monographs cited above, but these do not provide any really convincing interpretations. The detailed descriptions of the *tsantsa* ritual by Father Siro Pellizzaro, working among the Shuar Jivaros, now published in Spanish, are of a quite exceptional ethnographic quality – S. Pellizzaro, *Ayumpum. La reducción de las cabezas cortadas* (Sucua, Ecuador, Mundo Shuar, 1980), and *Tsantsa. La celebración de la cabeza reducida* (Sucua, Mundo Shuar, 1980). It was on the basis of these remarkable documents that Anne Christine Taylor recently suggested a particularly rich and original interpretation of head-hunting: 'Les bons ennemis et les mauvais parents. Le symbolisme de l'alliance dans les rituels de chasses aux têtes des Jivaros de l'Équateur' in E. Copet and F. Héritier-Augé (eds.), *Les complexités de l'alliance, IV. Économie, politique et fondements symboliques de l'alliance* (Paris, Éditions des Archives contemporaines, 1993); my own remarks on head-hunting in the present book owe a great deal to her.

On the opposition between modern societies, in which the individual is the touchstone of the social edifice, and those where the individual takes on meaning and value only in his/her subordination to a more encompassing totality, see Louis Dumont, *From Mandeville to Marx: The Genesis and Triumph of Economic Ideology* (Chicago, University of Chicago Press, 1977) and *Essays on Individualism: Modern Ideology in Anthropological Perspective* (Chicago, University of Chicago Press, 1986). As the reader will detect, my own position is more qualified than that of Dumont, for in my view it is possible to speak of individualistic values in pre-modern societies such as that of the Jivaros.

Chapter 19

On *arutam*, see, for the Shuar Jivaros: R. Karsten, *The Head-Hunters of Western Amazonas*, op. cit., part 5; M. Harner, *The Jivaros*, op. cit., chapter 4, and 'Jivaro Souls' (*American Anthropologist* 64, 1962); and S. Pellizzaro, *Arutam. Mitos y ritos para propiciar a los espiritus* (Sucua, Ecuador, Mundo Shuar, n.d.); on the Aguaruna Jivaros, see M. Brown, *Tsewa's Gift*, op. cit., chapters 2 and 6, and *Una paz incierta*, op. cit., chapter 11.

Chapters 20 and 21

There is a considerable volume of literature on shamanism, but it is of very uneven quality. The only real synthesis on the question is still – unfortunately – that of Mircea Eliade in *Shamanism: Archaic Techniques of Ecstasy* (Chicago, University of Chicago Press, 1951): unfortunately, because his point of view, at once mystical and reductionist, produces a very inadequate account of the complexity of the phenomenon. Eliade's theses have provided the starting point for many critical discussions on the nature of shamanism: E. Lot-Falck, 'Le chamanisme en Sibérie: essai de mise au point' (*Bulletin de l'Asie du Sud-Est et du monde insulindien* IV, 3, fasc. 2, 1979); Jean Malaurie, 'Note sur l'homosexualité et le chamanisme chez les Tchouktches et les Esquimaux d'Asie' (*Nouvelle Revue d'Ethnopsychiatrie* 19, 1992); Luc de Heusch, 'Possession and shamanism' in *Why Marry Her?*, translated by Janet Lloyd (Cambridge, Cambridge University Press, 1981); Roger Bastide, *Le rêve, la transe et la folie* (Paris, Flammarion, 1972); I. M. Lewis, *Ecstatic religion; an anthropological study of spirit possession and shamanism* (Harmondsworth, Pelican, 1971); G. Rouget, *La musique et la transe*, op. cit. From one author to another, the definition of shamanism can oscillate between a simple therapeutic technique – see M. Bouteiller, *Chamanisme et guérison magique* (Paris, PUF, 1950) – and a vast concept of the world that is supposed to be characteristic of many peoples – R. Hamayon, *La chasse à l'âme*, op. cit. A good synthesis of recent anthropological works on shamanism may be found in two special issues of the periodical *L'Ethnographie: Voyages chamaniques*, 74–5, 1977 and *Voyages chamaniques* 2, 87–8, 1982.

Although the term 'shaman' originated in Siberia, it is perhaps in South America that shamanistic practice has been the most perceptively observed. For this region, see D. L. Browman and R. Schwarz (eds.), *Spirits, Shamans and Stars. Perspectives from South America* (Paris and The Hague, Mouton,

1979); Jon C. Crocker, *Vital Souls. Bororo Cosmology, Natural Symbolism and Shamanism* (Tucson, University Press of Arizona, 1985); Alfred Métraux, *Religions et magies indiennes d'Amérique du Sud* (Paris, Gallimard, 1967); G. Reichel-Dolmatoff, *The Shaman and the Jaguar*, op. cit.; Jean-Pierre Chaumeil, *Voir, savoir, pouvoir*, op. cit.; Michel Perrin, *Les Praticiens du rêve*, op. cit. It is from Michel Perrin that I borrowed the neologism 'shamanery'. On Jivaro shamanism, see the already mentioned monographs by R. Karsten, M. Harner and M. Brown.

The shamanistic songs of the Achuar are not esoteric, unlike those of the Cuna shamans of Panama, for example, which have been analysed remarkably well by Carlo Severi in 'Le chemin des métamorphoses. Un modèle de connaissance de la folie dans un chant chamanique cuna' (*Res* 3, 1982). On the central role of tobacco in Amerindian shamanism, see Johannes Wilbert, *Tobacco and Shamanism in South America* (Yale, Yale University Press, 1987). Two texts by C. Lévi-Strauss are absolutely fundamental for an understanding of the symbolic dimension of shamanistic cures: 'Symbolic efficacy' and 'The sorceror and his magic', both published in *Structural Anthropology*, translated by C. Jacobson and B. G. Schoepf (Harmondsworth, Penguin, 1972). The thesis, now rejected, according to which shamans are neurotics, was originally defended in particular by I. M. Lewis, *Ecstatic Religion*, op. cit., and George Devereux, *Mohave Ethnopsychiatry: the Psychic Disturbances of an Indian Tribe* (Washington DC, Smithsonian Institution Press, 1969). On dietary prohibitions as an instrument of social classification, see C. Lévi-Strauss, *The Savage Mind*, op. cit., chapters 3, 4 and 5. The shamanism of the Quichuas of the Bobonaza is tackled in the two monographs already cited by N. Whitten; the shamanism of the Quichuas of the Napo is discussed in Blanca Muratorio, *The Life and Times of Grandfather Alonso, Culture and History in the Upper Amazon* (New Brunswick, Rutgers University Press, 1991). To clarify the difference between the trance of an ordinary shaman and the possession that is peculiar to the *panku*, see the definitions suggested in the already cited works by M. Eliade, L. de Heusch, I. Lewis and G. Rouget.

Chapter 22

The difficulties of missionary work among the Achuar and the problems of conscience that may result from it are raised with remarkable sincerity and frankness in the journal of a Salesian novice; it was originally written purely for himself but his superiors, having learned of it, persuaded him to publish it (entirely to their credit): José Arnalot 'Chuint', *Lo que los Achuar me han enseñado* (Sucua, Ecuador, Mundo Shuar, 1978); after living among the Achuar, the author left the order. Readers of Claude Lévi-Strauss's *Tristes Tropiques*, translated by J. and D. Weightman (Harmondsworth, Penguin, 1976) will perhaps have noticed that the lesson in rhetoric of Father Albo (a pseudonym, of course) was, in a way, a symmetrical inversion of the 'lesson in writing' (op. cit., chapter 28), in which a Nambikwara chief bolsters his authority amongst his people by pretending to write. Among the many books on the ideological effects of Catholic missionary work among the Amerindians, see in particular: T. Todorov, *La conquête de l'Amérique*, op. cit.; Serge Gruzinski, *La colonisation de l'imaginaire. Sociétés indigènes et occidentalisation dans le Mexique espagnol, XVIe– XVIIe siècle* (Paris, Gallimard, 1989) and Victor-Daniel Bonilla, *Serfs de Dieu et maîtres d'Indiens. Histoire d'une mission capucine en Amazonie* (Paris, Fayard, 1972).

The book by Frank and Mary Drown, a Protestant fundamentalist missionary couple who set up the Macuma mission among the Shuar Jivaros in the late forties, presents a total contrast to the journal of J. Arnalot: their triumphant apologia for the evangelist undertaking is accompanied by a veritable repulsion for the *mores* and beliefs of the Indians – *Mission among the Head-Hunters* (New York, Harper and Row, 1961). The economic aspect of Protestant evangelical work among the Achuar is tackled in P. Descola, 'Ethnicité et développement économique', op. cit., and A. C. Taylor, 'God-Wealth: the Achuar and the Missions' in N. Whitten (ed.), *Cultural Transformations . . .*, op. cit. The classic reference on the 'cargo cult' in Melanesia is the book by P. Lawrence, *Road Belong Cargo* (Manchester, Manchester University Press, 1951). Two books present a remarkably well-informed critical study of the activities and methods of Protestant fundamentalist sects in Latin America, in particular those of the well-known Summer Institute of Linguistics: Peter Aaby and S. Hvalkof (eds.), *Is God an American? An Anthropological Perspective on the Missionary Work of the Summer Institute of Linguistics* (Copenhagen, IWGIA, 1981), and David Stoll, *Fishers of Men or Founders of Empire?* (Cambridge, Mass., Cultural Survival, 1983).

The definitive disappearance of cultures in which ethnologists are interested has been regularly announced over almost a century. The most recent notorious example is *La paix blanche* (Paris, Le Seuil, 1970), in which Robert Jaulin vigorously condemns the ethnocide of tribal minorities perpetrated by the West, an operation of cultural (and all too often physical) destruction, now virtually completed, in which ethnology, he argues, has been partially complicit. The reader will have understood that while, along with him and, fortunately, many others, I condemn the ethnocide suffered by Amerindian cultures, my view of the future is more tempered and less pessimistic. The example of the Federation of Shuar Centres, a powerful indigenous organization created by the Shuar Jivaros in 1964 with the aid of the Salesians, shows clearly that the Indians are now capable of taking their own destiny in hand by discovering new forms of ethnicity and coexistence with the dominant societies – see *Federación de Centros Shuar: Una solución original a un problema actual* (Sucua, Ecuador, Don Bosco Press, 1976).

Chapter 23

The diversity of concepts of death and of the ritual operations that accompany it attracted the attention of ethnologists at an early date. See in particular: Robert Hertz, 'A contribution to the study of the collective representation of death' in *Death and the Right Hand*, translated by R. Needham and C. Needham (Aberdeen, Cohen and West, 1960); Louis-Vincent Thomas, *Anthropologie de la mort* (Paris, Payot, 1975); G. Gnoli and J.-P. Vernant, *La mort, les morts dans les sociétés anciennes* (Paris and Cambridge, Éditions de la Maison des Sciences de l'Homme/Cambridge University Press, 1985); Sally Humphreys and H. King (eds.), *Mortality and Immortality. The Anthropology and Archaeology of Death* (London, Academic Press, 1981); Maurice Bloch and J. Parry (eds.), *Death and the Regeneration of Life* (Cambridge, Cambridge University Press, 1982). On death in Indian cultures of the lowlands of South America, there are three works of fundamental importance: Michel Perrin, *The Way of Dead Indians: Guajiro Myths and Symbols*, translated by Michael Fineberg (Austin, University of Texas Press, 1987); E. Viveiros de Castro, *From the Enemy's Point of View*, op. cit.; and Manuela Carneiro da Cunha, *Os mortos et os otros. Uma análise do sistema funerário e da noção de pessoa entre os índios Krahó* (Sao Paulo, HUCITEC, 1978). Finally, on the Jivaros, see A. C. Taylor, 'Remembering to forget. Mourning, memory and identity among the Jivaro' (*Man* 28 (4), 1993).

Concepts of death are inseparable from concepts of personality. On this theme Marcel Mauss, once again, was a pioneer: 'L'âme, le nom et la personne' in *Oeuvres*, Vol. 2 (Paris, Les Éditions de Minuit, 1969; first published 1929), and 'Une catégorie de l'esprit humain: la notion de personne, celle de "moi" ' in *Sociologie et anthropologie*, op. cit.; first published 1938. See also *L'identité. Séminaire dirigé par Claude Lévi-Strauss* (Paris, Grasset, 1977) – in particular the articles by J. C. Crocker on the

Bororo and by Françoise Héritier-Augé on the Samo – and Marc Augé, *Génie du paganisme*, op. cit. On South America, see the above cited works of M. Perrin, E. Viveiros de Castro and M. Carneiro da Cunha, to which should be added J. C. Crocker, *Vital Souls*, op. cit. My readers will no doubt have realized that memories of my philosophical training – part and parcel of the equipment of any secondary school humanities student in their last year – helped me to formulate my interpretation of the Achuar cosmology and theory of knowledge. My critique of the Platonic interpretation of Jivaro cosmology is chiefly directed at M. Harner, *The Jivaros*, op. cit., chapter 4.

Chapter 24

There is no detailed description of the *anemat* ritual. R. Karsten mentions it briefly in connection with the Shuar Jivaros (*The Head-Hunters of Western Amazonas*, op. cit., part 4, chapter 4). My own interpretation of this ritual owes much to the ideas developed by C. Lévi-Strauss in his conclusion to *L'Homme nu* (Paris, Plon, 1971). On the function of *ujaj* in the *tsantsa* ritual, see S. Pellizzaro, *Tsantsa*, op cit.

Ethnological Writing

The relationship between ethnology and literature is fraught with ambiguity. The concern for precision, the importance of terse formulae and of narrative flow, the need to translate as accurately as possible concepts that do not always have semantic equivalents in other languages – all these constraints of a discipline committed to producing meaning using, essentially, the words of ordinary language mean that ethnology has to 'attend to its style'. But only rarely have authors, such as Claude Lévi-Strauss and Michel Leiris, done honour to the Republic of Letters and raised ethnology to the level of literature. Yet in many cases that is not for want of trying or even of talent. If most ethnologists are, as Edmund Leach put it, failed novelists, that is not solely due to the whims of the Muses. The rules for the writing of monographs have been fixed for sixty years or more, and they force any ethnologist aspiring to recognition from his peers to adopt a mode of expression absorbed early on in his career from reading the works of his elders, a mode that he ends up regarding as natural. The result is a certain standardization of forms of description, the virtually exclusive use of analytic categories that are recognized by the profession – kinship, religion or technology – and self-censorship of any judgements that seem too overtly subjective. For a science that aims to produce valid generalizations by comparing ethnographic data drawn from widely differing cultures, this in itself may be no bad thing. It is understandable that such an ambition should entail a homogeneous manner of presenting the data.

However, by proscribing any subjectivity, classical ethnology rules out exploiting the very element that makes its endeavour unique amongst the human sciences, that is to say a knowledge that is based upon the personal and continuous relationship forged between one particular individual and other particular individuals – knowledge that has emerged from a collection of circumstances which inevitably varies in each case but is, notwithstanding, perfectly legitimate. Yet the lay reader is almost always left in ignorance as to the conditions in which this knowledge was acquired. After all, historians refer to the archives they have used, which others are at liberty to consult, possibly to extract quite different interpretations from them; sociologists describe the questionnaires and statistical procedures that have enabled them to come to their conclusions; and psychologists do not hesitate to give long descriptions of their experimental procedures: in short, only ethnologists feel exempt from explaining how they have managed to extract from a unique experience a corpus of knowledge whose validity they require everyone to accept. An ethnologist's laboratory is himself and his relationship with particular people, his own naivety and cunning, the tortuous path he has intuitively followed, the chance situations in which he finds himself, the role that he is made to play, sometimes unwittingly, in local strategies, the friendship that may link him to the person used as a principal informant, his reactions of enthusiasm, anger or disgust – a whole complex mosaic of feelings, qualities and occasions that give our 'method of enquiry' its own particular hue. It is this essential part of our scientific procedure that the precepts of ethnological writing demand be passed over in silence. To be sure, dates and place names are given at the beginning of a monograph but, denied – as they are – any existential substance, their sole function is to establish a minimum guarantee of truth: 'I resided in such or such a village or community at such or such a time, so I know what I am talking about.' Apart from this statutory clause, the conditions of 'fieldwork' are thereafter evoked only in an allusive manner. This may be transparent to those who have been through similar experiences but, whether or not that is so, it is considered bad form to dwell upon them.

Quite apart from the fact that these canonical rules of monographic writing are epistemologically limiting in the scientific production of ethnology, they also severely limit its potential audience. Without presuming to recommend self-indulgent introspection, cheap exoticism or sensationalism, it seems reasonable to wonder why, with very few exceptions, ethnologists have not acquired the wide public that historians have managed to attract. Whereas the latter – including the most scholarly of them – write both for their peers and for the general public without, on that account, abandoning the rigorous criteria of their discipline, ethnologists – abetted no doubt by the lack of enthusiasm displayed by publishers – seem resigned to publishing less and less and for an increasingly restricted circle of professionals. It was in reaction to this state of affairs and in order to try to restore to ethnological literature a subjective way of proceeding previously denied by the conventions that, with the encouragement of Jean Malaurie, I decided to write the present book. I have backed a hunch that ethnology can escape from the ghetto in which it has allowed itself to be confined and still remain faithful to its original intentions; that it can be at once instructive, edifying and entertaining, it can fulfil a scholarly function while pondering the conditions in which it operates, retrace a personal itinerary, and at the same time reveal all the richness of an unknown culture. Only time will tell whether I have been successful. But of one thing I am already certain: it is that such an undertaking would have been virtually impossible without the framework provided by the series that originally encouraged it. Terre Humaine [the Plon series in which this book was originally published in French], which has no real equivalent either in France or elsewhere, has for forty years been offering a prestigious refuge to ethnologists left unsatisfied by the constraints of the university style. With the strength of a number of admirable precedents to support it, this series confers an air of legitimacy upon forays off the beaten track such as the present work; it has helped me to overcome the reticence that any ethnologist feels at the idea of talking about himself, thanks to the fact that, through a consensus unusual in our discipline, each of us regards it not so much as a series of works deliberately collected together, but rather as a genre in itself. In contrast to the 'post-modern' anthropology so fashionable in the United States, in which the ethnologist becomes his own object of enquiry and observation of oneself is more important than the observation of others, thereby leading to a narcissistic solipsism that is not always redeemed by fine language – in contrast to this new egoistical avatar of ethnocentricity, Terre Humaine reminds us, as book succeeds book, that it is possible for an individual experience of the diversity of others to convey universal perceptions that are accessible to all.

In the last analysis, the desire to reach a wider public stems from the double social responsibility that an ethnologist incurs: first, a responsibility to the people who gave him their trust over several years and whose uniqueness he is in a better position to celebrate with accuracy than those who simply specialize in exotic adventures; and secondly, to his own co-citizens who, in that they financed his research work (for whether a full-time researcher or teaching in a university, his position in France is that of a civil servant), have a right to expect him to reveal its full interest to them. However, ethnology is a more technical science than history, and many parts of it call for a language and methods that will always remain the prerogative of specialists. The problem of ethnological writing cannot be reduced to a choice between a scholarly publication and a work of popularization. Rather, it involves adopting modes of expression to suit the questions tackled and the aim in view. It is to the great credit of Terre Humaine that it has managed to create a forum for those who are committed to sharing with a wider audience the exceptional mode of learning about others that they are fortunate enough to profess.

445

Index

Academic study and fieldwork, 20–1
  see also Ethnology
Acculturation, 361–2
Achayat, 218
Achuar Jivaros, 3, 8, 13 17–18
  distinctive signs of 220–1
  their effect on Descola, 405–10
  the landing-strip, 55, 70
  see also Capahuari
Achuentza, 121
Adultery see Sexuality
Aesthetics, 104
Affinities, 156, 176–8, 278, 219, 415
Albo, Father 351–6
Amana, 125–6, 129–30, 133, 328
Amazonia
  appropriateness for study, 23–4
  colours of, 41–2
  in early morning, 44, 49
  in evening, 42
  from the air, 26
  ignorance of, 3, 17, 24
  Indians' knowledge of, 122–3
  lack of seasons, 65, 66
  legends concerning, 3–6
  walking in, 168–70
  weather, 65–6, 75
Amik see Friendship
Ampiur, 219
Anaconda, 67, 76, 77, 82, 111,
    142–3, 235, 239, 242–3, 324,
    325–6, 328, 398
Anasat, 218
Ancestors, 306
  see also Arutam
Anchumir, (Anne Christine) 71,
    153, 168
Andes, 1, 2, 12, 13, 75, 140, 149,
    158, 222, 255

Anemat ritual, 384, 386–93
Anent, 78–81, 86, 93, 99–100,
    117, 132, 185–7, 211, 312, 376
  and arutam, 307–9
  for the dead, 381
  for gardening, 89–90
  for healing, 317–22, 328–9
  for hunting, 121
  for love, 195–7
  used by missionary, 356
  for war, 391–2
  see also Music, Songs
Anger, 193–4, see also Emotion,
    Murder, Vendetta, Violence
Animals
  classification of, 76–7
  and communication, 375
  domestication of 130–2
  edible species, 77, 339
  guardian spirit (Jirijri), 130, 146,
    187, 323, 326–7
  shamanistic, 328, 335–6
  symbolism of, 328, 335–6, 395
  taboos concerning, 340
  and the wakan (soul), 367–9, 375
  list of species:
  acouchi, 88, 415
  agouti, 88, 106, 131, 415
  anaconda, 67, 76, 77, 82, 111,
    142–3, 235, 239, 242–3, 324,
    325–6, 328, 398
  anteater, 76, 77
  armadillo, 77
  brocket (red deer), 76, 114, 367,
    368
  cacique, 77, 415
  catfish, 302, 339
  cayman, 139, 143, 212, 324, 326
  coati, 76, 182–3, 416

crab, 77, 326
dog, 47, 50, 75–6, 78–9, 81–3,
    126–9, 130–2
dolphin, 326
hatchet fish, 77
howler monkey, 106, 168
jaguar, 82, 106, 111, 324, 325,
    326, 392, 394
kinkajou, 76
marmoset, 50
ocelot, 82, 328
opposum, 76
otter, 77, 142–3
paca, 88, 417
peccary, 76, 77, 106, 120–1,
    127–31, 133
raccoon, 77, 326
skunk, 77, 416
tamandua, 76, 418
tapir, 76, 79, 131
tayra, 79, 418
turtles, 139
vampire bat, 48, 327
water hogs, 326, 415
woolly monkey, 106, 125–6, 133,
    139, 212, 418
see also Birds
Ankuaji, Father, 351–6
Ankuash, 218
Antikiu, 240
Anne Christine see under Descola
Antunish, 187, 190, 203, 214
Apachentza, 218
Apupentza, 152, 279, 288, 345,
    364, 379
Arias, 191
Arms see Blowpipe, Guns, Hunting,
    War
Army and soldiers, 6–7, 253–4, 343
Arutam (visions), 123, 299–300,
    302–14, 355, 367, 384, 390
    and Christian prayer, 360
Asamat, 173, 371
Astronomy, 225
    Orion, 239, 376
    Pleiades, 225, 239, 376
Atinia, 174
Auju, 165, 171, 180, 181, 191, 249

Author see under Descola
Awananch, 280–1, 284, 326, 348,
    377
Awaritiur, 267
Awasant, 174

Bachelard, 21
Barter, 82, 245–7
    see also Exchange, Gifts, Trade
Birds, 66, 77, 368
    grosbeak, 262, 328, 367–8, 416
    harpy eagle, 181
    hoazin, 137, 416
    hummingbird, 86–7, 316
    macaw, 100, 339
    owl, 328, 365
    penelope bird, 77, 417
    toucan, 77, 133, 159, 197, 262,
        326
    trumpet-bird (agami), 50, 77, 418
    vulture, 392
    woodpecker, 77, 397
Blood, 94–5
Blood debt (tumash), 150, 251, 278,
    288, 294, 350–1
    see also Murder, Vendetta
Blowpipe, 159–60, 326, 335
Bobonaza River, 18–19, 158, 210,
    279, 281
Bolivian lowlands, 1
Boredom, 201–2
Borges, Jorge Luis, 100
Bouguer, Pierre, 20
Brazil, 155

Cabo Pozo 344
Canelos (area and tribe), 11–13, 15,
    18, 25, 28, 256
Cannibalism, 272
    see also Head-hunting, Shrunken
    heads
Canoe, 151, 152, 210–11, 239,
    252–4
Capahuari (river and village), 18, 29,
    33, 52, 55, 60, 74, 120, 167,
    201–2, 212–13, 240, 242
    landing strip, 55, 70
Capitán Chiriboga, 256, 265

Causality, 312–14
    see also Cosmology, Illness, causes
        of
Ceremonial friendship (*amik*), 149,
    153–64, 347–8
Cevallos, Jaime, 255–6, 266
Chalua, 105, 243, 342
Chango, 252, 263
Charms
    namur, 140–1, 337
    nantar, 84–5, 86, 90, 94, 116
Chawir, 89, 174–5, 177, 182, 196
Chayuk, 301
Children, 42, 47–8, 78, 88–9,
    106–8, 118–19, 141, 163–4,
    192, 193
    as apprentice shamans, 341
    development of, 367
    illnesses of, 232–4
    and the Iwianch, 369–71, 373–4
    orphans, 295
Chimpui (stool), 39, 43, 51, 69, 143,
    165, 278
Chinkianentza, 267
Chinkias, 90
Chinkim, 283
Chiriap, 220
Chirta River, 123, 241–2, 280
Chiwian, 44, 46, 138, 163
Chiwias, 268
Chistianity, conversion to, 357–8
    see also Missionaries, Prayer
Chuchukia, 301, 329–30
Chuint, 386
Chumapi, 162, 190
Chumpi, 174, 267
Chundaykiu River, 114, 142, 252,
    254
Chunji, 201, 391
Churuwia, 269
Classification
    of dreams, 106, 111–16
    of flora and fauna, 76–7, 85
    of illnesses, 231–2, 236
    of magical phenomena, 325–9
    of tribes, 220–3
    of *tsentsak*, 336
Climate, 65–6, 75, 138–9, 211

Colour, use of, 65–6
Colombia, 1, 14, 205
Communication, 105, 171–2,
    283–4, 372
    aujmatin, 165–8, 353, 355, 386
    sign language, 371
    slow talk, 53, 56, 62–3, 171, 179
    with the dead, 372
    see also Anent, Language
Conambo, 300, 330, 357
Conflict, 16–17, 160–1, 263, 277
    see also Vendetta, War
Coversation *see* Communication
Cooking, 40–1
Copataza, 150, 203, 300, 329, 330,
    347, 358–9
    see also Ikiam
Cosmology, 225–6, 375–6, 406
Costume *see* Ornamentation,
    Tarasap
Creation myths, 224
Curaray river, 38
Curare, 108–9, 125, 128, 158, 159,
    329, 342
Curses, 99–100

Dahua, 252, 263
Dancing, 259–60
Deaf-mutism, 371
Death, 111, 113, 203, 234, 363–83
    communication with the dead, 372
    dreams of the dead, 114–16
    dying, 365–6
    funeral, 376–83
    metaphors for, 395–6
    suicide, 295
    see also Iwianch, Murder,
        Shrunken heads, Spirits, Soul,
        Vendetta
Debt, 246, 251, 342
    see also Blood debt, Gifts
Defecation, 49
Descola, Anne Christine, 3, 7, 42,
    46, 70, 85, 94, 153–4, 165, 206,
    239, 257, 279, 336, 364, 385
    and face painting, 173
    and marriage, 198–200
    her native name, 71, 153, 168

Descola, Philippe
  acceptance by Achuar, 153–4,
    393, 395
  accuracy of this book, 401–2,
    404
  Achuar view of 71
  adaptation, 280
  his boredom, 201–2
  dancing, 260
  his detachment, 393
  his discouragement, 385
  lessons learned from the Achuar,
    405–10
  his marriage, 198–200
  nickname, 58, 71
  and relationships, 104
  selectivity, 402
  as shaman, 211–12, 316, 340,
    343, 347
  training, 21–2
  understanding the Acuar, 403
  and Wajari, 72, 103, 153–4, 162,
    369–71
Destiny, 310–11, 367, 406
Discourse see Communication
Disease see Illness
Dogs, 47, 50, 75–6, 78–9, 81–3,
    126–9, 130–2
Domestication of animals, 130–2
Dreams, 84, 105–19, 120–1, 294,
    376, 381
  as augury, 117, 294
  classification of, 106, 111–16
  of the dead, 114–16
  interpretation, 106–8, 118–19
  and myths, 325
  see also Sleep, Trance
Drink
  manioc beer (nijiamanch), 34–7,
    41, 51, 58–9, 165, 256–7,
    274, 391
  namuk, 384, 387, 391
  natem, 205–9, 305, 315, 316
  wayus, 44–5, 49, 104
Drugs, hallucinatory, 205–9, 299,
    305, 315, 316
  see also Healing, Shamans

Ecuador, 11, 14, 149, 205, 210,
    343, 362
Edible animals, 77, 339
Emotion, 170
  anger, 193–4
  expression of, 377, 408
  fear, 233
  grief, 377
  jealousy, 100, 184, 199, 219,
    289–90
  love, 194–8
  pity, 377
Entsakua, 219
Entza, 36, 40, 47, 69, 85, 86–90,
    93, 99–102, 116, 153, 165,
    174–5, 182, 184, 189
Ethics, 126
Ethnology, 21–5, 144–5, 401–5,
    408–10
  accuracy of, 401–2
  formalisation of, 144–5
  methods, 238–9, 404
  neutrality of, 192–3, 408
  subjectivity of, 404–5
Etza, 253
Evangelism, 357–62
  see also Missionaries
Exchange, 72–5, 247, 354–6
  see also Barter, Debt, Gifts, Trade
Expedition (1976), 4–5
Explorers, 15–21

Face painting, 165, 173, 174, 296,
    376
Family relationships, 54
  see also Kinship
Fat, 139–40
  see also Food
Fire, construction of, 45
Fishing, 134–46
Flornoy, Bertrand, 18
Food, 28, 40–1, 62, 180, 301–2
  black/white meat, 301–2
  breakfast, 51
  dietary prohibitions, 339–40
  exemption from barter, 74
  fat, 139–40
  funeral meal, 381

fruit, 139
manioc, 41
onions, 343
salt, 381
table manners, 36–7, 41
taboos, 339–40
tumpi (manioc and taro), 301
see also Fishing, Hunting, Illness
Freud, Sigmund, 119
Friends, 149
ceremonial (*amik*), 152–64
distant, 158
and enemies, 161–2
Furniture
chimpui, 39, 43, 51, 69, 143, 165, 278
kutank, 344
peak, 47, 378–9, 376

Garden, 84–102, 156, 180, 186, 288, 376
see also Food, Healing, Plants
Ghosts *see* Iwianch, Soul, Spirits
Gifts, 103, 243–6
Glass beads (*shauk*), 25, 158–9, 257
Godelier, Maurice, 22
'Godfather' relationship, 11–13
Godin des Odonnais, Isabelle, 18–20
Great man (*juunt*), 63, 175–6, 178, 290–2
see also Tukupi, Washikta
Guayaquil, 25
Guayas, Gulf of, 158
Guns, 149, 158, 180
rifle, 248, 250–1, 295–6, 384, 387

Hallucinations *see* Trance
Harner, Michael, 17–18
Harpoon-making, 136
Head-dress (*tawasap*), 159, 345, 385–6
Head-hunting, 272–9
see also Shrunken heads
Healing, 73, 232, 236–8, 240–2, 315–34, 336–7, 345–6
see also Shamans

Hegel, 5
History, 2, 67, 223
see also Identity, Mythology, Time
Hobbes, Thomas, 17
House
construction of, 45, 56, 59–61, 104, 165
position of, 60–1
as sepulchre, 378–9
of war (fortified), 165, 282–90, 364–5
see also Furniture
Huasaga, 241
Humboldt, Alexander von, 5
Hunting, 120–33, 156
ethics of, 126
lodge, 135–6
nocturnal, 288
see also Animals, Fishing

Iconography, 239
Identity, 275–6, 354, 367, 409
ethnic, 220–4, 407–8
geographical, 216–17
social, 178
Ikiam (murder victim), 61–3, 150–1, 171, 179, 203, 213–14, 223, 267
the full story, 248–50
Illness, 230, 231̇43, 315, 349
causes of, 231–5, 241–3
of children, 232–4
classification of, 231–2, 236
and death, 365
diagnosis of, 329–30
malaria, 210, 235
skin diseases, 237–8
Incest *see* Kinship, Sexuality
Inchi, 88–9, 163
Individualism, 138, 223, 293, 366, 406
aents, 221–2
concept of, 221–4
destiny, 310–11, 367
Initiation of shamans, 266, 337–8
Inkis, 191
Iquitos, 159
Irarat, 386

Irarit, 257, 259
Isango, 252–3, 263
Ishkui, 177
Ishpinkiu river, 114, 213, 242
Isolation, 213–17, 247, 280
Ishtik, 252
Iwianch, 91, 146, 328, 365–6,
    367–76
Iyun, 267

Jaime, Don 201–5
    see also Cevallos, Jaime
Jaramillo, 254–6
Jempe, 197, 267
Jerez, Juan, 255
Jimpikit, 174, 177
Jivaro tribes, 13
    western interest in, 14–20
    see also Achuar, Shuar, Tribes
Jung, Carl, 119
Jussieu, Joseph de, 20

Kaitian, 378, 379, 385
Kajekui, 213, 214, 252
Kamijiu, 218, 219–20, 241–2
Kaniras, 350–2
Kantuash, 295
Kapair, 220
Kapawi river and region see under
    Capahuari
Karsten, Rafael, 15–16
Kashpa, 378, 379, 386
Kashpaentza, 112
Katip, 393, 394–5
Kawarunch, 62, 63, 150–1, 165–8,
    170–2, 179–80, 203, 217,
    218, 249–50, 268–72
    his death, 267–8, 350–2
Kayap, 279, 281, 282, 283, 284
Kayuye, 174, 218, 219
Kinship
    affinity, 156, 176–8, 278, 291,
        415
    consanguinity, 177, 216, 291–2
    cross-cousins, 177, 416
    incest, 216
    levirate, 176
    marriage, 176–8, 184–200, 216

polygamy, 188–90
    tarimiat, 189–90
    waje, 176–7, 198
Kirimint, 294–5
Knowledge
    concepts of, 374, 407
    of shamans, 323
    and time, 407
Kukush, 385
Kunamp, 267, 352
Kunampentza, 104, 143, 201, 300
Kuniach, 219
Kupatentza, 104, 123
Kurientza, 151, 240, 377
Kusutka river, 134–5, 137, 139
Kuunt, 54, 56, 58, 350–1

Labour (work) patterns, 56
La Condamine, Charles de, 19–20
Land, 407
    ownership, 11–12, 67–8
    see also Identify
Language, 11, 13, 38, 72, 116–17,
    202, 371–2
    and love, 195
    and perception, 374–6, 405
    problems, 40
    sign (for deaf-mutes), 371
    and tribal identity, 221–3
    see also Communication
Legends concerning the Amazon,
    3–6
Lévi-Strauss, Claude, 22–3, 24, 40,
    113, 118
Literature, 15–17
    see also Ethnology, accuracy of
Loja, 20, 255
Love, 194–8
    philtres, 262, 336

Macas, 15
Magic
    of arutam (visions), 299–300,
        302–14
    charms, 84–5, 86, 140–1, 337
    and gardens, 90, 92–4
    of healing and illness, 241,
        315–18

and hunting, 126, 132–3
of love 262, 336
namur, 140–1, 337
nantar, 84–5, 86, 90, 94, 116
and war, 391–2
see also Anent, Shamans
Makatu, 219, 231, 235–6, 243–4,
    252, 253, 260
Makuma river, 55, 158, 343, 351
Makusar river, 153
Male bonding, 49
    see also Friendship
Mamati, 149, 187
Mamays, 252, 253, 346
Mangosiza, 45, 158, 222
Maps, inaccuracy of, 2
Marañon, 18, 20, 359
Marriage, 176–8, 184–200
    adultery, 191
    arranged, 197–8
    love, 194–8
    violence in, 187, 191–4
    waje, 176–7
Mashiant, 378, 385
Mashinkiash, 295
Masak, 191
Mashu, 301, 329–30, 347
Masurash, 210, 230
Materialism, 136–7
Mayanch, 363–6
    her funeral, 376–83
Mayaproa, 386–8
Maynas, 18
Medicines, 73, 236–8, 331
    see also Healing, Tobacco
Memory, lack of, 273, 314, 318
    see also History, Identity, Time
Mente Kusatka swamp, 168–70
Metekash, 379–81, 393
Michaud, Henri, 25
Military *see* Army
Mirijiar, 219, 252, 253, 258
Mirunik, 40–1, 47, 69–70, 135,
    189
Missionaries, 7–8, 15, 17, 55, 70,
    151, 161, 178, 199, 263,
    272–3, 349, 354, 356–62,
    368, 372

Don Jaime, 201–5
Father Albo (Ankuaji), 350–6
film show, 204–5
radio station, 202
sermons, 203
as shamans, 243
Montalvo, 18, 27–8, 30, 69, 158,
    195, 221, 255–6
Montalvo, Angel, 255
Morand, Paul, 25
Mosquitoes, 210, 242
Mukucham, 301, 315
Mukuchiwa (shaman), 242–3
Mukuimp (shaman), 180, 184, 300,
    359
    and *aujmatin*, 171
    building house, 56
    fishing, 134–42
    and Kawarunch, 165, 171–2
    relationship to Wajari, 54, 105,
        168, 174, 188
    as shaman, 205–9, 211, 240, 315,
        343, 348
Murder, 267–8, 281, 290–1, 295,
    300–1, 304, 311–12
    see also Blood debt, Ikiam,
        Vendetta
Music
    instruments, 259–60
    songs (*nampet*), 78–81, 206–7,
        257–9, 273
    tsayantar, 206, 257, 259, 315
    tuntui (drum), 45
    see also Anent
Mythology, 24, 118–19, 223–9
    Ajaimp, 226–9
    Hummingbird, 86–7
    Iwianch, 369–71
    Nunkui, 84–5, 90–1, 224
    Indians and Whites, 359
    Musach, 239
    Nettle, 346
    Pleiades, 239
    Sua and Ipiak, 95–8
    Sua and Tsunki, 324–5
    see also History, Legends, Spirits,
        Time
Naanch, 54, 95, 164, 178, 192–3,

Naanch – *cont.*
  195, 218–19, 227, 240, 305,
  347
Najur, 218
Nakaim, 214
Namoch, 78
Nampirach, 157
Nankiti, 265, 279–90, 294–6, 345,
  348, 364
  description of, 283
Nantar (charm), 84–5, 86, 90, 94,
  116
Napo, 222, 323, 342
Narankas, 61, 150, 248–50, 267,
  350–1
Nationalism, 407–8
Nature and culture, 405–6
  see also Animals, Birds, Plants
Nawir, 138, 163, 172
Nayapi, 151, 213, 230, 247–8, 268,
  324
  description of, 218
  and gifts, 243–6
  his history, 218–20
  at his house, 210, 243, 252–60
  and Makatu, 231, 235, 241
  and Tsunki, 141–2
  and malaria, 242
Nayash, 386
Naychap, 173
Neighbourhoods, 217, 292, 311,
  314
Nijiamanch (manioc beer), 34–7,
  41, 51, 58–9, 165
Nuis, 174
Nunkui (spirit of gardens), 84, 90,
  91–2, 94, 99, 117, 186, 224
Nurinska, 267, 350–1
Nusiri, 218, 219

Oligation, 231, 300
Omen (*pasun*), 67
  mesekramprar, 115
  see also Dreams
Oriente, 11, 27
Orinoco, 1, 24, 205, 247
Ornamentation, 51, 220, 257, 393
  of the dead, 276

wristbands, 310
  see also Face painting, Tawasap
Orphans, 295
Otalvo, 9, 342

Paantam, 46, 135, 163
Pakunt, 299–302, 310
Party (*namper*), 256–60
Pastaza river and area, 3, 13, 18, 61,
  170, 172, 199, 223, 248–9,
  279, 300
Peak (bed), 47, 378–9
  for the dead, 376
Peas, 280–1, 363, 378
Perception and language, 374–6,
  405
Person *see* Identity, Individualism,
  Kinship, Soul
Peru, 13, 27, 55, 149, 151, 241, 243,
  323
Phoebus, Gaston, 129
Physiology, 232
  blood, 94–5
  defecation, 49
  lactation, 232
  sperm, 141, 232, 366
Picham, 172, 182, 352, 354, 371
Pierre (Abbé), 7, 18
Pikiur, 385
Pinchu, 51, 54, 103–5, 108–9, 111,
  157, 214, 219, 308
  his appearance, 103
  as hunter, 120–33
Pincian, 190
Piniantza, 206–9
Pinik, 61, 150, 151, 213–14, 248,
  250
Pirisant, 177, 181
Plants
  classification of, 76–7, 85, 236–8
  garden, 85
  medicinal, 236–8
  poisonous, 135–8
  propagation of, 92, 131
  shamanistic, 336
  soul of, 98–9
  weeds, 86–7
  wild fruits, 139

list of species:
amaranth, 237
arrowroot, 85, 415
avocade tree, 85
banana tree, 85, 86, 87
bean, 85
bread fruit tree, 139
caimito tree, 85, 415
chambira palm, 139, 416
chirichiri, 237, 379–80
clibadium, 85, 416
cotton, 85
cocoa tree, 85, 139
genipa, 85, 97–8, 237, 274, 295, 416
ginger, 236
gourd tree, 85
granadilla tree, 139, 416
groundnuts, 85
guava tree, 85
inga, 85, 139, 416
iniayua palm, 159
ivory palm, 139, 254, 416
jeep, 301
kampanak palm, 60
kapok, 159, 273
kunkuk palm, 135
lianas, 135, 205
lonchocarpus, 85, 135, 137, 138, 212, 417
manioc, 85, 86, 87–8, 89, 92–3, 95, 131
nettle, 237, 346
palm trees, 60
papaya, 85
pineapple, 85
piripiri, 236–7
rocou, 85, 86, 97–8, 165, 417
rubber, 256
sapote, 86, 139
sesa, 237
squash, 85
stramonium, 75, 78, 85, 237, 274, 299, 305, 306, 418
sugar cane, 85
swamp palm, 139, 418
sweet potato, 85
sweetsop, 85

taro, 85
tobacco, 85, 232, 237 240, 241, 299, 373, 380–1, 397
turiyi palm, 60
wayus, 44–5, 49, 95
wild mango tree, 139
yaji, 205
yam, 85, 87, 88
yapaipa, 237
Poison
curare, 108–9, 125, 128, 158, 329, 342
lonchocarpus, 135–8
sunkipi, 219
Politics, 293
authority, 292
frontiers and borders, 253–4
and gift-giving, 244–5
great man (*juunt*), 63, 175–6, 178, 290–2
see also Status
Polygamy, 188–90
Prayer, 358–60
Prestige, 81
see also Status
Procreation, 366
Prohibitions *see* Taboos
Protocol, 46
and gifts, 244–5
and hospitality, 284
and food, 36–7, 41
Puanchir, 218, 219
Pujupat, 111, 218, 291
Pumpuentza, 351–2
Puyo, 2–14, 17, 24–6, 70, 201, 210, 342
description of, 9–11

Quichuas, 120, 243, 253–6, 262–4, 323, 335, 342–4
communication with, 375
Quito, 18, 20

Rainbow, 67
Relations between tribes, 55, 262–4
see also Tribes
Religion, 357–62
see also Missionaries

Rhetoric, 165–7, 171–2
Riobamba, 15
Rites of passage, 66
Ritual, 153–4
  anemat, 384, 386–93
  head shrinking, 273–6
  and missionary, 356
  ujaj, 393–9
Rufeo, 344–5

Samik, 252, 257–9, 264
Samiruk, 181
Sampico, 335–7
Sangay volcano, 26, 368
Santamik, 103, 105, 121–9, 157
Sasaïme river and region, 61–2, 63,
  173, 178, 216, 218, 221, 223,
  240, 249, 350–2, 371
Senkuan, 379
Senur, 34, 40–2, 47, 75, 78, 135,
  140, 163, 165, 174–5, 182,
  184–5, 188–9
  her appearance, 69
Seum, 267
Sexuality, 129, 182–6, 253, 260–2
  abstinence from, 181, 199, 253,
    340
  adolescent, 194–5
  adultery, 191, 260
  and dreams, 117
  homosexuality, 183
  in a house of war, 289
  incest, 216
  procreation, 366
  see also Love
Shakaim, 195
  see also Spirits
Shamans, 105, 112–13, 201,
  205–6, 209, 305, 315–34,
  335–49
  dangers of being, 347, 363
  and healing, 236–8, 241–3,
    315–34, 345–6
  initiation of, 337–8, 340–1
  limitations of, 348–9
  mother-saliva, 336, 337–8
  natem (drink), 205–8, 236
  panku (kind of shaman), 344–5

pasuk (spirit helpers), 208, 326–7,
  328–32
possession, 344–5
rivalry between, 280–1
shinki-shinki, 317, 329
status of, 340
sumai (kind of shaman), 322–3
tsentsak (magic darts), 104–5,
  316, 322–3, 330–3, 335–7,
  341–6
tsuakratin (healer), 281, 345
tunchi (sorcery), 236, 301, 305,
  330–1, 333–4
vocation of, 340–1
and water, 323–5
wawekratin (sorceror) 281, 345
see also Healing, Magic, Mukuimp,
  Soul, Spirits, Tunki
Shamich, 177, 218
Sharian, 294–5, 337–8
Shell-Mera, 26, 70
Shiki, 301
Shirmachi, 269–71
Shrunken heads, 14–15, 271–8,
  314, 398
Shuar tribe, 13, 14, 15–18, 55,
  160–1, 221, 268–72, 277,
  313–14, 335, 343, 361–2,
  368, 398
Shuwinia, 127–8
Sickness *see* Illness
Skills, 56, 131, 136
Sleep, 43, 210, 234, 305
  see also Dreams
Songs (*nampet*) 78–81, 257–9,
  273, 356
  ujaj, 393–9
  see also Anent, Music
Soul (*wakan*), 95, 99, 133, 233–4,
  307, 311, 322, 365–8, 373,
  380–2
  arutam, 299–300, 302–14, 355
  emesak, 396–8
Spanish conquistadores, 2
Spirits, 91
  amana, 125–6, 129–30, 133
  Amasank, 140, 146, 326
  communication with, 376

of the forest, 326
Iwianch, 146, 317–18, 322, 328, 365–6, 367–76
Jurijri, 130, 146, 187, 323, 326
Nunkui, 84, 90, 91–2, 94, 99, 117, 186, 224
pasuk, 208, 326, 328–32
Shaam, 132, 146, 327
Shakaim, 99, 117
Titipiur, 327
Tsunki, 134, 141–3, 145–6, 203, 254, 318–26, 342
see also Anent, Shamans, Soul
Status, 63, 175–6, 178, 290–3
of shamans, 340
of wives, 188–90
Storytelling, 46, 91
see also Mythology
Stramonium, 75, 78, 85, 237, 274, 299, 305, 306, 418
Suicide, 295
see also Death
Sumpa, 174
Sumpaish, 61, 150, 171, 203, 213–16, 248–51
Sunti, 341
Supinanch, 283
Surikentza, 174, 267
Surutik, 94
Suwitiar, 94, 174, 188
Symbolism, 312

Taanchim, 218
Taasham, 270–1
Table manners, 36–7, 41
Taboos
on foods, 339–40
and illness, 241
and weapons, 180
Taish, 149–52, 157–8, 161, 213, 216, 240, 242, 244, 252
Tarapoto, 159
Tarir, 54, 149, 152, 157–8, 161, 183, 211, 212, 214, 219, 241, 242, 244, 266, 268, 279, 287, 294, 296
Tawasap (head dress), 159, 345, 385–6

Tawaynambi, 152
Tayujin, 54, 58, 61, 123, 150, 249, 267, 330
Temperance, 51
Tentets, 283, 287, 288, 345
Tii, 143, 151, 247–8, 252, 259, 263, 267–8
Time, 67–8, 223, 225, 312–13, 406–7
see also History, Memory
Timias, 218
Tiriats, 114–15
Tirinkias, 240
Tiriruk, 174, 177, 218, 219
Titiar, 52–62, 153, 162–3, 174, 186, 190, 219, 223, 246, 267
Tobacco, 85, 232, 237, 240, 241, 373, 380–1, 397
Tourists, 15
Trade, 11, 69, 72, 152, 155, 158–60
and war, 161, 288
see also Barter, Exchange, Gifts
Trance and hallucinations, 299, 316
drugs, 205–9, 299, 305, 315, 316
see also Shamans, Spirits, Visions
Tribes, 220–3, 313–14
Achuar *see separate entry*
Aguaruna, 13, 15, 277, 313
Alamas, 11
Antuas, 342
Candoshi, 222
Canelos, 11–13, 15, 18, 25, 28, 256
Cocama, 159, 222, 322
Conibo, 323
Huambisa, 13, 277
Lamistas, 159
Mayn, 149, 152, 281
Pransis, 168
Quichuas, *see separate entry*
Shipibo, 323
Shuar *see separate entry*
Tupi, 156
Waorani, 222
Zaparo, 222
Tsamarin, 213, 214, 242, 248, 252
Tsanta ritual, 271–8, 398
see also Shrunken heads

Tsapak, 191
Tseremp 56, 62, 189, 211, 214, 241,
    257, 268, 279, 287, 294–6
  behaviour of, 183, 264–6, 358
  breaking taboo, 114–15
  description of, 54
  in dialogue, 283
  and gifts, 243–4, 245–6, 252
  as interpreter, 38, 40
Tsitsink, 174, 177, 182
Tsuink, 267
Tsukanka, 52, 58, 114–15, 165–74,
    178, 191–2, 240, 245–6, 249,
    267, 305
Tsunki, 134, 141–3, 145–6, 203,
    254, 318–26, 342
Tukupi, 63, 150, 168, 172–81, 182,
    203, 218, 225, 249–50, 267,
    305, 352, 353–6
  his appearance and character,
    173
Tumink, 219, 220
Tunki, 299–302, 305, 309, 311,
    315–23, 325, 327, 328–34,
    33543, 357
Tuntui (drum), 45
Tuntuam, 179, 267
Turipiur, 281, 345
  see also under Spirits

Ucayali, 247, 323
Uitiaj, 386
Ujukam (shaman), 248, 250
Unkush, 89
Untsumak, 393, 397
Unupi, 294–5
Ushpa, 391, 393, 394
Uweiti, 270–1
Uwejint, 191
Uyun (pouch), 309

Vampirism, 93, 95
Vendetta, 61–2, 64, 150, 161, 174,
    178, 203, 249, 277, 290
  see also Death, War
Violence in marriage, 187, 191–4
Visions
  ajutap, 313

arutam, 299–300, 302–14, 355,
    360, 367, 384
Vomiting, 49

Wajari, 30, 33, 44–5, 46–7, 70,
    100, 165, 168, 172, 189, 206,
    219, 265, 267, 326, 341, 347
  appearance of, 34, 48, 51, 52
  and the author, 72, 103, 153–4,
    162, 369–71
  his dream, 84
  as father, 48, 50
  first sight of, 30
  fishing, 134–43
  purging himself, 49
  as informateur, 37–41
  and sexuality, 182–5
  as warrior, 49–50
Wakan see Soul
Wampuash, 126, 128, 177, 181
Wampuik river, 153
War, 16–17, 277, 284–96
  anemat ritual, 384, 386–93
  head-hunting, 272–8
  house of, 282–90, 364–5
  impikmartin, 286–7
  with Shuar, 268–72
  shrunken heads (tsantsa), 14–15,
    271–8, 314, 398
  and trade, 161, 288
  tumash (debt or obligation), 150,
    251, 278, 288, 294
  vendetta 61–2, 64, 150, 161, 174,
    178, 203, 249, 277, 290
Washikta, 63, 150, 158, 161, 167,
    172, 173, 179–81, 192, 203,
    218, 245–6, 248–50, 305, 352
Water
  and shamanism, 323–5
  see also Tsunki
Wawar, 190
Wayurentza, 218, 300, 341
Weapons see Blowpipe, Harpoon,
    Guns
Weather, 65–6, 75
Week, 214
Whites, 140, 343, 355, 359–60, 375
  Father Ankuaji, 151–6

Winchikiur, 242, 252, 257
Wirisam, 190
Wisui, 315–22, 329–30, 331–2, 335
Wisum, 219, 220
Women
  and *arutam*, 305–6
  and dogs, 81–2
  as gardeners, 88–9
  and the Iwianch, 371, 373–4
  and politics, 293
  post-menopausal, 94
  as shamans, 325
  and war, 393–9
  widows, 79
  as wives, 184–200

Work, 56
  in garden, 86–8
  house building, 59–61

Yakum, 168, 267, 378, 385
  Descola's nickname, 58, 71
Yamanoch, 177
Yankuam, 281, 283, 287, 288, 363
Yapan, 91, 176
Yatris, 103, 105, 157
Yaur, 123, 150, 151, 171, 179, 203, 214, 248–50, 307, 391
Yujuentza, 279
Yurank, 174, 185
Yutsuentza, 281, 282, 288, 294, 345
Yuu, 105, 143